Indianapolis Board of Trade

The Industries of the city of Indianapolis

The advantages offered for business location and the investment of

capital

Indianapolis Board of Trade

The Industries of the city of Indianapolis
The advantages offered for business location and the investment of capital

ISBN/EAN: 9783337238681

Printed in Europe, USA, Canada, Australia, Japan

Cover: Foto ©Suzi / pixelio.de

More available books at **www.hansebooks.com**

THE INDUSTRIES

THE CITY OF INDIANAPOLIS

THE ADVANTAGES OFFERED FOR

BUSINESS LOCATION AND THE INVESTMENT OF CAPITAL

PUBLISHED UNDER THE AUSPICES OF THE

INDIANAPOLIS BOARD OF TRADE

[COPYRIGHT, 1889, BY A. N. MARQUIS & COMPANY]

A. N. MARQUIS & COMPANY

1889

STATE CAPITOL AT INDIANAPOLIS

THE STATE OF INDIANA.

THE nineteenth century closes upon Indiana, glorious in a realization of the sublime promise of her prophetic infancy. Within a hundred years a commonwealth has been created, savage domination has yielded precedence to our progressive civilization, and the shadows which darkened her pioneer days are only recalled and remembered, when contrasted with the sunshine of her present prosperity. Internal improvements have caused the waste places to blossom as the rose. An educational system has been established embodying the highest excellencies, a code of laws comprehensive and adaptive have been collated and are enforced for the prevention of wrongs and the protection of rights, while agriculture, manufactures and trade are pre-eminent sources of fortune, and all the agencies that can even remotely contribute to the welfare of the State or the Nation, or both, have been successfully enlisted. Indiana is bounded on the north by Michigan, east by Ohio, south by the Ohio River and on the west by Illinois. She has a total area of 36,350 square miles or 23,116,160 acres. La Salle is credited with the discovery of the country. The first settlement of the present State is disputed. Some authorities declare it was made at Vincennes sometime between 1700 and 1710, while others contend that no settlement was effected there until 1735, and still others insist that French traders located upon the present site of Fort Wayne as early as 1700. In 1763, Great Britain acquired title to the territory from France, and two decades later, it became the property of the United States. In 1787 the Northwestern Territory was organized and embraced within its area the present State of Indiana. In 1800 Indiana Territory was organized, there being at that time a population of 5,000 within its limits. In 1804 the land in the new territory was opened to entry, and in 1814 the number of the inhabitants had increased to upward of 20,000, with manufacturing industries, including grist-mills, saw-mills, tanneries, etc., principally, valued at $300,000 and over. The territorial capital was located at this period at Corydon, in Harrison County, where the constitutional convention was held in December, 1815, the proceedings of which paved the way for the admission of the State into the Union, during April of the year following. The population is stated to have then been 63,807. Walter Taylor and James Noble represented the State in the United States Senate, and William Hendricks in the Lower House. In 1825 the capital was moved to Indianapolis, and from that date the population steadily increased in numbers, coming chiefly from Kentucky, Virginia and Tennessee, with some from points further south and north. In 1831 the Indian title to lands was extinguished and in 1832 the Black Hawk War occurred, both of which incidents had the effect of peopling the State with inhabitants who have left the impress of their character upon the history of succeeding years. From 1840 to 1850, the State grew in prominence and influence. In the Mexican War Indiana furnished five regiments of soldiers who participated in the campaigns that were concluded by the treaty of Guadalupe-Hidalgo. In the war between the States that followed the firing upon Sumter, she sent into the field 208,367 enlisted men. The later history of the State is familiar to the world. Her wonderful growth and development are unparalleled. Religious and educational institutions abound in every section, and are largely attended. The State institutions are equal to the demands made upon their resources, and benevolent enterprises of a private character are numerous and well sustained. The fact is, as Mr. George J. Langsdale eloquently remarks, the State has "only entered upon a new era of development that is yet beyond our comprehension." The population of the State in 1850 was 988,416; in 1860, 1,350,420; 1870, 1,680,637; 1880, 1,978,301; 1890, 2,154,354 and in 1899 is estimated at 2,500,000.

THE GEOLOGY OF THE STATE.

The geological formation is, with the exception of superficial deposits, composed of rocks of the paleozoic age. The formation expressed throughout different portions of the State consists of lower silurian limestone and shales, upper silurian limestone and shales, Devonian limestone, sub carbonic rock lime and sandstone, and rocks of the coal measure series, which include coal seams and their accompanying rocks. The lower silurian rocks are found in the south-eastern part of the State; the upper silurian in the eastern, southeastern and extreme northwestern; the Devonian in the northern, central and southern; the sub carboniferous on the western and southern parts, and the St. Louis and Keokuk limestone in the western and southern portions of the State. The coal measure rocks are expressed in the southwestern portion of the State, and there is a general dip of strata running in a southwesterly direction of 25 feet to the mile, with considerable slate in the southern half of the State. In the northern part the dip is to the northwest. East and north-east of Indianapolis is the oolitic limestone, the most important mineral deposit in the State, an inexhaustible supply. In Washington County alone there is 200 square miles of this formation, much of which has an average thickness of 40 feet, and many other counties have equally as good deposits. This stone, which is unsurpassed for building purposes and will be a source of revenue for an almost endless period, exists chiefly in the counties of Putnam, Monroe, Owen, Lawrence and Washington. Lawrence and other counties also contain large deposits of kaoline or white clay and glass. Sand is found in good quantities in Washington and Madison Counties, with inexhaustible supplies of fine clay in the counties included in the coal belt. A line of quicksand runs through the State from the northeast to the southwest, crossing along the river, the latter following the line of the disturbance. The rocks along the river have been distorted to such an extent by this upheaval, that the natural gas once confined in them has all escaped. South of the river the disturbance has been of such a nature as to produce low arches and the gas is yet confined in the original recesses. The greatest amount of gas, however, is found in the area where Niagara limestone are the surface rocks.

COAL PRODUCING AREA.

There is a total of seven thousand miles of coal producing area in the State, located principally in Fountain, Vermilion, Park, Vigo, Clay, Owen, Sullivan, Greene, Knox, Daviess, Martin, Gibson, Pike, Dubois, Posey, Vanderburg, Warrick, Spencer and Perry Counties, throughout which a total of fourteen seams of coal, varying from a few inches to twelve feet in thickness, are to be found. Coal mines have been successfully operated in all these counties during the past year, though the statistics may show a slight falling off in the out-put, due to the substitution of natural gas throughout an extended territory that has heretofore been a consumer of coal. The following table shows the output of the mines for the years from 1879 to 1898:

1879	1,256,000 tons.	1891	2,500,000 tons.
1880	1,500,325 "	1893	2,375,000 "
1881	1,771,300 "	1895	3,000,000 "
1883	1,900,000 "	1897	1,251,705 "
1885	2,500,000 "		

TIMBER LAND.

At the close of the year 1886 the area of timber land in the State included a total of 4,000,606 acres. During that year the area had been reduced 359,133 acres. Taking this reduction as a fair criterion for the two years succeeding, the total area of timber land remaining not located in the State January 1st, 1889, was not far from 1,900,000 acres. The southern portion of the State has always been rich in the growth of hardwood lumber, with considerable amounts of oak, ash, sugar, beech, hickory, linn, sycamore, etc., in other sections, and large forests of oak and hickory yet standing in the eastern part of the State.

NATURAL GAS.

This subject is exhaustively treated in another part of this book under the caption, "Natural Gas in Indianapolis."

MINERAL SPRINGS.

The State is dotted with mineral springs, the waters of which have been proved to be invaluable for medical purposes, and are steadily growing in prominence and importance with invalids and pleasure seekers. Among the leading in this department are the Sulphur Springs at French Lick and Weisbaden in Orange County. These have become popular in all portions of the country. There also are the Indian Sulphur Springs in Martin County, the Chalybeate Springs in Warren County, the White Sulphur Springs at Lodi, in Fountain County, and at Lafayette, and other resorts of a similar character elsewhere in the State.

STONE QUARRIES.

The stone quarries located in the above designated sections of the State are steadily operated during the season. In 1888, 89 there were quarries worked, having a total capital of $340,805, giving employment to 1,161 hands, to whom a total of $534,000 wages were paid and turning out products valued at $1,073,675. The estimated value of products in 1888 was not far from $1,700,000.

AGRICULTURE.

The leading industry of the State is, of course, agriculture. The nature of the soil, its facilities for natural and artificial drainage, the equable temperature which prevails in this latitude, and other causes combine to furnish the most substantial returns for the labor of the husbandman and equally substantial inducements for investment in farm lands. The table at the bottom of this page shows in a condensed form facts relating to the extent and condition of this industry, also the amount and value of the leading productions.

At the close of 1888, there were estimated to be about 200,000 farms in the State, representing a total valuation of $446,461,548, not including fences, buildings, etc. Of the total acreage cultivated 7,157,665 acres were devoted to cereals, including flaxseed, buckwheat, etc., 3,161,832 acres to clover and timothy seed and hay, and 79,420 acres to potatoes, etc. There were 6,795,731 bearing and 3,143,037 non-bearing fruit trees embraced in the area devoted to orchards. The statistics declare the crop year of 1888 to have been an excellent one, and each of the important cereals except wheat a substantial increase in product, average yield per acre, and value of crop when compared with 1887.

THE SCHOOLS.

The system of education employed in Indiana is very comprehensive and complete. District schools at which the primary and elementary branches are taught, are available to residents to every city and town. Normal schools, six in number, are provided for the instruction of teachers. In addition to these, there is a completely equipped polytechnic school, and fifteen colleges and universities at which the higher branches are taught, the curriculum embracing prescribed and alternative studies, the pursuit of which equips students with a thorough classical or scientific education, as they may elect. The system which has obtained so successfully was established by men of intelligence, liberal views, and high appreciation of the needs of the service. Its development has been rapid and permanent, and the influence it has exerted in the development and growth of Indiana, as also in the promotion of the wealth and prosperity apparent to-day, cannot be too highly estimated. The following table shows the growth of the schools during the period from 1860 to 1889:

YEAR	SCHOOL POPULATION	SCHOOL ENROLLMENT	NO. OF SCHOOL HOUSES	NO. OF TEACHERS	VALUE OF SCHOOL PROPERTY	AVERAGE DAYS OF SCHOOL
1860	512,467	301,451	6,347	7,852		77
1865	552,291	413,354	7,301	9,313	$ 3,073,173.00	70
1870	672,449	482,522	8,507	11,406	7,262,630.30	98
1875	667,136	502,363	9,586	13,133	10,050,856.00	124
1880	703,524	511,283	9,617	13,357	11,935,954.00	136
1885	730,499	501,250	9,572	13,754	13,507,052.00	130
1889	756,960	512,163	9,614	14,302	14,754,614.53	133

The amount annually expended for school purposes approximates in round numbers five millions of dollars, derived in part from the State's apportionment to counties of the common school revenue, from interest obtained on the proceeds of sales of the sixteenth section in every congressional township, from the local tuition fund and from the sale of liquor licenses and from other sources. The total school revenue for the school year ending July 31, 1888, was $5,235,031.98. The average daily wages for the year throughout the State, were $2.26 per day to male teachers and $1.87 to female teachers. The average daily attendance of pupils was 54 per cent. of the enumeration and 70 per cent. of the enrollment.

STATE FINANCES.

The financial condition of the State as shown by the following statement of the State Treasurer, is excellent:

Balance on hand Nov. 1, 1887	$ 373,914.22
Receipts from all sources	4,173,617.98
	$4,547,562.19
The expenditures were	4,289,836.63
Balance in treasury Oct. 31, 1888	$257,725.56

The total outstanding indebtedness of the State at the close of the fiscal year 1888, amounted to $6,770,608.34, of which $4,388,783.22 was domestic and $2,381,825 foreign, the latter drawing $337,864.99 interest.

AGRICULTURAL STATISTICS.

ARTICLES	1885	VALUE	1886	VALUE	1887	VALUE	1888	VALUE
Wheat	lbs.				$33,419,738		$25,675,698
Corn								44,202,600
Oats								7,428,840
Barley								392,680
Rye								341,600
Buckwheat								56,813
Flax Seed								115,455
Clover								1,339,572
Timothy								73,230
Clover Hay								19,111,500
Timothy								23,844,482
Irish Potatoes								2,710,100
Sweet								156,129
Tobacco	lbs.							1,332,298
		$201,595,054		$113,905,687		$160,830,679		$109,523,803

MANUFACTURING.

The manufacturing industries of Indiana have been rapidly growing in volume for the past forty years, and are annually becoming more varied. According to the statistics made in this department, the State, in the value of her manufactured products and in the number of her citizens employed, ranks higher than many States whose facilities may be regarded as superior; and consequently the number of persons employed is increasing in a greater ratio than in many of her sister States. New industries are constantly being added to the list, and this alone justifies the conclusion that in the near future Indiana will become one of the leading manufacturing States of the Union. The following table, which does not, however, include those employed in mining operations, nor upon railroad work, demonstrates the steady growth of this interest:

YEAR.	ESTABLISH-MENTS.	CAPITAL INVESTED.	HANDS EMPLOYED.	WAGES PAID.	VALUE PRODUCTS.
1850	4,392	$ 7,750,402	14,440	$ 4,740,441	$ 18,725,423
1860	5,323	18,451,121	21,295	8,315,355	42,803,469
1870	11,847	52,052,425	58,852	26,366,740	108,617,278
1880	11,198	55,312,942	69,508	21,294,900	148,006,411
1885	11,885	51,890,716	60,861	26,290,920	156,562,724
1888	15,000	68,000,600	75,000	30,000,000	175,000,000

These figures, while indicative of a growth in production even in excess of the ratio of increase in population, do not even approximately foreshadow the augmentation in industry which is now going on, as the recent introduction of natural gas, and the many advantages it gives in the cheapening and improvement of the processes of manufacture, is affording an added impetus to production, which has no equal in the past history of the manufacturing enterprises of the State. It may, therefore, be fairly predicted that the next census will show an increased ratio of advancement in all productive lines.

VALUATION AND TAXATION.

The total assessed valuation of property in the State for 1888 was $956,742,606, of which $748,843,447 was on real estate and $220,931,558 was on personal property, being an increase of $48,941,874 over the assessed valuation of real and personal property of 1880.

RAILROAD INTERESTS.

Indiana contains thirty-two lines of railways. On the 1st of January, 1889, there were 5,731,575 miles of main track, 1086.62 miles of double track, and 1,236.11 miles of siding, making the total mileage 5,990.48. The capital stock of the incorporated railways of the State January 1, 1888, aggregated $87,926,604; the bonded debt was $46,929,782; the unfunded debt was $7,160,683, and the total cost of the road and their equipment, including 92.28 miles constructed that year, was $144,745,692. During the same year the total receipts from the passenger department, including express, baggage, mail, etc., were $7,019,522; from the freight department, $61,826,648; and the operating expenses were $62,553,879; making the net receipts $26,373,691. There were 5,103,286 passengers, and 55,411,824 tons of freight carried. In 1888 the passenger department received $15,342,435, and carried 27,884,213 passengers; the freight department $52,529,601, and carried 55,379,741 tons of freight. The total operating expenses were $73,892,845. The total assessed valuation of roads for 1888 was $64,211,717.

RELIGIOUS.

The piety said to have been characteristic of the pioneers of Indiana has been inherited and perpetuated by their descendants. The total number of church organizations in the State is stated in round numbers at five thousand and the value of church property at fifteen millions of dollars, a substantial increase over the statistics of 1885. In the latter year there were 4,564 church organizations, having a total membership of 478,416, and owning property valued at upward of twelve millions of dollars.

MASONIC TEMPLE, INDIANAPOLIS.

THE CITY OF INDIANAPOLIS.

NDIANAPOLIS, the capital and most populous city of Indiana, is located on the west fork of White River, in the center of the State. The city is peopled by the most enterprising and progressive classes of citizens, and is surrounded by a territory rich in agricultural, mineral, and other natural resources. As a manufacturing and distributing point she occupies a leading position, and unsurpassed transportation facilities place her in immediate communication with all sections of the country. Financially of the staunchest character, an educational center of conspicuous importance, "a city of churches," socially and in other respects invitingly attractive, Indianapolis offers inducements for business and residence that have found expression in her wonderful growth and prosperity, particularly during the past decade. Briefly told, her history is one of successful endeavor against obstacles and competition. The city was first settled in 1819 or 1820. In the latter year Indianapolis was selected as the State Capital, and in 1821 the present city site was platted by Alexander Ralston. During December of the same year Marion County was organized, and in 1832 the town was duly incorporated, though it was not until 1836 the action of citizens in the premises was confirmed and legalized by special act of the Legislature. On the 17th of February, 1838, an act re-incorporating the town was adopted, providing among other things for including within its corporate limits the four sections or "donations" of land made by Congress upon the admission of the State in 1816. The embryo city grew steadily and satisfactorily in influence and importance. Enterprising citizens identified themselves with the town, stores were opened, manufactories were established, weekly papers were issued, school houses were built, and religious services were conducted at frequent intervals. In February, 1847, a city charter was granted by the Legislature, and Samuel Henderson became the pioneer Mayor. From that date the building up of Indianapolis became an established fact, and since then its progress has been permanent and substantial. It is to-day a city containing a population approximating one hundred and twenty-five thousand, with a future brilliant with possibilities. The streets are broad, handsomely shaded, and many of them paved. The residence portion is specially attractive, the houses being among the handsomest in the State, a large number of them occupying commodious and elaborately decorated plats of ground, forming a landscape replete with natural and artistic attractions. The business structures and manufacturing industries are substantially built of brick or stone, and many of them triumphs of architectural finish. The public buildings, including the State House, Court House, the Union Depot, Tomlinson's Hall, Masonic Hall, State Institutions, etc., are distinguished features of the city's attractions. The transportation facilities embrace sixteen separate lines of railway, not including the Belt Road, and the street railway is one of the most perfectly equipped and appointed in the West. The commercial and manufacturing industries of the city, of vast proportions, are steadily increasing in number and resources, and each of the several banks in operation do a large business. All of these interests, however, are treated more at length under their appropriate heads, as also are other subjects of which no mention is here made.

THE POPULATION.

The early enterprises of the city and State are elsewhere stated. The precise population of Indianapolis at date when it was selected as the State Capital cannot be stated. In 1830, the city contained 1,085 inhabitants. Within the next ten years the number more than doubled, being quoted at 2,695. In 1850, the population was 8,091; in 1860 it was 18,611; in 1870, 18,244; 1880, 75,044; 1884, 88,000; 1885,

96,500; 1886, 106,000; 1887, 117,500; and in 1888, 125,000, including Haughville, West Indianapolis, North Indianapolis, Brightwood and Irvington, suburbs of the city. Of the present population fully sixty-six per cent. are native born, the remainder containing a strong German and Irish element, a sprinkling of Swedes and Norwegians, and from four to five thousand negroes.

THE MUNICIPAL GOVERNMENT.

Since the incorporation of Indianapolis as a city in 1847, the city's growth required new provision for the better conduct of the public service. The executive department of the municipality is vested in a Mayor, the legislative department consisting of a Board of Aldermen and a Common Council, the former being composed of ten members, two from each of the five aldermanic districts into which the city is divided, and the latter of one councilman from each of the twenty-five wards. They are elected biennially in October and are each paid $150 per annum for their services. The remaining city officials, except the City Clerk, who is also elected, are appointed by the Council with the advice and consent of the Board of Aldermen. The latter list includes the City Attorney, who receives an annual salary of $3,000; a City Engineer, who receives $1800 and perquisites; two Street Commissioners, one receiving $1600 and the other $600 per annum; and two Market Masters who are paid a per diem. The County Treasurer and Auditor also act in the same capacities for the city.

THE POLICE DEPARTMENT.

The city was without a regularly constituted police force until 1854. In that year a system was inaugurated employing 14 men. The year following the system was abandoned, but revived in 1856 with 10 men. During the war the force was increased and in 1865 consisted of 38 members, so continuing until 1883, when the metropolitan system was adopted. It is under the direction of a board of three commissioners appointed by the Governor, Secretary of State and State Treasurer. The department is made up of one superintendent, two captains, two doormen, two drivers and seventy patrolmen, the appointments of whom are made in equal numbers from the dominant political parties. The department also includes a well organized patrol system, its equipment consisting of twelve boxes located throughout the city, and one wagon manned by two patrolmen, available for immediate service day or night. The pay rolls for 1888 footed up $60,601; the annual expense for the maintenance of the department, however, will not exceed $58,000. During 1888 the total arrests numbered 3,795, of which 3,480 were males and 315 were females.

THE FIRE DEPARTMENT.

The first steps in the direction of organizing a fire department were taken in 1859, when a company was formed with limited equipments but sufficient for the service. Volunteer companies were subsequently established and continued in operation until 1860, when the paid system was substituted and has since been maintained. The present force is made up of one chief, two assistants, eleven captains, thirty-one pipemen, six engineers, six stokers and twenty-one drivers. The equipment embraces six steam engines, one single and one double chemical engine, three hook and ladder trucks, and fifteen thousand feet of hose. Fifty-four horses are required in the service and the total valuation of the property, including in addition to the above twelve two-story brick engine houses, is $350,000. The annual support of the department requires an outlay of $77,620, of which $59,936 are paid for salaries and $17,684 for repairs, expenses, etc.

MUNICIPAL IMPROVEMENTS.

Indianapolis is more than fairly well supplied with excellent streets, drainage and water facilities. The total mileage of streets in the city is stated at 450, of which five miles are paved with wood, thirty are paved with stone, two hundred and fifteen miles are graded and gravelled roadways, one hundred miles are graded and provided with gutters and one hundred and fifty miles are unimproved. The total cost of work done from January 1, 1885, to January 1, 1889, was $673,000. The repairs from January 1, 1879, to January 1, 1889, are estimated at $40,000 per annum, except during 1888, when $59,000 was expended in that behalf.

SEWAGE.

As early as 1860, provision was made for a complete sewage system, the work of platting the city and otherwise arranging prelimi-

six to forty feet and has a total capacity of 15,000,000 gallons. Water is supplied to the cisterns, at the foot of Washington street, through mains, thirty inches in diameter, and thence delivered throughout the city by an engine and water-power, having a total capacity for pumping 22,000,000 gallons every twenty-four hours. The city supports thirty public fountains and five hundred fire hydrants.

LIGHTING THE CITY.

The city is lighted by gas and electricity. The former is furnished by the Indianapolis Gas Light and Coke Company, a private corporation, organized in 1851; electric lights are also provided by a private corporation, employing the Brush system, and natural gas is utilized in addition. On January 1, 1889, gas lamps to the number of 2,650, 100 electric lights and 314 vapor lights were in use by the city at an annual cost of $63,000. The gas lamps are furnished at $15

BIRD'S-EYE VIEW OF INDIANAPOLIS, LOOKING EAST FROM THE COURT HOUSE.

naries being executed by an engineer from Chicago. Little was done, however, toward perfecting the plans then formulated until 1870, when what is known as the "Grand Trunk" chain of sewers was begun, and thus far includes portions of Kentucky avenue, Massachusetts avenue, Illinois, Washington, Pennsylvania, Delaware, Michigan, Reed, Broadway and south streets. There were 30 miles completed January 1, 1889, the largest proportion of which were of brick from eight to ten feet in diameter, the balance being of pipe or vitrified stone from 15 to 24 inches in diameter; the cost of construction and materials ranging from seven to fourteen dollars per cubic foot.

THE WATER SUPPLY.

Indianapolis obtains its water supply from the Indianapolis Water Works Company, first organized in 1870, and re-organized in 1881. The company owns 75 miles of mains and 50 miles of laterals that have been constructed at a total cost of $2,000,000. The reservoir is located two miles northwest of the city, at the junction of White River and Fall Creek. It is 2,000 feet long, varying in width from

per year each, the electric lights at $80, and the vapor lights at $18 each. Commencing at the above date, the expense for lighting the city was estimated not to exceed $50,000 per annum, which amount, owing to the facilities furnished by the presence of natural gas and electric light corporations, will hereafter be materially reduced.

THE CITY SCHOOLS.

The opportunities afforded for the acquisition of an education in Indianapolis are not surpassed by those of any city in the United States. The system which now obtains has been in progress of development since the city was originally settled. The first school taught was in 1821, by Joseph C. Reed. Three years later Mr. and Mrs. Lawrence conducted an institute of learning in the Presbyterian church. In 1832 Miss Clara Flick opened an academy here, and in 1834 the old County Seminary became established. In 1853 the free school system superseded the primitive methods heretofore employed, with Henry P. Coburn, Calvin Fletcher and H. F. West as trustees. The schools were opened the same year, throughout which there was an average daily attendance of eighty out of a school population of 1,100, giving employment to ten teachers, who were paid $2.25 per term for each scholar. In 1871 the present system was organized. It is under the direction of a Board of Directors, elected from each of the eleven school districts into which the city is divided and is maintained by the State; the funds therefor being derived from the common school fund, from a special tax levied by the city and from the amounts received for liquor licenses, dog taxes, etc. The course embraces twelve years of four years each in the elementary, intermediate and high school departments. The course also includes an industrial department, where the most approved system of manual is taught. The course of study in all the departments is adapted to the requirements of the service of furnishing a thoroughly practical education. In the high schools the course is arranged with a view to the wants of students who complete their education there, with additional studies calculated to qualify those who desire to enter either of the State universities, into which they are admitted upon their graduation at the high school, without an examination. The curriculum embraces fourteen prescribed and ten optional subjects, particular attention being devoted to the science, higher mathematics and the languages. In the intermediate department the course includes arithmetic, geography and grammar, and the primary studies of a preparatory character to which are added the best features of the kindergarten system. The city has 28 public school buildings and two high schools, the latter being respectively located on the North and South Sides. They are all substantially built of brick, commodious and well equipped, thoroughly lighted and ventilated, and provided with every auxiliary and facility for the service to which they are designed. They represent a total valuation of one million of dollars. There are at present 300 teachers employed, 25 males and 275 females, the salaries for principals being $1,200 per annum, for teachers in the seventh and eighth grades $600, and for those in the remaining grades $350 per year. The school enrollment is 15,000, with a daily average attendance of 12,000 pupils, and the annual expense for tuition is $250,000, in addition to which $50,000 is required for repairs, incidentals, etc. The accommodations are inadequate to furnish sufficient room for the requirements of the service, and negotiations are in progress for the erection of three additional school buildings to be completed during 1889.

In addition to the public schools, the city contains 33 religious and private schools, two business colleges, a training school and Butler University at Irvington, a suburb of Indianapolis.

TEMPERATURE.

The temperature at Indianapolis compares well with that of any other part of the country, as will be seen from the following table showing the average temperature by months for four years ending January 1st, 1889:

For	Jan.	Feb.	Mar.	Apr.	May.	June	July	Aug.	Sept.	Oct.	Nov.	Dec.
	33.4	25.4	35.1	52.7	64.1	78.6	76.6	71.8	56.0	34.1	41.0	30.5

The highest temperature during that period was upon July 30, 1886, when the thermometer showed 108.8, and the lowest on January 10, 1886, it being 15 below zero on that day. In 1885 the direction of the wind was from the south-west and the rainfall was 39.51 inches; in 1886 and 1887 the wind was south, the rainfall for the former being 49.88 and 33.08 for the latter, and in 1888 the wind was from the northwest with 34.36 inches rainfall. Statistics further show that droughts and excessive rainfalls are exceptional.

VITAL STATISTICS.

That Indianapolis is pre-eminently a healthy city is conclusively demonstrated by comparison of the city's mortality reports with those of contemporaries. They show Indianapolis as the healthiest city in the United States with two possible exceptions, namely, Minneapolis and Denver. This gratifying fact is due in part to natural advantages in respect to locality, the absence of diseases that can be charged to the climate or are indigenous to the country, to efficient sewage, pure water and to other causes the presence of which are promotive of good health. The diseases prevalent are either hereditary, brought to the city by the incoming population, or owing to excesses, and even these are an infinitesimal percentage of the population as shown by the death rate, which was 14.62 in 1,000 during 1886; 14.54 in 1887 and 14 and a fraction in 1888. In 1887 there was an epidemic of scarlet fever, diphtheria and measles. The total number of these cases reported was 3,673 and the total number of deaths 146.

It will be seen by the foregoing summary of the features and attractions of Indianapolis, that they are of metropolitan proportions, and that there are concentrated here all the varied institutions and advantages which contribute to make the city a desirable location for business or residence.

SOUTH MERIDIAN STREET.

Natural Gas in Indianapolis and the State.

NATURAL GAS DISPLAY IN THE INDIANA GAS FIELDS.

HE discovery of natural gas in Indiana was made first at the little town of Eaton, in Delaware County, about three years ago. From the date of that discovery prospecting and developing has been going steadily forward. Up to this date 980 gas wells have been sunk in the State, 75 per cent. of which have been gas-bearing wells. The Indiana gas field embraces 3,500 square miles, or about two million square acres, and if one well was sunk on each 100 acres of gas land, it would require twenty thousand wells to exhaust the field. The development thus far made shows that gas underlies the greater part of the counties of Hamilton, Hancock, Madison, Delaware, Blackford, Tipton, Howard and Grant, as well as one-half of the counties of Henry, Randolph, Jay, Clinton, Miami, and Wabash, the last named counties being on the rim of the gas field. This field extends into the State of Ohio and connects with what is known as the Findlay gas field in that State. The southwest rim of the field runs to within five miles of the city of

A NIGHT SCENE ON EAST MARKET STREET - NATURAL GAS ILLUMINATION.

These railroads are all connected for freight purposes with one Belt Road and union tracks and magnificent stock yards. Over 5,000 freight cars pass daily over this Belt Road, and from 300 to 500 car-loads of stock are handled daily at these yards, which do a larger business than the yards of St. Louis, Cincinnati or Louisville. The line of this Belt is rapidly filling up with large manufacturing establishments, which obtain, without expensive switch charges, direct connection with all the railroads entering the city, the switch charges on the Belt being only one dollar per car.

In consequence of the railroad connections, and large field for trade, the city has always been a good location for merchandising. Many merchants have amassed fortunes and retired from this field, while few have failed. The city has over 300 wholesale and jobbing houses, and over 1,000 doing a retail business in the various lines of merchandise. The sales for the past year at wholesale are estimated at nearly $20,000,000. The people of the tributary country being comparatively free from debt, there have been few bad debts made, and the business has been very remunerative. Our city is believed to have the most successful wholesale street in the country. In many departments the city has the largest and most complete retail stores to be found in America, and there is little, if any, occasion for our people to go away from home to do shopping, while hundreds come from nigh-boring cities daily to attend the numerous conventions held here, and while here make their purchases.

There has never been any systematic booming of the city of Indianapolis. What she is to-day and what she is likely to be in the future is the result of plain, substantial business methods. The growth of the city in the past two or three years has been simply wonderful; not a day but some new comer from the east or from the south, in the State takes up his permanent abode here. There is no city anywhere that is more beautiful, healthful and inviting as a place of residence. There is no smoke emerging from chimneys, and the white and delicate tints are being placed upon even the business houses, and the great comfort and economy resulting from the general introduction of natural gas has made the city so attractive that the thousands who yearly seek new locations are now steadily drifting our way, and the census of 1890 will give Indianapolis a population very close to one hundred and fifty thousand.

RAILROAD FACILITIES.

THE transportation facilities available at Indianapolis are not surpassed by those of any inland city in the world, unless it may be Chicago. They have been intimately associated with the city's growth and development. Capital, instead of being cautious, sought investments of this character with confidence in the future of Indianapolis as a railroad center. The result is that a railroad system is in operation here of the largest magnitude, controlling an almost unlimited mileage. Every scheme of railroad enterprise in the State has either originated at Indianapolis or designated that city as its terminus, and corporations, organized elsewhere have made the city either their objective point or include it upon their route. By means of the system now in operation here, the city is placed in immediate communication with every section of the country from the Atlantic to the Gulf, from the Dominion of Canada to the Mexican Republic, the number of competing lines creating a rivalry which finds expression in facilities for the carriage of passengers or freight reasonable and abundant. The original system consisted of eight roads, embracing the Madison & Indianapolis, the Bellefontaine, the Terre Haute & Indianapolis, the Indianapolis & Lafayette, the Indiana Central, the Indianapolis Junction, Peru & Indianapolis, and the Indianapolis & Vincennes. Other roads followed in rapid succession until the present system was established and is constantly appreciating the value and importance of the city as a railroad center.

The following railway lines now enter Indianapolis:

Jefferson, Madison & Indianapolis; Indianapolis to Louisville, Ky., 110 miles.

Terre Haute & Indianapolis, Vandalia Line; Indianapolis to St. Louis, 240 miles.

Cleveland, Columbus, Cincinnati & Indianapolis; Indianapolis to Cleveland, O., 283 miles.

Cincinnati, Wabash & Michigan; Indianapolis to Benton Harbor, Mich., 201 miles.

Cincinnati, Indianapolis, St. Louis & Chicago, Cincinnati to Indianapolis, 110 miles; Indianapolis to Kankakee, 139 miles; Kankakee to Chicago, 53 miles.

Chicago, St. Louis & Pittsburgh; Columbus to Indianapolis, 188 miles; Indianapolis to Chicago 162; Kokomo, 104 miles.

Lake Erie & Western; Indianapolis to Michigan City, 161 miles.

Indianapolis & Vincennes; Indianapolis to Vincennes, Ind., 117 miles.

Cincinnati, Hamilton & Indianapolis; to Cincinnati, 123 miles.

Ohio, Indiana & Western; Indianapolis to Peoria, Ill., 212 miles; Indianapolis to Springfield, O., 140 miles.

Indianapolis, Decatur & Western; Indianapolis to Decatur, Ill., 153 miles.

Indianapolis & St. Louis; Indianapolis to St. Louis, 261 miles.

Louisville, New Albany & Chicago; Indianapolis to Chicago, 181 miles; Indianapolis to Cincinnati, 123 miles; Indianapolis to Michigan City, Ind., 153 miles.

The following table shows the number of trains, regular and special, arriving at the Union Depot in 1888, also number of coaches handled:

MONTHS.	REGULAR TRAINS.	SPECIAL TRAINS.	COACHES.
January	3,003	121	20,011
February	3,051	29	22,164
March	3,292	28	22,621
April	3,607	36	23,311
May	3,551	96	21,133
June	3,511	214	25,455
July	3,516	141	23,003
August	3,515	192	23,062
September	3,251	261	25,041
October	3,118	203	25,990
November	3,256	89	21,826
December	3,386	96	21,002
Total	39,256	1,801	300,400

An average of 112 trains per day throughout the year. During the same period the total movement of cars, passenger and freight, numbered 1,057,835, being 66,349 less than in 1887, owing to the scarcity of rolling stock.

UNION RAILWAY COMPANY.

The Union Railway Company was organized in 1850, and the old Union Depot completed in 1853. On September 20, 1883, it was incorporated and re-organized under an agreement entered into between the Chicago, St. Louis & Pittsburgh; Jefferson, Madison & Indianapolis; Cincinnati, Indianapolis, St. Louis & Chicago; Terre Haute & Indianapolis, and Cleveland, Columbus, Cincinnati & Indianapolis companies, each company owning a one-fifth interest in the enterprise. Soon after the new organization was perfected bonds to the amount of $1,000,000 were issued to erect the new Union Depot, for which ground was broken in November, 1886, and the structure completed during the fall of 1888. A description of the building will be found elsewhere. The affairs of the company are directed by a board consisting of di-

member from each of the proprietary companies, supplementary to which is a board of managers composed of one each from the proprietary and association companies. The monthly expenses of the new depot are made up and prorated among the companies recipient of its privileges on a train basis, the charges against the Belt Road being assessed upon a mileage basis.

THE BELT ROAD.

The Belt Line Road was reorganized in 1876 for the purpose of leasing its road and terminal facilities in the city and vicinity to other companies for the carriage of freight, also to afford sites for the building of factories along its line at reasonable prices. In 1882, the Union Railway Company leased the franchise for 999 years at an annual rental equal to six per cent. of the appraised valuation of the same. The company's tracks connect with the Cincinnati, Indianapolis, St. Louis and Chicago Road, northwest of the city, extending also to L. R. & W.; I. D. & W.; I. & St. L. and T. H. & I. on the south and southwest; thence to the Stock Yards, thence south and east to the J., M. & I.; C., I., St. L. & C.; and C., St. L. & P. tracks; on the north it connects with the tracks of the C., C., C. & I. and the L., B. & W. Roads, and on the west with the tracks of the L. E. & W.; L., N. A. & C., and the Chicago division of the C., St. L. & P. roads, leaving a space north of the city two and one quarter miles between its tracks. The company owns and operates 14½ miles of track, six miles of which are double, also six miles of siding and ten locomotives. The business handled is that usually handled by private corporations for their own account, the charges being upon a mileage basis and one dollar for each car moved without respect to distance. As an encouragement to the location of factories along its lines, the company is prepared to build switches from their main tracks to the doors of factories at the bare cost of labor and materials. During the year 1888 the Belt Road handled a total of 600,350 cars, 58,948 being handled on switches leading to manufactories located on its line, of which number 17,352 were loaded cars, also handling 40,110 carloads of live stock. The Belt Road practically makes the railroad lines centering at Indianapolis one line, and offers inducements, particularly to manufacturers, in its facilities for prompt shipments, unrivalled by any city in the United States.

In addition to the foregoing it should be stated that extensive car shops belonging to the Pennsylvania system, the "Bee Line," the "Big Four," Indianapolis, Decatur and Springfield, and Indianapolis, Decatur and Western, are located in the immediate vicinity and give employment to an aggregate of 2,500 hands.

STREET RAILWAY SERVICE.

The street railway service of Indianapolis is conducted on the same liberal and comprehensive plan characteristic of public and private enterprise, for which the city has, since become pre-eminent. The first street railway here was operated along Illinois street in 1864; this was the beginning of the present extended and invaluable system. During 1864, the franchise, with its equipments, right of way, appointments, etc., was disposed of to W. H. English and others, from whom it was subsequently purchased by the Messrs. Johnson, who in turn disposed of it to C. B. Holmes and J. C. Shaffer of Chicago, during January, 1889, for a consideration of $4,500,000. The system embraces 14 separate lines, covering a total of 60 miles of trackage and extending throughout the city in every direction, as also to the surrounding suburbs, cars leaving the corner of Washington and Illinois streets for their various termini every ten seconds during the day. The company employs 250 cars, 500 men and 1000 horses in the service, and run on schedule time. The fare is five cents, entitling passengers to transfer tickets over any of the company's lines.

UNION RAILWAY STATION.

The Union Railway Station that occupies the site of the old union depot was completed in 1888 at a cost of more than $1,000,000. It is the finest structure of its kind in the United States, and except the State House, the most conspicuous public building in the State. The main edifice is of brick with stone trimmings and dressings, elaborately finished and otherwise a model of elegance. It is 150 feet square, three stories high with mansard roof extension and surmounted by a lofty tower, the summit of which is visible to residents of all portions of the city and the surrounding suburbs. The main floor contains elaborately furnished sitting-rooms for the convenience of passengers waiting the arrival and departure of trains and all modern equipments are provided for their comfort and accommo-

NEW UNION RAILWAY STATION—INTERIOR VIEW.

dation. The upper stories are used for railroad offices. East and west of the main building are baggage rooms, also of brick, in dimensions 25x150 feet each and two stories high. The train shed is of iron and brick, extending a distance of 740 feet east and west and 189 feet in width. It is provided with nearly two miles of trackage and contains every facility and equipment known to the service. A total of 130 trains and upward of 10,000 passengers are estimated to have arrived and departed from the Union Depot daily during 1888.

The city is in every respect situated admirably for the purposes of a great railroad center, its centrality to a rich productive region for agricultural and manufactured commodities, live stock, lumber, etc., supplying an amount of tonnage far in excess of that usual to cities of the same size. The comprehensive railroad system of the city has been an important factor toward securing the steady increase in population and wealth which has been a marked characteristic of the city's history, and its completeness furnishes every facility for extended and constantly augmenting growth.

FREIGHT RATES.

The rates of freight from Indianapolis to Eastern points are lower than from any point on the same meridian. The same may be said with reference to freight rates to points West, North or South. And while the inter-state law has proved disastrous to some cities, its operations have served to confirm the advantages enjoyed here in regard to location, the presence of competing lines, and in other particulars. The following tables show the rates from Indianapolis to the below designated points, in effect April 1, 1889:

98 per cent. of rates from Chicago to	Boston and Portland	New York.	Albany.	Philadelphia.	Baltimore & Washington	Buffalo.	Pittsburg.
1st class, per cwt.							
2d " "							
3d " "							
4th " "							
5th " "							
6th " "							

The rates to Southern points, the same as from Cincinnati, are as follows, according to Southern Railway and S. S. Association classification.

RATES TO SOUTHERN POINTS.	Meridian.	Memphis.	Vicksburg, Natchez, Port Gibson, Baton Rouge, New Orleans, Mobile.
1st class, per cwt.	122	75	98
2d "	107	60	81
3d "	89	55	71
4th "	75	40	58
5th "	62	35	44
6th "	54	30	36
A "	39	29	29
B "	31	19	25
C "	39	29	27
D "	32	17	22
E "	21	20	30
H "	23	21	30
F "	66	40	49

To Texas and Arkansas points Louisville rates prevail, which are equal to St. Louis rates, plus the following arbitraries:

CLASSES.	1	2	3	4	5	A	B	C	D	E
Arbitraries	11	9	5	3	4	4	3	3	3	2

The following are the rates from Indianapolis to

	1st.	2d.	3d.	4th.	5th.	6th.
Cincinnati	25	22	18	14	9	8
Louisville	27	24	20	15	11	10
Cleveland	25	22	21	16	11	11
Toledo	28	26	25	15	13	10
Chicago	28	26	22	14	11	9
Peoria	34	29	22	14	11	9
E. St. Louis	34	31	31	15	12	10

From the foregoing it is apparent that the merchants, manufacturers and shippers of Indianapolis enjoy the most substantial advantages in the matter of freight rates.

TAXATION AND VALUATION.

TAXES in Indianapolis for municipal purposes are lower than those of any city of equal population in the country, those for educational purposes being the largest, and the total corporate tax amounting to but ninety cents per $100 valuation, with an equal amount for State, county, township, library, special and road repair support combined. The valuation of property for 1887 was $50,385,650, and that for 1888 $51,760,535, the total assessment was as follows, both years it being the same:

STATE.	STATE SCHOOL.	INDIANA UNIVERSITY.						
.12	.16	.003						

The city budget for the year 1888 was as follows: Police, $91,885.12; fire department, $82,457.19; lighting the city, $66,603.82; interest account, $66,572.40; salaries of city officials, $32,773.54; street improve-

ments, openings and repairs, $57,127.01; water rent $34,673.27; sewers, $14,693.23; hospital, $22,574.01; town hall, $4,340.81; Illinois street tunnel, $15,640; health, $7,859.69; cisterns, $2,625.13; fountains, $57,120; insurance, $117.60, and $2,474.79 for all other expenses, making a total of $470,777.51.

The bonded indebtedness of the city amounts to $1,705,500, and is steadily declining. Five hundred thousand dollars of the bonded debt was incurred by the city's loaning its credit for that amount to the Belt Line road, to secure which the latter issued bonds and mortgages for a like amount, with interest at the same rate as that paid by the city, payable fifteen days before the interest on the city bonds becomes due. The city's assets, consisting of the school property, worth $1,500,000; fire department buildings and equipments, $350,000; parks, $500,000; Tomlinson hall and city markets, $500,000; tunnel, $150,000; police equipments, $20,000; water and gas equipments, $50,000, etc., shows the city owning nearly $4,000,000 in excess of all liabilities, and is financially reliable as the most exacting could desire.

THE JOBBING TRADE.

HE jobbing trade of Indianapolis dates its inception back more than thirty years. Prior to that period, small sales of goods may have been made by houses here in connection with their regular business, but no special efforts were made in this field of commercial enterprise until late in the fifties. In 1857 A. & H. Schnull sold considerable invoices of groceries in bulk to be sold by the purchasers at retail. In 1860, some dry goods were disposed of to jobbers in these lines. In 1862, Wright, Bates & Maguire engaged in jobbing and later Andrew Wallace. These mentioned are the pioneer jobbers of Indianapolis, but it was not until about 1870 that the jobbing trade may be said to have been fairly commenced. From such a beginning, there has been a steady and substantial growth, not only in the original lines but in other branches of trade, until the annual transactions amount to millions where they formerly were limited to hundreds.

THE NUMBER OF JOBBING HOUSES.

The growth of the business is attested by the rapid increase in the number of houses thus engaged. The panic of 1873, while it produced no particularly disastrous effect, was not without results depressing, if not discouraging; and it was not until 1876 that the reaction set in. Since that year, the houses have become numerous, now numbering more than two hundred, employing upward of six hundred travelers, and making total sales which in 1888 aggregated $38,430,000 in value.

THE TERRITORY COVERED.

When the jobbing trade was first undertaken by merchants of Indianapolis, the business now controlled from here was in the hands of merchants of other cities, principally Chicago and Cincinnati. Much of this territory has been gradually acquired by Indianapolis, in addition to that secured by the development of unsettled sections as also of that once included in the limits of other markets. Beginning with a territory of the most limited dimensions, the jobbing trade of Indianapolis now controls the State, portions of Illinois, Ohio, Michigan, Kentucky, as far south as Tennessee, besides in special lines considerable territory west of the Missouri River. The trade is reported satisfactory in every particular; especially is this the case in the facilities enjoyed here for the prompt acknowledgment and shipment of orders. And while it is represented by an exceptionally varied class of houses, there are yet fields for enterprise that might be advantageously occupied. The opportunities for openings are worthy the attention and investigation of capitalists seeking investments for their money; and every encouragement and aid will be offered new comers, by citizens and the Board of Trade.

IMPORTS.

The importation of goods by Indianapolis merchants and manufacturers during 1888 was quite extensive. Those received were valued at $506,700, upon which duties amounting to $133,986.62 were paid.

The accompanying table does not show the total amount of sales made, or the capital invested in the various lines represented by the jobbing trade, but those only of houses principally engaged in the lines to which they are credited. For example, all jobbing grocers carry seeds in stock, but their sales in this line are not included in the sales of two exclusively seed houses which amount to $125,000; and many goods not enumerated are embraced in more important lines. For instance, guns, willow ware and surgical instruments

being included in the hardware, grocery and drug lines respectively, it should also be added that the operations of jobbers in grain, live stock and ice were received too late for publication in the present edition of the INDUSTRIES.

JOBBING HOUSES.

Section		No. of Firms	Travelers	Employes	Capital Invested	Sales for 1888
5	Agricultural Implements			218	$ 125,000	$2,800,000
2	Bakers			90	100,000	285,000
2	Barbers' and Dental Supplies	6		16	75,000	100,000
4	Boots and Shoes	23		52	250,000	1,300,000
12	Builders' Material			200	140,000	1,000,000
2	Canned Goods, Oyster and Fish			10	50,000	240,000
3	China, Glass and Queensware	22		76	200,000	1,000,000
5	Cigars and Tobacco	25		20	100,000	240,000
1	Clothing			10	32	200,000	150,000
4	Coffee, Spices and Baking Powder	21		91	225,000	740,000
25	Commission (Produce)			20	300,000	2,500,000
5	Coal			125	250,000	800,000
5	Confectioners	27		200	75,000	730,000
1	Dressed Beef			6	50,000	100,000
1	Drugs	20		196	610,000	1,500,000
1	Dry Goods	30		121	200,000	1,800,000
1	Flour and Feed			47	84,000	425,000
14	Grocers			181	1,525,000	7,000,000
9	Hardware and Iron	54		140	985,000	3,000,000
2	Hats and Caps			32	165,000	240,000
2	Hides and Pelts			60	200,000	1,000,000
3	Jewelry	7		20	85,000	250,000
2	Leather and Findings			18	115,000	600,000
10	Liquors	31		84	410,000	1,200,000
20	Lumber			200	250,000	3,000,000
2	Millinery	20		60	150,000	1,000,000
3	Notions and Toys	29		20	350,000	1,000,000
2	Paper	13		20	275,000	425,000
2	Rags and Iron			20	80,000	150,000
2	Railroad Supplies			16	70,000	320,000
1	Roofing Slate			10	20,000	40,000
1	Roofing Material			11	20,000	115,000
1	Rubber Goods	4		11	25,000	45,000
1	Scales	3		18	75,000	45,000
6	Seeds			61	80,000	135,000
6	Stationers	30		187	385,000	600,000
6	Stoves	13		81	150,000	350,000
5	Tinners' Supplies	8		40	100,000	350,000
6	Tobacco Leaf			12	25,000	100,000
2	Vinegar	2		8	20,000	70,000
2	Yeast			5	5,000	60,000
225	Total		600	3280	$10,025,000	$38,430,000

For the purpose of exhibiting the volume of the business in distributive lines carried on in the city there can be no more valuable method than the particular mention of the more prominent firms which have contributed to and continue to promote the importance of Indianapolis as a trade center. For this purpose the notices which follow have been prepared, and will be found to contain valuable information in regard to the history, growth and present status of many of the leading mercantile establishments of the city. In the aggregate, they exhibit a gratifying activity in nearly every branch of distribution. In detail, the houses which have been selected, while the list is not claimed to be exhaustive of all the meritorious firms, will be recognized as representative of the best elements of the business life of the city, and worthy exemplars of its commercial importance.

MURPHY, HIBBEN & CO., 97 AND 99 S. MERIDIAN STREET AND 26, 28, 30, 32, 34 AND 36 E. GEORGIA STREET.

MURPHY, HIBBEN & CO.

Wholesale Dry Goods and Notions, 97 and 99 South Meridian Street, 26, 28, 30, 32, 34 and 36 E. Georgia Street (annexed).

This, the oldest and most important jobbing dry goods and notion house in the State, has for more than twenty years maintained the highest position in the esteem and confidence of the trade, steadily retaining its supremacy through the several changes of title and interest occurring in this period and surviving the decline or retirement of various competitors in this and adjoining markets. Concentrating their energies in the prosecution of the business and limiting the employment of their resources to its constantly widening field, their present ample capital and assured financial position have been acquired by no doubtful methods, but are the direct result of prudent and attentive business methods, combined with a broad spirit of commercial enterprise. As noted above, Messrs. Murphy, Hibben & Co., occupy the premises numbered 97 and 99 South Meridian street, a five-story stone trimmed brick building, to which are annexed in the rear the five brick stores numbered 26 to 36 East Georgia street; these are connected with the main building by a large tunnel in the basement and convenient bridges on upper floors, affording in their entirety more than double the space employed by any similar business in the State. The merchandise offered in the various departments includes all desirable lines required in a first-class modern store, covering a wide range of foreign and domestic dry goods, notions, hosiery, white goods, linens, woolens, floor oil cloth, hemp carpetings, mounted window shades, overalls, working shirts, jeans and cassimere pants of their own manufacture, etc. Liberal use has been made by the firm of the facilities for direct importation offered by the Indianapolis Custom House, as evidenced in recent reports of the collector, and as

distributors they have attained an enviable position with some of the best known foreign manufacturers, enabling them to compete with any market on the class of goods brought out. Special attention has been given to the products of western and southern mills, with the most encouraging results, as both the consumer and the trade hold these lines in constantly increasing favor. Messrs. Murphy, Hibben & Co. control in the territory the general lines as well as special fabrics manufactured by "The Tennessee M'f'g Co.," Nashville, Tennessee, brown cottons, shirtings, grain bags, cotton batting, etc.; "Eagle and Phœnix Mills," Columbus, Georgia, heavy, medium and light weight cotton ades; "Mississippi Mills," Wesson, Mississippi, capital over $1,500,000, jeans, super-extra doe-skins, diamonds, tweeds, flannelettes, cheviots, cotton and woolen knitting yarns, sewing thread, etc., etc.; "Springfield Cassimere Mills," Springfield, Illinois, cassimeres, suitings, etc.; "South Bend Woolen Mills," South Bend, Indiana, cassimeres, skirtings, yarns, etc.; "New Albany Hosiery Mills," New Albany, Indiana, hosiery, yarns, etc.; "Seymour Woolen Mills," Seymour, Indiana, blankets, yarns, flannels, etc.; "Janesville Cotton Mills," Janesville, Wisconsin, sheetings; "Sibley Mills," Augusta, Georgia, plaid shirtings; "Sea Island Mills," warps, sheetings and bleached cottons; "Haw River Mills," Haw River, South Carolina, checks, stripes and shirtings, etc., etc. The wide acquaintance of the house and its well known reputation for solidity and fair dealing gives it as a representative of the best element of commercial character and activity, and the firm is conceded to stand at the head of the strictly jobbing interests of the city.

GRIFFITH BROTHERS' BUILDING, AS VIEWED FROM MAIN ENTRANCE OF THE NEW UNION STATION.

Griffith Brothers Wholesale Millinery, Importers and Jobbers.—This firm is representative in the broadest and truest sense, and the house is prominently known to the trade in every direction, and its position and influence are substantial and powerful factors in the development of Indianapolis's prosperity.

Krull & Jenkins Wholesale Dealers in Candies, etc., 21 and 23 West Maryland street. In 1888, Albert Krull, who had been for sixteen previous years connected with the wholesale confectionery of Daggett & Co., embarked in the same line of business on his own account, and in 1889 the present firm was formed. Both are men of experience in this special field, and the firm is rapidly acquiring prominence and commercial importance. They are located in a building 50x80 feet in size, admirably equipped for the transaction of business. They carry large and varied lines of candies, nuts, chewing gums and flavoring extracts, all carefully selected and of the best quality. They employ a force adequate to the demands of the trade, which is steadily appreciating in volume and value in the city and vicinity, and this house holds a leading and enviable position with patrons and the public.

Hoover & Gamble Miamisburg, O., Manufacturers of Excelsior Harvesting Machinery; Milton Daily, General Agent, No. 6 Chamber of Commerce. The firm of Hoover & Gamble have works located at Miamisburg, O., where they were established in 1876, and which have since advanced from small beginnings to a position of prominence and importance second to no similar undertaking in the United States. They employ a large force of operatives in the manufacture of machinery generally, making specialties, however, of

the Excelsior No. 8 Steel Folding Binder, and binder twine. The former is pronounced by experts to be the newest, neatest, most simple, strongest and best binder in the world. The binding attachment is original, as also are the main frame and gearing, and because thus differing from all other harvesters and binders, and because of its conspicuous merit in contrast with other machines, is not in ordinary competition. The same may be said of their Excelsior No. 2 Mower. Their binder twine is made from the best quality of manila and sisal fibre, extra strength and clear stock, and which, in addition to being even and strong, is insect proof and subjected to the severest tests before being offered for use. All of their manufactured articles are equally superior in materials, workmanship and capacity for durable service. The Indianapolis branch of the enterprise has been in charge of Milton Daily since 1881, the demand for the machinery of the Excelsior make in Indiana, Illinois, Western Minnesota and Dakota being supplied from this city. He occupies premises 25x80 feet in dimensions for office purposes, also warerooms and repair shops adjoining of similar proportions, shipments of machinery being made generally from the works direct, and all orders being promptly and satisfactorily filled. He employs from five to ten traveling salesmen, and does a large trade throughout the territory included within his jurisdiction.

McKee & Co.—Wholesale Dealers in Boots, Shoes and Rubbers, 93 and 95 South Meridian street.—Among the leaders in the wholesale boot and shoe trade of Indianapolis is the firm of McKee & Co., composed of Edward L., J. Robert and Robert S. McKee. The house was first established in 1861 by Vinnedge, Jones & Co., subsequently becoming Jones, Armstrong & Co., Jones, McKee & Co. in 1879, and adopting the present style upon the death of Mr. Jones, in January, 1888. They occupy four floors, well arranged and appointed, and provided with every convenience for the display, sale and shipment of their large and full lines of stock. Their goods are the products of the most reliable eastern manufactures, including the output of a factory at Lynn, Mass., in which they are largely interested, and the product of which they practically control. They handle boots and shoes for men, women, misses, youths and children, in leathers of the best quality, made up in the latest styles of the prevailing fashion and embodying beauty of design and finish, superior workmanship, comfort and durability. They are also sole agents here for the Boston Rubber Shoe Co., an organization of established reputation; also of the Lycoming Rubber Co. (Limited), and carry full lines of rubber boots, shoes, etc., in great variety and attractive assortment. They employ seven travelers and a full force of clerks and assistants, and do a large and constantly increasing jobbing trade throughout Indiana, Illinois and Ohio. The house is leading and representative in commercial circles and a valuable factor in the development of prosperity in the city and State.

Browning & Son—Dealers in Drugs, Medicines, Etc., 7 and 9 East Washington street, Apothecaries' Hall. The oldest, largest and finest stocked and equipped drug emporium in the State, and one of the oldest west of the Alleghenies, is that of Browning & Son. It was established by David Craighead nearly fifty years ago, and was for some length of time carried on under the firm name of Craighead & Browning. In 1854 Robert Browning succeeded, and in 1864 G. W. Sloan was admitted as a partner, and during 1886 the present firm, composed of Robert Browning and Robert C. Browning, was formed. The senior member of this firm has been a partner in the enterprise almost from its establishment. The firm occupies the main floor, basement and fourth floor of Apothecaries' Hall, 40x150 feet, and also a two-story annex, 25x80 feet in dimensions, extending back to Pearl street, which is used for warehouse purposes. The firm carry full stocks and complete lines of the purest and freshest of drugs and chemicals, proprietary medicines, druggists' sundries, physicians' supplies, surgical instruments, hospital appliances, paints, oils, dye stuffs, fancy glassware, etc.—in fact everything kept in stock by a first-class drug house. They deal at wholesale and retail, and the superiority of their goods and honorable methods employed in their transactions have acquired for the house a high and firmly-established reputation. They employ a force of fourteen experienced pharmacists and assistants, besides two traveling salesmen, and do a large jobbing business throughout Indiana, in addition to their large wholesale and retail trade in the city and vicinity.

Schnull & Co.—Wholesale Grocers, Coffee Roasters, Etc., 62, 64, 66 and 68 South Meridian street. The largest and most influential wholesale grocery house in the State, is that of Schnull & Co. It was founded in 1855 by A. & H. Schnull, the commercial pioneers of Meridian street. Upon the organization of the firm they purchased and demolished a church edifice at the corner of Georgia and Meridian streets, upon the site of which they erected the first business block on Meridian street. They subsequently purchased two residences adjoining their place of business, which they also demolished, building in their stead the business block occupied by the present firm. In addition to these improvements, and solely with a view of making Meridian street the trade center of the city, they purchased all the available property in their vicinity, which was re-sold on reasonable terms, the purchasers stipulating that the improvements to be made thereon should be for business purposes only. The result is that Meridian street is the leading wholesale street in Indianapolis, and is such through the enterprise and foresight of the Schnull Bros. Shortly after the war, the firm dissolved, Albert Schnull

returning to Europe and the head of the present firm becoming the founder and president of the Merchants' National Bank, also establishing a cotton mill, The Eagle Iron Works, and other manufacturing industries. In 1878 he became a partner in the wholesale grocery house of Severin, Schnull & Co. He disposed of his interest in that concern during 1872 to Mr. Ostermeier, and securing the interest of Mr. Over, of Over & Krag, established the firm of Schnull & Krag, which continued in operation until December, 1888, when G. A. Schnull succeeded to the Krag interest, and the present firm was organized. The premises consist of a four-story and basement building, 70x200 feet, with an annex to the rear, also four stories high, and 35x100 feet in dimensions. The house is provided with improved elevator and telephone service, also with every convenience for the display, sale and shipment of goods. The annex is occupied for the roasting and grinding of coffee and the compounding of spices. It is equipped with the latest improved machinery and appliances, and nothing is left to be desired that will contribute to promote the quantity and quality of the output. Their specialties are cigars, and among other brands, their "Schnull's Famous" is especially popular—over 1,000,000 having been sold in 1888. It is a clear Havana filler and conceded to be the best five cent cigar in the market, which they job very extensively. Their coffees are also in great demand all over the west and northwest; their lines of staple and fancy groceries, including every description of articles handled by a first-class grocery house, supplying the trade throughout Indiana, Illinois, Kentucky, Ohio and in States more remote. They employ from 30 to 40 assistants and seven traveling salesmen, and their business amounts to hundreds of thousands of dollars in value annually. The growth of the house has been remarkable, but not disproportionate to the enterprise and liberality displayed in its management. The senior member of the firm, in addition to the undertakings with which he is connected, is one of the heaviest real estate owners in the city; his present holdings including the Occidental Hotel block, part of the Schnull block, the Meridian street business block, and many other properties in the residence and commercial portions of the city.

A. Kiefer & Co.—Wholesale Druggists, 72 South Meridian street.—This business was established in 1866 by Kiefer & Vinton, by whom it was conducted until 1871, when Mr. Kiefer became sole owner and so continued until January, 1884, when W. B. Schmidt was admitted, forming the present firm. They occupy a double store, four stories, 30x100 feet in dimensions, at 72 South Meridian street, and a two-story warehouse, 40x100 feet. They carry large and assorted stocks of drugs and chemicals, proprietary medicines and compounds, druggists' supplies and sundries, medical and surgical instruments, paints, oils, brushes, artists' supplies, perfumeries, soaps, etc. They have also a special department for cigars, which is stocked with extensive lines of imported Havana, also with Key West and other favorite domestic cigars. They make specialties of Brown's Expectorant for coughs and colds, Laraxine for the liver, Lyon's Kozodiann, an infallible remedy for baldness, and Deming's Discovery, of which they are sole proprietors and manufacturers, and which are sold through jobbers and the trade in all parts of the country. They employ from 35 to 40 competent chemists, clerks and salesmen and six travelers and do a large trade in the city and State, as also in portions of Illinois and Ohio. Messrs. Kiefer and Schmidt are members of the Board of Trade, and representative citizens and merchants, and their house is in high standing with the trade.

Dickson Storage & Transfer Co.—Storage, Transfer and Warehousing, 170 South Pennsylvania street.—This company, composed of H. B. Dickson and L. Dickson, was established in 1887. They occupy the two lower floors of the block above located, each 100x115, also the two upper floors of the same block, each 165x115 feet in dimensions. The premises are fitted up with large elevators, railroad tracks to enable the rapid and safe handling of freight and its transfer without exposure to the weather, and are provided with other facilities and conveniences necessary to the efficiency of the service and the secure warehousing and protection of consignments. They make a specialty of storing and carrying stock for agricultural implement and

was a prosperous future in store and carry the stock of twelve such houses, besides acting as agents for the Rock Valley Manufacturing Company, engaged in the production of agricultural implements at Lancaster, Ohio, also for the Eclipse hand wagon factory of Racine, Wisconsin, and can fill the orders in the region of each. This branch of the business is managed by H. E. Dickson, who was for seventeen years one of the most successful salesmen in the employ of the Oliver Plow Co., the remaining departments of the enterprise being directed by his son and partner, E. Dickson, for many years a conductor on the I. P. W. & C. R. R. prior to embarking in the present undertaking. In addition to the supply of these lines, they do a general storage business for all descriptions of commodities not explosive, including furniture, pianos, etc., handling supplies in the most careful and systematic manner and upon the most reasonable terms. They enjoy special advantages in low rates of insurance, a reduced transportation tariff and easier emoluments, and their business is managed according to the most honorable and approved business principles. They employ a force of from eight to ten warehousemen and their trade is drawn from all points tributary to Indianapolis and vicinity.

Pearson & Wetzel.—Importers and Jobbers in China, Glass and Queensware, 119 and 121 South Meridian street. The establishment of the house of Pearson & Wetzel dates back to 1882, and the firm is composed of Charles B. Pearson and Henry Wetzel. They are among the most extensive dealers in china, glass and queensware in the city. In 1887 their present store was erected and taken possession of by the firm. The building is one of the handsomest on the street. It is four stories in height, with a frontage on Meridian street of 30 feet and a depth of 200 feet, well appointed and supplied with all modern improvements. They are the sole agents in Indianapolis for Johnston Bros.' granite ware, of Hanley, England, in which, as also in all other imported and domestic stocks, they make a very fine display. These latter include china, glass and queensware of the most celebrated manufacture; stoneware from the best-known potteries, chandeliers, lamps, kerosene fixtures, table and pocket cutlery, plated goods, fruit jars, flasks, prescription vials, etc., etc. They employ a large and experienced staff of assistants, including five traveling salesmen, and minister to the wants of an extensive trade in Indiana, Illinois and Ohio.

Hays Bros.—Wholesale Boots and Shoes, 36 South Meridian street. This firm, which was organized in July, 1887, is composed of Joseph Hays and L. E. Hays. In 1872, Mr. Joseph Hays began business here as a retail boot and shoe dealer, and for many years conducted operations with a success that annually became more and more prominent and prosperous. Deciding to extend their field of operations and usefulness, they embarked in the wholesale trade at the date above stated, and have since devoted their attention to that department of the business, for which they enjoy superior facilities, including a branch house in the same line at 169 Bedford street, Boston, Mass. The premises occupied in this city consist of a four-story and basement brick structure, 28x125 feet in size, equipped with every modern convenience, and furnishing commodious accommodations for the storage and display of the large and varied lines they carry in stock. These embrace the best makes of ladies', misses', children's, men's, youths' and boys' boots and shoes, selected with care from the products of leading eastern manufactories, and enjoying a deserved reputation for their material, finish and durability. They give employment to a full staff of clerks and assistants, including three traveling salesmen, and are constantly adding to their trade and influence throughout Indiana, Ohio, Illinois and Kentucky. The Hays Bros. are enterprising and experienced men, and their "new departure" has acquired prominence among the representative business houses of Indianapolis.

F. C. Huntington Co.—Seed Merchants, 78 and 80 East Market street.—This establishment was founded in 1860, by J. P. Mendenhall & Co., to whom the present management succeeded in August, 1886. They occupy a two-story and basement building, 30x100 feet in dimensions, well appointed for the storage and protection of stock, and the filling and shipment of orders. They carry heavy stocks

and full lines of agricultural, horticultural and garden seeds, embracing a total of more than 2,000 varieties, also delicate roots, plants and flowering shrubs, in addition to special varieties of flowers indigenous to the tropics and peculiar to European cultivation. They also handle garden tools of every description, and fertilizers of the best quality, and issue, quarterly, a 25,000 edition catalogue of their stocks, beautifully illustrated and printed, which is mailed free to customers, dealers and cultivators in all portions of the country. No house in the business enjoys better advantages for securing the most desirable commodities and they do a large trade in the city and State, besides supplying patrons in every section of the United States, with special seeds, bulbs and plants.

Kothe, Wells & Bauer.—Wholesale Grocers; 128 and 130 South Meridian street. An important recent addition to the wholesale grocery trade of Indianapolis is the house of Kothe, Wells & Bauer, composed of George Kothe, late of the large insurance house of Richardson & Kothe, William Kothe, Jr., Charles W. Wells and George Bauer, and which was organized in January, 1889. Previous to that date, Mr. Kothe, Jr., had been for eleven years a traveling salesman for the grocery house of Schnull & Krag, with whom Mr. Wells and Mr. Bauer had also been similarly engaged, the former for fifteen and the latter for nine years. The continued experience and large acquaintance and connections thus acquired eminently qualify these gentlemen for the same line of work for this house, which they will undertake, assisted by Messrs. James Blizzard, W. J. Griffin and Frank Blount. The firm is located in the heart of the wholesale trade district, where they occupy a handsome four-story building, 35x150 feet and containing all modern facilities and improvements for the storage, display, sale and shipment of stock and the transaction of business. They carry full lines of staple and fancy groceries, making specialties of teas, coffees and sugars of the choicest grades and varieties. In their department of fancy groceries they include canned and potted meats, fruits and preserves, sauces, pickles, spices, baking powders, etc., also handling the best brands of smoking and chewing tobaccos and cigars, with other articles appertaining generally to the business. The house is already acquiring an important line of trade throughout Indiana and adjoining territory. The members of the firm are men of enterprise and business ability, and the affairs of the house are conducted upon liberal and honorable methods.

D. S. Morgan & Co.—H. E. Rose, General Agent, Manufacturers of Triumph Harvesting Machinery, No. 8 Cleveland Block.—The establishment of D. S. Morgan & Co., at Brockport, N. Y., was founded in 1844, completing in that year the first practical reaper built in the world. Since then improvements have been perfected in rapid succession until they now manufacture the latest and most improved grain harvesting implements of the kind known to the trade. In 1882 the company was incorporated with the main office and factory at Brockport, and agencies throughout the United States, Canada and Europe. The premises occupied cover a very large area, upon which have been built machine shops, moulding rooms, wood working shops, setting up and painting departments, etc., fully equipped with the latest improved machinery and appliances and ample warehouse accommodations and shipping facilities. An immense force is employed, and the annual output is of corresponding magnitude. Their products embrace the "Triumph" Steel Frame Folding Binder No. 8, different in construction from any other binder, the only practical folding binder on the market, made of steel, simple and durable, easily handled and efficient in operation; the "Triumph" Mowers, cutting a swath of from four feet three inches to five feet wide, for one or two horses; binders in wood or steel frame, cutting from five and one-half to six and one-half foot swathes, and other machinery, embodying more points of excellence in materials, lightness of draft, perfection of work and durable wear, than any other mower ever invented. The present officers of the company are; D. S. Morgan, President; George H. Allen, Treasurer; E. T. Lamb, Secretary; H. S. Malden, Manager of Agencies, with H. E. Rose General Agent for the State of Indiana. The latter assumed charge of this territory in 1884. He occupies handsome offices and is provided with exceptionally complete facilities for fully meeting the requirements of the trade in this State, which, under his fostering care, has steadily grown. He is prepared to fill orders with the least delay for the company's supplies, machinery, etc., and extra parts for them, shipping same securely packed and by the most expeditious route. He also furnishes catalogues, price lists and other valuable information, and is well known and highly esteemed in all portions of the State for the liberal and honorable methods that characterize his management of the business.

Hollweg & Reese— Direct Importers of China, Glass and Queensware, 84, 86 and 88 South Meridian street.— The largest, best stocked, and most elegantly equipped china, glass and queensware jobbing house in the State of Indiana, is that of Hollweg & Reese located as above. Mr. Louis Hollweg, who established the business in 1868, is the only surviving partner, Mr. Charles E. Reese being deceased. The firm occupies a handsome five-story and basement building, 75x130 feet in dimensions, as salesrooms and office, and the two adjoining buildings, each four stories high and 30x120 feet in dimensions, are used for the storage of heavy stock, the packing and shipment of goods, etc. The premises are equipped with every facility for the accommodation of the trade. They handle very heavy stocks, chiefly the products of the most famous European potteries, of which they are direct importers, embracing Limoges, Dresden, Carlsbad, and other celebrated chinas; English, French, Belgian, Hungarian and Bohemian glassware, in crystal, cut and colors, and are agents for Meakin's ironstone china, made in Staffordshire, England. They also carry full lines of the choicest American manufacture of white and decorated wares, American glassware, lamps of every description in glass, porcelain, pottery, etc., plain and decorated, lamp goods, supplies, etc., novelties, ornaments, bric-a-brac, etc., of the finest quality. Their stocks are carefully selected and they are prepared to fill and ship orders promptly. They employ fourteen travelers and a force of competent clerks, and their trade extends throughout Indiana, Illinois, Ohio and Kentucky.

Geroe, Wiggins & Co.— Wholesale Produce and Commission, 43 and 45 South Delaware street. One of the leading houses engaged in the commission business in this city, is that of Geroe, Wiggins & Co., which was established many years ago and is composed of W. R. Geroe, T. P. Wiggins, J. C. Bigelow and William Kiefaber. They occupy a basement and two floors, each 25x120 feet in dimensions, well appointed and equipped with all available conveniences for the display, sale and storage of consignments, and provided with a complete and efficient shipping service. They handle large quantities of foreign and domestic fruits, vegetables and country produce generally, received direct from importers and producers, and enjoy superior advantages for quick sales and prompt returns, owning similar establishments at Cincinnati, Dayton and Toledo, which are distributive points for the trade within the territory contiguous and dependent upon those cities as their source of supplies. The firm solicit consignments, and are prepared to furnish patrons with all information with reference to the demand for their special lines of commodities the condition and fluctuations of the markets, and other points of value. They employ a large force of assistants and their operations for account of customers are handled judiciously, closed up without delay and immediate returns of the proceeds made to consignors. The house is widely known for its honorable business methods, and its efficiency and enterprise have made it a substantial and reliable factor in the trade of Indianapolis.

M. O'Connor & Co., Wholesale Grocers, 47 and 49 South Meridian street.—Mr. M. O'Connor, the principal of this firm, has been an active and influential resident of Indianapolis for over 21 years, establishing his present enterprise in 1876. The firm occupies a handsome and well equipped four-story and basement building, 35x200 feet in dimensions, at one of the most available corners in the wholesale trade section of the city. They carry large stocks and complete lines of staple and fancy groceries, selected with care and purchased from first hands. These embrace teas, coffees, and sugars of the best qualities, spices, baking powders, canned goods, potted

meats, preserves and fruits, smoking and chewing tobaccos of the most celebrated manufacture, imported and domestic cigars, substantial and delicacies of every description and in general assortment, pure and fresh and in all respects suited to the demands of an exacting class of patronage. Their supplies in every department are unsurpassed for their uniform superiority and high standard of excellence, and the enterprising methods which characterize the management of the house place it in a leading and prominent position. All orders are filled promptly and shipped securely, and the business of the house is annually increasing in volume and value. The Messrs. O'Connor & Co. employ a large force of assistants, besides six traveling salesmen, and do a large trade throughout Indiana and along the borders of Illinois and Ohio.

Gordon, Kurtz & Co.— Wholesale Saddlery Hardware, 128 and 130 South Meridian street.— Among the leading concerns, doing

an exclusively wholesale trade in the lines of saddlery hardware is that of Gordon, Kurtz & Co. The firm is composed of Irving S. Gordon and William E. Kurtz, and in 1877 succeeded the firm of J. S. Gordon & Co., organized in 1872. They are located in a three-story and basement building, 25x200 feet in size, perfectly equipped and appointed, furnished with the Reedy elevator and other conveniences, and supplied with all modern facilities for the display, storage and shipment of goods. They carry full lines of stock, embracing every article of utility or ornament appertaining to saddlery hardware, and control the output of establishments manufacturing horse collars. They also handle saddles, and supplies of every description, and of the best make. Prompt attention is paid to all orders, particularly to mail orders, the firm being prepared to make shipments to all points at the shortest notice, while they offer the best inducements in quality and price. They employ a large staff of clerks, assistants, etc., also five traveling salesmen, and supply a large local demand, besides doing a large trade in Indiana, Ohio, Illinois and in territory more remote. The members of the firm are public spirited, and the firm is in every respect reliable and representative.

Newark Machine Co., of Columbus, O.,—Manufacturers of Agricultural Implements, Indianapolis Office, No. 3 Masonic Temple. This company, one of the most influential organizations engaged in the manufacture of clover huller and straw stacking implements in the world, was established at Hagerstown, Md., in 1877. The plant was removed to Newark, O., in 1881, and on July 27 of that year the company was incorporated, with a capital stock of $50,000. Their success was complete, and, during 1883, they declared a stock dividend of 35 per cent, and paid a cash dividend of eight per cent. In 1884, the works, warehouses, etc., were destroyed by fire with a loss of over a quarter of a million of dollars. The plant was then removed to Columbus, O., where the old "Gill Car Works" buildings have been since occupied, and will be retained until the company can secure a desirable location and erect works adapted to their requirements. Their specialties are The Victor Clover Huller, The Victor Manure Spreader and The Imperial Straw Stacker. The former, with patent seed cleaner and bagger, is conceded to be the best equipped, most efficient, durable, economical, profitable and satisfactory machine of its kind, and unsurpassed for rapidity of work, simplicity of construction, ability to save seed, prevent waste, and to handle damp, wet and tough clover seed. Over 200 machines were sold in 1888, and there are now between 4,000 and 5,000 in use throughout the States and Territories, and over 600 have been sold in this State alone. The manure spreader is the only one made that can be attached to the running gear of an ordinary farm wagon and can also be used without such ends. It is made in four sizes, holding from 33 to 45 bushels according to the size, graduated so as to spread from six to 35 loads per acre, evenly distributed, and enabling the straw and sheets to benefit by the compost. It combines economy in price, lightness in draft, simplicity and durability, and is the only perfect machine of the kind manufactured. The large sized Straw Stacker is equally reliable, effective and satisfactory. It saves from five to seven men's labor every hour it is in operation, and will deposit more straw in a stack, of a given height, than any other stacker made. These specialties are manufactured exclusively by the Newark Company, who also include in their output, fanning mills, corn shellers, cutting boxes and other agricultural implements. Their market is the world, the shipment of stock requiring trains of 25 cars each to transport from Columbus to all points in the United States. Their prices are low and the superiority of their products is

Kentucky copper distilled whisky, including all the favorite brands of Anderson and Nelson Counties, noted for their purity, volume and medicinal properties. In addition to these, they carry in full supply Monongahela and Kentucky rye whiskies, California wines and brandies, imported French brandies, champagne, claret, madeira, port, sherry, Burgundy and Rhine wines, Holland and English gins, cordials, etc., in great variety and of superior quality. They are prepared to respond to all orders promptly and their relations with producers and importers are such that they are able to offer unsurpassed inducements to customers. They employ two travelers and a force of assistants, and do an increasing trade throughout the city and State, in which their wide experience and honorable dealings long since procured for them an enviable reputation.

A. Booth Packing Co.—Oysters, Fish and Canned Goods, 40 North Illinois Street. The A. Booth Packing Company is the largest, most perfectly equipped and best appointed enterprise engaged in the packing and shipping of oysters, fish, canned goods, etc., in the world. It was established at Chicago in 1850, by A. Booth. The firm subsequently became A. Booth & Sons, and in 1887 was incorporated with a paid up capital stock of $1,000,000. They have branch houses at Chicago, Denver, St. Paul, Baltimore, Kansas City, St. Louis, Louisville,

WASHINGTON STREET—LOOKING EAST FROM ILLINOIS STREET.

attested by gold and silver medals awarded by the Cotton Exposition, Southern Exposition, Cincinnati and Chicago Expositions, as also from the State Fairs and Agricultural Societies of every State in the Union. The Western agency of the company has been, since 1882, in charge of E. L. Williams as general manager, who includes within his territorial jurisdiction the State of Indiana, and portions of Illinois, Kentucky and Michigan, giving employment to from eight to ten salesmen, and doing a large and increasing trade with dealers and farmers in all directions. To his ability and enterprise the large trade of the company, in the territory controlled by him, is in no small degree due. The company's officers are: J. P. McCune, President; T. J. Picard, Vice-President; F. S. Wright, Treasurer; J. M. Knodle, Secretary, and J. M. Kailer, General Superintendent.

H. Sweeney & Co.—Wholesale Dealers in Pure Copper Distilled Kentucky Whisky, 212 South Meridian street. H. Sweeney & Co. began operations here in 1874, continuing in the trade until 1885, when Mr. Sweeney abandoned the field to engage in other pursuits, but resumed his present business in November, 1888. The firm occupy a handsome three-story and basement brick building, 25x120 feet in dimensions, and equipped with every convenience and facility for the transaction of business. They handle very extensive lines of pure

Omaha, Duluth, Minneapolis, Bayfield, Escanaba, Manistique, New Orleans, Port Arthur, Canada, and Astoria, Oregon. The headquarters are at Chicago, from which and other points they send out the largest fleet of fishing vessels on the lakes. At Astoria, Oregon, they conduct an immense establishment devoted to the canning of salmon, also an equally extensive canning depot at Chicago, with very commodious refrigerating capacities there and at Winnipeg, Manitoba, for the preservation of their commodities. They also own and operate very large oyster beds at Baltimore and New Orleans, and their annual business in all lines foots up millions in value. The Indianapolis branch is under the management of Mr. C. E. West, who, prior to taking charge of this branch, had been connected with the company for two years at their Minneapolis branch, and is intimately familiar with the business and the requirements of the large trade. The local branch occupies the basement and main floor, each 25x100 feet in dimensions, with a fish and oyster packing house in the rear, recently completed, 25x75 feet, provided with a freezer of five tons capacity and accommodations for the canning of oysters and other facilities for the advantage of the service. In this department they handle upward of 4,000 gallons of oysters and 1,000 pounds of fish per diem. Mr. West also includes under his management a retail branch of the business at the corner of Delaware street and Massachusetts avenue. Their lines of supplies embrace Oval Brand, Diamond Brand and other well known brands of oysters, salmon, canned and fresh, salt and fresh water fish and bivalves, delicacies, etc., in the same lines, pure, fresh and sweet, and enjoying a reputation for their superior qualities in all parts of the world, where, particularly in England, France, Germany and the United States, they have received the highest metals and awards over all competing displays from houses similarly engaged.

The Spray Medicine Co.—C. R. Crow, General Manager, No. 23 West Circle street.—This company was organized in 1886 for the purpose of enabling the public throughout all portions of the United States to avail themselves of the benefits of "Minnehaha Spray," a recent medical discovery for the purification of the blood, and the cure of other diseases, and which is declared by chemists and the afflicted to be of unsurpassed efficiency and value. Their headquarters are in this city, with branches at St. Louis and St. Paul, and agencies in all the leading cities of this country and Canada. The "Spray" is a vegetable compound, warranted to contain no iron, iodide, potassium, opiates of any character and no mercury in any form whatever, but two of the finest nerve foods known to scientific development. It infallibly cures all primary and secondary forms of blood diseases, dyspepsia and stomach disorders, ulcerated sore throat, insomnia, hysteria, nerve diseases, catarrh, headache, neuralgia, etc., acting powerfully on the mucous coatings, rousing up the torpid liver, promoting perfect digestion and thorough assimilation of food, restoring lost vitality and otherwise assisting nature to perfectly renew the system. The medicine is tasteless, being put up in capsules, 50 in each box and sold by agents only, at $1.00 per box. Mr. C. R. Crow, the general manager of the company and to whose enterprise and efforts the introduction and popularity of the "Spray" is largely due, is located as above, where he occupies handsomely fitted up offices. He carries large stocks of the specific, in which he deals exclusively, and is prepared to ship medicines to any part of the United States either by mail or express. He employs four travelers and supplies a steadily increasing demand throughout the North, South and West, as far as Washington Territory. The virtues of the "Spray" are attested by 9,000 references in St. Paul and other cities where its reputation has already become established, and the honorable and liberal management of Mr. Crow has contributed to secure the deserved prominence and prosperity enjoyed by the enterprise here and elsewhere.

L. L. Norton—Jobber of Watchmakers' Tools and Materials, Dueber Cases, Hampden Movements, Trenton Watches, Roll Plate and White Metal Chains, Silk Guards and Welch Clocks, No. 14 Hubbard Block, 12 South Meridian street.—The business conducted by L. L. Norton, that of jobbing in watchmakers' tools and materials, Welch clocks, Trenton watches, Dueber cases and Hampden movements, roll plate and white metal chains, was established by that gentleman in 1886, and now enjoys a monopoly of the trade in those lines, being the only house in Indianapolis making them a specialty. He occupies premises 20x50 feet in dimensions, attractive and well appointed and supplied with every facility and convenience for the business. His range of stocks embrace watchmakers' tools and materials, rolled plate and white metal chains, jewelers' sundries and supplies and novelties in great variety. His stocks are imported direct from Europe and are the products of the leading manufactures both there and in America. They are unsurpassed in their lines in the West and every effort is made by Mr. Norton to meet the demand of the trade. He employs a competent force of assistants, including one traveling salesman, and does a large and steadily increasing trade throughout the city and State, and in portions of Illinois, Ohio and other States.

Bradley, Holton & Co. Manufacturers of Agricultural Implements, 177, 179 and 181 East Washington street.—This company was incorporated in 1886 as successors to the David Bradley Manufacturing Company, located here during 1880, as a branch of the same concern having its headquarters at Chicago, where the manufacture of their products is still carried on, giving employment to several hundred operatives. At the date of the incorporation under the laws of Indiana,

there was no material change made in the membership, Mr. David Bradley remaining President of Bradley, Holton & Co., with J. Havis Bradley, Vice-President, and W. B. Holton, Secretary and General Manager. The premises occupied embrace a three-story and basement brick building with 50 feet front on East Washington street and extending back 200 feet to commodious premises fronting on Pearl street, and utilized for warehouse and shipping purposes. They carry very large stocks and an endless variety of agricultural implements, including The Bradley and other patterns of cultivators, The Bradley Self Dump and other hay rakes, plows of every description and for every purpose, from those for breaking up the prairie to those intended for the most delicate work, harrows, drills, cotton planters, farm and church bells, etc., etc., of their own manufacture. In addition to these productions, they carry very extensive lines of corn planters and shellers, the Eagle hay, straw and fodder cutting boxes, corn, wagon, and sack elevators, The Bradley mowers, cider mills, corn and cob mills, steam engines and generators, buggies, carriages, phaetons, surreys, buckboards and business wagons, spring, delivery, milk and farm wagons, and other implements, tools, conveyances and appliances adapted to agricultural use. They fill orders and furnish information in the most prompt and satisfactory manner. The quality of their goods, their low prices and honorable methods have secured for them precedence over competing houses in the same lines, among the agricultural communities and dealers of the West, Northwest and South. They employ twenty assistants and six travelers, and from Indianapolis supply a very large demand throughout Indiana, Ohio and Kentucky.

Chas. M. Raschig. Importer and Dealer in Cigars and Tobacco, 21 East Washington street.—This is one of the oldest houses in its line in the city, having been established by Mr. Charles M. Raschig in 1856, and for nearly a third of a century has been successfully conducted. He occupies the main floor and basement, each 25x100 feet in dimensions, at the above site, handsomely fitted up and attractively appointed and also owns and manages the cigar stands in the Grand Hotel and the Hotel English. His specialties are the "C. M. R.," a five-cent cigar that has met with an almost unparalleled demand, for the sale of which he is sole agent; the Raschig No. 21, Seidenberg & Co.'s "La Rosa Española," and other five-ten cent cigars, in addition to carrying heavy stocks and full lines of Havana cigars, which he imports direct, his selections including a dozen of the leading brands; Key West and other domestic makes of cigars, cigarettes, etc., together with the best qualities of smoking and chewing tobaccos, meerschaum, briar and other pipes, and smokers' articles and novelties in great variety. His stocks are large and complete, and orders are filled promptly and at the lowest market prices. Mr. Raschig does a large and steadily increasing jobbing trade in the city and vicinity, and the house is regarded as a leading and representative one.

Taylor & Smith. Manufacturers and Dealers in Leather, Findings, Belting, Hose, Packing, Etc., 137 and 139 South Meridian street.—One of the representative houses in the metropolitan city of Indianapolis, is that of Messrs. Taylor & Smith, manufacturers and dealers in leather, findings, shoe store supplies, belting, hose, packing and all kinds of rubber goods used for mechanical purposes. This is a very old business concern, one of the oldest in the city, having been established in 1858. The present proprietors Messrs. William A. Taylor and William H. Smith, have been connected with the house for over 20 years. Both gentlemen are well and favorably known to the trade, are widely experienced in the business, have ample facilities, and give to the business, in all its details, their close personal attention. The firm occupies a substantial three-story brick building with a handsome stone front, located at Nos. 137 and 139 South Meridian street, where may be found a full and complete stock of goods. Special attention is given in all of their various departments, to securing the best grade of goods, and it is a matter of particular attention with this firm to see that all goods sent out by them shall be fully satisfactory as to quality. Messrs. Taylor & Smith are the sole agents in Indiana and Eastern Illinois for Messrs. Mooney & Sons' celebrated oak tanned harness leather, for which they have an extensive sale on this and adjoining States. There are also large-ly engaged in the manufacture of chestnut oak tanned leather belting, orders for which they are prepared to fill on short notice. For many years this concern has had the sole agency in Indiana of the Boston Belting Company, of Boston, Mass., widely known as one of the oldest and most extensive manufactories of rubber goods for mechanical purposes, including belting, hose, packing, etc. A full line of the manufactures of this company is carried by Messrs. Taylor & Smith, who are in correspondence with parties who sell to use this class of goods. The gentlemen comprising this firm are to be congratulated upon the large measure of success already attained, and upon the material value of their establishment to the city of Indianapolis.

The Bowen-Merrill Co. Importers and Publishers; Jobbers of Books, Papers, Etc., 16 and 18 W. Washington street. This company, which was incorporated in 1885, was the consolidation of the businesses of the old established firms of Bowen, Stewart & Co., and Merrill, Meigs & Co., houses that had their origin in this city over fifty years ago. The company is officered as follows: Silas T. Bowen, President; Samuel Merrill, Superintendent; Charles D. Meigs, Jr., Secretary; and William H. Elvin, Treasurer, who manage and direct the largest jobbing house in their line in the State. They occupy one of the handsomest business edifices in the city, comprising a four-story and basement iron front building, 40x150 feet, handsomely appointed and equipped with all requisite facilities and appliances, and owned by the President of the company. Their printing, binding and other mechanical work is done elsewhere, owing to lack of room. Their specialties are law books, embracing the codes, digests, statutes and reports of the various States, as well as elementary works, Sabbath-school records and publications, class books, blank books, etc., appropriate to every department of commerce, manufactures or trade. They carry very extensive stocks of paper of every description, including wrapping, printing, commercial, legal and note, stationery and druggists' sundries and other supplies generally, in great variety and of the best quality. The affairs are administered according to a most liberal and judicious policy, and its history has been that of progress and prosperity. A staff of fifty assistants and eleven travelers is employed and their trade is throughout the United States, in Canada, England and Continental Europe, and even to Australia and British India.

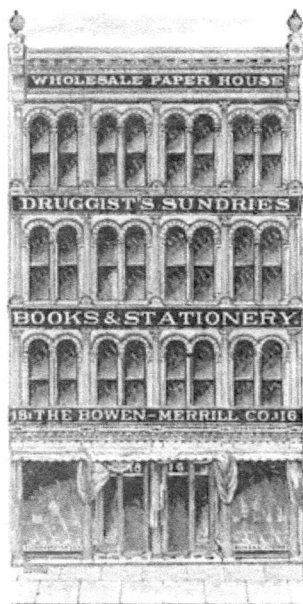

Mullaney & Hayes Wholesale Liquor Dealers, 123 South Meridian street. The firm of Mullaney & Hayes is composed of P. J. Mullaney and Thomas Hayes, and was organized in 1892. Since that date, they have carried on a successful business, annually increasing in volume, and constantly extending their field of operations. The premises occupied consist of a four-story building, 25x150 feet in dimensions, containing superior accommodations for the sale, display and storage of stock, and equipped with the fullest complement of conveniences for shipping. Their specialty is "Mullaney & Hayes' Old Crow Bourbon," a very superior brand of hand-made sour mash whisky, made specially to the order of the firm, and enjoying a widespread and well merited reputation for body and purity. They also carry extensive lines of the most celebrated makes of Kentucky, Pennsylvania and other American brands of Bourbon and rye whiskies (free and in bond), fine imported brandies, gins and liquors, foreign and American wines, cordials, etc., and other articles adapted to the business, which they sell at the lowest prices consistent with quality. They employ a large staff of clerks and three traveling salesmen, and do a large business in the city and throughout the State, which territory is closely covered. The members of the firm are enterprising, public-spirited merchants and citizens, whose liberality and fair dealing have acquired for the house a substantial popularity and valuable patronage.

A. B. Gates & Co. Wholesale Fancy Grocers, Coffee Roasters and Spice Grinders, 31 and 33 East Maryland street. The firm of A. B. Gates & Co. are successors to the firm of A. B. Stevens & Co., who began operations here during 1862. In 1871 the present firm, composed of A. B. Gates, H. B. Gates and W. N. Gates, was organized, and purchased the interest of the former firm, and since that date the affairs of the establishment have been managed with ability, productive of gratifying returns. They occupy a three-story and basement brick structure, 40x110 feet in size. The office and salesrooms are on the main floor, the upper stories being used for storage purposes. To the rear of the salesroom, from which it is separated by a ten foot alley, are the spice mills, occupying a three-story building, 30x50 feet, of brick, and equipped with all necessary machinery and appliances for the manufacture of spice and the roasting of coffee, driven by an engine of forty horse power. Their specialties are baking powder, roasted coffees and ground spices, all of their own preparation. They also carry extensive and select lines of fancy groceries, embracing canned goods, fruits and preserves, potted meats, sauces, relishes, pickles and dainties, foreign and domestic, of the best manufacture and unsurpassed purity. They employ a force of twenty-three clerks and salesmen, and do a large wholesale trade throughout the State, their baking powder especially being in demand in all parts of the United States. The Messrs. Gates are natives of Indiana and pioneers in the business in which they are engaged. They are members of the Board of Trade, and their enterprise, equitable dealings and liberal terms have promoted their house to a front rank.

Wiles, Coffin & Co. Wholesale Grocers, 71 and 73 South Meridian street. This house was founded during 1863 by the firm of Jay, Cox, Fitzsimmons & Co., becoming Conley, Wiles & Co. in 1865, subsequently Wiles, Coffin and Smith, and in 1878 Wiles, Coffin & Co., composed of Messrs. William D. Wiles and David W. Coffin. The premises occupied by the firm consist of a four-story building, 30x160 feet in dimensions, thoroughly equipped and appointed for the accommodation of the trade, containing commodious sample rooms for the display of the lines of stocks carried, a handsome suite of offices for the transaction of business, with storage capacity and shipping facilities ample and complete. They handle every description of staple and fancy groceries, including teas, sugars, coffees, spices, delicacies, canned goods, fruits and preserves, cigars, tobaccos, etc. They are prepared to fill and ship orders without delay, and the quality of their goods, their reasonable prices and liberal terms, have ever commended them to a liberal patronage. They employ six travelers and a full force of clerks and assistants, and cover closely Indiana and the adjoining States. The members of the firm are energetic, representative men of business and enterprising citizens, and the house possesses a merited reputation for its honorable methods continued throughout its career of over a quarter of a century.

Johnson Paper Co.—General Paper Dealers, 127 South Meridian street.—The Johnson Paper Company was established in 1886 by John W. Johnson, who at that date purchased the old established house of Hubbard & Anderson, and has since owned and managed the business. He occupies a commodious four-story building 35x100 feet in dimensions, fully equipped and furnished with accommodations and appointments adequate to the business. He carries large and varied supplies of all kinds of commercial and wrapping papers, twines, etc., as well as paper bags, of which he carries four different lines, embracing 35 separate styles or sizes. He employs a large staff of clerks and three traveling men, and his trade extends over Indiana, Illinois and Kentucky. He also does an extensive and extending local trade, especially in paper bags. Mr. Johnson is an experienced man in this business, and attends personally to the affairs of the concern, and his enterprise is a deservedly prominent and prosperous one. It is one of the leading in the State and its value, as a factor of commercial development and importance is well attested by the large and annually increasing patronage that is being acquired by the house.

J. C. Perry Wholesale Grocer, 26, 28 and 30 West Georgia street. This house was founded by Wright, Bates & Metcalfe in 1862. During 1869 the firm became J. E. Robertson & Co., and in 1874, Robertson & Perry, so continuing until January, 1888, when Mr. Perry succeeded to the sole ownership and management, directing the operation and details of a very large and valuable business. He occupies a conveniently arranged structure, four stories in height, 50x200 feet in dimensions, and supplied with all necessary improvements and facilities. He carries very extensive and comprehensive lines of staple and fancy groceries and grocers' supplies, imported and domestic, besides cigars and tobaccos of the best manufacture. Great care is taken in the selection of stock to obtain only the best grades and qualities, and this fact, together with the prices at which they are sold, and the liberal methods employed by the house in all its operations, have secured a large and firmly established trade throughout Indiana and Illinois, also a considerable portion of Ohio and Kentucky, besides an extensive trade in Indianapolis and vicinity. Mr. Perry's merited success is due to his enterprising management and faithful care of the interests of his patrons.

Elder & Harmon Agents for all kinds of Farm Implements, 69 West Washington street.—This firm, composed of James M. Elder and Willard Harmon, was organized during the latter part of 1867. Both members had been for years previous engaged in the same line of business and are familiar with the wants of the trade in all its minutest details. They occupy a three-story and basement brick structure, 20x80 feet in dimensions, well appointed and equipped, and furnished with every available facility for the business, and possess superior conveniences for filling and shipping orders promptly and securely. They are agents for the leading makes of plows, rakes, mowers and reapers, also handling engines, threshers and clover hullers, the Jackson wagon and other vehicles for farm work. All these implements are noted for their standard worth and adaptability and are obtained from first hands in such large invoices as to enable the firm to offer the most attractive inducements in the matter of prices. They do a large trade in the city and surrounding country, as also among the farming districts of the State, and their house has achieved a pronounced and permanent success upon the basis of absolute merit.

W. J. Holliday & Co. Wholesale Dealers in Iron, Steel, Etc., 39 and 61 South Meridian street. One of the oldest and most influential iron and steel houses in this city is owned and managed by W. J. Holliday & Co., composed of W. J. Holliday, John W. Murphy, John A. Ferguson and Henry Voight. The house was established in 1858 by Murphy, Holliday & Co., senior members of the present firm.

Messrs. Ferguson and Voight were made partners later, and the change in the firm name dates from 1862. They occupy a double four-story and basement brick building, having a frontage of 40 feet to a depth of 200 feet, erected for the special accommodation of the firm, and completely equipped with all the latest modern improvements and labor saving devices. Their stocks embrace iron and steel from the leading furnaces of the world, springs, axles, nuts, bolts, hubs, felloes, spokes, carriage trimmings, blacksmiths and machinists tools and supplies, with other articles of a character germane to those leading and above cited. Their lines are severally complete, and comprehensive, imported and domestic, and of unsurpassed quality. Their prices and terms are reasonable and liberal, and their shipping facilities perfect. The inducements offered the trade are substantial, and they supply a large and steadily increasing demand throughout Indiana, Southern Illinois and Eastern Ohio, giving employment to four travelers and a large staff of clerks and assistants. The members of the firm are representative merchants, Messrs. Murphy and Holliday being also members of the great dry goods house of Murphy, Hibben & Co., while Messrs. Ferguson and Voight are prominently identified with other commercial and manufacturing industries here.

Geo. H. Talbott Merchandise Broker and Storage Warehouse, No. 78 South Pennsylvania street. In the year 1886, Geo. H. Talbott began the business of merchandise brokerage in this city, at the same time accepting the agency of leading mercantile and manufacturing firms located in various portions of the country, but desirous of competing for the Western trade with Indianapolis as their base of supplies. His efforts in both lines of commercial endeavor have been successful, and through his enterprising agency, jobbers are today supplied with goods without the delays incident to shipments from a distance. He occupies premises three stories high, 25x135 feet in dimensions, departmental and equipped with all modern conveniences, including improved telephone and elevator service. He handles staple and fancy groceries, canned and bottled preserves, soaps, starch, syrups, lard, flour, cigars, tobacco, etc., of established repute and of unrivaled quality, which are sold at the lowest manufacturers' prices. His operations are extensive, and steadily appreciating in value and importance in the city and throughout the State.

A. H. Frank—Dealer in Leaf Tobacco, 35 South Pennsylvania street.—Mr. Frank had long been engaged in the cigar and tobacco business here, owning a number of stores dealing in these lines distributed in various portions of the city, and actively directing their operations, until May, 1888, when he established himself in the leaf tobacco business, to which he has since devoted his attention. He occupies commodious accommodations and has built up a large city trade, which is steadily extending and prospering. He handles all descriptions and grades, for wrappers and fillers, including Havana, Sumatra, seed leaf tobacco, etc., and is thoroughly familiar with all qualities and values. In addition, he is well known to the manufacturers of cigars throughout the State, with whom he enjoys a well merited reputation for honorable dealings, and to producers with whom he holds relations, so enviable, that he is able to offer superior inducements to both in the matters of price and quality of stock.

Brooks Oil Company, Cleveland, O., and Indianapolis, Ind.—Manufacturers of Fine Machinery Oils; Headquarters at Cleveland, O.; Indianapolis Branch, East Michigan street and Bee Line Railway. No industry is of more importance to the manufacturing interests than that having for its object the supplying of lubricants for machinery. In this line of business one of the leading establishments in the country is the Brooks Oil Company, established over twenty years ago at Cleveland, O., where its works and headquarters are still located. Six years ago this company established its Indianapolis branch, and now occupy a brick warehouse 40x100 feet in dimensions on East Michigan street and the Bee Line Railway, the tracks of which afford superior facilities for the receipt and shipment of goods, to which additional facilities for handling and storage will be added during the summer, necessitated by the increased demand for their oils. The production of the company's refinery at Cleveland includes High Grade Cylinder, Engine and Dynamo Oils, of which **Col. Drake's Cylinder and Valve Oil, Brooks Oil Company's Corliss Engine Oil, Sperm Dynamo and Engine Oil,** and **White Seal Burning Oil** are especially favorably known. The acknowledged superiority of these oils has earned for them a high reputation with consumers and the trade throughout the Union, Canada and Europe, and it is on the Indianapolis branch a large trade is done in the States of Indiana and Illinois. Large and complete stocks of all the products of the company are carried in their warehouse in this city, and six traveling salesmen visit the customers of the house in the territory controlled from this city. The company makes a specialty of fine cylinder and engine oils and all their products give a degree of satisfaction only accorded to merit. Mr. J. F. Burt, who has charge of the company's interests at this point, is thoroughly conversant with every detail of the business, and efficiently looks after the business in the territory assigned to his charge. The house enjoys a large and steadily growing trade.

McCann & Co.—Successors to McCann & Allison, Wholesale Commission Merchants, 76 and 78 East Maryland street.—The wholesale commission house of McCann & Co. was originally established by A. A. Barnes in 1869. The business has since been conducted under the firm names of Mann & Bradley, Bradley & Co., McCann & Co., McCann & Allison until 1888, when the present firm took charge and have continued the management and ownership of the enterprise. They occupy a two-story and basement building, 30x100 feet in dimensions, well departmented and equipped for the storage and sale of stock, as also for its shipment, and the transaction of business. They are also provided with rooms for ripening green fruits; also rooms where bananas, oranges, grapes and other delicate fruits can be preserved for an indefinite period without affecting their quality in the slightest degree. Their rooms are kept at the different temperatures required, and their facilities for handling bananas are not equaled in the city. The handling of bananas by the firm will average at least one car per week, which shows somewhat the extent of their trade in that line. They do a large commission business, buying and selling for their own account and to order, exclusively at wholesale, in large round car-load lots. Their specialties are bananas, apples, potatoes, cabbage, onions, pears, grapes, cranberries, with other fruits, vegetables, berries, esculents, etc., indigenous to this climate; also Creole, Florida and California oranges, lemons and oranges from the Mediterranean; Aspinwall bananas, and other productions from the tropics, etc. The firm members are particularly qualified to dispose of consignments to the best advantage, being long experienced in and familiar with the requirements of the trade, and execute orders promptly. They refer to R. G. Dun & Co., the Indiana National Bank, Y. R. Wysong & Co., A. A. Barnes, and other leading houses here and elsewhere. Consignments receive immediate attention, remittances are made to consignors without delay, and the management of the house is directed by liberal and honorable methods, commending it to the fullest confidence.

J. A. Everitt & Co. Seed Merchants, 141 West Washington street. The seed house of J. A. Everitt & Co. is one of the best and most completely equipped in the United States. Their trade-mark "K" is known and recognized as evidence of the worth of articles with which it is identified, while their motto: "Our business is national, our facilities unequaled and our ambition to excel," is the synonym of all that the terms imply. They located here in 1886, coming from Watsontown, Northumberland County, Penn., where they had been

similarly engaged for six years previous. They occupy a three-story and basement building, 25x100 feet, provided with all requisite facilities and conveniences, and carry full lines of seeds of every description, grown to their special order, chiefly in the North and East, and embracing the standard varieties, such as bean, beet, cabbage, carrot, celery, sweet corn, cucumber, lettuce, melons, onion, parsnip, pea, radish, spinach, tomato, turnip, etc., of the choicest character, with novelties and specialties in the same lines; the plants from which show superior growth, producing qualities and better average results than those obtained from any other source. Their floral department is equally select and desirable. The list contains every seed known to the lexicon of florists, put up in handsome packages, each package containing the firm's trade-mark and full directions for sowing and cultivating. Their small fruit and plant departments, their departments of farm seeds, of lawn and grass seeds, of clover seeds, of esculents, including the great early potato "The Everitt," garden tools, etc., are likewise unsurpassed in variety and completeness. They also deal in choice breeds of poultry, and have in stock everything in the lines required for garden use or floral ornamentation. They issue an elegant catalogue, of 150,000 copies, annually, and are publishers of *The Agricultural Epitomist*, issuing 75,000 copies per month. They are prepared to fill all orders promptly, offering the most substantial inducements in the way of prices and terms to cultivators and the trade, and ship by the most expeditious and reliable means of transportation. A force of six assistants is constantly employed, the number being increased to 20 or more during the busy season, and they do a large and steadily increasing trade in the United States and Canada, besides exporting extensively to customers in all portions of Europe. The concern is leading in its lines in the country, and owes its success, among other things, to the enterprise and honorable dealing which characterize its management.

Frank M. Dell—Dealer in Coal, Coke and Lime; Office and Yards, No. 27 East Georgia street.—The present extensive coal, coke and lime enterprise owned and managed by Frank M. Dell was founded sometime during 1858 by Valentine Butch, the firm subsequently becoming Butch & Dickson; about 1863, Butch, Dickson & Dell, and later still, William Dell, the latter being succeeded in 1883 by the present proprietor, his son. He owns and occupies over half a block of ground, and is fully equipped with every facility for the expeditious and successful handling of the large trade supplied. He carries full and select lines of coal and coke, Huntington and Delphi lime, plaster paris, cement, lath, hair, white sand, sewer pipe, patent chimneys, fire brick and clay, and other contractors' and builders' materials. He employs a full force of assistants, and enjoys a large trade in the city and State.

East St. Louis Dressed Beef Co.—Wholesale Dressed Meats; J. M. Copeland, Manager; corner McGill and Louisiana streets.—The East St. Louis Dressed Beef Company, with headquarters at the National Stock Yards, at East St. Louis, Ill., located a branch house in Indianapolis during November, 1888. Mr. J. M. Copeland manages the business here, and occupies premises 25x100 feet in dimensions, the front portion of which is used for office purposes. To the rear of this is the refrigerating room, 25x80 feet in size, with a capacity for preservation of 100 head of dressed beef, besides large consignments of lamb, mutton, pork, etc., and during the summer months between 80 and 100 tons of ice are consumed per week in keeping the room at a temperature sufficiently cold for the perfect care and security of its contents. The products are slaughtered at East St. Louis, whence they are transported hither in the latest improved pattern of refrigerator cars, from which they are unladen

at the doors of the refrigerating room, into which, by means of a patent elevated beef tramway, they are transferred direct. When sold, they are conveyed to the salesroom by the same agency, where they are automatically weighed and then delivered to customers, thus avoiding the necessity of handling the meat, and other disagreeable features, the ordinary accompaniment of the business. Mr. Copeland, employs six hands, besides operating three wagons for the free delivery of stock, and does a large and increasing wholesale business in the city and vicinity.

Messick, Cones & Co.—Manufacturing Confectioners; 27 and 29 East Maryland street.—The industry conducted by Messick, Cones & Co. is one of the largest in its line in the State of Indiana. The firm is composed of J. F. Messick and J. T. Cones. They became associated as partners in 1881, commencing business with but limited capital and comparatively limited stock and equipments. Since then, however, they have increased their facilities, enhanced the value

The house is representative, reliable and responsible. Its supplies are noted for their purity, its prices reasonable, its terms liberal and its reputation is attested by the confidence it enjoys with the trade.

The Piano Manufacturing Co.—Manufacturers of Light Plano Twine Binders and The New Plano Mower, J. T. Southern, General Agent; Cleveland block. The Plano Manufacturing Company, organized in 1881 as successor to the oldest-established Marsh Harvester Works, has been the agency through which the greatest improvements in harvesting machinery of the present decade have been introduced and utilized. The company's headquarters are at Chicago, Ill., their works being located at Plano, in the same State, where they employ an immense force of operatives, and though equipped with every pattern of labor saving machinery, were unable to supply the demand made upon them for their output during the season of 1898. They maintain distributing agencies in all the leading cities of the United States, as also at Milan, Italy; Paris, France; Buenos Ayres, S. A., and

VANCE BLOCK.

of their productions, extended their trade and influence and now represent an investment of between $50,000 and $75,000. They occupy a four story and basement brick edifice having a frontage of 25x120 feet, supplied with the latest patterns of labor saving machinery, driven by steam and furnished with every convenience for the manufacture, sale and shipment of their large and varied lines. Their specialties are hand-made creams and penny goods, though they manufacture all grades and descriptions of candy, also handling imported bonbons and candies and carrying large invoices of dates, figs, nuts, raisins and other commodities adapted to their business. Their trade is large and steadily increasing in volume and extent. Their specialties are in constant demand in all directions, dealers in Buffalo, Toledo, Cleveland, Kansas City and at other points east, west and south making the firm their source of supply for these articles, which, with their general lines, are also extensively sold throughout Indiana, Ohio, Illinois, Kentucky and Tennessee. They employ a force of 85 operatives, clerks, etc., in addition to four traveling salesmen, and their annual business aggregates large amounts.

elsewhere, and their annual business is of phenomenal proportions. Their range of production embraces The Light Running All Steel Plano Twine Binder, The Plano All-Steel Harvester and Binder, The New Plano Mower, The Jones Chain Drive Mower and The Short Stroke Rustler Chain Power Mower. They are unsurpassed in their excellence of material, simple in their construction, efficient in their operation, easily handled, perfect in all their parts, possessing lightness, ease of movement and a capacity for durable wear, and are pronounced by farmers and expert judges to be in all respects unequaled. The Indianapolis agency, for supplying the demand throughout Indiana, Southeastern Illinois and certain districts in Ohio, has been established here for many years, and is now managed and directed by Mr. J. T. Southern. He occupies a handsome suite of offices and commodious warehouse accommodations in the Cleveland block, the premises consisting of the main floor and basement, each 65x110 feet in dimensions. He carries large stocks of the various pieces for all the lines of manufacture of the company from the earliest made, and is amply prepared to fill orders for same or for binders, mowers, etc., completed at the shortest notice. The stock of the company for 1889, ... and ... and ... of ... periods ... and parties requiring any article in their lines should not hesitate communicating with Mr. Sullivan. He will, upon application, furnish illustrated catalogues, price lists, and other information of value to customers. He employs ... in pursuit of ... and his honorable management of the company's business has been procured for the latter a very extensive trade and the public confidence in a marked degree.

J. Platt & Co. Wholesale Dealers in Oysters, Fish, Etc.; 43, 45 and 46 Kentucky avenue. Telephone 212.—Among those who have attained to prominence and prosperity in a comparatively brief period, by the exercise of enterprise and honorable dealing, the house of J. Platt & Co., established in 1882, occupies a leading position. They occupy premises 50x100 feet in dimensions, divided into departments corresponding to the lines of commodities in which they deal, supplied with every convenience and facility for the prompt and satisfactory response to the large requisitions daily made upon their stocks by customers here and elsewhere. The premises are also provided with refrigerating rooms of large capacity, for the preservation of goods and specially converted for the uses to which they are appropriated. They handle large quantities of oysters from the Atlantic seaboard and the Gulf, like fish, game, poultry and eggs, with other articles in their line, unsurpassed in quality and sold at low prices, and orders either in person, transmitted over their telephone No. 212—or by mail, receive immediate attention. They employ from eight to ten experienced assistants besides two traveling salesmen, and do a large trade in poultry, game, etc., in New York, Albany and other leading cities of the East, with an equally extensive trade in fish and oysters throughout Indiana, Illinois and Southern Ohio, constantly augmenting in volume and value.

Holland & Co. Wholesale Cigars; 54 North Pennsylvania street. This prominent firm, composed of Benjamin B. Holland, John H. Holland and L. F. Holland, was organized in 1881, and has since pursued a successful career. They occupy a fine store, 25x100 feet in dimensions, into which they removed during the fall of 1888, from their original location on South Illinois street. The premises are well fitted up and provided with ample facilities for the conduct of business, and the display and shipment of their stocks. Their specialty is high grade five cent goods, of which they carry in stock over 50 brands, which are manufactured especially for them of the very best qualities of tobacco, and are well and favorably known to the trade. They also carry in stock full lines of the superior grades of Key West and other cigars of domestic production. Their relations with sources of supply are such that they are able to offer superior inducements to customers, and with the aid of four traveling salesmen, do a large trade throughout Indiana, as also in portions of Ohio and Illinois.

Burkhardt Lumber Agency—Dealers in all kinds of Hardwood Lumber; D. B. Burkhardt, Manager; 360 East Michigan street. This important recent addition to the lumber enterprises of the city was inaugurated in 1888, by Mr. D. B. Burkhardt, a practical and experienced lumber merchant, who had previously been engaged in the same business for a number of years at Covington, Ind. He has a commodious yard and large sheds, covering about half a block of ground on East Michigan street, with railroad tracks facilitating the receipt, handling and shipment of lumber. He maintains the most favorable relations with manufacturers, receiving constantly large consignments of lumber from mills located within a radius of seventy miles from Indianapolis, and from mills located in Tennessee, Kentucky, Ohio and Illinois. He carries on hand, at all times, large and completely assorted stocks of walnut, oak, ash, cherry, sycamore, poplar and all kinds of hardwood lumber, and does an extensive trade in the city and throughout the State, and also ships in car-load lots to Chicago, Cincinnati and other cities. He is prepared at all times to fill orders for all dimensions of lumber in quantities to suit

the trade, his facilities being of the best character. Mr. Burkhardt has already established his business on a firm footing, and his trade steadily grows as a consequence of the accuracy and reliability of his business methods.

Van Camp Hardware and Iron Co.—Wholesale Hardware; 78, 80 and 82 South Illinois street. The Van Camp Hardware and Iron Company, which is in every respect a representative establishment, was organized in 1885, as successor to the firm of Hanson & Van Camp Co., established in 1876, when they succeeded to the wholesale hardware house of Anderson, Bullock & Schofield, and the iron industry of Mass & Bergundthal, both large and influential enterprises dating their origin back many years. They occupy an elegant four-story and basement brick block erected for the uses to which they are at present devoted, and equipped with all requisite conveniences and facilities for the storage and display of stock, as also for the prompt filling and shipment of orders. On Chesapeake street and near the rear portion of the main store, is a well ordered warehouse one story in height and 60x100 feet in dimensions, for heavy goods. They carry very large and comprehensive

lines of stock of imported and domestic manufacture of standard qualities, and in all respects meeting the requirements of the trade. They embrace shelf and heavy hardware, wagon and carriage makers' wood and iron work and supplies, tin plate and tinners' stock, guns and revolvers and equipments, mechanics' tools and appliances of every description, table and pocket cutlery, bar and sheet iron, steel and other lines appertaining. The house is the largest of its kind in the State, and one of the leading ones in the country. The officers are men of large interests, and experienced and public spirited merchants and citizens. Mr. Cortland Van Camp, the President, also conducts in conjunction with his father and brothers, the Van Camp Packing Co., of this city, packers of fruits and vegetables and the largest canners of tomatoes in the world. The remaining officers are H. G. Carey, Vice-President, and D. C. Bergundthal, Secretary.

Tanner & Sullivan. Importers of Tin Plate and Metals; 135 South Meridian street. The firm of Tanner & Sullivan, composed of George C. Tanner and George R. Sullivan, is one of the most extensive and prominent in its line in the city or State. The house was established in 1878, and has grown in importance and prosperity from its inception. They are located at No. 135 South Meridian street, whither they removed in January, 1888, from premises on the opposite side of the street, which were burned during that month. They occupy a commodious four-story building, 25x180 feet in dimensions, well equipped and supplied with machinery and appliances necessary to the manufacture of tinware, etc., and furnished with conveniences and appointments for the display and shipment of their stocks. They are direct importers of tin plate and metals and wholesale dealers in tinners' supplies; also manufacturers of tinware of every variety and adapted to every use. They employ a full force of workmen, clerks, salesmen and assistants, and do a large trade in Indiana and the border States, besides supplying an extensive local demand. Their facilities are complete in every detail of the business, and they are prepared to fill all orders promptly and at the most reasonable prices. The members of the firm are enterprising merchants and citizens, and their house is a prominent and representative one.

Holliday & Wyon Wholesale Manufacturers of Harness; 77 South Meridian street. The largest manufacturers of harness and leather products in the same line in Indianapolis, if not in the State, is the firm of Holliday & Wyon. It is composed of J. D. Holliday and A. F. Wyon, and was organized and began operations in 1878. From comparatively small beginnings they have become leading and representative. They occupy a four story building, 25x100 feet in size, the main floor being used in part for the display and sale of leather and findings, and in part for that of saddlery, harness, etc. The manufactory, fitted up with harness manufacturing machinery of the most approved pattern, and the stock rooms occupy the upper floors. Their specialty is the "Perfection Saddle," an invention of the firm for adjusting the weight of harness more equable, and which is widely known and in general use by stablemen and horsemen in all parts of the country. They also manufacture harness, gig saddles, halters, etc., in great variety, all of the best qualities of material and workmanship. They employ from 40 to 50 hands, three travelers and other assistants, and do a large trade in Indiana, Ohio, Illinois and Michigan. Both members of the firm give their personal attention to the business and their long experience and honorable careers have contributed to the success of the house wherever it is known.

H. Rikhoff — Superintendent for J. C. Yuncker, Rectifier; Wholesale Dealer in Foreign and Domestic Liquors; 188 South Meridian street. The wholesale liquor business conducted by H. Rikhoff is old and well established, and his commodities are extensively known to the trade for their superior quality. He began operations here during 1864, and his place of business, which is admirably located, consists of a three-story and basement brick building, 25 feet front on South Meridian street, by 120 feet in depth, well arranged and appointed, and provided with every facility for the storage, display and sale of his large and select lines of goods. He carries extensive stocks of the best brands of Kentucky whiskies, California and other native wines, brandies, etc., the finest lines of imported champagnes, Burgundies, Rhine wines, sherries, ports, Madeiras, cordials, etc., Holland and English gins, with other articles usually handled by first-class houses in the same field of operations. Mr. Rikhoff does a large trade, which is exclusively wholesale, in the city and State, also filling orders from Ohio and Illinois, and is known as a business man of enterprising and honorable methods. In addition to his present enterprise he is superintendent of the rectifying establishment of J. C. Yuncker, and is otherwise prominent in undertakings designed for the prosperity of the city and surrounding country.

Gale Manufacturing Co. of Albion, Mich. — Manufacturers of the Gale Chilled and Steel Plows; 63 West Maryland street. This business was founded by the Gale family over forty years ago, and in 1887 the enterprise was reorganized, and has since been directed and controlled under its present corporate title with H. K. White, of Detroit, Mich., President, and Horatio Gale, Vice-President. The same year they invented and patented the new "Big Injun" sulky plow, an implement absolutely unrivaled for the uses for which it is designed, and which, since its introduction, has been in constant demand, taxing the resources of their immense facilities to even moderately supply. The headquarters of the company are at Albion, Mich., where, on October 1, 1888, they completed new works, covering a vast area of territory, equipped with new and improved machinery, and provided with every facility for manufacture and shipment. They employ a large force of hands there, and turn out 125,000 plows per annum of

the best material, constructed in the most skilful and scientific manner and handsomely finished. Their range of production embraces the Gale Walking Plows, right and left hand turf and stubble plows, steel and steel beams, and chilled walking plows in all sizes, besides right and left hand steel and chilled bottoms for the "Big Injun" sulky plows. E. H. Stuntz, their general agent here, established this branch in the spring of 1888. He had been for six years previously connected with the Minneapolis Harvester Works and is an experienced man in the business. He occupies the main floor of premises 30x50 feet, with two basements adjoining, each 30x50 feet in dimensions, and carries full lines and complete stocks of the company's manufactures. His territory includes Indiana and Kentucky, in which, owing to his enterprise, liberal management and honorable business methods, he has already acquired a large and rapidly increasing trade, and gives employment to from three to six traveling salesmen. He fills orders promptly, and will furnish catalogues on application.

Fairbanks & Co. Standard Scales and Eclipse Windmills; L. W. Drew, Manager; 26 South Meridian street. The reputation of the Fairbanks scales is almost universal, and their successful service in the department of commercial and manufacturing industry is so much above their value is beyond criticism. They are the standard scales of the world for weighing the most delicate ingredients of medicine, preparations and the bulky articles of demand in every line of business and productive industry. The Indianapolis branch of this enterprise was established here in 1862, and is in charge of an agent who has had 24 years experience in this and other fields. He occupies a three-story and basement brick building, 25x120 feet in dimensions, and carries a large and complete stock of Fairbanks' scales, railroad water tanks, fixtures and pipes, hand cars, push cars and railroad velocipedes, letter and way bill presses, baggage barrows, trucks and warehouse wagons, wind-mill towers, United States standard weights and measures, coffee mills, stock books, alarm cash drawers. Hancock's inspirators for feeding stationary, marine and locomotive boilers, "Culbert Universal" wood split pulley, etc. From this point a very large business is done, covering the entire State.

Geo. A. Woodford & Co. — Wholesale Dealers in fine Kentucky Whiskies; 63 and 65 South Meridian street. The business conducted by Geo. A. Woodford & Co. was established in 1875, and the present firm was organized in 1883, and is composed of Geo. A. Woodford and John Pohlman. They occupy the main floor and basement, 25x125 feet in dimensions, and well equipped with facilities and accommodations for the sale and shipment of goods and the transaction of their large operations. They are the sole proprietors of "Brooks Buckridge Whiskey" and Woodford & Dean's "L. A. D." a choice hand-made sour mash whisky from Anderson County, Ky., also distillers' agents for the famous Wm. H. McBrayer, Green Hollow, and other W. S. Stone hand-made sour mash whiskies, and they handle other reliable brands of Bourbon and rye whiskies which they sell in bond, tax paid, and are special dealers in peach, apple, grape and imports of French brandies, wines, gins, cordials, liqueurs, etc. Their lines are always full and complete, and they sell at prices and upon terms reasonable and liberal, to a large and steadily increasing trade throughout Indiana and in Southern and Central Illinois. The members of the firm are citizens and merchants representative of Indianapolis. Their business affairs are managed judiciously and conservatively, and the purity of their stocks, and other features of excellence, have acquired for their house an influential and valuable trade constituency.

Eastman, Schleicher & Lee — Carpets, Draperies and Wall Paper; 6, 7 and 9 East Washington street. This firm, which was organized in 1885, is composed of Walter H. Eastman, Adolph Schleicher and Fielding T. Lee and is leading and representative in every respect. They occupy a four-story and basement building, 25x120 feet, also two floors, each 30x135 feet in dimensions in the building adjoining, to the east, and the premises in their entirety are exceptionally equipped and provided with conveniences for an elaborate display of their stocks, as also with facilities for their shipments and the transaction of business.

A. M. McCleary—Dealer in Coffees, Sugars and Groceries; No. 78 South Meridian street. Mr. McCleary established himself here during 1879, and having previously by large experience become possessed of a thorough knowledge of the requirements of the trade, he has built up a large patronage which is steadily increasing, and extending in the city and throughout the State. He represents a extensive line of importing and jobbing houses at the East, handling staple groceries, and sells to jobbers here and in the general trade. He carries at No. 78 South Meridian street, where he carries samples of coffees, sugars and grocers' supplies generally. His facilities for filling orders at the lowest rates are unsurpassed, and he is at all times prepared to furnish dealers with the lowest quotations. Mr. McCleary is a representative business man, and to his personal efforts is largely due the increase and development of the brokerage business here. He is a member of the Board of Trade, and enjoys a well-deserved and enviable reputation for fidelity in the discharge of contracts with the trade.

H. F. Solliday—Manufacturer of Baking Powder, Etc.; 98 and 100 South Pennsylvania street. Mr. Solliday began business during 1881 and has constantly enlarged his facilities and extended his trade, now also combining a similar establishment at Wichita, Kan. In this city he occupies a three story and basement building, 25x100 feet in dimensions, and equipped with compounding and roasting conveniences, and other machinery and appliances required in the manufacture of his output. The branch house at Wichita, where it is known under the firm name of Solliday Bros. & Lamphere, is fully as complete in its appointments and equipments. His specialties are the "Incredible" and "Bakers' Delight" brands of baking powder, composed of superior ingredients, and enjoying a well established reputation for purity and adaptability to the uses for which they are designed. He also manufactures fruit extracts, vinegar and spices extensively, and carries complete lines of all these articles. He is prepared to ship in package or in bulk to any point, and his prices, considering the character of his products, are among the lowest on the market. He employs a force of from 15 to 20 assistants and three travelers, and a similar number at Wichita, and supplies a large demand throughout Indiana, Illinois, Ohio, Kentucky, Tennessee, Alabama, Missouri and Michigan, the trade in the West, as far as the Pacific Coast, obtaining their goods from the branch house at Wichita.

J. E. Bodine & Co.—Dealers in Dental Supplies and Barbers' Supplies; 27 and 29 Circle street. The firm of J. E. Bodine & Co. is composed of J. E. Bodine, John B. Ransom, Thaddeus F. Randolph and I. S. Wooth. The firm of Ransom, Randolph & Co. of Toledo, O., with which Mr. Bodine was formerly connected, was established in this city in 1877. During 1884 the Indianapolis house was established under the direction of Mr. Bodine, and three years later the firm name of the latter was changed to that by which it is now known, the Toledo house, however, being conducted under the name of Ransom & Randolph, and extensively engaged in the manufacture of barbers' chairs, cabinet ware, etc., also dealing in barbers' supplies, in every line of which they export largely, and carrying full lines of dental supplies handled by J. E. Bodine & Co. The latter occupy the entire floors of premises each 20 feet front on Circle street and 65 feet deep, containing every facility and convenience for the advantageous display of stocks, with ample accommodations for the storage of goods and the transaction of business operations. They carry the choicest lines of dental goods and supplies generally, embracing instruments, artificial teeth, etc., and do a large trade in supplying graduates of the Indiana Dental College of this city with outfits, in addition to their regular trade throughout an extended territory. They also carry extensive lines of barbers' chairs, furniture, etc., manufacturing the celebrated Indianapolis and Toledo razors, and keeping in stock every description of barbers' supplies of the best make and quality and do fine grinding and decorating to order. They have recently fitted up the barber shops of the Bates House, Union Depot, Young Men's Christian Association and other resorts in this city, besides well known establishments of a similar character in other portions of the West. The house is highly representative

and distinguished in its field of usefulness, prepared to respond promptly to all orders, selling at the lowest prices consistent with superior material and workmanship and one of the most desirable in all respects with which to establish business relations. They employ a full staff of clerks and three travelers and supply the demands of a large and increasing trade throughout Indiana, Kentucky, Tennessee and portions of Ohio, the trade in Pennsylvania, the balance of Ohio and elsewhere in the East being met by the Toledo house.

Kipp Brothers—Importers and Jobbers of Fancy Goods, Etc.; 37 and 39 South Meridian street.—A prominent and representative jobbing and importing house is that of Kipp Brothers, located on the leading business street of the city and occupying a building 45x200 feet in dimensions, and supplied with every convenience and accessory for the prosecution of their business. They do an exclusively wholesale business aggregating more than half a million dollars annually. Their different departments represent full lines of musical instruments, cutlery and fancy hardware, stationers' sundries, druggists' sundries, pipes and smokers' articles, fishing tackle, sporting goods, base ball supplies, jewelry, clocks, optical instruments, Yankee notions, traveling satchels, etc., fancy china and glassware, toys of every description, baby carriages and express wagons, flags, fireworks, etc. The house is the largest of its kind in the United States, importing their goods direct, and in many lines controlling the products of factories at home and abroad. They employ twelve traveling salesmen who cover all leading towns in Indiana, Illinois, Kentucky, Tennessee, Alabama, Georgia, Ohio, Michigan, Iowa, Kansas, Nebraska, Missouri, Colorado, etc., and they also have a large force of clerks and assistants. The firm has, for the convenience of Southern customers, a branch, with complete sample lines, at 533 West Main street, Louisville, Ky.

Fahnley & McCrea—Importers and Jobbers of Millinery, Straw and Fancy Goods; 140 and 142 South Meridian street.—One of the oldest wholesale millinery houses in Indianapolis, and one of the most extensive in its lines between New York and Chicago, is that of Fahnley & McCrea. The firm is composed of Fred Fahnley and

R. H. McCrea, and for nearly a quarter of a century they have contributed to the wants of a large and select trade throughout the West, Southwest and Northwest. They became established in 1864, and now occupy a handsome and most conveniently located stone front building, four stories high, with a frontage of 35 feet and a depth of 130 feet, extending to a wing 25x80 feet in dimensions, fronting on Louisiana street. The premises are most thoroughly equipped and the varied and complete lines of stock carried include millinery and milliners' supplies, hats, ribbons, feathers, tips, plumes, artificial birds and flowers, laces and other novelties, of the latest European styles, imported direct from Paris and Berlin, also obtained from first hands at New York and other Eastern depots of supply. Every article adapted to the trade is to be procured at this house, and the choicest description and at the lowest prices commensurate with the quality offered. They employ a force of forty clerks and salesmen, in addition to ten travelers, and do a trade approximating over half a million dollars annually in Indianapolis and throughout the States of Indiana, Illinois, Iowa, Ohio, Kentucky and Tennessee. Messrs. Fahnley and McCrea are members of the Board of Trade, and leading and influential merchants and citizens. Their success is the result of enterprise, judicious management and honorable dealings.

Walter A. Wood Machine Company—Manufacturers of Harvesting Machinery, No. 4 Cleveland block. This company, which was incorporated in 1853, has headquarters at Hoosick Falls, where their office and factory are located, with branch offices in all the leading cities of the United States, Europe, Germany, Italy, France, Australia, South Africa, South America, and elsewhere, and their total output of harvesting machines for the past thirteen years foots up 726,530. Their great works are among the largest in any of the lines of industry carried on in the world, are equipped with all the latest improved drilling, milling, reaming, planing, turning and other machinery, and employment is given to 3,000 hands. Their manufacture embraces mowers, reapers, harvesters and binders, attachments for same, hay rakes, bundle carriers, and other agricultural implements. They are made of the best materials, combining strength, lightness and simplicity, more perfectly than the productions of any similar industry

in the United States, and have been awarded the highest prizes at the International Expositions held in Europe and America, in addition to 1,200 medals from agricultural and mechanical societies. The Indianapolis branch, covering the business throughout Indiana, has been under the exclusive control and direction of W. H. Walter since 1883. He occupies commodious and finely appointed offices in the Cleveland block, with a thoroughly equipped repair shop adjoining 3000 feet in dimensions, and large warehouse accommodations at the North street crossing of the "Big Four" road. He carries heavy stocks of pieces and attachments for the machines manufactured by the company, and employs from six to ten traveling salesmen. He is prepared to fill orders promptly, and upon the most satisfactory terms.

Oliver Chilled Plow Works—Manufacturers of Oliver Chilled and Steel Plows, 160 South Pennsylvania street.—The Oliver Chilled Plow Works, located at South Bend, this State, are owned and operated by an organization of which James Oliver is President, J. D. Oliver, Treasurer, and George Ford, Secretary, with H. B. Smith manager of the agency in this city. The works are very large, embracing foundry, machine shop, blacksmithing, finishing, setting up and paint shops, warehouses, etc., amply equipped and employing 1,200 hands. The specialty of the manufacture is the Oliver Chilled Plow, without comparison the best plow for general purposes offered to the farmers of America, and which, in durability, lightness of draft, ease of management, range and quality of work and superiority of material and workmanship, has no equal. Perfect fitting duplicate parts are made and the care to make exact duplicates of the various repairs has made this plow a universal favorite. It is made in all the various sizes necessary to adapt it to the different classes of work and has the largest sale of any plow made in this country. The company also manufacture the "Steel Walking" plows, divided into four classes. The 205 series, for work in sections where clay land and rich, black soils prevail, the Southern steel series, in which the plows are designated by numbers 6, 61, 62, 63, 64 and 65, for alluvial bottoms and upland soil; the Special steel plows numbered 58 and 14 A, for stubble, heavy, sticky clay and hard baked ground; and garden plows known as "K" and "M" expressly for gardening and truck farming. The Indianapolis agency was opened here in 1866, to supply the trade

in Indiana, Illinois, Ohio and Kentucky. Mr. Smith has been the manager in charge for many years. He occupies a handsome four-story and basement brick building, 165x115 feet in dimensions, owned by the Messrs. Oliver. Here a force of twelve hands and several travelers are employed, and a very large trade is carried on. Catalogues and price lists will be furnished by Mr. Smith upon application, and all orders meet with prompt and satisfactory attention. His efficient and honorable management of the business has secured marked advantages for the firm he so ably represents.

Hide, Leather and Belting Co.—G. W. Snider, Proprietor, Dealer in Leather and Belting; 125 South Meridian street. This is one of the oldest establishments of its kind in the State. It was founded over thirty years ago, by John Eshback, who conducted the enterprise until about 1870, when Mr. Snider purchased the premises and has since remained sole proprietor. He occupies a well equipped building, four stories high and 25x200 feet in dimensions, provided with every facility and convenience, mechanical and otherwise, adapted to the business. His specialty is the manufacture of oak-tanned leather belting, in which he turns out annually a very large supply of the best goods in their line in the market, and which are sold at the most reasonable prices. He also carries full and complete lines of leather and findings, shoemakers' tools, oils, rubber hose, gum belting, steam packing, garden sprinklers, moveable fountains, hose trucks, etc., etc., of superior quality. During the summer of 1888 he sold upward of 100,000 feet of three-quarter inch rubber garden hose, with sales in other lines proportionately large. He employs a large number of hands in the manufacturing department of experience and ability only, also a full staff of clerks, assistant and traveling salesmen, and does an exclusively wholesale trade in the city and State, as also in States contiguous. Mr. Snider is a member of the Board of Trade, and an active, public-spirited and influential citizen.

M. M. Reynolds—Dealer in Brick, Lime, Lath, Cement, Sewer Pipe, etc.; Coal, Coke and Wood; 464 Massachusetts avenue. Mr. Reynolds established this business six years ago, and from that time to the present has enjoyed a large and active trade. Until recently the coal and coke department of his business was its most prominent feature, but the decrease in the demand for these products has made that branch subsidiary to his larger trade in brick and building materials of all kinds, although he still carries large and well assorted stocks of coal, coke and wood, and is prepared to fill orders for the best quality of these goods in all grades. He has extensive yards covering half a block of ground on Massachusetts avenue, with commodious storage sheds, and railroad tracks throughout the premises afford superior facilities for receipt and delivery. In these yards he carries large and complete stocks of common, pressed and ornamental brick, fire brick, fire clay, lime, Louisville and imported Portland cements, plaster paris, plastering hair, lath, sewer, drain and culvert pipe, and all kinds of builders' and contractors' materials. He gives employment to ten hands, and utilizes eight teams in delivering goods. He also handles lumber, but the branch of his business is confined to car load lots. Mr. Reynolds is thoroughly experienced in all the details of this business and carefully selects his goods so as to insure the quality of his stock, and his accurate knowledge of the needs of the trade, and reliable methods, have been prominent factors in building up his enterprise to its present gratifying condition of popularity and success.

The McCormick Harvesting Machine Co.—Manufacturers of Harvesting Machinery; Works and Headquarters at Chicago, Ill.; J. B. Heywood, Manager for Indiana, 107 and 109 East Washington street. In connection with inventions in agricultural machinery, the name of Cyrus H. McCormick stands out pre-eminent, his invention of the harvesting machine having done more to promote the production of grain than any other device ever formulated by human ingenuity. His invention was the initial idea of the modern and perfected McCormick Harvesting Machines, which are beyond comparison the most complete and useful machines offered for the use of the agriculturalist. These machines are manufactured by the McCormick

Harvesting Machine Co., of Chicago, Ill., operating the largest works in the world, and having the largest output. The machines made and marketed include the McCormick Light Draft Steel Harvester; the McCormick Light Binder, noted with the new and improved McCormick Knotter; the McCormick No. 4 Steel Mower; the McCormick No. 4 Steel Mower; the McCormick Big 4 Mower; the Daisy, a machine solely for reaping; the McCormick Basket Carrier; the McCormick Steel Tongued Carrier, and the McCormick Binder Truck. The various kinds of harvesting machines made by the company excel all others in the simplicity and economy of their operation, and that these points of superiority are recognized by the farmers of the world is attested by the fact that the sales of these machines are far in excess of those of any other make, and reached, in 1888, to the enormous number of 70,544. The demand for these machines extends all over the world, including, in addition to a heavy trade in the United States and Canada, an extensive export business to Australia, New Zealand, Africa, England, France, Italy, Russia, and all parts of Europe and South America. The Indiana agency for these machines was established thirty years ago, and since 1879 has been managed by Mr. J. R. Heywood. He has steadily increased the business in the territory assigned to his supervision, the sales in Indiana having increased from 426 in 1879 to 3497 in 1888. The warehouse now occupied by the company in this city is a two-story and basement building, 50x150 feet in dimensions, but the importance of this field is recognized by the company, and they now have in contemplation the erection at the corner of South Pennsylvania and Maryland streets of what will be the finest business block in Indianapolis—an imposing seven-story structure fronting 200 feet on South Pennsylvania street by 108 feet on Maryland street. At the warehouse here a complete stock of the McCormick machines and all repair parts is carried, and all orders are filled promptly. Under Mr. Heywood's management, the business of the company in Indiana has faithful and watchful care.

J. G. Rose & Co. Distillers' Agents; Room 7, Board of Trade Building.—The firm of J. G. Rose & Co., distillers' agents for the leading brands of the best qualities of hand made sour mash bourbon and rye whiskies, was organized in the fall of 1888. They carry heavy stocks of whiskies in bond, from whence they buy and sell for and to account of customers, and are also Western agents for the genuine Blue Lick water, the invaluable qualities of which, as a remedial agent, have been familiar to the public since their discovery years ago. The firm occupy handsome office accommodations, 25x100 feet in dimensions, in the Board of Trade Building, provided with every facility for the prompt execution of orders for the purchase or sale of goods in their lines, and for the immediate shipment of consignments to all portions of the country. Among the famous brands of whisky for which they are the agents in this city and section are: Anderson, Attraction, William Berkley, Blue Grass, Chickencock, Double Springs, Nat. Harris, Hermitage, Hugely, Old Gray Bourbon and Rye, Wathen Rye, and many other brands which are sold at distillers' prices and are of unsurpassed qualities. The business, which is largely local and steadily increasing in volume and value, offers superior inducements to dealers and jobbers, to whom the leading standard articles are available at the cost of production, thereby saving to purchasers the expenses incident to handling and transportation.

The Island Coal Co.—Miners and Shippers of Island City Coal; Office, 32 East Market street.—One of the most extensive, thoroughly equipped and widely known representatives of the coal mining industries of Indiana is the Island Coal Company, organized in 1884, of which S. N. Yeoman is President, W. W. Hubbard, Treasurer, and A. M. Ogle, Secretary. Their mines are located at Island City, in Greene County, this State, and are steadily increasing in value as also in the volume of their output. Three shafts have been sunk on the property, each of which is manned in the most skillful manner and equipped with all the latest applicable machinery, driven by steam. The total output of the mines now in operation is 4,000 tons of coal daily, which has acquired an extended reputation for its intrinsic worth for the uses to which it is designed. It is semi-block, grading the Blocking, and excelling in many repeated tests all

Indiana coals. Being free from sulphur and slate, it is superior for grates, domestic use and steam purposes; warranted to burn to a white ash without leaving clinkers behind, and to make a coke with less than one per cent. impurity. These claims are borne out by the experience and testimony of those who have personally tested their reliability, including among others the superintendent of the Indianapolis City Hospital, the building and supply agent of the city schools, and other officials equally prominent, reliable and disinterested, here and elsewhere. The company is amply provided with railway facilities, thus facilitating the prompt filling and shipment of orders to consumers in all parts of Indiana and the surrounding country, at prices as low as is consistent with the conceded superior quality of the commodity. The company's transactions are very extensive, selling at wholesale only, and are principally with dealers, manufacturing corporations, supply agencies, etc., in the West and Northwest, notably at Chicago and other large interior cities, as also in cities along the chain of lakes. The sales in Indianapolis are by car-load lots, the company not occupying yards, but delivering from the track. The executive board is made up of enterprising men whose management is characterized by ability, and their annual operations represent large amounts in value.

Indiana Paper Company—Manufacturers of Paper and Paper Bags; 21, 23 and 25 East Maryland street.—This company was established in 1880. In 1884, it was incorporated with a capital stock of $150,000, with mills at South Bend and headquarters in this city. They occupy a three-story and basement brick edifice, 60x70 feet in size, and carry a large stock of paper of every quality and for every purpose, including book, printing and manila among the finer grades; also rag and straw wrapping paper for packing purposes. They also manufacture paper bags, and do a large and growing trade in the Middle, Western and Southern States.

Slocum & Gage—Wholesale Dealers in Hardwood Lumber; corner of New York and Pine streets.—This business was inaugurated seven years ago by Mr. E. E. Slocum, changing to its present style in February, 1888, upon the accession of Mr. L. H. Gage to the firm. They carry on an extensive wholesale business as dealers in walnut, quarter-sawed and plain oak, ash, poplar, and all kinds of hardwood lumber adapted to interior finish of buildings and the manufacture of furniture, etc., dealing in car lots only and shipping to the leading eastern markets. They carry large and completely assorted stocks, having extensive lumber yards covering about two squares of ground, with railroad switches and every facility for the receipt, handling and shipment of lumber. They receive their stock principally from mills within a radius of 60 miles of Indianapolis, but have lately also bought large quantities of ash lumber in Tennessee. The firm maintains the most favorable relations with manufacturers, and is thereby enabled to offer the best inducements in equitable prices and carefully selected stock, carrying large assortments constantly on hand and filling all orders in the most prompt and satisfactory manner. Both of the members of the firm are men of practical business experience, and the methods upon which their affairs are conducted commend them to the favor of the trade, and have secured for them a steady and gratifying increase in the volume of their business.

McCune, Schmidlap & Co.—Wholesale Coffee, Teas and Grocers' Sundries; Indianapolis Coffee and Spice Mills; 74 and 76 South Meridian street.—This business was established 16 years ago by the firm of McCune & Sons, changing eight years later to its present style and membership, Messrs. H. B. McCune, L. Schmidlap and J. T. McCune now being the individual members of the firm. They occupy a three-story and basement building, 25x208 feet in dimensions, with light on three of its sides, and containing every convenience and facility for the prosecution of the business, including a complete equipment of coffee and spice mill machinery. Among the specialties of the firm may be prominently named the "Real" Baking Powder and Spices, their McCune's Package Arabian and McCune's Package Golden Santos coffees, roasted from selected green stock and of the finest flavors. In addition to these specialties, all of which are in large and popular demand, the firm does a large jobbing business in teas, green and roasted coffees, dried fruits, canned fruits, fish and vegetables, pickles, condiments, cereal goods, cigars and tobaccos and all kinds of fancy groceries and grocers' sundries. A full force of hands is employed in the house and six traveling salesmen represent the firm in its trade territory, covering the States of Indiana, Ohio and Illinois. The firm, by the accuracy of its business methods, has earned a large trade which is constantly increasing in volume.

J. S. Buck—General Agent Wm. Deering & Co., Chicago, Manufacturers Harvesting Machinery; 192 to 200 West Market street. The Deering agricultural machinery works at Chicago are among the largest and most productive in their lines in the world. William Deering & Co., by whom the works were established in 1860, was organized at that date, and still own and direct the operations of an industry than which there is none in any of the departments of manufacture more universally known or exerting a more powerful influence upon the prosperity, not alone of the West, but of every section of the country. Their works, on Fullerton avenue, Chicago, cover 50 acres, occupied by buildings for manufacturing their output, from the rough material to the finished production of their superior grain cutting and grass cutting machinery, giving employment to nearly 2,500 hands and turning out upward of 50,000 binders, mowers and reapers annually, all of which have received the highest expressions of commendation, and a larger patronage than any other implements of their

W. H. Russe & Co.—Wholesalers of Lumber; Bee Line Railway and East Michigan street. This firm, which is composed of Messrs. W. H. Russe, Henry Ludson and George D. Burgess, is of recent formation, having been established in November, 1888, but Mr. Russe, of this firm, had previously been for a number of years engaged as a dealer in hardwood lumber, and Mr. Burgess had carried on business as a merchant in pine lumber for a considerable period prior to becoming a member of this firm. All of the members bring to the prosecution of the business the requisites of experience and capacity, as well as a large and extended acquaintance with the trade and the best facilities for carrying on the business. They occupy commodious yards, eligibly located on the Bee Line Railway and East Michigan street, with railroad tracks throughout, affording all conveniences for the receipt, handling and shipment of lumber. They carry large and complete stocks, embracing every description of hardwood lumber, which they are prepared to supply in all dimensions to order, handling oak, walnut, ash, cherry, sycamore and poplar in large quantities. They do a large business with New York, Boston, Philadelphia and other Eastern cities, shipping direct in car-load lots from country mills located within a radius of from fifty to sixty miles from the city. They sell large amounts of pine and poplar lumber in car-load lots to dealers in this and neighboring cities and towns. All orders are promptly filled, and the accurate and reliable methods which characterize all the firm's transactions commend it to the favor and confidence of the trade.

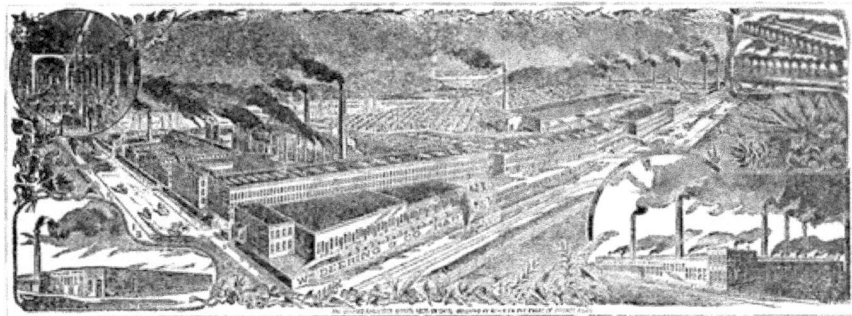

kind manufactured in America. Their range of production embraces the Deering All-Steel Twine Binder, five, six and seven foot; the Deering Light Reaper, with and without folding platform; the Deering Binder Twine, the New Deering Mower, the Deering Front Cut Giant Mower, the Deering One-Horse Mower, the Deering attachment to mowers and the Deering attachments for twine binders, all of which have been successful at expositions, tests being made of their efficiency, capacity and durability in comparison with the machinery of competing concerns in the same lines of manufacture. An important addition to the manufacturing is the making of twine, for which purpose they have erected special buildings, and disposed of 20,000,000 pounds last season. The agency for the Deering Company was established in this city in 1879, by J. D. Truett, who was succeeded in February, 1889, by J. S. Buck, who has since remained in charge, including within his territorial jurisdiction the State of Indiana. He is a gentleman of long continued experience in the business, and is conceded to be one of the best informed men in the United States on harvesting machinery. He occupies a two-story and basement building 30x75 feet, well appointed and provided with unsurpassed facilities for the receipt and shipment of stock, railroad tracks being at the doors. He carries large stocks, and during the season employs a staff of twenty-five traveling salesmen, covering the State of Indiana thoroughly in all directions, and doing a business that is annually increasing in magnitude, extent and value.

Nichols & Shepard Co., Battle Creek, Mich., Manufacturers of The New Vibrator Thresher Machine; office, 22 Kentucky avenue. The Nichols & Shepard Co., manufacturers of vibrator engines and threshing machines, was established at Battle Creek, Mich., in 1848, and was incorporated in 1869 as Nichols, Shepard & Co., and in 1887 the title became Nichols & Shepard Co. Their headquarters are at Battle Creek, Mich., where the works cover seven acres of ground, upon which have been erected extensive buildings, equipped with all necessary machinery and appliances of the latest improved pattern and where a force of 900 hands are employed. They are the patentees and originators of vibrator threshers and in their forty years' experience have made many improvements in their original machine. They have controlled the largest and best trade on the continent and their vibrator is recognized by intelligent threshers and farmers as the highest standard of excellence in the line of harvesting machinery. For several years past they have been working out the details of a new and improved thresher, which they have called "The New Vibrator," and in the season of 1896 put four at work in the grain fields of the country, in 1887 twenty-two were in service, and in 1888 one hundred were originally built but the increasing demand necessitated the building of one hundred and seventy-five more, and two hundred and seventy-five were sold. The success of this new and improved machine has been marvelous and substantial and they have adopted it as their exclusive machine for the future and will put the resources of these large factors, together with the determination that his superiority of material, workmanship, efficiency and durability will not be surpassed by any other dealer in the world. The range of manufacture also includes plain and traction engines, and they make a specialty of their self-guiding traction engines, which is as checked by experts and engineers to be the aim of mechanical invention. The Indianapolis agency was established at first in 1854 by W. S. McMillin, the present manager, whose territory includes Indiana, Kentucky and Tennessee. He is located as above, also occupying a commodious salesroom and warehouse at the South street crossing of the Bee Line Railway tracks, and employs several traveling agents, and his enterprising and liberal management has greatly promoted the company's influence and prosperity in the territory within his jurisdiction.

Arthur Jordan—Wholesale Produce Dealer and Shipper; Corner Maryland and South Delaware streets and Virginia avenue; Branch Houses, Terre Haute, Ind.; Worthington, Ind.; Oakland City, Ind.; Franklin, Ind.; Crawfordsville, Ind.; Nokomis, Ill. The produce business of Arthur Jordan, of the corner of Maryland and South Delaware streets, is one of the most valuable adjuncts to trade interests in Indianapolis, besides drawing the attention and trade of all classes of country merchants, and thereby contributing largely to the trade of all the wholesale business of the city. The business was established by Mr. Jordan in 1876, and during the intervening years has been constantly increasing in magnitude and influence in all directions. In order to meet the demands of his trade, six branch packing houses have been established at leading produce supply points in this State and Illinois, and two extensive creameries in adjoining counties, contributing to the supply of pure butter for his city trade, and are under the direct supervision and control of the main office at Indianapolis. The business in this city is located on one of the best sites for commercial purposes and occupies three entire floors of this commodious building, which was erected and fitted up by him with special reference to his business. The building occupies the entire half square, is fully equipped and appointed with all modern improved facilities for handling and shipment of produce of all kinds. He is peculiarly in a position to meet the requirements of his large trade, having refrigerators and freezing rooms equal to any in the West. His specialties are poultry, eggs and butter. The poultry is killed on the premises by skilled workmen, and prepared for shipment under the most competent management. Finest grade of butter and eggs are also handled largely, and the "A. J." brands of poultry, eggs and butter are well established, and have a special demand in the New York, Boston and other Eastern markets. His relations with producers and consignors are such that

he is prepared to offer every inducement and superior qualities of goods to a large and exacting patronage, while the prices his brands command, together with his superior facilities, enable him to pay for this line of produce the leading prices at all times, and has made this for years the principal poultry and egg market in the West. His

annual business foots up over half a million dollars, and requires the employment of about sixty men. The supplies are drawn largely from Indiana and Illinois, but of late his purchases have extended into several of the adjoining States. Mr. Jordan is an enterprising, public spirited merchant and citizen, and one of the Board of Governors of the Board of Trade, and has always been prominent in public matters designed to aid in the development and prosperity of Indianapolis and Indiana.

H. C. Smither—Dealer in Roofing Material and Coal Tar Products; 169 West Maryland street. Among the prominent and leading concerns that have contributed materially to the development and promotion of the trade in roofing materials in this city, that of H. C. Smither occupies an advanced position. The business was

established by the firm of Sims & Smither in 1873, and was conducted under their joint administration until 1887, when Mr. Smither became sole proprietor, in which capacity he has since remained. He is conveniently and otherwise desirably located for the trade, as above, his premises being 35x150 feet in dimensions; well equipped with all requisite facilities for the business, including telephone service for the prompt acknowledgment of orders. He carries full and complete lines of goods adapted to the requirements of the trade, including gravel roofing materials, two and three ply ready roofing, waterproof sheathing, plain straw board, asbestos fire-proof felt, roof and metal paints and other commodities of the same character, in great variety. They are the products of the leading manufacturers in their several lines, composed of the best and most effective materials for the uses to which they are designed, and for sale in quantities to suit at the most reasonable prices. Mr. Smither is experienced in the business, enjoying the most favorable relations with producers of superior grades of goods in his lines, and is in a position to offer the most liberal inducements to the public and the trade generally. He does a large business with builders, contractors and others in the city and vicinity, and the house is universally recognized as a depot of supply, in every way reliable and managed according to the most honorable methods. Mr. Smither also handles the genuine Trinidad asphalt roofing and paving materials, and he feels that there should be more of these materials used for roofing purposes, as they are more durable and will last longer than any other composition roofing, and it is far better than tin or iron. And to any one wanting a good asphalt roof he would be glad to receive their orders, and will apply the roofing himself or see that it is done by good and responsible workmen, and to also further the interests in genuine Trinidad asphalt roofing, he would specially call the attention of all architects and builders to this roofing, and would be too glad to answer any and all communications that may be sent to him at his place of business, 169 West Maryland street.

The Fostoria Buggy Co.—Wholesale Manufacturers of Buggies, Etc.; 82 East Market street.—The factory of this company is at Fostoria, O., where they operate very extensive works, giving employment to a large force of skilled assistants and turning out a correspondingly large product for which there is a constant and steadily increasing demand. The Indianapolis branch is an important factor in the sum total of their yearly business. Mr. R. Silver, its manager, has been intimately identified with the buggy trade in this city for the past five years. He is experienced in the business, acquainted with wants of customers, and by his liberal and honorable enterprise has measurably advanced the company's prosperity throughout Indiana and Illinois, the territory assigned to his exclu-

sive direction. He occupies the main floor and basement of premises 25 feet front on East Market street and 100 feet deep. They are well adapted to business occupation, being commodious, well lighted, with ample accommodations for the business. The line of productions of the company, carried in full supply by Mr. Silver, embraces stationary and jump seat surreys, buggies, delivery, roundabout and other patterns of light wagons, carts, etc., in great variety and of standard worth, for the retail trade only. The best materials only are used, and the most skillful hands employed in their design, make and finish, and when completed are substantial, reliable and in every respect models in their line.

George K. Schofield—Sale Stables; 76 North Delaware street.—Mr. Schofield, who is, without doubt, the largest live stock dealer in Indianapolis, devoting his operations principally to the purchase of driving and draught horses, and mules, for the Eastern markets, began the business here in 1875. His success was instant and has continued increasing in proportions and values annually. He occupies conveniently arranged and well appointed offices, adjoining which is a commodious stable with accommodations for 30 head of stock; and he also has stables on Wabash and West Washington

streets, with a total capacity for 100 horses. They are substantially constructed, with particular regard to sanitary arrangements and for the security of horses in case of fire, in which event their escape can be accomplished promptly and effectually. His specialties are the purchase, in large, round lots, of the best strains of horses and mules for his own account and to order; also carriages and other vehicles. Auction sales are held daily at the Washington street stable, the

stock coming chiefly from Kentucky, Ohio, Illinois and Indiana, and, as stated, sent to the Eastern markets of supply. His carriage repository, at 82 East Market street, is one of the best appointed and most heavily stocked of any in its line in the city, in the way of light carriages, buggies, road wagons, and vehicles generally, the products of the best makers in the country, and unsurpassed for beauty, durability and workmanship.

Charles Mayer & Co. Importers and Jobbers of Fancy Goods, Toys, Etc.; 29 and 31 West Washington street. The house of Charles Mayer & Co. is probably the largest general emporium for fancy goods, toys, notions, etc., in the State. It was established in 1840, by Charles Mayer, Sr. During 1864, the present firm name and style was adopted. The firm is composed of Charles Mayer, Sr., Ferdinand Mayer, Fred Berger, Charles Mayer Jr., and Louis Mayer, men of experience, enterprise, and familiar with the demands of the trade to which they minister. They own and occupy an elegant five-story and basement building, 20x200 feet in dimensions, and also a three-story warehouse, 20x150 feet, fronting on Pearl street. The store proper is perfectly lighted and ventilated, heated by steam, provided with hydraulic passenger elevators, also with parcel and cash electric railways and other facilities and conveniences for the accommodation of the trade. In addition to the usual sales-rooms, the basement is also devoted to that object, being lighted by natural gas through the Welsbach pattern of burner and otherwise rendered available for the uses to which it is adapted. They carry very large stocks of druggists', stationers' and grocers' sundries, fancy leather goods, autograph and photograph albums and frames, scrap books, pictures, birthday, Christmas and New Year cards, Japanese and Chinese novelties, musical instruments, boxes and wares, majolica, fancy china, Bohemian glassware, brass and bronze goods, toys, children's carriages, velocipedes, bicycles, tricycles, girls' propellers, fireworks, Chinese lanterns, sporting goods and notions generally, in great variety. They import foreign goods direct, and buy domestic manufactures for spot cash. They are also State agents for A. G. Spalding & Bros.' (Chicago) sporting goods, and in all their lines handle none but the best, which are sold to customers and the trade at the lowest prices. They employ from 75 to 100 assistants, besides eight travelers, and do a large and constantly augmenting business throughout Indiana, Illinois, Iowa, Kentucky and Ohio, as also in portions of Texas and California, in all of which the house enjoys an established reputation and a distinguished prestige.

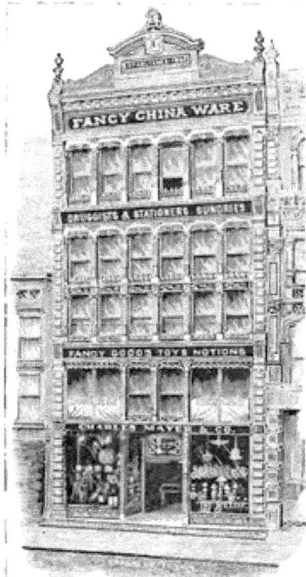

BANKS AND BANKING.

INDIANAPOLIS was without banking facilities until 1835, when the Indianapolis Insurance Company was organized and engaged in a general banking and insurance business until 1842, finally becoming the Bank of Commerce. Edward S. Alvord & Co. became established thereon, and in 1847 the Bank of the State of Indiana was organized at Indianapolis, with seventeen branch banks distributed throughout the State. Upon the establishment of the national banking system it was succeeded by the Indiana National Bank. The later history of banking in Indianapolis is a familiar story. The city now contains four national and two private banks, the solvency and reliability of which are beyond comment, as is shown by the accompanying tabulated statement. They are closely identified with the commercial and industrial interests of the city and State, and wield a powerful influence in the development and maintenance of the public prosperity. In this department there is also a field for the employment of additional capital, and overtures with that object in view will meet with substantial encouragement from citizens and capitalists. The following table shows the condition of the banks at the close of the last fiscal year:

BANKS	CAPITAL	SURPLUS	DEPOSITS	LOANS AND DISCOUNTS
Indianapolis National	$ 300,000	$ 75,000.00	$1,500,000.00	$ 900,000.00
Indiana National	500,000	300,000.00	2,500,000.00	1,300,000.00
Merchants' National	300,000	80,000.00	807,162.00	375,000.00
Meridian National	250,000	160,000.00	1,300,000.73	700,000.00
Bank of Commerce	200,000			
Fletcher's	1,000,000		2,500,000.00	1,500,000.00
Total	$2,500,000	$615,000.00	$8,731,572.73	$4,875,000.00

THE CLEARING HOUSE.

The clearances at the clearing house for the year 1888 were $80,537,502.53, against $45,381,194.45 in 1887, and $66,078,012.12 in 1886.

BUILDING AND LOAN ASSOCIATIONS.

There were eighty-nine building and loan associations in operation in Indianapolis January first, 1889, with a capital stock aggregating $26,355.00, having a large membership and in prosperous condition.

SAFETY DEPOSIT COMPANIES.

Ample facilities for the storage of valuables are available by two companies, provided with all modern equipments for security against burglars or fire.

S. A. Fletcher & Co.—Bank and Safety Deposit Vaults; 30, 32 and 34 East Washington street. Among the financial institutions of Indianapolis none is more strongly intrenched in the confidence of the people than the banking house of S. A. Fletcher & Co., which, with a record of honorable history extending back for more than a half a century, now deservedly ranks as one of the most solid and substantial of the banking institutions of the State. It was established in 1839 by Mr. Stoughton A. Fletcher, who was joined in 1852 by Mr. F. M. Churchman, when the style of S. A. Fletcher & Co. was assumed. In 1882, upon the death of the founder, Mr. Stoughton A. Fletcher his son, Mr. Stoughton J. Fletcher, who had been connected with the bank for fifteen years previously, succeeded to his interest, the firm now being composed of Messrs. S. J. Fletcher and F. M. Churchman. No change has ever been made, however, in the style of the firm,

which has long been so well known and highly regarded that the expression, "as sound as Fletcher's bank," has become a familiar household word in Indianapolis. The building occupied by the bank and safety deposit vaults is a four-story and basement structure, 22x150 feet in dimensions, with a handsome front of oolitic lime-stone, and is one of the most attractive and imposing business edifices in the city. Its interior is elegantly and conveniently fitted up, affording every facility for the successful prosecution of the business. A general banking business is transacted, the bank receiving the deposits of banks, bankers, business firms and corporations, and the public, loaning money on acceptable security, discounting approved paper, issuing exchange on the leading cities of America and Europe, and attending to all the usual details of legitimate banking business. The bank has a working capital of $1,000,000, and its statement made at the close of 1888 showed its deposits to amount to $2,700,000 and its discounts to $1,500,000. The bank has some 7,500 depositors, including the wealthiest capitalists of the city and a number of country banks in this and surrounding States. The bank numbers among its correspondents the most substantial banks of the leading cities and has every facility for the transaction of its business. The firm's safety deposit vaults, which were opened to the public in 1888, combine all the most highly improved appliances for securing the safety of deposits and the convenience of safe renters, and affords a reliable means for securing the safety of money, valuables and documents. The members of the firm are gentlemen of the highest character and standing, and Mr. S. J. Fletcher, in addition to his interest in the bank, is a large owner of real estate and houses in the city and its suburbs, and along the line of the Belt Railway. The bank is the oldest in the city and does the largest business. It has earned this position of leadership by a steady adherence to the highest principles of financial integrity throughout the long period covered by its history of honor and usefulness.

Indiana National Bank—11 and 13 East Washington street.

The Indiana National Bank, one of the leading and representative monetary institutions in the State, was organized in 1865, under the National banking law, as successor to the Branch Bank of the State of Indiana. Mr. George Tousey was President and D. E. Snider Cashier. The former was succeeded by William Coughlen, who served from 1878 to 1882, when he was in turn succeeded by Volney T. Malott. Mr. Snider was followed by D. M. Taylor, and the latter by W. E. Coffin, who remained the incumbent until 1885. During that year the charter of the bank expired by limitation, and a re-organization was perfected with V. T. Malott, President; William Coughlen, Vice-President, and F. B. Porter, Cashier, who still occupy the several positions to which they were at that date elected. The bank was successful from its start, and that success has accompanied its career ever since. It transacts all business pertaining to general banking; receives deposits, discounts commercial paper, makes collections, deals in national securities, has correspondents at financial centers, buys and sells foreign exchange and issues drafts and letters of credit on the leading banks of the world. It is prominently identified with commercial interests here, and is of valuable assistance to the promotion of the prosperity of all deserving undertakings. The report of the condition of the bank at the close of business December 12, 1888, shows the loans and discounts were $1,329,393.30, the deposits were $2,329,684.03, and the surplus and undivided profits $252,928.87. The capital stock of the bank is $500,000, paid in, and the New York correspondents are the Bank of America, and Importers'

FLETCHER'S BANK—SEE OPPOSITE PAGE.

and Traders National banks. It is centrally located, in a building owned by Mr. Malott, occupying commodious and handsomely appointed offices, and enjoys an extensive patronage, as also a reputation for the magnitude of its transactions, and the adoption and enforcement of a policy that has secured for it a conspicuous position among the banking institutions of the State. The following leading Indianapolis business men and capitalists compose the present directory : R. S. McKee, George Merritt, W. J. Holliday, George T. Porter, Chas. H. Brownell, Volney T. Malott and William Coughlen.

The Indianapolis National Bank— Corner of Washington and Pennsylvania streets.—The Indianapolis National is one of the oldest National banks in the West, if not in the country, and one of the most prosperous and flourishing in the city. It was organized in 1865, with T. P. Haughey, President, and H. Latham, Cashier, and re-organized in 1885, upon the expiration of its original charter, with the same gentlemen occupying the same positions respectively to which they were elected when the bank began operations twenty years previous. In November, 1888, Mr. Latham retired from the cashiership, owing to ill-health, and was succeeded by Edwin E. Rexford, who has been in the employ of the bank since 1872. The capital stock is $500,000, and the surplus and undivided profits amount [...] $125,000, and a general banking business is done such as issuing money on first-class security, discounting commercial paper of approved values, caring for the accounts of individuals, corporations and banks, making collections, the purchase and sale of foreign and domestic exchange, and other lines of legitimate banking operations. It is managed according to its own ideas, but liberal policy, giving it the highest character of order and reputation for it the reputation of a substantial financial institution of the highest character. The condition of the bank at the close of business December 12, 1888, showed its capital stock and surplus as above, its total deposits to be $1,700,000 or so, and its total resources $2,137,078.88. Its present officers are: Theodore P. Haughey, President; Edwin E. Rexford, Cashier, and W. F. Croft, Assistant Cashier. The Board of Directors consists of the President, also of C. F. Meyer, of Chas. Meyer & Bro., wholesale cigars, Scott Butler, of Professor Butler's College, Henry Sattersdale, President of the First National Bank of Martinsville, Ind., and R. B. F. Pierce, all well-known citizens and capitalists. The bank is the United States depository for this district. Its correspondents are the Third National and Chase National Banks of New York City, the Commercial National of Chicago, and Third National of Cincinnati. It is conveniently located at the corner of Washington and Pennsylvania streets, and these premises are being enlarged by taking in the adjoining store, which will make it the largest and most complete banking house in the city.

Merchant's National Bank

Designated U. S. Depository; southwest corner Washington and Meridian streets. The organization of the Merchants' National Bank of Indianapolis was effected in 1865, with Henry Schnull, President, and V. T. Malott, Cashier. Its capital stock was $100,000. In 1881, the charter, which expired during that year, was renewed, the capital stock remaining unchanged. The bank building, located as above, occupies a site of unsurpassed advantage for the purposes of business, and is in all respects adapted to that object, being provided with all requisite facilities and appointments for the safe and expeditious conduct of operations. A general banking business is transacted, including the carrying of deposits for individuals, corporations and foreign banks, the discount of commercial paper, purchase and sale of foreign and domestic exchange, loans, collections, etc. Its regular correspondents are: The National Park Bank of New York, Everett National Bank, Boston; First National Bank, Chicago; Fourth Street National Bank, Philadelphia, and Merchants' National Bank, Cincinnati. Banking institutions of national celebrity. The bank is also the designated depository for United States funds in this district, and has the vaults of the National Trust and Safe Deposit Company, a separate corporation, in which the Merchants' National directory is largely interested, in connection with its banking premises. The operations of the corporation have been successful since their inception, the deposits, loans and discounts steadily increasing in amount and importance, due to the able and judicious character of its management. Its present surplus and undivided profits amount to $46,203.14, and during 1888 the loans aggregated $5,104,410.48, the deposits, $607,363.58. The executive board consists of J. P. Frenzel, President; O. N. Frenzel, Cashier, who, with James F. Failey, Paul H. Krauss and Christ. F. Bals, constitute the Board of Directors. They are men of extensive business experience and reputation, and the condition of the bank, as also its prospects, are in the highest degree satisfactory.

The National Trust and Safe Deposit Co.

10 South Meridian street. This company was organized in 1888, for the special purpose of doing a trust and safe deposit business. The premises occupied consist of the ground floor, divided into an office and waiting room, a private consultation room and apartments for ladies and gentlemen for the private examination of boxes. The vault, constructed by the Herhold Safe and Lock Company, rests on a foundation of solid masonry and is surrounded by solid brick walls. The lining, composed of welded steel and iron, is two inches thick. The

outer doors are guarded by twenty-two bolts operated by spring bolt machinery; the inner doors are locked with two double combination locks. The capacity of the vault is 1,800 individual apartments, each side or apartment provided with key or combination lock, as may be preferred, each lock being different from all the others and changed upon every re-renting. Proper regulations are enforced with regard to the identity of lessees or their deputies, and ample facilities are provided for the convenience and seclusion of patrons in their examinations of papers, bonds and stocks. Thoroughly reliable watchmen are employed day and night, and electric appliances are available for instant communication with the city police in case of emergency. The vault is absolutely fire and burglar proof and the

INTERIOR VIEW—NATIONAL TRUST AND SAFE DEPOSIT CO.

apartments are leased at from $5.00 to $25.00 per annum according to size. The enterprise is addressed to the notice of capitalists, bond owners, merchants, bankers, brokers, manufacturers, tradesmen, mechanics, clergymen, physicians, lawyers, widows, owners of plate, jewelry, souvenirs, family relics, securities, valuable papers, etc., as offering an absolutely safe place of deposit for same. In addition to renting boxes the company receives for safe keeping plate, bullion, jewelry, notes, bills, deeds, abstracts, manuscripts, letters, and securities generally at low rates. The officers, all well known capitalists and business men, are James F. Failey, President; E. G. Cornelius, Vice-President; Otto N. Frenzel, Secretary and Treasurer, who, with N. S. Byam, J. P. Frenzel, P. H. Krauss and C. H. Bals, constitute the Board of Directors. Many of these gentlemen are connected with the Merchants' National Bank, a separate and distinct corporation, however, from the present company.

Meridian National Bank

8 East Washington street.—The Meridian National is a substantial representative of the banking interests of Indianapolis, as also of the conservative but liberal policy which has always characterized their management and business operations. The organization of the bank was perfected in 1871, with John Farquar, President, and George F. Hogate, Cashier. In 1887 William P. Gallup succeeded to the Presidency, and is still the incumbent of that responsible position, A. F. Kopp, the cashier since 1885, has been in the service of the bank since 1873. They are located as above, at one of the most available points on East Washington street, where they occupy commodious accommodations, and are fully provided with all necessary requisites and appointments for the transaction of the business in all its various departments. They receive deposits, discount approved mercantile paper, deal in foreign and domestic exchange, also in Government, State and local securities, issue circular and commercial letters of credit, and in all business relations extend important and to the financial, commercial, and manufacturing interests of Indianapolis. Its chief correspondents are the Fourth National Bank of New York; The Merchants' National of Chicago; Maverick National, Boston; First National, Cincinnati; and the Central National Bank of Philadelphia. A prosperous business has been done since the organization. The capital stock is

$300,000 paid up, the surplus fund $100,000, and the total resources $1,577,620.62. The business for the fiscal year 1888 showed loans and discounts amounting to $788,078.84, and deposits, individual and otherwise, aggregating $1,169,895.73, with undivided profits approximating $20,000. A large and experienced staff of assistants is employed, and the list of customers includes the leading capitalists and business men of the city and vicinity. The officers are: Wm P. Gallup, President; D. A. Richardson, Vice-President; A. F. Kopp, Cashier. These gentlemen, with Charles Mayer, Fred Fahnley, J. P. Robertson, R. S. Foster, R. H. McCrea and Charles Scholl, compose the Board of Directors.

The Bank of Commerce — Junction South Pennsylvania street and Virginia avenue.— This bank was chartered by the State Legislature February 8, 1896. Its capital stock is $200,000, and by the provisions of its charter, the stockholders are individually liable to the same extent as those of National Banks. Over seven-eighths of the stock is held by the estate and heirs of the late W. C. DePauw,

of New Albany, who purchased a controlling interest some ten years ago, and directed its management up to the date of his death in Chicago, sometime during 1887. By the terms of his will, the closing up of his estate is deferred for fifteen years, and upon the final settlement being made, 14 per cent. of the stock and that percentage of the bank's earnings for the same period, are to be credited to the DePauw University, of Greencastle, this State. Its executors and directory boards have always been composed of men of financial ability and experience (John W. Ray, the Vice-President was eight years Cashier when the outlook was most unpromising, during which time the stock advanced from fifty cents on the dollar to a par value). The present officers are: Needham T. DePauw, President; John W. Ray, Vice-President, and William Rosson, Cashier, who, with William Wallace and Charles W. DePauw, constitute the Board of Directors. The Messrs. DePauw, sons of the late W. C. DePauw, reside at New Albany; Messrs. Ray, Rosson and Wallace being residents of this city.

PUBLIC BUILDINGS.

AMONG the prominent features of Indianapolis are the number and extent of the public buildings which decorate the city and vicinity. As the Capital of the State, the State institutions, embracing the Capitol, Insane Asylum, Deaf and Dumb Asylum, Blind Asylum and Female Reformatory are conspicuous examples of architectural development and finish. To these should be added the buildings inspired by public and private enterprise, notable among which are the Marion County Court House, Union Railway Station, Tomlinson's Hall, Fletcher's Bank building, the New Denison, and other structures, Federal, commercial and theatric, illustrative of the growth and prosperity of the city, as also of the enterprise and liberality of citizens.

THE STATE HOUSE.

By far the handsomest structure in the city is the State House, occupying the square bounded by Ohio, Tennessee, Washington and Mississippi streets. The building is of Bedford stone, three stories high, 492x196 feet in dimensions, and 283 feet from east to west through the center, with a dome of solid stone from foundation to apex, 72 feet in diameter and 234 feet in height. The basement is occupied for storage purposes and the State Armory, the main floor with the executive and administrative offices of the State, the second

Y. M. C. A. BUILDING.

floor by the Legislative department, the Supreme Court, State Library, Treasury, School Superintendent, Auditor and other offices, and the third floor by the Geological department, committee rooms, etc. The premises are heated by natural gas, and lighted by gas and electricity. They were commenced in 1878 and completed ten years later, at a cost of $1,983,000, exclusive of the furnishings, which cost an additional outlay of $182,000. It was erected upon plans furnished by a local architect, and is pronounced one of the most complete edifices of its kind in the United States.

MARION COUNTY COURT HOUSE.

The County Court House of Marion county is not surpassed in respect to architectural proportions, finish, coloring and general detail, by that of any similar corporation in the country. The building, which is of Bedford stone, is located in the square bounded by Washington, Delaware, Market and New Jersey streets, with a frontage of 276 feet 6 inches and a depth of 196 feet 3 inches. It is located in the business center of the city and is one of the most massive public buildings in the State. The style of architecture is the modern French *Renaissance*. The work of construction was begun in 1870, and the building completed in 1876 at a cost of $1,500,000. The basement is occupied by city

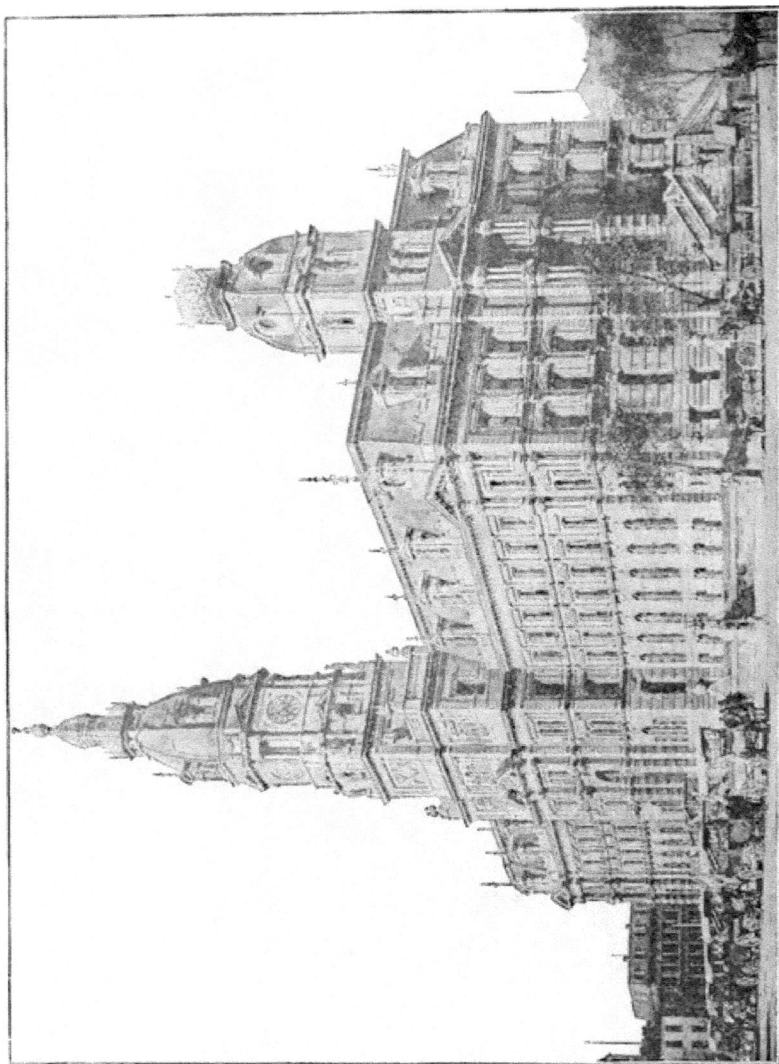

MARION COUNTY COURT HOUSE.

offices, the upper floors being used by the county offices and court rooms. Each suite of rooms, with the walls and ceilings of the entire building, are frescoed, the floors are laid with tile, and other appointments have been provided for the convenience of the public appropriate to the character of the edifice and expressive of good taste.

TOMLINSON'S HALL.

Tomlinson's Hall is a commodious brick structure fronting 120 feet on Market street, with a depth of 195 feet on Delaware street. It was erected in 1886 at a cost of $125,000, the proceeds of a bequest made to the city for the purpose by Stephen Tomlinson some years ago, and allowed to accumulate until sufficient in amount to commence operations.

The building is two stories high, the main floor being occupied as a vegetable market and the second story as a public hall, with capacity to accommodate an audience of five thousand. East of this is a market house completed the same year. It is a one-story brick, 100 feet front on Market street and 195 feet deep, and cost the city thirty thousand dollars.

FEDERAL BUILDING.

The Federal building is situated at the corner of Pennsylvania and Market streets. It is three stories high and was commenced in 1857. The main building was completed in 1860, at a cost of $160,000; the annex in 1872. The main floor is occupied by the Postoffice, the second story with the United States Court room, Judge's, Marshal's and other offices, and the third story with the offices of the Collectors and other Federal officials. Additional ground, adjoining the present site on the east, was purchased by the government in 1888, and the structure will be materially enlarged immediately an appropriation is made by Congress.

MASONIC TEMPLE.

Masonic Temple is located at the corner of Washington and Tennessee streets. It is a four-story edifice of stone and brick, and one of the handsomest buildings in the city. The ground floor is used for stores, the second floor being devoted to offices and the third floor to lodge rooms; the fourth story being occupied exclusively by the commandery. The building prepared for occupation, cost $175,000, not including the furnishings.

YOUNG MEN'S CHRISTIAN ASSOCIATION.

The handsome stone building on Illinois street owned and occupied by the Young Men's Christian Association was completed in July, 1887. The style of architecture is Romanesque or round arched Gothic, executed in rough stone from the quarries at Romano, on the

Vincennes road. It is 71 feet 3 inches front on Illinois street with a depth of 120 feet, and the interior is handsomely finished in hard woods. The main floor is devoted to stores, the three upper stories by the association, and are divided into offices, reading, parlors and amusement rooms, with an audience room in the rear 70x68 feet in dimensions, with a capacity for seating an audience of ---. The total cost of the building was $125,000, the furnishing equipment of the same being done at an expense of $11,000 additional.

ODD FELLOWS' HALL.

Odd Fellows' Hall was built in 1854, and reconstructed in 1874, at an expense of $85,000. It is three stories in height, 65x102 feet in dimensions, and composed of brick, with a covering and ornamentations of stucco. The main floor is occupied with stores, the upper floors being used for offices and lodge room purposes.

BOARD OF TRADE.

The Board of Trade building occupies the south-east corner of Maryland and Tennessee streets, having a frontage of 60 feet on the former and 120 feet on the latter thoroughfare. The building is of brick, with stone facings, and Renaissance in style of architecture. The main floor and second story are occupied by stores and offices, the Exchange being upon the third floor. The building cost $80,000, and was completed in 1874.

THE ARSENAL.

The Arsenal is located in the northeastern portion of the city adjoining Woodruff Place, in the midst of a tract of 75½ acres. The building is of brick, 183x63 feet in dimensions, and fronts on both Michigan and Clifford avenues. The premises are used for the storage of arms and ordnance by the general government. Adjoining the Arsenal are officers' quarters, barracks, storehouses, magazine and other buildings, also of brick. The improvements are valued at $645,031.72.

EXPOSITION BUILDING.

The Exposition Building was erected during 1873, in the northeastern part of the city, upon plans furnished by the late Edward May. The building is 150x390 feet in dimensions, built of brick in modern style of architecture and surmounted by a cupola 150 feet in height. The total cost was $75,000.

Besides those mentioned, there are a number of smaller halls available for society and other purposes, and three theatres: The Grand Opera House on North Pennsylvania street, the English Opera House, on the Circle, and the Park Theatre and Museum, at the northwest corner of Tennessee and Washington streets.

TOMLINSON'S HALL. (CITY HALL.)

RESIDENCE PORTLAND VAN CAMP.

RESIDENCE FREDERICK PARSLEY.

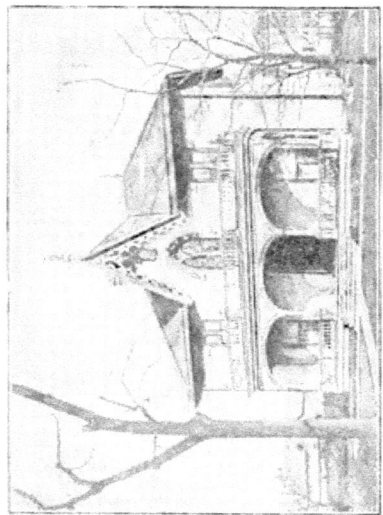

RESIDENCE C. H. FITZGERALD.

RESIDENCE A. H. SORBYNE.

MANUFACTURERS.

ANUFACTURING industries were established in Indianapolis when the present city was first settled. Since 1821, when they embraced undertakings of the most primitive character, their number has grown into large proportions, with results that have annually contributed more substantially to the city's prominence and prosperity as a commercial center, than any other single agency employed in that behalf. It is unnecessary to more than refer to the early efforts ventured in this field of usefulness. They were numerous, and while many fell by the wayside, many survived and became the founders of the present elaborate system, a system that has attained to its present significance under the fostering influence of a class of business men to whom in all the departments of life, civilization is indebted for the creation, development and promotion of enterprises designed for the public welfare. Indianapolis is a manufacturing city, and known as such in every State of the Union, as also throughout the Canadian provinces, South America, Europe, Australia and elsewhere beyond the seas, for the products of the city's 560 factories are sold in all the markets of the world.

PORK PACKING.

Probably the most important industry of Indianapolis in the amount of capital invested and the value of the annual product, is pork packing. The establishments thus engaged here give employment to 1,200 hands, control $2,000,000 of invested capital, and the value of their products for 1888 was $10,000,000. Their houses and equipments are unsurpassed in every particular, and their lines of production, which are of the best quality and description, are shipped to all the depots of supply in this country and Europe, where they command the highest prices.

LUMBER PRODUCTS.

Another leading industry in the value of its annual products, amount of capital invested, etc., is the manufacture of furniture. Among the many advantages possessed by Indianapolis for the success attained in this direction is the city's proximity to an almost inexhaustible supply of hardwood, the amount of which available to such uses can hardly be estimated. Indianapolis has for years supplied the markets of the world with walnut, oak, cherry, ash and poplar, and yet controls the hardwood lumber trade of the country. The manufacture of furniture on a large scale was commenced here about 1855, and has steadily increased in volume from that year. The business is owned and conducted by men of enterprise, the factories are not surpassed in size and appointments by those of any similar industry in the west, and the facilities enable the manufacture of every description of household and office furniture, rapidly and with the most satisfactory results. The growth of this industry, and the increase in the number of manufacturers, together with the quality of the output and amount of sales annually made, is phenomenal. In 1882, the value of the product was $2,000,000. That amount represented the capital alone invested in the business in 1888, the output for which year aggregated $4,000,000 in value. Next to furniture manufacture, the manufacture of lumber and building materials is an important industry of the city, and of comparatively recent origin, having been introduced here about the period of the breaking out of the war. The ample supply of raw material within easy reach of manufacturers, and the facilities for shipment to every portion of the world at low rates for freight, gave an early impetus to the business which has constantly appreciated in value through the years that have followed. There are now twenty-one firms and corporations engaged in the manufacture of lumber and building materials, with a total capital of $4,500,000, giving employment to 1,000 men, and producing an annual output valued at $3,100,000.

The manufacture of wagons and carriages, wheels, staves, woodenware, car-woodwork, boxes and other articles composed mainly of wood, come properly under this division of the city's industrial resources, among which they are prominent and leading. There are now fifty-seven factories devoted to these lines, employing an aggregate of $2,221,000 capital and 2,598 hands. The total value of their products for 1888 was $3,632,000. The largest of these industries, thirty-five in number, employs 990 men and turned out wagons and carriages, valued at $1,500,000, in 1888, though the stairs manufactured for the year were valued at $2,000,000 and the wooden wheels at $750,000. The establishment, growth and progress of these industries will be found in the notices of houses and companies therein engaged.

METAL WORKING INDUSTRIES.

Under this head is included the factories which manufacture articles, the constituent properties of which are metals, such as steel, iron, copper, brass, etc. The origin of these industries dates back to the establishment of the Eagle Machine Works in 1850. Other foundries and machine shops followed, to which large additions have been made in value and capacity from time to time as the service demanded, and nearly all have enjoyed a prosperous career. There are now sixty-seven of this description of factories in the city, with an aggregate capital of $3,105,000, and the value of their annual product for 1888, during which they employed 3,224 hands, was $10,411,000. Their output embraces engines, mill and other machinery, architectural iron work, springs, bolts, malleable iron work, saws, stoves, surgical instruments, wire, and other commodities in the same line, which enjoy a national reputation for superiority in respect to materials and workmanship. Among the largest industries not specified above, are the agricultural works, car works, railroad shops, etc., giving employment to 2,460 hands and $3,050,000 capital, and producing an annual output valued at $5,500,000. The field for business is extensive, and the opportunities afforded to capitalists for profitable investments are abundant.

MISCELLANEOUS INDUSTRIES.

There are upward of 350 firms, corporations, etc., carrying on manufacturing industries of a miscellaneous character, giving employment to nearly 9000 hands and $10,000,000 capital, and turning out annually goods and wares valued at more than $20,000,000. The leading among these are grist mills, seven in number, producing flour valued at $3,000,000; breweries turning out $2,000,000 worth of malt liquors annually; tanneries, $1,500,000; bricks, $1,800,000; overalls, $800,000; fruits, $800,000; textile fabrics, $700,000; stone work, $1,000,000; pumps, tiles, starch, hominy, and other lines, $500,000 each; also manufacturers of boots and shoes, tiles, canned goods, linseed oil, medicaments, tin ware, varnishes, etc., with large capacity and correspondingly productive, both in respect to materials and values.

ROOM FOR ADDITIONAL INDUSTRIES.

The location of Indianapolis, in the center of a rich agricultural country, near to supplies of iron, wool, stone, coal, etc., possessing unsurpassed transportation accommodations, supplied with an abundance of the best quality of coal, available to consumers at the lowest prices, the distributing point for natural gas, which will be furnished to industries free, with other conveniences and appointments, make the city one of unlimited advantages for manufacturing purposes.

There are still openings in this city for men of enterprise and capital to engage in the manufacture of articles, the production of which is hardly sufficient to equal the demand. Among these may be mentioned boots and shoes, paper, potteries, show cases, glassware, stained glass, straw goods, upholsterers' goods, willow ware, beveled and silvered mirrors, licorice, oils and dyes, brooms and broom handles, organs and sewing machines, lead pipe and sheet lead, safes, fluid extracts, marble tops, photographers' materials, locomotives, bolts, chromos, glue, etc. The following table contains a list of manu-

facturing enterprises at present in operation in Indianapolis and the suburbs. It does not, however, contain the entire variety of goods produced here, the entire capital employed, nor the total product of the lines named, these figures being included in the classification in which the firm is principally engaged. The manufacture of oils and gas is carried on extensively in Indianapolis, but the figures in their connection were not obtained in time to be included in the table below. Neither is mention made of shoemakers, bakers and small industries generally who manufacture for consumers only.

LIST OF FACTORIES.

No. of Factories	Employes	Capital Employed.	Product for 1888.	No. of Factories	Employes	Capital Employed.	Product for 1888.
Advertising Novelties	10	$10,000	$100,000	Jewelry	12	$5,000	$20,000
Agricultural Implements	550	500,000	1,000,000	Lightning Conductors	30	25,000	100,000
Architectural Iron	40	175,000	2,000,000	Linseed Oil	30	125,000	750,000
Artificial Limbs	6	5,000	20,000	Lumber and Builders' Material	1,000	1,000,000	2,000,000
Awnings and Tents	12	16,000	70,000	Marble and Stone	115	125,000	500,000
Bed Springs	20	40,000	150,000	Malleable Iron	700	300,000	600,000
Belting (leather and chain)	20	100,000	275,000	Mattress	20	20,000	75,000
Bicycles	20	1,500	60,000	Medicine	115	15,000	500,000
Bolts	40	20,000	50,000	Nail	40	50,000	100,000
Book Binders and Blank Book Manufacture	300	325,000	1,500,000	Natural Gas Supplies	90	250,000	1,000,000
Boots and Shoes	50	20,000	100,000	Organs	6	5,000	25,000
Boot and Shoe Uppers	20	10,000	35,000	Overalls	500	150,000	400,000
Bottling (soda, pop, beer, etc.)	65	75,000	200,000	Paper	40	30,000	75,000
Box (cigar)	15	8,000	25,000	Paints and Oils	60	65,000	175,000
Box (packing)	162	100,000	200,000	Planes	20	25,000	60,000
Box (paper)	60	8,000	60,000	Plumbers	620	125,000	250,000
Brick	120	215,000	1,000,000	Pork Packers	1,200	2,000,000	10,000,000
Brick Machinery	15	16,000	70,000	Potteries	15	15,000	25,000
Brass Founders	20	30,000	100,000	Pumps	350	300,000	500,000
Brewers	210	1,000,000	2,000,000	Pulleys (paper)	15	25,000	100,000
Brooms	200	30,000	100,000	Railroad Shops	3,050	2,000,000	2,000,000
Cars	500	500,000	2,500,000	Regalia	15	8,000	40,000
Carpet Goods	40	60,000	300,000	Rubber Stamps	12	5,000	35,000
Carriage Woodwork	60	220,000	325,000	Saws	325	100,000	600,000
Carriages and Wagons	500	500,000	1,500,000	Shirts	100	95,000	135,000
Chemist	100	130,000	250,000	Show Cases	15	13,000	50,000
Cigars	212	150,000	500,000	Stoves	150	50,000	100,000
Cooliers	30	25,000	150,000	Starch	150	250,000	500,000
Coffee	8	40,000	75,000	Stained Glass	8	5,000	35,000
Coopers	325	100,000	600,000	Stoves and Heading	250	410,000	2,000,000
Cracker Machinery	25	10,000	40,000	Stone Quarries	350	60,000	1,000,000
Chemical (dental)	25	20,000	100,000	Straw Goods	60	10,000	90,000
Electric Light	100	250,000	300,000	Soap	300	10,000	100,000
Electrotype	25	15,000	50,000	Surgical Instruments	25	25,000	100,000
Engines, Boilers, Founders and Machinists	1,005	1,000,000	3,000,000	Terra Cotta	50	50,000	100,000
Engravers	15	8,000	10,000	Tinners	175	150,000	250,000
Knitting	25	20,000	65,000	Tiles (encaustic)	150	300,000	500,000
Fertilizers	100	30,000	250,000	Trucks (store)	10	10,000	25,000
Flour Mill Machinery	500	650,000	1,250,000	Trunks	40	15,000	125,000
Furs	10	20,000	50,000	Upholsterers	25	10,000	50,000
Frames and Mouldings	140	100,000	350,000	Varnish	40	150,000	250,000
Fences (patent)	20	30,000	25,000	Veneer	50	50,000	100,000
Flour Mills	160	500,000	3,000,000	Vinegar and Cider	10	10,000	35,000
Forge and Switches	40	50,000	200,000	Water Works	100	500,000	250,000
Fruit Packers	20	20,000	400,000	Warp (cotton)	40	50,000	300,000
Furnaces	20	40,000	150,000	Wheels (wooden)	75	60,000	750,000
Furniture and Fixtures	250	2,000,000	1,000,000	Wire Works	30	8,000	50,000
Glue	25	50,000	80,000	Willow Ware	40	8,000	20,000
Harness	100	125,000	300,000	Wooden Ware	100	150,000	300,000
Hosiery	30	40,000	500,000	Woolen Mills	110	25,000	300,000
Hoops	25	10,000	35,000				
Hosiery and Knitting	115	5,000	120,000				
Ice Cream	20	2,000	60,000	Total	21,225	$21,725,000	$50,586,000

Kingan & Co. (Limited)—Pork Packers.—The commanding position held by the vast establishment of Kingan & Co. gives it a notable prominence as one of the foremost representatives of the important industries of Indianapolis. The fame of its products have long extended beyond national boundaries, and they are as popular in Canada, Great Britain and Continental Europe as in this country, fully half of the trade of the house being its export business. The enterprise was established about thirty years ago, and it has been conducted under its present corporate style for the past fourteen years. The plant, more than ten acres in extent, and enclosed within its walls, is in itself a miniature city, alive with activity and business vigor. A large number of buildings from three to seven stories in height are contained within the inclosure, to which entrance is obtained through large gates and driveways leading to a spacious courtyard around which the vast buildings utilized in slaughtering, packing and storage houses, as well as the office and other buildings, are located. The machinery equipment includes all the latest appli-

being utilized which is calculated in any way to aid or expedite the operations of the business, and to keep the product up to the high standard of quality by which its celebrity has been attained. The vast resources of the company and the wide area covered by its trade rank it among the leading American manufacturing houses, and its prominence and prosperity attest the wisdom of its management.

Eli Lilly & Co.—Eli Lilly, President; James E. Lilly, Vice-President; Evan F. Lilly, Secretary; Josiah K. Lilly, Superintendent; Pharmaceutical Chemists, McCarty street.—For the extent of its business, the wide range and admitted excellence of its products, and the expensive area covered by its trade, there is no manufacturing concern in Indianapolis which stands more prominent than that of Eli Lilly & Co. The business was established in 1876 by Mr. Eli Lilly, who, in 1881, became the President of the company upon its incorporation under its present style. The company's laboratory,

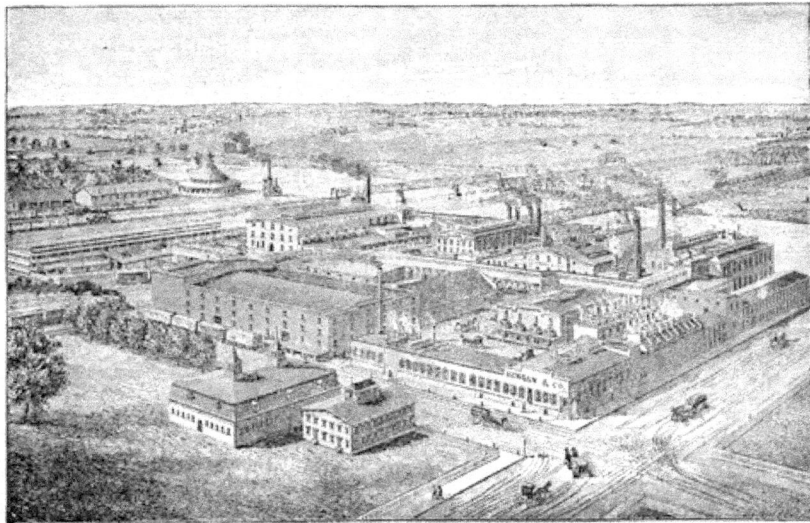

KINGAN & CO. (LIMITED), INDIANAPOLIS, IND.

ances which modern invention has supplied to aid or expedite the operations of this department of industry; and here an average of about 600,000 hogs are annually slaughtered and converted into pork products by the aid of the most approved modern processes. The outlay for hogs amounts to from $6,000,000 to $7,000,000 per annum; a capital of $1,500,000 is invested, and the product reaches to from $8,000,000 to $9,000,000 annually. Employment is given to a force ranging from 500 to 1000 hands, according to the season, and the storage capacity of the warehouses amounts to about 11,000,000 pounds. The company, in addition to its premises here, has other extensive packing houses at Richmond, Va., and Kansas City. The brand of "Reliable" hams and other pork products is justly popular and in large demand in all parts of the Union and Canada, while for the export trade they put up their "Kingan" brand, specially put up in accordance with the requirements of the English and European markets and in large and constantly growing demand. Vast as the business is, all of its details are under the close supervision of experienced superintendents in every department, every accessory

occupying a three-story and basement brick building, 90x175 feet in dimensions, with an "L," 70x25 feet, is notable for its convenient arrangement and its perfect equipment of improved machinery, much of which is of a special character, while the motive power is supplied by an 80-horse power engine, fed by two large boilers. The company gives employment to a force of about 100 skilled employes in the manufacture of standard medicinal products and pharmaceutical preparations, including fluid extracts, standard tinctures, gelatin coated and sugar coated pills and granules, medicinal elixirs, syrups and wines, compressed tablets and lozenges, solid extracts, powdered extracts, concentrations (resinoids), and a varied list of miscellaneous preparations. Not only all the officinal preparations of the United States Pharmacopœia, but also all approved unofficinal extracts and other preparations are included in the products of the laboratory, and there are also here prepared a number of specialties which have secured the approval of the highest medical authorities and the profession at large. Included in the latter class are Succus Alterans (McDade), of great value as an alterative mixture for syphilis and

President of the company. The trade of the company steadily increases with each succeeding season, and the high position it holds is the deserved result of the energy and enterprise of the President, Mr. Eli Lilly, and his associate officers, the careful supervision of the processes employed in the laboratory, and the uniform excellence of all its products.

Van Camp Packing Co.

Packers of Extra Tomatoes, Corn, Peas, Beans, Strawberries, Pumpkins and Tomato Ketchup.

Van Camp Preserving Co.

Manufacturers of Pure Fruit Preserves, Jellies, Fruit Butters, Mince Meat, Sauces, Etc. Gilbert C. Van Camp, President; Frank Van Camp, Secretary and Treasurer, 330 to 400 Kentucky avenue. This establishment, which has grown from comparatively small beginnings to a position of leadership in its line, has earned a position in the favor of the trade and consumers second to no manufacturing concern in the country. The business was established in 1861 by Mr. Gilbert C. Van Camp, the firm later assuming the style of G. C. Van Camp & Co., who were succeeded in 1882 by the Van Camp Packing Co., and in April, 1889, the Van Camp Preserving Co. was incorporated as a distinct institution, Mr. Gilbert C. Van Camp and Frank Van Camp continuing as the officers of both companies, which occupy the same offices and works. The plant, to which additions have been made from time to time as the growth of the business demanded them, now covers four acres, and includes the main building, a two-story and basement brick structure 100x100 feet in dimensions, with a wing 150x30 feet; and two large storage sheds, in dimensions 160x100 feet and 60x60 feet respectively; and the manufacturing equipment includes five boilers; two of 80-horse power each, two of 60-horse power each, and one of 25-horse power; two caps, one of 40-horse power and the other of 25-horse power; large tanks and kettles with a capacity of 4000 bushels of tomatoes per day, 25,000 solderers, with a quantity of 200,000 cans per day, and a vast amount of improved machinery and appliances specially adapted to the purposes of this business. A force ranging from forty to fifty hands is steadily employed, and this force is augmented in the packing season to from 600 to 700 hands; and five

active and experienced traveling salesmen represent the house to the jobbing and wholesale trade in all parts of the Union. The Van Camp Packing Co. are the largest packers of tomatoes in the world, and put up, on an average, about 3,000,000 two and three-pound cans of tomatoes, peas, string beans, corn, strawberries and pumpkins in the packing season of about fourteen weeks annually. The Van Camp Preserving Company has a productive capacity for 100,000 pounds of jellies, preserves, fruit butters, mincemeat, etc., per day, and are large producers in all of these lines. The house has ever based its claims to success upon the purity of its goods, and by maintaining the highest standard of quality has secured its present firmly established position as a leader in this branch of industry. This excellence of quality, and the enterprise of Mr. Gilbert C. Van Camp, the President of the company, have been factors in the success of this great establishment, and the office and financial affairs of the company are efficiently supervised by Mr. Frank Van Camp, a gentleman of thorough business training, and in all its details the management is characterized by progressive and sagacious methods.

Eagle Machine Works Co.

L. W. Hasselman, President; W. J. Hasselman, Vice-President; Manufacturers of Agricultural and Saw Mill Machinery and Engines; Missouri street and Kentucky avenue. The development of the resources of the great West, which in the rapidity with which a wilderness has been changed to a prolific agricultural region is the greatest marvel of modern history, is the result of numerous causes, none of which have been more potent than the progress made in the invention and manufacture of improved agricultural machinery. These labor-saving appliances have increased productive power and lessened its cost, lightened labor, and made possible enterprises in agricultural development of a magnitude greater than any previously known to history. One of the early firms engaged in the improvement of the appliances of agriculture was that organized in 1848 as Watson, Voorhees & Co., who were succeeded in 1850 by the firm of Hasselman & Vinton, of which Mr. L. W. Hasselman was a member. This firm continued the business until 1865, when the Eagle Machine Works Company was incorporated under a charter for twenty years, upon the expiration of which, in 1885, the charter was renewed for fifty years. At that time the works of the company were located on Meridian street, but two years later the new works of the company, on Missouri street, were occupied. These premises, with additions since made, now constitute one of the most modern, thoroughly equipped and conveniently arranged establishments of its kind in the country. The numerous buildings comprised in the plant are for the most part three-story brick structures, and cover an area of two acres of ground, including a completely equipped machine shop, 175x60 feet; wood-working shop, 175x60 feet; paint shop, 170x50 feet; blacksmith shop, 100x60 feet; a lofty, well-lighted foundry, 60x90 feet; two store rooms, each 50x175 feet in dimensions, and to these are now being added a four-story brick building, 60x60 feet. The machinery equipment of the works includes a 100-horse power engine, fed by two 45x16 feet boilers, 700 feet of shafting, and a complete outfit of large planers, lathes, boring machines, drills, steam punches, etc., all the machinery being of the most modern and improved make, and especially adapted to the requirements of the business. A force of 150 workmen is given employment. The products of the works include a number of the most valuable of modern labor-saving machines, including the celebrated "Hustler" Thresher, unequaled in simplicity of construction, ease of mechanism, perfection of its grain separation, and economy in operation; the "Eagle" Straw-stacker (Hasselman's patent), the most substantial, simple and practical stacker in the market; circular saw mills of various improved makes, mill dogs, head blocks, edging saw tables, swinging saw cut-offs, drag saws, wood saws, portable farm engines, traction engines and skid engines. All of these meritorious machines are made by expert workmen, under the most careful supervision, the best materials being used, and every provision made for securing their durability and efficiency. Their merit is attested by a steadily increasing demand, and the trade of the company is annually augmented, an extensive business being enjoyed, covering the States of Indiana, Ohio, Illinois, Kentucky, Missouri, Arkansas, and all the Northern and Northwestern States. The President of the company, Mr. I. W. Hasselman, who has been at the head of the business for nearly forty years, holds a recognized position as a progressive and representative American manufacturer and to his accurate knowledge of the business and sagacious management of its affairs is due the commanding position which the company holds among the important manufacturing corporations of the country. Mr. W. J. Hasselman, the Vice President, has also, during his extended connection with the company, largely contributed to its success, and the expansion of its business.

The Wm. F. Piel Co.—W. F. Piel, Sr., President; W. F. Piel, Jr., Vice-President and Treasurer; H. W. Piel, Secretary; Starch Manufacturers; Office, 17 South Meridian street. In the lines of production for which Indianapolis has secured a recognized prominence, the manufacture of starch is a notable one, and the activity in this branch of manufacture is due to the establishment of the Wm. F. Piel Co., recognized as a leading and representative one, excelling in the amount and quality of its product, the completeness of its manufacturing facilities and the extended area covered by its trade. The business was established in 1867 by W. J. Piel & Co., and continued under that style until 1887, when the present company was incorporated; the founder of the business remaining at its head as President. The works of the company are located at the corner of

Morris and Dakota streets, where a tract of thirty-five acres, of which three acres are covered with buildings two and three stories in height with basements. These premises are fitted up with all the latest and most improved machinery, including, in addition to a large Corliss engine of great power and four smaller ones, a large quantity of special machinery, by which the most favorable results are obtained in the improvement of the product and the saving of labor. The works have a capacity for the utilization of three thousand bushels of corn per day, and employment is given to a force of 150 hands in the manufacture of the various grades of starch. The works are the largest in the United States exclusively devoted to the manufacture of starch, and have long been noted for the superior excellence of their product. The special brands are "Champion Gloss Lump," for laundry purposes; "Refined Pearl," for steam laundries and manufacturing purposes generally; "Germania," for export trade, and "Improved Corn Starch," for culinary use. The uniform superiority of the product has secured for these brands the favor of consumers and a consequently universal demand by the trade in all parts of the Union, which is regularly visited by a large staff of traveling salesmen, and agents of the company located in the leading cities; while a large export trade is also enjoyed, extending to all parts of Europe and other countries. The establishment is a representative of the highest order of industrial activity, and its leading position has been

attained by close attention to every detail, by maintaining the product at the highest standard of excellence and uniformity and by propriety of methods in the conduct of the business.

Thomas Madden—Manufacturer of Lounges, Parlor Furniture, Chairs, Etc.; English avenue and "Big Four" Railroad. One of the most prominent names connected with the development of the furniture manufacturing industry is that of Mr. Thomas Madden. He was a member of the firm of Ott & Madden for a number of years prior to 1884, in which year he established his present enterprise and inaugurated what has grown to be one of the largest and most successful furniture manufactories of the West. The premises occupied for the purpose of the business embrace a four-story brick building, 60x110 feet in dimensions, completely equipped with all the most highly improved machinery and appliances adapted to the manufacture of furniture, with special reference to the production of the specialties of the house, including every description of lounges, parlor furniture, reclining chairs, platform rockers, etc. A force of workmen, averaging about one hundred in number, are constantly employed under competent supervision, the most careful selection of materials is made, and the product embraces every element of desirability and perfection in workmanship, elegance of design and finish, and durability in construction. The trade is supplied with these goods either in the white or upholstered, and they are in great favor with dealers throughout the Union on account of their salability and merit. As a consequence of maintaining the quality of the product at the highest standard of excellence, Mr. Madden has secured a steady augmentation in the volume of his trade from the inception of his business to the present time, and is accorded a prominent place among the representative furniture manufacturers of Indiana. His practical experience and progressive and reliable business methods have been prominent factors in the success which has attended his efforts.

J. B. McElwaine & Co. Manufacturers and Dealers in Natural Gas Supplies; 50 South Illinois street. The firm of J. B. McElwaine & Co., composed of J. B. McElwaine and M. M. McElwaine, was organized at St. Petersburg, Pa., in 1874. They located here in 1887, and have branch establishments at Findlay, O., Bradford, Pa., and at other points in the natural gas districts and oil regions of the country. They are located at the corner of Illinois and Maryland streets, occupying the basement and main floors, each 20x80 feet, with a warehouse fronting on Maryland street, two stories in height, and 20x200 feet in dimensions. The former premises are occupied as an office and sale-room, and the latter for storage purposes, and they are now building the McElwaine block, on West Maryland street, which they will occupy when completed. They are complete in all their appointments and equipments, and the firm are prepared to furnish all facilities and fixtures adaptive to the utilization of natural gas, for lighting, heating and domestic conveniences. Their lines embrace steam and water goods, cordage and drilling tools, etc., etc., also handling plumbers', gas and steam-fitters' tools and supplies, of the best qualities and grades, embodying all the latest improvements and the products of the most skillful and competent operatives. They publish a very full and elaborate catalogue of their manufactures and materials, and their prices are exceptionally low. They employ from ten to twelve hands in their works, also four travelers and a force of assistants, and their trade is extensive and increasing throughout Indiana, Ohio, Illinois and Kentucky. The members of the firm are men of enterprise and leading representatives of the industry with which they are identified, an industry of comparatively recent development, but which in its varied ramifications is an invaluable aid to the resources of the city and State.

Indianapolis Wheel Co.—Manufacturers of Carriage Wheels, Hubs, Etc.; Office and Works, corner First and Howard streets.—The Indianapolis Wheel Company, an industry typical of the enterprise, progressive spirit and genuine importance characterized the city and the numerous factors connected were established in 1875, so F. F. Coffin, one of Anderson, its present proprietors, through whose individual efforts the plant has attained to a distinguished success and prosperity. The premises occupied cover three acres at the above described site, and are accessible by the Illinois street cars and in other respects convenient to the trade. Within the area recently used these lots have erected the factory proper, a three-story and basement brick building, 125x50 feet in dimensions, with buildings adjoining of smaller size for finishing and other purposes, also large and well arranged and appointed watch-use and storage accommodations, and complete facilities for the receipt of stock and the shipment of orders. The mechanical equipment embraces the latest and best improved patterns of wood-working machinery, including lath and spoke machines, a specially superior Sarven wheel machine, with other appliances calculated to promote the volume and quality of the products, driven by an engine of 125-horse power, fed from a battery of three boilers, each 30x5 feet in dimensions. Their specialties are the Sarven wheel, bent hubs and plain wood hubs, their lines of production, however, comprehending every description of carriage, cart and wagon wheel hubs, also spokes, rims, felloes and other articles in these several departments. They are composed of the best quality of second growth hickory and other hardwoods, adapted to the requirements of the service, thoroughly seasoned and otherwise prepared for durable wear, and in all respects models of workmanship and finish. They enjoy a widespread reputation for their standard worth, and fully justify the verdict of the trade respecting their unsurpassed value. A force of from 125 to 150 experienced hands are employed, and an annual business of very large values is done in all the States of the Union, besides extensive transactions with manufacturers and dealers in Europe. The firm conduct one of the leading important industries in the State, and their enterprise has proved an invaluable factor in the promotion of the city's interests and prosperity.

The Indianapolis Cabinet Co. John Roberts, President; F. A. Coffin, Secretary and Treasurer; Manufacturers of Desks and Tables; Office and Factory, head of Malott avenue. — The magnitude of the manufacturing establishment of the Indianapolis Cabinet Co., and the widely extended area covered by its trade, fully entitle it to classification among enterprises standing in the front rank of importance. The works were established in 1879 by the Sewing Machine Cabinet Co., of Bridgeport, Conn., and were run in connection with the business of the Wheeler & Wilson Sewing Machine Company until they were purchased in 1880 by the Indianapolis Cabinet Co., incorporated in that year, who have greatly enlarged the

works, and have built up a most extensive business in the manufacture of office desks and tables. The plant covers over five acres of ground, and the buildings need cover a ground floor space of nearly three acres. The main building, comprising three-story and basement brick structures, front 325 feet on Malott avenue and 350 feet on House avenue, and railroad switches, with room for over 100

cars, run into the grounds and buildings and afford the most complete facilities for the receipt of materials and the shipment of manufactured goods. The equipment of the works includes three powerful engines of 175-horse power, 100-horse power and 50-horse power respectively, seven large boilers, and thirty miles of steam pipe, in addition to a complete outfit embracing more than $100,000 worth of the most highly improved machinery adapted to this branch of manufacture. The vigilance exercised to keep the manufacturing facilities of the company abreast with modern progress is demonstrated by the fact that from $7,000 to $10,000 worth of wood-working machinery and tools are annually discarded, though yet in good condition, to make room for more perfect and recent inventions. Everything connected with the works is on the largest scale. The company's drying houses have a capacity for 500,000 feet of lumber, and the thirty miles of steam piping, before referred to, is utilized in the heating and drying departments of the business. The company uses up an average of 7,000,000 feet of walnut lumber, and an equally large quantity of whitewood, annually, besides vast quantities of oak, ash, cherry, mahogany and other woods. In their shipping department they use over 100,000 yards of burlaps and 300,000 pounds of excelsior per annum, and in the other departments their operations are conducted on an equally extensive scale. In the factory a force ranging from 375 to 400 hands is employed, and the products include all kinds of office desks and tables, embracing roll curtain desks in various styles, library desks, cylinder desks, flat and bevel top desks, standing desks, letter press stands, filing cases and cabinets, and office tables of all sizes and styles. Its patented roll curtains made by this company and fitted to its desks are lined with spring sheet brass instead of canvas, and are superior to any other roll curtain for desks, being more flexible, more elastic, absolutely dust and vermin proof, and combining many other advantages found in no other roll curtain. The trade of the company is not only extensive in all parts of the United States and Canada, but also includes a heavy export shipping business to England and British colonies in Australia and South Africa, and to Spain and all the Spanish colonies, the export business consuming fully half of the product of the works. The business is so systematized, by daily reports from every department, that an accurate account of the material used and goods produced is kept, and on this close supervision the company mainly rely for their profits. The company employs no traveling salesmen, selling only to one large house in each of the leading cities and thereby avoiding all risk of bad debts. The business has steadily grown from year to year and is now so large as to make this the largest establishment in the world devoted exclusively to the production of office desks and tables.

Indianapolis Car and Manufacturing Company — Charles S. Millard, President and Treasurer; Charles E. Gore, General Manager; George A. McCord, Secretary; Manufacturers of Freight Cars of Every Description; Hadley avenue and Belt Railroad, West Indianapolis. — Among the diversified industries that contribute to the prominence of Indianapolis as a manufacturing center, that of the production of railway freight cars, as carried on by the Indianapolis Car and Manufacturing Company, is one of the most important. The company, which was incorporated in 1882, utilizes a plant fifteen acres in extent, and enjoys facilities for the efficient prosecution of this branch of manufacture not excelled by any similar concern in the world. The works include two foundries, 222x80 feet in dimensions; one for soft iron, with a smelting capacity of forty-five tons per day, and the other for chilled iron, turning out 1,000 car-wheels, each of 600 pounds weight, per week. The wood-working shop, which is 225x80 feet in dimensions, has a complete equipment of the most modern and improved wood-working machinery, and the machine and blacksmith shops, of about the same size as the wood-working shop, are outfitted with every appliance and machine necessary to their perfect and expeditious operation, including the largest shear and punch machines manufactured, hammers of great power, bending machines, bolt cutters and headers, drills, wheel-boring machines (with a capacity for boring 100 wheels per day), a powerful Westinghouse pump, for testing their air-brakes; seven furnaces, fed by natural gas; three engines, two of 80-horse power each and one of 50-horse power; four boilers, each 4½x18 feet; lathes, planers, and a profusion of other machines. Other buildings included in the plant are construction and finishing shops, each about 500x100 feet, paint shops and other structures, while railroad switches throughout the premises give every facility for the receipt, handling and shipment of materials and manufactured products. In the various departments of the business employment is given to a force aggregating 800 hands, and the output of the works averages 100 first class freight cars each 34 feet in length and of a carrying capacity of 30 tons per week, and twenty coal cars, of the most improved construction, daily. Railways in all parts of the Union are supplied with cars from these works, and while cars are built to order only, the company has at all times contracts on hand sufficient to keep their works in active operation. The greatest care is exercised in every detail of the manufacture, and the highest reputation is maintained for the products, which answer every requirement of sound materials, perfect workmanship and faultless construction. Vast as the business is, its operations are

an interest. Business steadily increased, and to supply the present corporation was organized, with ample capital, and an executive board, composed of A. H. Nordyke, President; A. K. Hollowell, Treasurer, and D. W. Marmon, Secretary. They own and occupy an area of territory in West Indianapolis eleven acres in extent, with railroad tracks and other valuable shipping facilities on the ground. The improvements consist of buildings devoted to the lines of manufacture carried on, including the foundry, machine shop and other departments, iron and woodworking shops, finishing and test rooms, warehouses, shipping department and offices. The machinery equipment embraces all the latest improved mechanical implements and labor saving devices, necessary to the service of the most approved model known to inventive genius or accessible to purchase, driven by engines with a total of over 500-horse power. Their specialty is the patent Nordyke & Marmon roller mill, and all other machinery necessary to complete the outfit of mills for effective service, also grain elevators and other mill appurtenances. Their products are in use and take precedence over those of all other similar establishments, not only

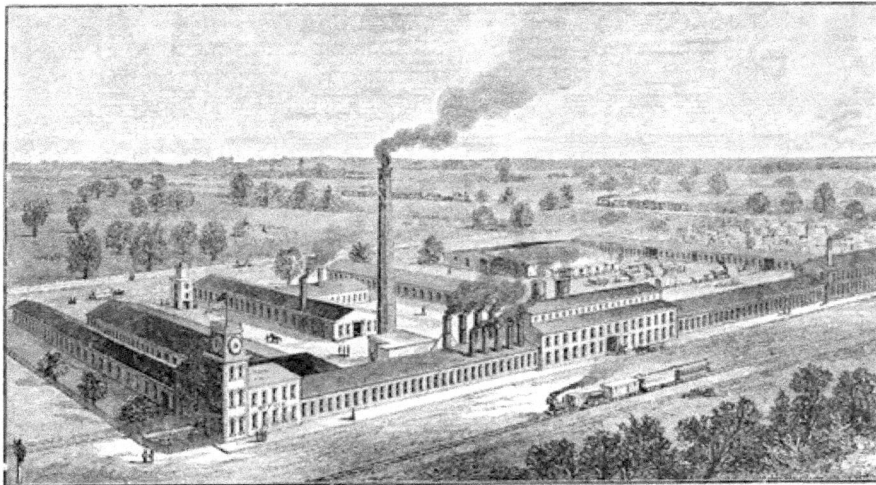

NORDYKE & MARMON COMPANY BUILDING.

characterized by an exact regularity, which gives evidence of the most capable and sagacious management. Mr. Charles S. Millard, the President of the company, directs its affairs with the highest order of executive ability, while the general management is confided to Mr. Charles E. Gore, whose intimate knowledge of the business has been an important factor in its success. Mr. George A. McCord, the Secretary, is a gentleman of superior business attainments, who efficiently supervises the office affairs of the company. Thus officered and managed, the company holds an important place among the representative manufacturing corporations of the country.

Nordyke & Marmon Co.—Manufacturers of Flour Mill Machinery; West Indianapolis. The largest enterprise in the country, devoted to the manufacture of flour mill machinery, the products of which are in use throughout the civilized world, is the Nordyke & Marmon Co. The undertaking was established during 1851, by Ellis and A. H. Nordyke, under the firm name of Nordyke & Son. In 1855, D. W. Marmon was admitted as a partner into the house, and upon the death of Mr. Nordyke, Sr., in 1871, A. K. Hollowell succeeded to

throughout the United States, but in the Canadian Dominion and Europe, also in Russia, Australia, New Zealand, and the wheat producing countries of South America. Their reputation is too well established and extended to even elicit comment, their general adoption by all leading mills being an expression of commendation more eloquent than words. They employ a force of 450 experienced operatives, and their annual business approximates $1,000,000 in value. The executive officers are the same as when the company was incorporated, and their administration through succeeding years has resolved the enterprise into the most influential and substantial of its kind in existence, and made it a factor in the development and promotion of manufacturing industries, potent and pre-eminent, throughout the Northwest.

Knight & Jillson, Manufacturers and Dealers in Iron and Brass Goods; 75 and 77 South Pennsylvania street.—The largest dealers in iron pipe, gas and steam-fitters' supplies and specialties in the city, are Knight & Jillson, the business being first established in 1872, by John Knight, and the present firm, composed of the latter and William M. Jillson, being organized in 1880. The escape premises, two stories high, 50x90 feet in size, and located as above, in the manufacturing center of Indianapolis. The building is divided into offices, warehouses and machine departments, each being commodious, well appointed and equipped for the purpose to which it is devoted, including all the latest and most approved implements and appliances, and equally complete facilities for the receipt and shipment of stock. They carry in stock the products of the **National Tube Works Co.**, embracing wrought iron pipe, boiler tubes, drive pipe, casing and tubing and the whole range of gas, steam and water goods, such as valves and cocks, fittings, brass goods, sinks, bath tubs, closets, pumps, gauges, regulators, tin, lead, solder, hose, belting, packing, waste, engine trimmings, etc., for all of which the establishment is the acknowledged headquarters in the city. In brief, its stocks, supplies, and lines of production are among the most complete, varied and indispensable in their lines in the State, and in constant demand here and elsewhere in districts where natural gas has been utilized for any purpose. They employ from twenty-five to thirty hands, also a full staff of salesmen and travelers, and supply the demands of a large trade in Indiana, Illinois and Ohio.

L. Neubacher & Son—Brass Founders and Finishers; 92 and 94 East Georgia street. The brass foundry and finishing works of L. Neubacher & Son were established by Mr. Louis Neubacher, senior member of the present firm, in 1878. During 1885, Frank O. Neubacher, son of the above, was admitted into partnership, and the firm name was changed to that under which operations are now conducted. They are located as above, at an available point, and are supplied with every facility for the receipt of material and the shipment of their lines of manufacture. The premises occupied consist of a finishing shop 30x50 feet in size, equipped with all necessary tools and appliances for the work in hand, also a building, 25x80 feet, and used for the purposes of a foundry. The latter is provided with three furnaces with a capacity of 1,000 pounds per diem, and equally well appointed and supplied with means for rapid and superior production. The plant is in all of its departments complete and thoroughly adapted to the uses for which it is occupied. They manufacture brass goods for every line of service, making railroad castings a specialty, and including in their output equipments for engine builders, plumbers, natural gas fitters, water-works cocks, brewery supplies, etc., in all of which their workmanship is of a superior character and has acquired for them the commendation and patronage of a large constituency. They also make a specialty of repairing and testing steam gauges, and in addition do an extensive business in repairing of brass products generally. Their materials are of the best description and their prices and terms are low and reasonable. They employ a force of from ten to fifteen operatives and supply a large trade throughout Indiana, Illinois, Ohio and Missouri and other States. The members of the firm are men of experience and enterprise, and their establishment is among the leading and representative manufacturing industries of Indianapolis.

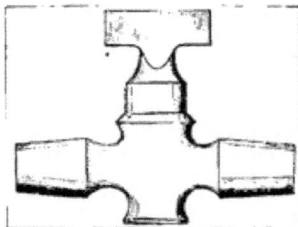

Wm. B. Burford—Manufacturer of Blank Books, Lithographer, Printer and Stationer; 21 West Washington street. There are many patrons of Wm. B. Burford who have never seen his establishment, and to them the first sight of its exterior would no doubt prove a disappointment. It does not boast an imposing front, but the entrance is in a modest four-story building which would scarcely be noticed except for its contrast with the handsome structures surrounding it. Once within the door, however, the visitor is convinced that outward appearances are often deceptive, for he finds that he has entered a veritable bee-hive. It was once said that this establishment was like a mine, for although its entrance was small, it was full of life and business, and after wandering through its labyrinths, a guide was necessary to show the way to the outer world. No one can enter the storeroom without observing the immense stock of blank books which occupies the greater part of one side of the room and makes a beautiful display with its rich bindings of russia leather finished with gold. A novel feature of this display is that the stock is so covered, and so arranged in shelves lined with Brussels carpet that the customer can readily see and indicate just the book he desires. On the other side of the room is stocked a full line of stationery and office supplies, while the rear is devoted to the offices for the correspondents, book-keepers and accountants. It is here that the busy character of the house begins to show itself, for its business extends from New York City to San Francisco, and from the Lakes to the Gulf, and a large force of men is necessary to give it proper attention. The basement of the building is used partly as an engine and boiler room, and for the storing of heavy paper and other stock. Of course the machinery begins where the engine stands and near it are found an automatic knife grinder, for the sharpening of the knives used in the many paper cutting machines through the house; a tag machine, which prints, eyelets and counts shipping tags taken from a roll of proper material, and is as great a curiosity as a pin machine; also a machine for making pasteboard tubes for mailing show cards, which, although simple in construction, does its work quickly and well. The type-press room occupies spacious quarters in the two rooms numbered 22 and 24 West Pearl street, at the rear of the store room, and is filled with the latest and most improved printing machinery. This is a noisy department, and a conversation can scarcely be heard for the heavy rumbling of the ponderous book printing presses and the rapid thumping of the speedy job presses as they throw out from 1,000 to 2,500 printed sheets per hour. It can scarcely be believed, but is nevertheless a fact that one of these presses is capable of producing 450,000 printed book pages in the short space of nine hours. The entire second floor is occupied by the lithograph department, and is well worth careful inspection. The designers and engravers have the well lighted room over No. 23 West Washington street, and can only be reached after the visitor has passed through long avenues of lithograph stone and machinery. The presses for printing from stone are necessarily heavy, for many of the stones weigh from three to five hundred pounds, and the presses in which they are carried vary from five to eleven tons in weight. Five steam and eleven hand litho presses are continually running, and other machinery, consisting of a stone planer, ink mills, reducing, shading, cutting and bronzing machines, are full of interest to the observer. From this department has emanated some of the most beautiful work used in mercantile circles, while its productions in menu cards, opening announcements, etc., are perfect gems of art. Here was also made the portrait of President Harrison, which was pronounced by friends and critics

alike a wonderful triumph of lithographic art, and with the portrait of ex-President Cleveland, its companion piece of work, reached the enormous sale of nearly 600,000 copies. The bindery covers the entire third floor, and is replete with ruling, folding, book sewing, wire stitching, numbering, perforating and other machinery used in the manufacture of blank books and the publication of edition work. One of the ruling machines is the largest in the country, being wide enough to rule a sheet of paper five feet in width, and much of the machinery is full of interest, which could only be appreciated by being seen. The fourth floor is devoted to type setting, and although it contains no machinery other than human hands, is still worth a visit, for otherwise one cannot understand how much type nor how many busy men are needed in this branch of such an extensive establishment. About 150 persons find continual employment in this house, some of them having been in its service for from five to twenty years, and among them are many of the most expert men in their various branches of the business. After many years of life together the employes have formed a relief association for their mutual benefit in case of disability, and an idea of its extent may be gained from the statement that it has a membership of over 150 and receives into its treasury over $600 per year. Our description of this establishment has necessarily been meagre, but the widespread reputation of Wm. B. Burford is based upon the magnitude of his business and the quality of his productions, and from this it can readily be understood that he is well equipped with competent men and effective machinery to give entire satisfaction to his steadily increasing trade.

The Cleaveland Fence Co.

The Cleaveland Fence Co.— J. B. Cleaveland, Patentee; Manufacturers of Yard and Farm Fencing; Office and Factory, 23 Biddle street.— Every addition to the manufacturing enterprises of a city is a valuable acquisition, and this is distinctively the case when the product of the new establishment is a specialty meritorious one. Among recent additions to the industries of Indianapolis that of the Cleaveland Fence Co., inaugurated in 1886, is one of the most notable. The factory premises include a machine shop, 60x90 feet in dimensions, a foundry 60x100 feet, and a blacksmith shop, 20x60 feet, as well as a large yard for the storage of materials. In the factory, which is furnished with a full equipment of machinery specially designed for the purposes of the business, employment is given to a force ranging from fifteen to twenty hands in the manufacture of yard and farm fences from a tubular iron and steel ribbon combination, the invention of Mr. J. B. Cleaveland, and protected by patents dated November 13, 1888, and February 5, 1889. This fence combines, in the highest degree, all the requisites of utility and beauty, being at once economical in price, strong and durable, and

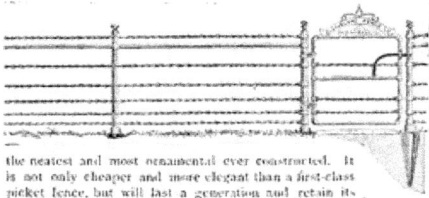

the neatest and most ornamental ever constructed. It is not only cheaper and more elegant than a first-class picket fence, but will last a generation and retain its attractive appearance. By an ingenious device known as the Cleaveland Automatic Tension Governor, the strands of ribbon or wire are kept constantly taut, while during the contraction caused by excessively cold weather the governor yields automatically to a sufficient extent to prevent breaking, without loosening the strands where it is necessary to keep the fence in perfect trim under all atmospheric conditions. In addition to fencing, a neat and durable style of iron hitch post is manufactured at the works. The superior merits of the Cleaveland fences have already secured for them a large demand, and although the enterprise was started late in 1886 there was put up in the year 1888 over 20,000 feet of lawn fence in this city alone, and in the first three months of 1889

orders were received for more than 40,000 feet. The demand for these fences has already extended throughout Indiana, Ohio, Illinois, Missouri, Kansas, Georgia and other States, and is rapidly increasing. Mr. J. B. Cleaveland, the inventor of this superior fence, is a practical and experienced man, and is prepared to contract for erecting these fences in a workmanlike manner, employing a large force of hands in this branch in addition to those engaged in the manufacture. He is a thorough business man, and his energy and ability, backed by the great merit of his product, are earning for him a deserved success in his important enterprise. The increase of the business has necessitated increased facilities and they will within a few months erect extensive works, 208x183 feet, on the "Big Four" Railroad, south of Seventh street, in addition to their present plant, and will increase their force to 200 men.

The Sinker-Davis Co.

The Sinker-Davis Co.—Manufacturers of Band and Circular Saw-Mills, Engines, Etc.; Office and Works, 111 to 139 South Pennsylvania street. This extensive and widely known manufacturing industry was founded in 1850 by the firm of Sinker & Kellshaw, becoming Sinker, Davis & Co. subsequently, and incorporated during 1871. In April, 1888, the present corporation succeeded to the possession of the enterprise, and have since conducted operations.

They occupy nearly an entire block, admirably situated for the purposes to which it is devoted. The improvements consist of a machine shop 250 x 50 feet in dimensions, a foundry 150x100 feet, a pattern shop and other buildings, all of brick, of adequate dimensions, built in the most substantial manner, and making up the most complete and best appointed works of the kind in the State. The equipment embraces the largest and latest improved pattern of hammers, lathes, drills, punches, etc., driven by steam; with facilities in the foundry for turning out the largest castings, and other appurtenances and conveniences indispensable to the service. Their specialties are large engines and saw-mill machinery and supplies. Their range of production also embraces all sizes of shafting, pulleys and hangers, head blocks, dogs, engine supplies, etc., with other articles of utility and value included in the outfit of a thoroughly equipped saw-mill, and latterly they have engaged extensively in the manufacture of natural gas supplies for the Citizens Gas Trust and other corporate enterprises of a similar character. Their productions are all noted for the superior material of which they are composed, as also for their finished workmanship and durable qualities. Their manufacture is under the supervision of skillful and careful managers, giving employment to from 125 to 150 experienced operatives, and the demand supplied comes from every section of the United States in all directions. The present officers are: J. H. Hooker, President; H. R. Bliss, Secretary and Treasurer.

Indianapolis Coffin Co.

Indianapolis Coffin Co.— Manufacturers of and Dealers in Wood Coffins and Caskets, Cloth Covered and Metallic Caskets, Hardware, Robes, Linings, Etc.; Office and Salesroom, 17 West Market street, Factory, corner of Sixth and West streets. In no branch of industry has there been more gratifying progress made of recent years than in the manufacture of coffins and all the necessary fittings for the purpose of the decent, orderly and appropriate conducting of funerals. In this, as in other manufacturing lines, the aid of modern machinery has been invoked to cheapen and at the same time improve the product, with the most beneficial results. The only establishment of this kind in the city, and one of the best managed in the country, is that known as the Indianapolis Coffin Company, of which Messrs. D.

Hazzard and W. H. Hazzard are the proprietors. Their business premises are located at the corner of South and West streets, and with adjoining yards for lumber, etc., cover an area of two acres. The works include the main building, a three-story brick structure, 45x95 feet in dimensions, with an L, two stories in height and 25x45 feet in dimensions, in addition to which the company has ample storage sheds, etc. The works are complete, fitted up with all the necessary machinery and appliances for carrying on the manufacture in all its details, with a forty-horse power engine. Natural gas is used as fuel, and employment is given to a force ranging from twenty-five to thirty hands. The manufactures embrace every description of wood and cloth covered caskets and coffins, and they are dealers in metallic caskets, coffin and casket hardware, linings, robes, wrappers, gowns, etc., in fact, everything in the line of funeral furniture and undertakers' supplies. The office and salesrooms occupy the main floor and basement, 20x50 feet in dimensions, at 57 West Market street, where is carried a large and complete stock embracing everything in the line. The Messrs. Hazzard, who have carried on the business from its inception fifteen years ago, are thoroughly practical and experienced men in this business, conversant with the needs of the trade, and highly regarded for their accuracy, and honorable business conduct. The product of the establishment is uniformly of the best quality, and a large and steadily growing trade in Indiana, Ohio and Illinois is enjoyed by the company.

Indiana Paint and Roofing Co. G. C. Forsinger, Proprietor; Manufacturer of Rubber Roofing, Sheathing Paper, Mixed Paint, Marbleized Slate Mantels, Etc.; 42 South Pennsylvania street; Telephone No. 417. The importance of a good roof to a building is recognized by all competent builders and every prudent house-owner, and the selection of good roofing material possessing the requisites of durability, fire-resisting qualities and imperviousness to moisture, is an important consideration. To the manufacture of roofing material possessing, in addition to these characteristics, that of economy, the Indiana Paint and Roofing Company is devoted. Mr. G. C. Forsinger, the proprietor of the business, is a practical and experienced roofer, and has been continuously engaged in that line of business since 1865. The company is engaged in the manufacture of rubber roofing, prepared from felt of a pure wool fibre saturated in a compound of rubber and other ingredients which render it entirely impervious to water, and then rolled and re-rolled under hydraulic pressure until it presents a strong, compact, cleanly and pliable material, suitable for roofing buildings of every description, and which when properly laid and finished is superior to shingles, tin, iron or any other material, is more durable, and is fire-proof and water-proof. It steadily hardens when exposed to the rays of the summer sun, will not crack or break in the coldest winter weather, and is not affected by any atmospheric conditions however severe. Other products of the company are slate paint, unequaled as a preservative to roofs, and which, used in connection with slate cement, also manufactured by this company, will effectively stop all leaks. It can be used for tin, shingle or iron roofs, and is also used as a finish for the rubber roofing made by the company. In addition to these articles the company manufactures and handles a full line of roofing materials, including water-proof building paper, sheathing paper, mixed paints, roofing brushes, pitch, resin, tar, black and asphaltum varnish, for iron and foundry buildings, as well as roofing of all kinds. An important part of the business is that of laying rubber, gravel or composition roofs, and repairing iron, tin, shingle or gravel roofs. The long and practical experience of Mr. Forsinger in this line enables him to execute orders in the most prompt and efficient manner, and the uniform satisfaction given by all work executed under his supervision has secured for him a leading position in this branch of industry, and a large and steadily growing trade. The premises occupied by the business embrace the main floor and basement, 20x100 feet in dimensions, at 42 South Pennsylvania street, and also a commodious warehouse on West street, which is utilized for storage purposes. A large and complete assorted stock is carried, and orders for the roofing materials manufactured by the company or embraced in its stock are promptly filled. Mr. Forsinger carefully supervises all the details of the manufacture

of his superior roofing, and is thereby able to maintain its quality at the high grade of excellence by which its reputation has been earned. He is a gentleman of superior business attainments, who, by the uniform propriety of his business conduct, has earned the favor and confidence of the trade and the public.

Lowe Carey — Manufacturer of Hominy, Grits and Corn Goods; Mills, corner of Alabama street and Fort Wayne avenue.— Among the milling enterprises of Indiana the hominy mills now conducted by Mr. Lowe Carey have obtained a special and deserved prominence as a result of the uniformly superior quality of their product. The business was established in 1882 by Mr. J. M. Kelly, a practical miller of long experience, who carried it on until January, 1889, when he sold the business to Mr. Lowe Carey, its present proprietor. The enterprise, however, still enjoys the advantage of Mr. Kelly's supervision over the milling department, of which he still has charge. The mill premises embrace a three-story building, 40x80 feet in dimensions, equipped with all the necessary machinery for the business, the motive power being supplied by a 50-horse power engine. The mills give employment to a full force of hands, and have a productive capacity of 100 barrels daily of hominy, grits, pearl meal and mill feed. Only the finest selected corn is used, and as a consequence the product is kept at the highest standard of excellence, the specialty of the establishment being its justly celebrated Challenge Pearl Hominy, which is in demand not only in the city, but also throughout Indiana, Ohio, Illinois, Kentucky and Pennsylvania. Mr. Carey, the proprietor, is a capable business man, whose methods of dealing invite the favor and confidence of the trade, and who fills all orders in a prompt and accurate manner.

Indianapolis Veneer Works — Adams & Williamson, Proprietors; Manufacturers of and Dealers in Veneers, Burls and Fancy Woods; terminus of Massachusetts avenue.— The central position of Indianapolis with reference to the most important regions of production in domestic hardwoods has led to the establishing here of several important industrial enterprises which utilize this prolific hardwood supply as their raw material. One of the most important establishments of this character is that conducted by the firm of Adams & Williamson, under the style of the Indianapolis Veneer Works. This firm, of which Messrs. G. F. Adams and M. D. Williamson are the individual members, inaugurated their business about ten years ago, and bringing to its prosecution the necessary pre-requisites of practical knowledge and business capacity, have since conducted the works with a marked and steadily growing success, building up a firmly established trade and earning a deservedly high reputation both for the excellence of their product and the accuracy of their business methods. The premises occupied by the business are new structures, those formerly used having been destroyed by fire in June, 1888, with a loss of $40,000. The works were at once rebuilt, and the plant now occupied, covering three acres of ground, includes a lofty, well-lighted brick workshop, 80x125 feet in dimensions, and a three-story and basement brick building, 20x150 feet, of which the ground floor is used as a stock room and the two upper floors as drying rooms. The equipment of the works includes every convenience and accessory calculated to aid or expedite the operations of the business, embracing a 100-horse power Corliss engine, fed by three tubular boilers 45x16 feet, and all the most modern and improved machinery for the manufacture of veneers. The veneer cutting is done by machines of the latest improved make, which cut from the log solid sheets seven feet wide, and these are sent to the sizing power knife machines, by which the veneers are cut into the desired sizes, including all thicknesses up to one-fourth of an inch, the latter being used for drawer bottoms. The drying is effectively done with the aid of two Sturtevant blowers, and eight large steaming vats provide the facilities for steaming logs before passing to the veneer cutting machines. Much of the machinery used is of a special character, invented for these works, and used by no other establishment. Ample light is provided by incandescent lamps supplied by the firm's own electric lighting plant. Railroad switches at the front and side of the works afford the most superior facilities for the receipt of materials and shipment of the manufactured product. Logs are received from the north, and veneers are manufactured from walnut, oak, ash, cherry and all kinds of hardwood. A force of from sixty to seventy workmen is employed, and an extensive trade is done, principally with furniture manufacturers in the East and in supplying manufacturers of sewing machines and other large consumers of veneers. The trade of the works is so firmly established as to require no canvassing, and consequently no traveling salesmen are employed. The firm owes its success to the maintainance in its product of the highest standard of quality, to close supervision of every detail of manufacture, and to uniform reliability in all its dealings with the trade.

T. W. Gardner—Manufacturer of Jewelry, Watches, Etc., and Dealer in Diamonds and other Precious Stones; Room No. 20, Hubbard Block.—The manufacture of jewelry and watches is an industry that is gradually becoming more and more prominent in Indianapolis, attracting large investments of capital and enlisting the most experienced and practical operatives in its pursuit. One of the leading

work. His business has been successful from the start, not only among the high-class jewelry houses of the city, but throughout the State, in addition to acquiring a considerable patronage from private residents of the same territory. He is an energetic and progressive manufacturer, also an enterprising citizen, and his management has secured for his house a confidence and prominence established and deserved.

Geo. Merritt & Co., Woolen Manufacturers and Wool Dealers; 411 West Washington street.—This firm, consisting of Geo. Merritt and Worth Merritt, woolen manufacturers and dealers in the State. The house was established by the firm of Merritt & Coughlen in 1856, and continued under their administration until 1881. In that year, Mr. Coughlen, the present Vice-President of the Indiana National Bank, retired, and Mr. Merritt succeeded to the vacancy and the present firm was organized. Their woolen mills are three stories in height, 10x70 feet in dimensions and fully equipped with all the latest improved patterns of looms, spindles, etc., with

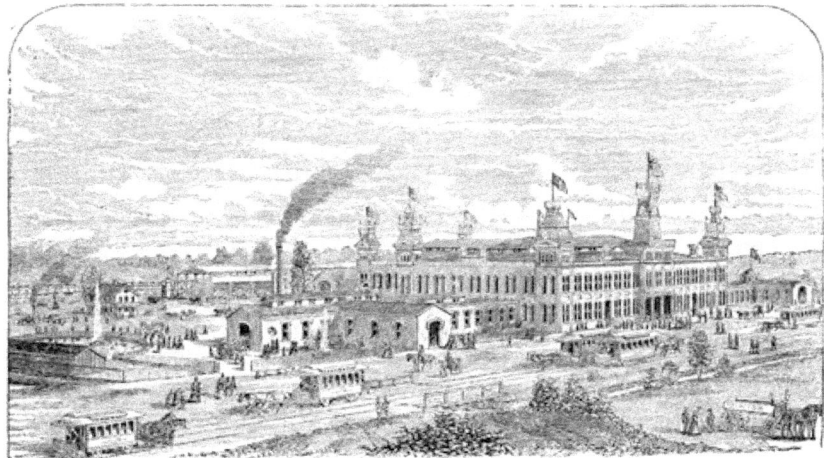

THE EXPOSITION BUILDING.

establishments engaged in these lines of useful and ornamental productions, demanding the application of skill, taste and originality to the work carried on, is that of T. W. Gardner, in the Hubbard Block. He began the business here in 1880, having been with the jewelry house of Bingham & Walk for five years previous, and bringing to his aid, in his present undertaking, a complete familiarity with the art to which he is devoted, as also an intimate knowledge of the requirements of the trade. The premises occupied by Mr. Gardner are fitted up for the purpose to which they are applied, equipped with all necessary tools and appliances, and otherwise furnished with facilities and appointments. His specialties include the manufacture of watches and jewelry to order, and also repairing of the same. To this important branch Mr. Gardner gives his personal attention, and he also carries large stocks of diamonds and other precious stones, and is prepared to mount the same in any style to the taste and desire of the purchaser. In all of these particular and special departments he is an expert and skillful craftsman, the knowledge of which fact by the trade, together with his promptness in the filling of orders, keeps him constantly occupied in the designing and execution of fine

other machinery and appliances adapted to the requirements of the service. Adjoining the mills is the drying department, a one-story structure 80x30 feet in size. Opposite these, from which it is separated by a gateway, the warehouse is located, a three-story and basement building 80x60 feet, containing commodious storage accommodations and being otherwise adapted to the uses for which it is appropriated. Large quantities of raw wool and equally large supplies of manufactured stocks are here in readiness for the demands of the trade to which the firm ministers. Their range of production embraces flannels, blankets, yarns, dress goods, suitings, etc., in great variety and of the best quality, fully equal in such respects as also in the superior workmanship displayed in their manufacture, to the best foreign woolens. The mill is the most comprehensive and available in its line in the State, and the enterprise which has characterized its management, together with the liberality and equity that have been displayed toward the trade, has acquired for the undertaking an invaluable reputation in all parts of the United States and Canada. Orders are promptly filled at prices and upon terms consistent with the quality of goods purchased and according to commercial usage, and they do a large and steadily increasing trade in all portions of the country, north, south, east and west, to meet the demands of which the services of eighty hands and a large force of assistants and travelers are in constant requisition.

The Indianapolis Frog and Switch Co.

J. E. McGettigan, President and General Manager; C. H. Bosworth, Secretary and Treasurer; Manufacturers of Railroad Frogs, Crossings, Switches, and General Track Material; Willard and Merrill streets. Of recent accessions to the manufacturing interests of Indianapolis that made

by the inauguration, in 1888, of the works of the Indianapolis Frog and Switch Co. is one of the most important. The buildings utilized cover about one-fourth of a block of ground, and are completely equipped with all the latest and most highly improved machinery and appliances adapted to this branch of manufacture, and including much that is of a special character. The present force employed ranges from twenty-five to thirty hands, and from present indications within a short time the force will be increased to 75 or 100. The company's productions include, in addition to ordinary grades of goods, a line of improved specialties. Prominent among these are railway frogs and crossings with Perry's Patent Easing Blocks for guttered wheel tread. By this improvement is made the only "T" rail frog that will carry guttered wheels smoothly across the point and wing rail members, and combined with this advantage is the highest degree of durability, safety and economy. In addition to frogs the company has a line of specialties in split switches, ground, automatic and standard switch stands and signals, combining all the latest improvements in mechanism. These goods are possessed of the highest order of merit, and have already secured a large demand from railway and construction companies and firms in all parts of the Union—a specially large demand coming from railroads centering in Indianapolis. The company enjoys the advantage of practical and experienced management. Mr. J. E. McGettigan, the President and General Manager, has had practical experience in the operation and construction of railroads, and is also a member of the prominent railroad supply firm of Dawes & McGettigan. Mr. C. H. Bosworth, who has charge of the office and financial affairs of the company as Secretary and Treasurer, is a business man of superior attainments whose efficiency contributes, in an important way, toward the extension of the trade of the company. This company is one of large resources and the most complete facilities, and the promptness and accuracy which characterize its dealings commend it to the favor and confidence of the trade throughout the country.

The J. S. Carey Works

Dealers and Manufacturers in Tight Barrel Cooperage, Staves and Headings; corner of Georgia and West streets. This large and representative manufacturing enterprise was established twenty-five years ago, by J. S. Carey, whose name is still retained in the name of the works, although for the past few years Messrs. George P. Wood and A. H. Smith have been the sole proprietors of the business. The premises occupied by the firm, embracing their works, stock sheds, piling yards, etc., cover two blocks of ground, and are conveniently located upon railroad tracks, which afford every facility for the receipt, handling and shipment of raw

materials and manufactured products. The works are outfitted with a 100 horse-power engine, fed by two large boilers, and a complete equipment of all the most modern and improved machinery and appliances adapted to the manufacture of cooperage upon an extensive scale, and employment is given to a force ranging from 100 to 125 hands. A specialty is made of the manufacture of tight barrel cooperage, although they also make slack work and also deal largely in staves and headings. Great care is taken in the selection and seasoning of materials, and a close supervision is maintained over every detail of the manufacture. The product of the establishment has a recognized reputation for superior quality and is in large demand, not only by an extensive trade in the city and adjacent States, but also cast as far as Baltimore and west to Iowa. The works have a capacity for the production of 2,000 pork or whisky barrels per week, and are kept constantly busy with large orders. The members of the firm, Messrs. George P. Wood and A. H. Smith, are both business men of high character and superior attainments, and practically conversant with every detail of the business. They have commended themselves to a large and growing trade by uniform accuracy in their dealings, promptness in filling orders, and by honorable business conduct. They have surrounded themselves with the means and instrumentalities for the efficient prosecution of their branch of manufacture and have given to their works a recognized position among the leading industrial enterprises of Indianapolis.

Moore Desk Company

Winfield Miller, President; Charles E. Barrett, Secretary; George A. Emerson, Treasurer; Manufacturers of Office Desks; Office, 84 East Market street; Factory, near Brightwood. Devoting its energies to a special branch of manufacture, the Moore Desk Company has secured a trade not only covering the entire Union but also including a considerable export trade to Australia, Europe and South America. The company was incorporated fifteen years ago with ample capital, and has since kept steadily improving its plant and facilities until it now occupies a five-acre tract of ground, part of which is devoted to use as a lumber yard, while one acre is covered with buildings, including a three-story and basement brick factory, large store houses, an engine and boiler house, etc. The working equipment includes a 120-horse power engine, two large boilers, and a complete outfit of the best woodworking machinery, including all recent improvements. A force of seventy-five hands is employed in the manufacture of office desks in seventy different styles, of which over 4,000 are annually turned out, as well as letter-press stands, lawyers' and library book racks, etc. A specialty of the company is its new type-writer desk, in which the type-writer is secured by clamps to a shelf, which, by a device owned by the company, recedes as the lid closes and locks, shielding the type-writer from dust and presenting a sloping-top desk for ordinary uses. All of the operations of the works are conducted under careful supervision, the best materials are used, and the products are of unsurpassed workmanship and finish. No establishment in the country produces better desks, and it is by maintaining the quality of their goods at the highest standard of excellence, and by offering a variety of designs suited to the wants of all kinds of offices that the company has secured its prominence and prestige. The business is managed upon the most accurate and reliable methods, and the company holds a high place in the confidence of the trade.

Earnshaw & Wright

Proprietors of the Patent Coil Elm Hoop Works; corner of Biddle street and Bee Line Railway.—As a prominent manufacturing enterprise, which has earned a superior reputation and an extensive trade as a consequence of the uniformly high character of its products, the Patent Coil Elm Hoop Works of Messrs. Earnshaw & Wright deserve special mention. The business was originally established seven years ago by the firm of Earnshaw & Taylor, who carried on the business until November, 1888, when Mr. Joseph Earnshaw bought out the interest of his partner, Mr. Taylor, and continued the business until January, 1889, when Mr. Walter B. Wright became associated with him under the present firm style. The premises occupied embrace the mill building, 100x100 feet in dimensions, with yards and piling grounds about half a block in extent along the railroad tracks, superior facilities being thereby afforded for the receipt of raw material, handling of stock and shipment of manufactured product. The equipment of the mill includes a 40-horse power engine, a large boiler, and a complete outfit of the latest and most highly improved hoop-making machinery. Employment is given to a force ranging from thirty to thirty-five hands, and a large trade is enjoyed, 575 car-loads of lumber being handled and 6,000,000 hoops manufactured annually. The elm used is bought in the log, at points within a radius of seventy-five miles of Indianapolis, sawed into lumber at mills near the points of purchase and thence shipped to this city. The specialty of the firm is the manufacture of flat hoops, used for sugar barrels, and they have a large trade in the West, Southwest and South. Both of the members, in addition to a practical knowledge of this industry, are gentlemen of superior business attainments, and the firm has commended itself to the favor of the trade, not only by the uniform merit of its product, but also by the accuracy and reliability by which its business conduct is characterized.

Barnard & Leas Manufacturing Co. — Manufacturers of Flour Mill Machinery, Room No. 3, Chamber of Commerce Building. This company was founded as a private enterprise in 1860, and in 1872 was incorporated, with ample capital, and headquarters at Moline, Ill. It is the only establishment in the United States manufacturing the equipment, in its entirety, of modern flour mills and elevators. The factory at Moline is an immense affair, provided with all requisite machinery and appliances, and giving employment to a force of 300 men, at a total weekly compensation of $4,000. Their output is correspondingly large, embracing roller mills, Gorton's centrifugal reels and flour bolt, Barnard's Middlings Purifiers, aspirators, bran scourers, wheat cleaning machinery and flour and bran packers; Victor corn shellers and cleaners, Little Victor combined shellers and cleaners, shafting, couplings, hangers, pulleys; Barnard's dustless wheat separators, and other mill equipments in great variety, also conveyor flights, journal boxes, drop hangers, clutches, elevator heads, boots and legging, elevator buckets, turn heads, flexible spouts, steel conveyors, scoops, elevator horse power, etc., etc. They also build and equip flour mills and elevators. Their products are of the best character of materials and unsurpassed for efficient service, superior workmanship and durable wear. The present officers are J. A. Barnard, President; J. S. Leas, Vice-President; W. C. Bennett, Secretary and Treasurer, with J. F. Payne, Manager of the Indianapolis agency. He took charge in 1881, having been in the employ of the company for six years previous in a prominent fiduciary capacity. He is familiar with the business, and his honorable and liberal management has contributed to greatly extend the trade of the company throughout the States of Indiana and Ohio. During 1888, twenty-two complete mills at an average cost of $4,000 each, and fifteen elevators at an average cost of $750 each, were built upon orders obtained by him, and he also effected some eighty-five sales of incomplete mill equipments during the same period. Mr. Payne was the first man to introduce the short system of milling in the West, applying the same to a milling industry of which he is half owner, located on the Vincennes Railroad in this State. When this system was first mooted, the Barnard & Leas Manufacturing Company anticipated all other indorsements of its efficiency and value, by guaranteeing its success with their name, money and commercial standing, and enjoy the distinguished honor of "pushing" to a successful finality an enterprise that was at first declared by prominent millers and the press to be "a short shrift to bankruptcy." The short system is to-day not only in general use throughout the country, but commands universal confidence. Mr. Payne employs two traveling salesmen, and five gangs of millwrights, each gang averaging five men, and does a very large and annually increasing business. He fills all orders, and upon application will furnish catalogues, price lists, terms, etc.

Hall & Lilly — Hominy Mills; Hadley avenue and Belt Railroad, West Indianapolis. The milling enterprise established in 1862 by the firm of Hall & Lilly, of which Messrs. Charles E. Hall and George Lilly are the individual members, holds a prominent place among the representative industries of Indianapolis. The mill building occupied is a three-story and basement structure, 110x70 feet in dimensions, and the equipment includes two powerful engines and all the latest and most highly improved milling machinery for the production of hominy, grits, corn flour, corn meal, pearl meal and other products of white and yellow corn, and a specially superior quality of

Zealine, for brewers' use. A large force of hands is employed, and an average of 7,000 bushels of corn is daily utilized in the production of the various kinds of goods manufactured. The processes employed in the manufacture are of a special character, and designed to retain, to a degree not attained by any other method, the nutritive qualities of the corn. As a consequence of this excellence, the demand for the product of the mills has extended to all parts of the Union, and the establishment enjoys a trade which taxes its capacity. The members of the firm are practical and experienced millers, and all of the operations of the mills are conducted under their close personal supervision, resulting in a steady maintainance of that high quality in the product which has been the most prominent factor in their success. Added to their accurate knowledge of the wants of the trade and the public, they possess business qualifications of a high order, and have commended themselves to favor by promptness and reliability in all their business transactions.

C. C. Foster Lumber Co. — C. C. Foster, President and Treasurer; L. A. Budenz, Secretary; Manufacturers of Doors, Sash, and Blinds; Dealers in Lumber, Lath and Shingles; 404 to 420 North Mississippi street. — This important manufacturing and mercantile firm had its origin in 1870, in which year it was established by C. C. Foster & Co., changing in 1883 to its present corporate style. The facilities for the prosecution of the business, possessed by the present company, are of the most advanced character, the company occupying as a planing-mill, and sash, door and blind factory, a two-story building 100x180 feet in dimensions, equipped with every description of modern and improved machinery, propelled by a 100-horse power engine, fed by a 4½x18-feet boiler, the furnace of which is arranged to burn either natural gas or the surplus of shavings accumulated in the mill. The plant includes all the latest labor-saving devices, and every convenience and facility for the operation of the most complete and commodious mill and factory of its kind in the State of Indiana.

A force, ranging from fifty to sixty hands, is constantly employed, the product of the establishment including all kinds of planed and finishing lumber, and sash, doors, and blinds of all styles and dimensions. The company also has a commodious yard, covering over three acres of ground, and filled up with storage sheds for dry and finished stock. In these yards a large and completely assorted stock is carried, embracing all kinds of rough and dressed lumber, from which orders are filled in a prompt and satisfactory manner. Shingles, lath, and other lumber goods are also carried in large stocks, and the facilities enable the company to respond to the demands of the trade upon the most advantageous terms. A large trade is enjoyed in the city and surrounding towns, and the company holds a high place among the leading lumber corporations of the State. Mr. C. C. Foster, the President and Treasurer of the company, is a business man of distinctive prominence, one of the Governors of the Board of Trade, and a representative business man of the city.

W. H. Chamberlin, Sr.—Manufacturer Self-Loading Barrel Trucks; 66 Chesapeake street. William H. Chamberlin, Sr., inventor and manufacturer of the self-loading barrel and box trucks, and dealer in scales, embarked in business for himself during 1887, having been for ten years previous foreman for the Fairbanks & Co. scale house in this city. His undertaking has been successful and he has built up a large trade. He occupies premises 25 feet front on Chesapeake street, and 100 feet deep. They furnish ample accommodations for display and sale purposes, also for the manufacture and repair of his line of productions, and are well equipped for the supply of the trade. His specialty is the self loading barrel and box trucks, an ingenious invention discovered by Mr. Chamberlin, light, strong and durable, that enables the handling, loading and unloading of barrels, boxes and other bulky materials with the least expenditure of strength or labor. The accompanying cut will give some idea of the usefulness of this truck, showing the ease with which one man can load and handle a barrel or box weighing 800 or 1,000 pounds. They have met with general adoption here, and their popularity and employment is being rapidly extended in all directions. He carries a full supply in stock, and complete lines of scales of the best make, from the most delicate chemical balances to scales of the largest capacity, adapted to the requirements of every service and to every standard. His equipment includes all necessary machinery and his facilities are of a character so comprehensive that he is able to offer inducements to the trade in prompt service, low prices and other particulars of equivalent value. His scale repair department is a feature not to be overlooked. Most people think that when a scale refuses to weigh accurately it is worn out, when, in fact, by remodeling and putting in a new steel pivot and bearing, it will weigh as accurately as ever. Mr. Chamberlin employs from five to ten assistants, and does a large and increasing business throughout the city and surrounding country.

D. E. Stone & Co.—Manufacturers of Fancy Cabinet Ware; Office and Sale-rooms, 184 South Meridian street. This house was founded by Mr. Stone in 1877, and is to-day one of the largest and most favorably known industries in its line in the United States, coming under its present title in 1884. During June, 1888, their plant was destroyed by fire but rebuilt and occupied with the least possible delay, and in January, 1889, the firm was reorganized, being now

made up of D. E. Stone, O. L. Neisler (who succeeded to the interest of C. R. Ellis), and Charles T. Stone. The Messrs. Stone are practical cabinet-makers and manage the manufacturing department, Mr. Neisler having charge of the office and sales departments. They occupy an attractive three-story and basement brick building, 25x100 feet, used for office and warehouse purposes, where they carry large stocks, and are provided with facilities for the transaction of business, and the prompt execution and shipment of orders. Their factory is situated on Christian avenue and is fully equipped with all modern machinery for the promotion of the quality and volume of their lines of production. They also maintain branch offices at 24 and 26 Van Buren street, Chicago, of which C. A. West is manager, at 32 Elizabeth street, New York City, and at 818 and 820 Mission street, San Francisco, where they are known as the "Indianapolis Manufacturing Co.," besides having agencies in the chief remaining cities of the United States. They manufacture every description of book cases and desks for office, parlor, library, etc.; parlor, boudoir, library and office tables; music desks, cabinets, stands and racks; commodes, foot rests, blackers, etc., in many different varieties, of fine and medium grades of walnut, cherry, antique oak, antique ash and other hardwoods, with either natural or mahogany finish, and for sale at the lowest prices compatible with the quality of material and workmanship employed in their manufacture. For variety, originality, elegance of design and finish the products are without a rival in the market, and the popularity of the house and its lines is shown by the rapid increase in their sales, which during 1888 exceeded those of the previous year more than 40 per cent. They are prepared to fill orders promptly, packing to suit the wants of the trade without charge for boxing, and shipping at a saving of from 50 to 75 per cent. to buyers. They employ from sixty to seventy-five hands and their trade is throughout the Union in every direction.

Remington Standard Typewriter—Wyckoff, Seamans & Benedict, Proprietors and Manufacturers; G. E. Field, Manager for Indiana ; 51 North Pennsylvania street.—The spirit of invention, which is the most marked characteristic of this progressive age, has evolved a large number of meritorious labor-saving devices, among which the typewriter takes deservedly high rank for its general utility, and the numerous ways in which it facilitates clerical work of all kinds. Although many attempts had been made during the preceding century to invent a machine for writing, none had proved of any practical utility until 1867, when a writing machine, called the typewriter, was patented in Milwaukee, Wis., by C. Latham Sholes, Samuel W. Soule and Carlos Glidden. This invention, though crude, was the initial idea which has since been perfected in the excellent machine known as the Remington Standard Typewriter. The machines were for a number of years manufactured in the gun shops of E. Remington & Sons, of Ilion, N. Y., and in 1886 the New York firm of Wyckoff, Seamans & Benedict, who had been sole sales agents for these typewriters since 1882, purchased of E. Remington & Sons the extensive plant at Ilion, and all the franchises and rights of manufacture, and, in connection with a few of their friends, organized the Standard Typewriter Company, by whom the machines are now made. As now improved, the machine contains every requisite to perfect work, and is a triumph of modern invention. Although other writing machines have since come into the field, the Remington is still recognized as the standard of excellence in writing machines, surpassing all others both in quality of work and the speed with which it is executed. The superiority of the Remington has been recently demonstrated in a number of speed tests, notably at Cincinnati, July 26, 1888, where it was awarded the victory in a contest for highest speed in legal work ; at New York, August 1, 1888, for highest speed on correspondence, and in the International Tournament for the World's Championship at Toronto, August 13, 1888, where the Remington was awarded the first and second prizes for business correspondence, and the first and second prizes (gold

and silver medals) for legal testimony. The Remington has a larger sale than all other typewriting devices combined, and is in use by the largest firms and corporations in all parts of the United States and Europe. An agency for the sale of these machines has been conducted in this city since 1876, and in 1885 Mr. G. E. Field, who had previously been connected with the Chicago branch, came to Indianapolis, and has since controlled the sale of these machines in the State of Indiana. He occupies an eligibly located store at 34 North Pennsylvania street, opposite the Postoffice, where he carries a full assortment of the Standard Typewriters, Nos. 1, 2, 3 and 4, typewriter desks and cabinets, typewriter attachments, copy-holders, typewriter and manifold papers, ribbons, and all typewriter supplies.

machine shops, spoke turning, rim bending, finishing, blacksmithing, and other departments, together with complete storage and ware-house accommodations. Their equipment embraces the latest and most reliable machinery and appliances, adapted to the manufacture of wheels, driven by an engine of 500-horse power, fed from a series of eight boilers of the most approved pattern. In addition to this, and in order to more perfectly meet the requirements of the trade to which they minister in all parts of the world, they are erecting a new plant on the line of the Belt Railroad that will cover, when completed, seven acres of ground, and is furnished with more complete facilities and equipments, requiring two engines of 350-horse power each to operate, and increase their annual output, already phenomenally large, to

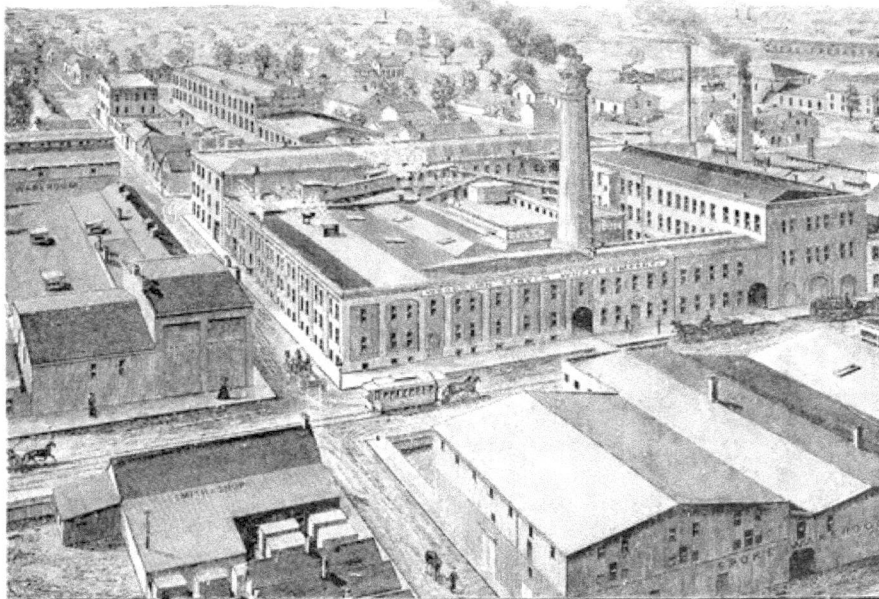

THE WOODBURN "SARVEN" WHEEL COMPANY'S BUILDINGS.

Mr. Field, the Manager, is an experienced and efficient business man, to whose energy and accurate methods is due in a large measure the notable increase in the demand for these machines in the State of Indiana.

The Woodburn "Sarven" Wheel Co — Manufacturers of Vehicle Wheels; Office, 210 South Illinois street.—This business was established in 1850, and, twenty years later, the present company was incorporated. They occupy a vast area of territory fronting on Illinois and other streets in the central portion of the city, upon which, from time to time, buildings have been erected, as the same became necessary to the increase of business which has steadily accompanied the undertaking from its inception. These improvements include the

much greater proportions. Their specialty is the Woodburn "Sarven" wheel, for every description of conveyance, and embodying in its construction strength, durability, elasticity and economy more perfectly than any other article of its kind known to the trade. The hub and spokes are mortised and tenoned like the common wheel, the spokes being united so as to form a solid arch outside the wheel after which two flanges of malleable iron are fitted to the hub and spokes, and riveted through, which sustains the arch formed by the spokes, yet preserves the same elasticity of wood in the hub and spoke which obtains in the common wheel. The "Sarven" is the only wheel having a mortised wood hub with tenoned spokes supported by flanges, connected by rivets. They also manufacture Brown's shell band, Warner patent, plain wood hubs, and compressed band hub wheels, in addition to other styles of wheels, hubs, spokes, rims and wheel materials generally, in every variety, made of the best materials and carried in full supply, thereby enabling them to fill orders promptly. They employ over 500 hands at the works, in addition to 100 at the new plant, which will be fully occupied during the Fall of 1884, and their trade in every State of the Union as also in Canada, Australia, Europe, South America, etc., is only measured by their capacity to supply its demand. Addison Bybee, President, and J. P. Pratt, Vice-President and Treasurer, are citizens of enterprise and public spirit. During 1898, Mr. Pratt was the President of the Indianapolis Board of Trade, honoring in the discharge of his official duties the association, extending its reputation and enlarging its field of operations and usefulness. Illustrated catalogues, price currents and other information are mailed promptly upon application.

E. Rauh & Sons—Dealers in Hides, Tallow, Pelts, Etc., and Manufacturers of Fertilizers, 219 South Pennsylvania street.—This firm, which occupies a distinguished prominence in its line of industry, is composed of Messrs. Leopold Rauh, Henry Rauh and Samuel E. Rauh, sons of E. Rauh, by whom the business was established at Dayton, O., in 1862. The Dayton house is still successfully carried on as well as the Indianapolis house, which was established in 1874. The premises here include a two-story brick warehouse at 219 South Pennsylvania street, where they carry large stocks of hides, pelts, tallow, etc.; and a tract of three acres on the line of the Belt Railroad, where their fertilizing works are located. Their factory has a complete equipment embracing all the improved machinery and appliances necessary for the prosecution of the business upon an extensive scale, and here is manufactured a superior quality of pure bone fertilizers, upward of 3,000 tons being produced annually. The firm gives employment to fifty hands at their factory and twenty-five at their warehouse, and enjoy a large trade in hides, which they sell in all the Eastern and Western markets, while their fertilizers are in large demand in Indiana and surrounding States and throughout the South. The members of the firm are all thoroughly practical and experienced men, conversant with every detail of the business, to which they devote their care and attention and in which they have secured a marked and gratifying success.

Coffin, Greenstreet & Fletcher—Pork Packers; Office and Packing House, corner of West and Ray streets.—An old established and prominent pork-packing establishment is that now conducted by the firm of Coffin, Greenstreet & Fletcher, of which Messrs. Albert W. Coffin, Jason H. Greenstreet, James L. Fletcher and Lafayette Fletcher are the individual members. The business was originally established in 1863 by Mr. B. Coffin (father of Mr. Albert W. Coffin), and in 1869 the firm became Coffin, Wheat & Fletcher. In 1896 Mr. B. Coffin died, and the following year the firm assumed its present style and membership. The premises occu-

pied for the business cover about five acres of ground, upon which are located the packing house, a three-story brick building, 200x250 feet in dimensions, a lard-house, slaughtering house, smoke-house, ice houses, etc., and the equipment includes all the most modern and improved machinery and appliances necessary for the prosecu-

tion of the slaughtering and packing industry upon an extensive scale. The firm does a large business as packers of every description of pork products, giving employment to a force of from 150 to 160 hands, and having three traveling salesmen who visit the trade as well as resident agents in all the large cities. Their facilities are of the most complete character, including a capacity for killing and packing 1,200 hogs per day, and a storage capacity of 7,000,000 pounds. Their "Primrose" brand of hams, shoulders, breakfast bacon, etc., bear a merited distinction for superior quality, and command an extensive trade in all parts of the country, but especially in the States of Indiana, Illinois, Ohio, and the South generally, while in lard they also do a considerable export trade. The firm, throughout the quarter of a century covered by its history, has ever conducted its affairs upon principles of accuracy and honor, and is a representative and deservedly prosperous house, ranking among the leaders in this branch of industry.

Indianapolis Chair Manufacturing Company—E. G. Cornelius, President; N. S. Byram, Vice-President; E. H. Cornelius, Secretary and Treasurer; Frank E. Helwig, Superintendent; Manufacturers of Chairs; 184 to 198 West New York street.—The tendency of modern industrial progress is toward specialties, and, as a consequence articles which were formerly made by hand and sold at prices only possible to the rich, are now turned out by machinery, and, while

improved in appearance, are so cheaply produced as to be obtainable by people of moderate means. An apt illustration of this tendency is made by the furniture industry, which is divided into many special lines, of which the manufacture of chairs is the most important, and engages the energies of many substantial and prosperous corporations. Among the companies so engaged in various parts of the Union are of the most prominent, both as to the extent of its business and the conceded superiority of its product, is the Indianapolis Chair Manufacturing Company, of this city. The business was originally established in 1874 by Charles Helwig, W. D. Hoffman and Frank E. Helwig, who incorporated it under its present title. In April, 1888, the company was re-organized with its present officers and largely increased capital and facilities. As now organized and operated the company takes rank among the largest of the concerns engaged in this manufacture. The manufacturing premises comprise a number of three and four-story brick buildings, covering an entire block of ground, with rear on the canal and railroad tracks, affording unequaled facilities for the receipt of raw materials and the shipment of the manufactured product. Across the canal is the lumber yard of the company, half a block in extent, well stocked with selected lumber suitable for their manufacture. The factory is furnished with a 150-horse power engine, three large boilers, and a complete outfit of the most highly improved modern machinery adapted to the manufacture of chairs upon an extensive scale. To this equipment the company, since its re-organization, has been making important additions and intend to increase the present output, averaging about 1,000 chairs daily, to from 1,800 to 2,000 per day. Employment is given to a force of more than 200 hands, and the products include all the latest styles and designs in upholstered, cane and wood-seat chairs and rockers. The company is especially noted for the elegance in finish, richness in design and excellence in workmanship in its finer grades of goods, by which they have secured a recognized leadership as manufacturers of fancy chairs. The trade of the company extends to every part of the United States, and a large staff of traveling salesmen represent these goods to the trade. The officers of the company, Messrs. F. G. Cornelius, President; N. S. Byram, Vice-President, and E. H. Cornelius, Secretary and Treasurer, are all business men of high standing, in whose hands the affairs of the company are sagaciously and efficiently managed, and Mr. Frank E. Helwig, the Superintendent, who has charge of the mechanical operations, is a thoroughly practical man, conversant with every detail of this branch of manufacture, and supervises the operations of the factory with a degree of skill and knowledge which contributes largely to the success of the company and the recognized excellence of its product. The efficiency of the official board of the company, the ample resources it controls and the unexcelled facilities it enjoys, entitle it to a leading place among the representative manufacturing establishments of the city.

Bryce's Bakery—Peter F. Bryce, Proprietor; Steam Bread and Crackers; 14 and 16 East South street.—The model bakery of the city and State, and in many respects the model bakery of the country, if not of the world, is that of Peter F. Bryce, located as above, employing the most perfect equipment available and manufacturing an annual product of the largest magnitude. Mr. Bryce is a native of Scotland, where he was born in 1826, and whence he immigrated to this country during 1843. In 1870, he established his present enterprise in Indianapolis. Ten years later, or in 1880, in response to the growing demand made upon his productive resources, the premises occupied were measurably enlarged and his facilities materially increased. They now consist of a two-story and basement building, 60 feet front on East South street between Meridian and Pennsylvania, and 100 feet deep, with large yard room adjoining, upon which storage sheds, stables and other improvements have been erected. The bakery is furnished with the new patent bread-making machinery of very large capacity, invented by Mr. Bryce, and declared by experts to be the most simple in construction, economical and efficient in its operation and results, of any device of a similar character yet discovered, in addition to large dough mixers of his own importation, together with other appliances required in the service. Seven ovens, some of which are among the largest in the world, are necessary to even approximately meet the wants of the trade, and his daily production averages 10,000 loaves of bread, in addition to other lines of edibles, such as crackers, cakes, etc. They are made from the best grades of materials, carefully selected and of guaranteed purity and excellence, and enjoy a widespread reputation for their superiority in every respect. His facilities are such, that Mr. George H. Bryce, manager of the establishment, is able to handle all orders promptly and satisfactorily and his administration of affairs has substantially promoted the success of one of the most important and productive industries in the State. Mr. Bryce, Sr., has been repeatedly elected a member of the Indianapolis Board of Councilmen, besides holding other offices of honor and trust, and is everywhere known as one of the most enterprising and honorable business men of the community. A force of from twenty-five to thirty men, and sixteen horses, are employed in the business, and a large and steadily increasing trade is done throughout the city and State, as also in portions of Ohio, and other States adjoining.

Henry T. Hudson—Sanitary Plumber, Natural Gas Fitting; 26 Massachusetts avenue.—Conspicuous among the sanitary plumbing establishments of Indianapolis, that owned and managed by Henry T. Hudson stands deservedly high. He located here during 1883, coming from Boston, where he had enjoyed an experience of eighteen years in the same line of operations, and embarked in business in this city during 1885. He is situated as above, occupying a two-story and basement building, 20x80 feet in dimensions, divided into office and workshop, and supplied with all modern appliances and conveniences for the transaction of business and the production of his line of supply. His specialties are improved systems of house drainage and ventilation, by the adoption of which, residences, public buildings, etc., are absolutely freed from the presence of sewer gas and other noxious agencies destructive of the health and comfort of occupants. In the matter of sanitary plumbing his work is equally efficient and permanent, and in the piping and equipping of houses for the introduction of substitution of natural gas it is unsurpassed. Among the recent jobs in the latter line recently completed by Mr. Hudson, was the piping in the State Asylum for Insane, also for Deaf and Dumb Asylum, both of which institutions are located in this city, and accessible to those who desire to examine the superior workmanship done under his supervision. He also did the plumbing and natural gas fitting work at the Blind Asylum, the plumbing work for the government at the Postoffice, and also the plumbing work at the Marion County Workhouse. He is prepared to fill all orders for materials or undertake the execution of contracts at the shortest notice, and he employs from fifteen to twenty skilled workmen. He gives personal attention to every department of his business, and substantial results are assured. He does a large and steadily increasing trade in the city and vicinity. Mr. Hudson is a representative citizen as also of the industrial interests of the State, paying the highest wages for services in his lines of operations in the city, prominent in all movements tending to the promotion and dignifying of labor, and in the Fall of 1888 received an expression of the high esteem in which he is held, by his election as a member of the State Senate. He is, in fact, as the public asserts "A remarkable man," and the house he manages with such equity and liberality has the confidence and patronage of a large constituency.

The Sun Vapor Street Light Co., Canton, O.— John M. Brubaker, Contracting Superintendent; Joseph A. McGuire, General Agent; Contractors for Lighting Streets; 32 Virginia avenue.—The Sun Vapor Street Lighting Company was incorporated in 1888 under the laws of the State of Ohio, as successors to the Sun Vapor Light and Stove Co., the Ohio Street Lighting Co. and the Belden Burner Co. Its capital stock is $500,000, with headquarters at Canton, O., and branches in this city. Charleston, S. C., Minneapolis, Minn., and Wichita, Kan. The company's line of operations is the lighting of the streets in cities, towns and villages with the famous Sun Vapor gas street lamps, which are secured to their exclusive ownership by United States and Canadian patents; also the manufacture of same with their equipments. In addition to brilliancy, purity and volume of light furnished, not only are they economical, but their introduction or substitution is accomplished without digging up the streets and the laying of expensive pipes and connections, as when coal or natural gas is used. Only a simple, cheap, plain, practical, common-sense post and neat lantern are required to furnish a satisfactory light, at low prices, and guaranteed to work as represented. The company has been very successful, employing over 100 hands at Canton, and upward of 300 subsidiary distributed throughout the Southwest and Northwest, and working 3,300 lamps at Cleveland, O., 1,300 at Minneapolis, 400 at Wichita, and 241 in this city, all of which are spoken of in the highest terms and even said to be better and cheaper than gas light. In Wichita the Common Council recently countermanded orders for electric lights previously given, in favor of the Sun Vapor light. The Indianapolis branch was established in 1889 under the management of Joseph A. McGuire as General Agent, with J. M. Brubaker Superintendent of the contracting department. The former is occupied in traveling throughout the South and West, contracting with municipal, town and village corporations for their partial or entire lighting at so much

per lamp per annum, Mr. Brubaker having charge during his absence. They are prepared to make estimates, furnish plans and specifications and execute contracts for work in the lines mentioned, providing all necessary equipments and appointments requisite to a complete and satisfactory service at the lowest prices and upon the most liberal terms. They are enterprising representatives of the important industry in the substantial promotion of whose objects and prosperity they are enlisted.

South Side Foundry Co.

Thomas Markey, President; Peter Zeien, Treasurer; August Weber, Secretary; Manufacturers of Gray Iron Castings; 28 Shelby street. This prominent manufacturing establishment began business about two years ago. The foundry occupies a building 60x225 feet in dimensions, with all the necessary machinery and appliances. The operations of the foundry are confined to the production of light gray iron castings to order, in which line the orders of the foundry keep a force of from thirty to forty hands constantly employed. These orders are for the most part from cus-

tomers in the city and throughout the State of Indiana, but outside orders are also frequently received from every portion of the Union. Not only are the products of the foundry of the best quality, but the prices charged for them are uniformly low. The members of the company are all thorough and practical business men, and they have commended themselves to favor by promptness and accuracy in filling orders and by uniform reliability in all their transactions.

Indianapolis Bolt & Machine Works

Manufacturers of Iron Construction Work for Buildings; 10, 12, 14 and 16 Garden street. The Indianapolis Bolt and Machine Works were established here in 1887, by O. R. Olsen and George W. Moore, and though of comparatively recent development, enjoy a reputation as a representative iron industry, second to none in the city, similarly engaged. A large amount of capital is invested in the enterprise, employment is given to a large force of experienced founders and machinists, and the annual output is of correspondingly large proportions. They occupy commodious premises, 60x130 feet in dimensions, upon which have been erected blacksmith shops, pattern and finishing shops, in addition to a three-story building, of very large dimensions, for a machine shop, equipped with lathes, boring machines, drills, punches and auxiliary machinery and appliances adapted to the purposes for which they are supplied, driven by steam. The pattern, finishing and blacksmith shops are equally well appointed, with facilities for the conduct and completion of the work, with the least delay and in the most reliable manner. Their lines of production embrace heavy and light machinery, iron construction work for buildings, bolts, lag screws, bridge rods, pulleys, shafting and hangers, which they also carry in full supply, and other articles required by the trade. They also repair all kinds of machinery in the most skillful manner and at the shortest

notice, and manufacture caustic tile presses in addition to complete outfits for tile mills, including dies, etc. The best materials only are used and every care is taken that their products shall conform in every particular to the exacting requirements of the service for which they are designed. They employ from forty to fifty skilled mechanics and assistants, and do a large and increasing trade throughout Indiana, Ohio, Kentucky, Missouri and Georgia, as also in the Eastern and Western States. Mr. Olsen, who is long experienced in the business, supervises and directs the departments devoted to manufacture, while Mr. Moore has charge of the office. Both are enterprising citizens, and their undertaking is managed in a manner so liberal and judicious as to have become a prominent base of supply for an extensive and extending territory.

Kimberlin Manufacturing Co.

Manufacturers of Harrows, Rakes, Etc.; 10 to 16 Garden street. This company was incorporated in 1881, with a capital of $50,000, for the manufacture of a special line of agricultural implements in constant requisition by farmers, on account of their indispensable utility and value for the service they are designed to facilitate. The business had been established the year previous by R. P. Kimberlin and L. F. Kimberlin, the former becoming charter President of the company, which also adopted his name, and Mr. L. F. Kimberlin is now President, and George W. Moore, Secretary and Treasurer. They occupy a three-story brick building, 60x130 feet in dimensions, containing thoroughly equipped machine, pattern, blacksmith shops, etc., provided with all requisite machinery and labor-saving devices of the most modern improved pattern, for successful manufacture of the products. The specialties offered the trade embrace the "Corn King," "Queen," and "Tip-Top Tongueless" cultivators, the most simple and practical in their construction of any on the market, and unequaled for lightness, strength and durability; the "Iron Duke" harrow, the best harrow ever made for general purposes, and especially adapted for use on sod, heavy clay soil, foul, trashy ground, or rough, stony land; the "Bonanza Force-Drop Corn Planter," that will plant corn in straight rows both ways, whether the team goes fast or slow; the "Star" and "Bonanza Sulky" hay rakes, for one or two horses; Frederick's patent equalizers, Davis' patent cultivator attachments, lifting jacks, check-rowers, etc., for which the demand is very extensive. Their productions are of the best grade of materials, and in every department are subjected to the most exacting tests before placed in stock. As models of proportion, arrangement, efficient service, capacity, durable wear and superior workmanship they are unrivaled, a fact that is conclusively established by testimonials of appreciation from those who have used them in all parts of the country. From forty to fifty hands, in addition to five traveling salesmen, are employed, and a large and growing trade is supplied throughout the United States in every direction.

R. G. Harseim

Manufacturer of Model Pantaloons, Overalls and Shirts; 23 and 25 East South street. One of the most active and enterprising manufacturing enterprises in this city, is that of R. G. Harseim, devoted to the manufacture of clothing, including the perfect fitting Model vest, of which he is the inventor. The establishment was founded by the present proprietor in 1884, and he has built up a trade commendatory of his industry and managerial ability. He occupies a two-story and basement brick building, 200x100 feet in dimensions and in every way completely equipped for the business, and provided with steam power for the operation of seventy-five sewing machines and other mechanical appliances, requisite to his lines of production. These embrace the Model pantaloon overalls and shirts, the Model vest, cassimere trousers, in style, material, workmanship, finish and appearance equal to custom-made work, etc., also lustre, seersucker, flannel and cottonade coats and vests, and other articles of wearing apparel of equal utility and durability. In addition to 125 hands employed at the present establishment, he employs a large force at the Reformatory, where thirty-five machines are operated, and his total output daily approximates 1,500 garments, of the best qualities of material and unexcelled in all their essential requirements by the manufacture of any similar industry in the West. He does a very large business, and during the last presidential campaign, furnished to order nearly, if not quite all, the uniforms worn by the political organizations of the State. A large staff of clerks and six traveling salesmen are required for the conduct of his operations among the trade in all portions of the United States, especially in the South and West, and he enjoys the confidence of commercial and financial circles in all directions.

Wm. P. Myer—Manufacturer of Elevator Buckets, Tinware, Etc.; 17 to 23 East South street.—This representative industry was established by William P. Myer in 1876, at Terre Haute. Realizing the invaluable opportunities available in this city for the increased production and distribution of his output, he removed his works to Indianapolis during 1880, and has since conducted large operations in his lines. He owns the property at the above location, the same

consisting of a two-story and basement building, fifty feet front, on East South street, and 160 feet deep, whereby occupies the main floor and basement, divided into an office and sales-room 30x100 feet, with a workshop 50x60 feet in dimensions. The upper floor with the premises adjoining, which are of like dimensions, are also owned by Mr. Myer. His equipment is complete, embracing all requisite tools and appliances necessary to the manufacture of his stock, and his facilities and appointments are equally full and available. His specialties are elevator buckets, rain-water cut-offs, etc. The former are for handling grain in mill or warehouse, also for handling ear corn, corn and cobs, clay, bones, malt, crushed coke, etc., substantially made of sheet steel, ordinary and of extra heavy grades, and unsurpassed by any other buckets in the market. The cut-offs are made in all sizes from two inches up, of tin or galvanized iron, for use in any position without extra pipe or elbows, and, though but three years on the market, are the favorites of the trade throughout the United States and Canada. He also manufactures elevator cups for mills and handling light materials, of tinned steel plate with iron bands; tin stove-pipe rings from five to seven inches in diameter, pie-plates, cups for patties and pieced tinware in great variety, and carries large stocks of stamped and japanned ware. Only the most skilled labor and best materials are employed by Mr. Myer, and his productions enjoy a reputation for superior workmanship and substantial durability, that has extended and established the trade in every direction. He employs from ten to fifteen hands and supplies the demand for specialties in every State of the Union and in Canada, for his tinware, etc., throughout the city and surrounding country. He furnishes complete catalogues of all his various products and price-lists upon application, and all orders are filled promptly and satisfactorily.

Armstrong Bros.—Boiler and Portable Engine Builders; 51 to 99 East Georgia street.—The most extensive of the boiler industries of Indianapolis is the boiler works of Armstrong Bros. The firm is composed of James J. Armstrong and W. C. Armstrong,

and was organized in 1878 at Springfield, O., whose their sons and direct works of a character similar to those here, and among the largest of the kind in the United States. In September 1, 1886, they located in Indianapolis, and succeeded the firm of Stokes, Davis & Co. in this line, being persuaded to revive this line of industry by the superior facilities afforded by this city as a manufacturing and railroad center. The works have a frontage of 350 feet on East Georgia street, with a parallel depth of 200 feet on South Pennsylvania and South Delaware streets. They are conveniently located for shipping and receiving purposes, and provided with machinery and appliances that will adequately promote the volume and value of production. The boiler shop is a commodious brick building 200x100 feet in dimensions, the sheet-iron works and machine shops are 150x50 feet, and the remaining structures requisite to the establishments in chief are of proportionately large dimensions. They are also provided with extensive yard room and other accommodations. The machinery equipment embraces powerful steam punches, some of which will force a space six inches in diameter through metal three-quarters of an inch in thickness; a full set of the Wilber flanging apparatus, for flanging heads up to eight feet in diameter; heavy rools, from the smallest sizes to eighteen feet in length; a complement of riveting machines, with other appointments necessary to the service, of the latest pattern and powerful capacity. Their specialty is heavy work; their range of manufacture includes steam boilers, stationary and portable engines, feed-water heaters and purifiers, gray iron castings, light and heavy sheet iron work, etc. Every device that can facilitate the work in hand is here utilized, every article in their line is included in the output, and characterized by the superiority of its material and workmanship. The works furnish employment to a force of from 75 to 100 experienced artisans, and the products are sold in the Northern and Western States, the trade throughout other portions of the Union being furnished from the Springfield works, where from 150 to 200 men are constantly employed. A full force of clerks and travelers are also employed here under the direction of James J. Armstrong, the resident partner and General Manager. Their office is at 101 South Pennsylvania street. The gentlemen who have undertaken this enterprise are of the highest order of public spirited citizens, and have given to the Capital City additional prominence and importance as one of the leading cities west of the Alleghenies.

H. Lieber & Co. Manufacturers and Dealers in Pictures, Frames and Mouldings; 33 South Meridian street. The art emporium of H. Lieber & Co. was established by Mr. Lieber in 1854, at 82 East Washington street, whence he removed to his present site in the Fall of 1888, and is now conducting the pioneer establishment and the largest enterprise of its kind in the State. The premises occupied consist of an elegant four-story and basement building, fronting 25

feet on South Meridian street and running back 100 feet, where it connects with a structure 100x80 feet in dimensions, four stories high and fronting on Pearl street. This latter was erected by the firm during the season of 1888. Their moulding and picture frame factory occupies a three-story and basement building 25x125 feet in size, erected upon grounds on Madison street, the area of which is 160x225 feet. The premises are equipped with all modern machinery and devices, and provided with ample accommodations for the various mechanical operations, as also for the storage and shipment of their varied lines of production. The range of manufacture embraces mouldings, frames, cornices, mirrors, etc., etc., using only the best seasoned woods and other materials, and employing experienced and practical operatives, under competent direction. The display, ware and alesrooms, fronting respectively on South Meridian and Pearl streets, are handsomely furnished, supplied with all the latest improved conveniences and well departmented. The main floors are devoted to the retail trade in fine pictures, mirrors, frames, mouldings, architects', painters' and artists' supplies, also containing a special and complete department for the firm's specialties, viz., photographers' materials; the second floor are used as the wholesale department and crowded with general stock; the third floors are occupied with mouldings, and the fourth with mirrors. Their stocks are very choice and complete, including the products of the leading manufacturers in Europe and America, and in every way models of artistic elegance and superior workmanship, on which accounts, as also on account of the low prices charged, the liberal terms offered and the facilities for large production, the care in great demand in all parts of the country. A force of forty-six clerks, salesmen and assistants are employed at the main house, the trade of which is distributed throughout the West and Northwest. At their factory, the services of fifty hands are in constant requisition, and the output goes East to their resident agent in New York City, who supplies the demand in that section, besides shipping extensively to England. The affairs of the concern are managed with liberal and intelligent enterprise, and the establishment in its entirety is one of the most prominent and prosperous in its line in the West.

Miner & Elbreg—Manufacturers of The Perfection Physicians' Chair; 224, 226, 228 and 230 South Delaware streets.—The Perfection Physicians' Chair, a recent development in the line of surgical appliances, has met with the universal commendation of the profession, since its introduction at a recent period, to whom it has since been known as "The Perfection" in every respect. Its purpose is to facilitate the conduct of examinations and operations with the least inconvenience to both patient and operator, and the evidence of its efficiency and value is daily attested, by the demand for them from all portions of the country, as also by the testimony of physicians, surgeons, oculists and specialists throughout a territory as widely distributed. In appearance it resembles a handsome parlor rocker.

Its mechanism is so arranged as that its operation is simple, easy and perfect; after the patient is seated in the chair, the latter can be adjusted to any desired position, without the slightest annoyance to the occupant or operator, and so balanced that the patient properly seated therein can recline at any angle without assistance, the operator being only required to secure the chair at the proper angle. All other chairs for a similar purpose, as is well known, must first be elevated and arranged, and the patient must climb into position by use of a step or be elevated by means of a rack and pinion movement. This is avoided. The back is lowered easily from an angle of 45 degrees to a level plane, the act of which elevates the seat from 23 to 29 inches, the required height for operating. It meets all the requirements of the surgeon, gynæcologist, oculist and artist, among whom it is rapidly coming into general use. Their manufacture was begun here in October, 1887, by Hopper & Elbreg. In May, 1888, Benjamin D. Miner purchased the interest of Dr. Hopper, and the present firm, consisting of himself and Henry H. Elbreg, was organized. They occupy a two-story and basement building, 100 feet square, divided into sales and display rooms, and containing the manufacturing department, where from ten to twelve operatives are employed and are made by hand work, under the personal supervision of Mr. Elbreg, the inventor. Their line of production is limited to "The Perfection Chair." Its frame work is of either antique oak, walnut or cherry, finished in oil or varnish, and in its construction neither time nor expense has been or will be spared to attain as nearly to perfection as possible. The stirrups are adjustable to different lengths and widths, automatic in action and always ready for use. The chair is provided with anti-friction casters, and is

upholstered in leather or extra mohair plush, besides being handsomely carved. It is six feet in length, 20½ inches wide between the arms, 30 inches over the arms, and weighs, when packed for shipment, 120 pounds. They are sold at prices ranging from $65 to $75, with a liberal discount for cash, and are, without doubt, the cheapest and best chairs in the market. The members of the firm are representative men. Mr. Elbreg is also the inventor of other surgical chairs, and has the benefit of years of experience in their manufacture. The business is managed upon the most liberal and honorable principles, and a large trade is done throughout the United States and Canada in every direction.

The Chandler & Taylor Co.—Manufacturers of Self-Contained Stationary Engines, Etc.; 370 West Washington street.—The Chandler & Taylor Company is one of the largest and most prominent representative industries in the State. The business was established by Wiggins & Chandler in 1858, the firm becoming Chandler & Taylor in 1863, and so continuing until 1888, when the present company was organized, with Thomas E. Chandler, President; Franklin Taylor, Vice-President, and W. M. Taylor, Secretary. The works occupy 170x250 feet, and consist of the machine and wood working shops, two stories high, 60x200 feet in size; the foundry, 100x150 feet, with new cupola of six tons capacity and equipped for turning out the heaviest patterns of castings; also commodious finishing, painting and pattern shops, and warehouse facilities, the latter on Washington street, opposite the machine shop. The plant is supplied with full lines of the latest improved machinery, including lathes, boring machines, steam punches, drills and other appliances requisite to the business conducted, also a large assortment of special machinery employed in the manufacture of their self-contained stationary engines. The latter are made in ten sizes of from 12 to 100-horse power each, and is the company's specialty. Their manufacture was commenced in 1887, and their superior merits have been constantly demonstrated by the large and increasing demand that is made for them. They are the embodiment of new principles governing the working of steam engines, and have shown the most marvelous results in the way of economy, power, simplicity and the highest efficiency. All the parts are interchangeable, like the constituent parts of an American watch, constructed of the best materials and subjected to the most exacting tests before offered for sale. Their lines of production also embrace saw machinery, muley and circular saw mills and their accessories, for use in local supply mills among lumber districts where water-power is the available motor. A large number of this line of machinery is sold on the Pacific Coast. In addition, they manufacture all descriptions of the works and brick making machinery, which are also in large demand and unsurpassed for the service for which they are designed. They employ 100 hands and a large force of assistants here, with agents at all important points throughout the United States. They are prepared to fill and ship orders promptly, and their trade is large and influential in all the States, also throughout Canada and in South America. During January, 1889, seven carloads of engines and saw mill machinery were shipped to their agent at Portland, Ore., in response to orders from that Territory. The company's officials give their personal attention to the work, and the enterprise is one of the most powerful for the promotion of prosperity in the city and State.

Udell Wooden Ware Works—A. A. Barnes, Proprietor; Calvin G. Udell, Superintendent; Manufacturers of Ladders, Wooden Ware, Fancy Cabinet Ware, Etc.; Addison and Canal streets, North Indianapolis.—The extent of its output, the variety of its products, and the wide territory covered by its trade, gives to the Udell Wooden Ware Works a recognized place among the leading industrial establishments of Indianapolis. The business was originally located at Chicago, from whence it was removed to this city in 1873, and conducted under the style of the Great Western Ladder Works, until 1882, when it assumed its present name, Mr. A. A. Barnes becoming the proprietor. The works, consisting of factories, warehouses, drying houses, engine and boiler houses, are conveniently arranged for the business, and with the extensive lumber yards cover an area of over six acres, and the machinery equipment comprises all the most improved wood-working appliances and every accessory calculated to facilitate the processes of manufacture. Employment is given to a force averaging about 180 hands, under the immediate and experienced supervision of Mr. Calvin G. Udell, a gentleman thoroughly conversant with every detail of this industry, and the inventor of many of the specialties produced at the works. The products include Udell's Extension Ladders, combining many excellencies which are not found in any other devices of their class, and every feature of utility and durability. In various designs and sizes the ladders produced at these works are adapted to every use to which ladders may be put, and are in vast and steadily increasing demand. In wooden ware the productions include towel arms, towel rollers, scouring boards, meat blocks, patent besom stands and racks, patent rope reels, clothes line props, salt boxes, scrub boards, ironing boards and stands, folding wash benches, extension brush handles and a large variety of other useful articles. In cabinet ware the products include commodes, umbrella stands, hat racks, medicine cabinets, trays, tables, cutting boards, etc. The trade of the works extends to all parts of the Union, and the goods made are popular in all sections. They are distributed from the works and through agencies in New York, St. Louis and San Francisco to the jobbing trade, and are also exported in considerable quantities. Mr. Barnes, the proprietor, is a prominent business man, and endowed with all the qualifications of experience and sound judgment necessary for the successful management of an enterprise of this character and importance. Mr. Udell, the superintendent, is, in addition to his position in this enterprise, connected as Treasurer with the McCoy Manufacturing Co.

Krause-Kramer Manufacturing Co.

Manufacturers of Lounges, Platform Rockers and Reclining Chairs; corner of New Jersey and Merrill streets. The tendency of the furniture industry toward specialties has resulted in the establishing of a number of important establishments, which, confining themselves to certain lines and enjoying a special equipment for them, are enabled to turn out large quantities and superior qualities of the goods to which their activity is devoted, and at prices far below those which formerly obtained. A noticeable illustration of this is found in the establishment conducted by the Krause-Kramer Manufacturing Co. at the corner of New Jersey and Merrill streets. The business was established in 1879 by Mr. George F. Krause, who still remains at its head, the present style having been adopted in January, 1889. The premises occupied

embrace the main factory, a four-story and basement brick building, 40x160 feet in dimensions, a three-story warehouse, 50x130 feet, large yards, etc. The factory is fitted up with the most modern and improved machinery and all appliances calculated to aid or expedite the operations of the business. Here a force ranging from fifty to sixty hands is employed in the manufacture of all kinds of lounges, platform rockers and reclining chairs, made in the most improved styles, of first-class materials and of the most expert workmanship.

All the operations of the factory are conducted under the careful supervision of Mr. George F. Krause, and the quality of the goods is maintained at the highest grade of excellence. The products of the factory are in large demand, and the trade of the house extends to every portion of the Union, and is especially large in the West and South. The house is represented to the trade by fifteen traveling salesmen, and the volume of the business steadily grows from year to year.

R. R. Rouse

Inventor of Improved Driven Wells; 11 and 13 West Maryland street. R. R. Rouse, inventor of improved driven wells, has made a twenty years' study of the subject of driven wells, and most of the steam power used in Indianapolis, both locomotive and stationary engines; also of hotels, breweries, pork houses, factories, mills, and all State and charitable institutions, for elevators, fire protectors, etc., get their water from his driven wells. A 16-inch well is now in successful operation, and 12-inch, 10-inch, 8-inch, 6-inch, and many thousand smaller ones, and he is conceded to stand at the head of his profession. His office and sale-rooms occupy the basement and main floor of the building, having a front of fifty feet on Maryland street, with a depth of 100 feet, and to their rear are the work-shops, 60x100 feet in dimensions. His range of manufacture embraces the general lines of tools and implements for sinking driven wells, pumps of every capacity and description, and fittings, and many specialties of his own invention, which are illustrated and described in his catalogues. He employs a force of skilled operatives, and his trade extends from Maine to California, and in parts of Canada and Europe. A branch establishment is conducted at Philadelphia, and an agency in New York City, and his services in the cause of internal improvements have been invaluable to the city, the State and the country.

The Hadley Shoe Co.

Wholesale Manufacturers of Fine Shoes; 79, 81 and 83 South Pennsylvania street. The Hadley Shoe Company is one of the most successful manufacturing establishments in the State, turning out a large annual product and rapidly distancing Eastern concerns in their competition for the Western trade. The business was established by Barnett & Elliott in 1881, becoming a joint stock company during 1886, with a paid-up capital of $50,000, with J. W. Hadley, President. They occupy the building at the above number, on South Pennsylvania street, convenient and convenient for the trade. Their premises are 80x100 feet in size, well lighted and ventilated and provided with every facility for the manufacture, display, sale and shipment of their products. Their specialties are fine shoes for ladies, misses and children, in which only the best qualities of calf, morocco and kid are used, and which in style, fit and finish are not surpassed by the custom-made work of professional boot-makers. They enjoy an extended and established reputation for delicate symmetry, appearance and durability, and are available to dealers and customers at prices but slightly more than the cost of manufacture. They employ from thirty-five to forty expert operatives, in addition to six travelers, and their trade, which averages $150,000 annually, is distributed throughout Indiana, Illinois, Michigan, Kansas and Missouri.

F. A. Miller

Successor to Hollenbeck & Miller; Manufacturer of Wire Cloth and Wire Goods; 47 South Illinois street. This important and successful business was established in 1874 by T. P. Hollenbeck, the present proprietor becoming a partner in 1883, and so continuing until May, 1888, when he succeeded to the sole ownership. He occupies the main floor and basement of premises 25x60 feet, containing a well equipped and appointed workshop, giving employment to from five to eight experienced operatives, and also having complete facilities for the transaction of business and the prompt and satisfactory execution and shipment of orders to any portion of the country. This range of production includes wire goods of every description and for every service, such as wire cloth, bird cages, flower stands, vases, arches, trellises, lawn chairs, store fixtures, bank and office railing, balcony railing, fences, window guards, stall partitions, floral designs for social or funeral occasions, grave guards, moss baskets, coal screens, upright and revolving ornamental signs, poultry coops, appliances for zoological gardens, etc., with other articles in great variety and general assortment. Among the work recently completed by Mr. Miller are the wire elevators at Pettis-man, Schloss her & Lee's store, the Moore building, etc.; the wire work and window guards of the Asylum at Crawfordsville, this State, also at the Fletcher Asylum, besides other large contracts in his general lines. He also made the wire work and put up the elevators in the Vance block, Fletcher & Sharp's building, Masonic Temple, and other buildings, and furnished them with Zimbul's Pneumatic Bells. In conjunction with his wire work, he carries on a stencil cutting and stamp making business, and does a large and steadily increasing trade in the city, and also throughout the States of Indiana, Ohio, Kentucky and Missouri. His products are of the very best materials and sold at the lowest prices. He is a man of enterprise, who has enjoyed a long experience in the business, with a thorough knowledge of the needs of the trade and public in his lines.

Roberts & Allison—Manufacturers Surgical Chairs, Throat Speculums, Plates, Etc.; 85 and 87 East South street. A very large manufacturing industry is owned and managed by the firm of Roberts & Allison. It was established by Clark & Co. In 1884, Richard B. Roberts and William D. Allison succeeded to the ownership, and the present firm was organized. They are admirably located, occupying a three-story and basement brick building 30x100 feet in dimensions. The premises are divided into office, display and salesrooms, with large manufacturing accommodations, fully equipped with all the

latest patterns of improved machinery and labor saving devices, driven by steam. Their lines of production include the Clark Physicians' Office Chair, an unique and beautiful piece of furniture for surgical and gynecological purposes, simple in its adjustment, absolutely noiseless, and can be placed at any angle with the patient in or out of it, without embarrassment to physician or occupant in cases of emergency. It is of adequate dimensions, made from selected walnut, oak, cherry or imitation mahogany, nicely carved and oil finished, and upholstered in extra fine mohair plush or leather. It is in short, the only plain, common-sense chair made, and the low price, considering its superiority, places it within the reach of every physician. They also manufacture parlor reclining chairs, made of selected walnut, and finished, provided with adjustable backs and suitable for parlor, sitting room or study. They are sold at prices ranging from $10 to $40 each, with a liberal discount to the trade, and

are not excelled by anything of the kind in the United States for the money. In addition to these, they manufacture Cole Bros. Throat Speculums and other special instruments for physicians and surgeons, and in 1887 began the manufacture of the Roberts & Allison Upright Pianos. They are full 7 1/2 octaves, with three-stringed treble, full iron frame and ivory keys, and are conceded by artists and the musical profession to be matchless instruments, unsurpassed by any in purity and refinement of tone, elasticity and delicacy of touch, as also in durability and capacity to stand in tune. They are elaborately finished in rosewood and other fancy woods, and are sold to the largest dealers in the South and West. Their departments are each supervised by a competent and experienced foreman, and the management of the house is characterized by the most liberal, honorable and progressive methods. They employ a force of thirty assistants in addition to tree travelers, and their large trade throughout every State in the Union is steadily increasing and extending.

Pioneer Brass Works—Manufacturers and Dealers in All Kinds of Brass Goods; 110 and 112 South Pennsylvania street. This leading and representative metal-working industry owes its origin to the enterprise of J. C. Brinkmeyer (deceased), who established it in 1875; subsequently becoming incorporated with a capital stock of $10,000, and by him managed and controlled until his death, during 1885, since when the works have been ably managed by J. H. Brinkmeyer, nephew of the founder and original proprietor, though still owned by the latter's estate, of which F. A. W. Davis is the executor. The premises occupied by the foundry, etc., are eligibly located, and consist of a commodious two-story building, 80x120 feet in dimensions, adapted to the purposes for which it is used, and equipped with all necessary machinery and appliances for speedy and economical manufacture, driven by an engine of 40 horse power. The products, the annual output of which is very large, embrace car bearings, a specialty of the concern, also sheet brass, brass tubing and rods, heavy and light castings, railroad castings, natural gas implements, plumbers' and gasfitters' brass supplies, and brass goods generally. They also do repairing and job work extensively, in which lines they are constantly employed. The works are the largest and most completely equipped in the State, and universally patronized by the railroads centering here, for railroad machinery and specialties to be obtained at no other establishment of the kind between New York and Chicago. Daily employment is furnished to twenty-five hands, and the trade supplied is distributed throughout Indiana and the States adjoining in every direction.

Soehner & Hammel—Plumbers and Natural Gas Fitters; 97 North Illinois street. The plumbing firm of Soehner & Hammel is one of the leading and most influential in that line of scientific and industrial development in Indianapolis. The business, to which they devote their special attention and services, was commenced in 1887, by W. H. Wright & Co., Mr. Charles Soehner, head of the present firm, being a partner. In 1888, the latter succeeded to the sole ownership, and in January, 1889, Louis Hammel was admitted to an interest, and the firm of Soehner & Hammel was organized. They are well located, occupying available and finely appointed premises, consisting of the main floor and basement, each 25x125 feet, with an adjoining "L" 25x30 feet in dimensions. They are divided into office, display and salesrooms, also containing a commodious workshop, fully equipped with all requisite machinery and labor saving devices. Their specialties embrace the piping of houses for natural gas, sanitary plumbing and steam and gas-fitting. They are specially prepared to fill orders in either and all of these departments, also to furnish plans and specifications and estimates for work to be done. They carry full lines of natural gas piping, materials and supplies, including natural gas cooking and heating stoves, gas fixtures, plumbers' materials, sundries and supplies, and other articles essential to superior service. They executed the work necessary to the piping and substitution of natural gas in the residence of President

Harrison, also in the store and residence of L. S. Ayers, Sullivan's large dry goods house, Fahnley & McCrea's store, *The Journal* office, Smith's printing establishment, and in many other private residences and public buildings in this city and elsewhere in the State. In addition to his present undertaking, Mr. Sochner is half owner of Blakley's Patent Natural Gas Enricher, an ingenious invention for instantly increasing the illuminating power of natural gas many fold. They employ from twenty-five to thirty experienced assistants, enabling them to properly respond to the large and increasing demands of their trade in the city and State.

The J. B. Allfree Co.—Mill Builders and General Mill Furnishers; corner Pennsylvania and Georgia streets. Mr. J. B. Allfree commenced business under the name of The J. B. Allfree Co, in November, 1887, for the manufacture of flour mills and general mill furnishings, making automatic engines and flour milling machinery special features of his line of production. He began operations at the corner of Missouri and Georgia streets, but in May, 1888, the premises were destroyed by fire, when he removed to the present site on South Pennsylvania street. In December, 1888, the J. B. Allfree Co. was incorporated with a capital of $50,000, and are now carrying on business at the same place, where they are provided with all the necessary appliances for promoting the quantity and quality of their output. They occupy a building 50x150 feet in dimensions, divided into office and manufacturing departments, the latter being used for the fashioning of the wood and iron work necessary. Mr. Allfree was for many years employed in the capacity of Manager and Superintendent of the mill building department of Sinker, Davis & Co., of Indianapolis. Their range of products embrace the "Keystone" wheat and corn mills, J. B. Allfree & Co.'s new bolting chest, the "Success" bolter and dresser, the Allfree purifier, the Allfree sieve scalper, the "Little Hoosier" corn cleaner, the "Keystone" huller and pearler, the "Climax" bran duster, the Allfree flour packer, the Allfree centrifugal reel, automatic engines, and other first-class lines of flouring mill machinery, and are prepared to contract for an entire equipment on either the short, medium or long systems. Their manufacture is from selected materials and embodying all the latest improvements in their several departments. They are made according to Allfree's patents and are symmetrical in design, elaborate in finish, effective in work, requiring less power, running cool and noiseless, needing little attention and producing greatly improved results. With the company *merit* has been the standard of value, a principle their strict adherence to which is conclusively demonstrated by the large and steadily increasing demands of a trade with which the Allfree Company's manufacture is the recommendation of its superior worth. They fill orders promptly, and, owing to their greatly increased facilities for manufacture, at extremely low prices. The present officers are Robert Shriver, of Cumberland, Md. (where he is President of the First National Bank), President; J. B. Allfree, Vice-President and General Manager, and Matthew H. Escott, Secretary and Treasurer. A force of from forty to fifty skilled operatives are employed, and the trade is with flouring mills all over the United States in every direction.

Indianapolis Cabinet Makers' Union—Valentine Schlosser, President; George A. Albrecht, Treasurer; G. G. Stark, Secretary; Manufacturers of Bedroom Suites and Extension Tables; Market and Pine streets.—Among the manufacturing establishments which have contributed in an important way to securing for Indianapolis its present prominent position as a leader in the furniture industry, none has a higher or more firmly established reputation than the Indianapolis Cabinet Makers' Union. It was originally established in 1862

as a co-operative association under the style of the Cabinet Makers' Union, with a twenty-five years' charter. Upon the expiration of the charter in 1887, many of the members having in the meantime dropped out of the association, the business was re-incorporated as an ordinary joint stock company, having but six or seven stockholders, and the present style was adopted. The premises occupied embrace a four-story and basement brick factory, fronting 180 feet on Pine street and 50 feet on Market street; a four-story and basement brick warehouse with a frontage of 125 feet on Market street by a depth of 50 feet, and the remainder of the half-square of ground occupied by the company and running back to Ohio street is utilized as a lumber yard. The factory has a complete equipment, including a 75-horse power engine, two large boilers and all the most approved woodworking machinery and appliances, affording the most complete facilities for the prosecution of the business upon an extensive scale. Employment is given to a force ranging from 80 to 100 workmen in the manufacture of bedroom suits and extension tables in walnut, oak, cherry and other fine woods, including all medium grade goods in the line, made in the most approved designs, of the finest workmanship and the best materials. No inferior or shop work is turned out, the most careful supervision being maintained to keep the product up to the high standard of excellence by which its reputation has been earned. All of the members of the company are practical cabinet makers, and the management is conducted in accordance with progressive business principles, which have secured for the company the favor and confidence of the trade.

Steel Pulley and Machine Works—D. L. Whittier, Proprietor; 79, 81, 83 and 85 South Pennsylvania street. An important iron industry, extensively equipped for productions in its line, and directed and managed with enterprise, is the Steel Pulley and Machine Works. They were established in 1875, by the firm of Newcomb & Olsen & Co., who held possession until 1889, when D. L. Whittier acquired ownership of the plant and adopting the name by which it is now known, has since managed the enterprise. He is located at one of the most available points on the city's manufacturing center, the works occupying a two-story building 100x200 feet in size, completely supplied with machinery and labor-saving devices necessary and valuable to the work carried on, propelled by steam. His range of manufacture embraces steel rim pulleys, heavy and light machinery, shafting, hangers, couplings, bolts, bridge and truss rods, etc., making a specialty of the first named (the steel pulley), which is protected by letters patent here and in Great Britain. It combines strength, increase of power, lightness of weight and other specific and general advantages that are attested by its use in preference to the iron pulley by manufacturers located in all parts of the country. In conjunction with the machine works, Mr. Whittier operates the Indianapolis Manufacturing Company, located on the second floor of the building above described. This department is splendidly equipped with machinery, and an extensive nickel plating plant, and the output embracing the patent "milk-shake" machines, ice-shaving machines, patent churns, patent flush rails for buggies, gasoline flat irons and other products of utility and value. The products are of the best materials and in construction and workmanship are not surpassed by those of any similar establishment in the country. He employs from 150 to 175 hands, three travelers and a competent force of assistants, and supplies a large demand in the United States, also extensively exporting to the European markets.

H. B. Cole & Co.—Manufacturing and Wholesale Confectioners; 62 South Pennsylvania street.—The firm of H. B. Cole & Co., composed of H. B. Cole and D. L. Whittier, was organized in 1888, as successors to Theo. Moench & Bro., who established the enterprise in 1882. Mr. Whittier is proprietor of the Steel Pulley and Machine Works, and Mr. Cole gives his personal and undivided attention to the management and manufacturing departments of this business. They occupy a handsome and prominent location at 62 South Pennsylvania street, which they have completely remodeled and refitted, the premises consisting of a brick building three stories high and 22x100 feet in dimensions, also two floors in the building at 60 Pennsylvania street, adjoining. Their site is unexceptional, and their premises are furnished with machinery and appliances for the manufacture of the line of goods in which they deal, operated by steam. They embrace all descriptions of candy from penny goods which the firm make specially for their extensive and growing trade in that feature of confections, to the choicer varieties of cream, stick and bar candies, French bonbons, made candy, sugared fruits, etc., in great profusion. The house enjoys a reputation for the purity of its products and the substantial and desirable manner in which they are furnished to dealers and customers. Nothing is lacking to complete the requirements of a business demanding such constant attention and careful management. They employ a large force of competent confectioners, in addition to a full staff of clerks and salesmen, and a number of travelers who are kept continually upon the road. Their trade is throughout Indiana and the States adjoining.

Victory Buggy Co.

Victory Buggy Co. F. M. Simmonds, Proprietor; Wholesale and Retail Carriages, buggies, Etc.; 174 and 176 South New Jersey streets. The Victory Buggy Company, owned and managed by F. M. Simmonds, was established here during 1884. He is located as above, where his works, display and salesrooms, office, etc., occupy a commodious two-story building, 90 feet front on South New Jersey street and 100 feet deep, containing all necessary machinery and labor-saving devices distributed throughout the blacksmith, painting and finishing shops for the promotion of production and making the concern a model of its kind in all respects. The aim of the company is to furnish a better and finer class of work for the same price than can be offered by any similar undertaking in the country, and nothing that will even remotely aid in the realization of such determination is either neglected or omitted. Their line of work embraces carriages, buggies, phaetons, and spring wagons principally, in which the best materials and workmanship and the most superior finish only are employed. The materials are selected with great care, being purchased direct from manufacturers for cash, and the most experienced mechanics are enlisted in the service, thereby enabling the company to guarantee the durable wear of their vehicles for one year from the date of purchase. If any part of same fail within that period, by reason of imperfect material or workmanship, they agree to make the necessary repairs without charge. They also make a specialty of leather and rubber buggy tops, cloth or leather back rubber curtains, extra seats, cushions, shafts, poles, neck-yokes, etc., at prices as low as are consistent with good workmanship and materials. They employ from thirty-five to forty hands, doing a large and growing trade in the city and State, also in Ohio, Illinois, etc.

Lilly Varnish Co.

Lilly Varnish Co. —Charles Lilly, President; Shelby Compton, Vice-President; Fred. Revely, Secretary; John M. Lilly, Treasurer; Manufacturers of Fine Varnishes, Rose street. —This prominent manufacturing concern was established in 1865 by the firm of Mears & Lilly, shortly afterward becoming J. O. D. Lilly & Sons, under which latter style the business was conducted until the incorporation in 1888

of the present company. The works, which have a complete equipment of all the most improved appliances for the prosecution of the business, occupy a brick building, for warerooms and office,

100x50 feet, and a brick factory building, 400x60 feet in dimensions, where a full force of hands is employed in the manufacture of railroad and carriage varnishes, japans, etc. The trade of the company extends to all parts of the country, but is especially large in the States of Indiana, Ohio, Illinois and Michigan, and a considerable portion of their business is with railroad companies. The products of the company enjoy a deservedly high reputation for their superior quality, and this excellence steadily maintained has been the most

prominent factor in building up the trade of the company to its present gratifying proportions. The house is represented on the road by seven competent and experienced traveling salesmen, and has commended itself to favor by the promptness and accuracy with which orders are filled, and the uniform fairness and reliability which characterize all its transactions.

George W. Killinger

George W. Killinger —Manufacturer of Bar Fixtures, Store and Office Furniture; Office, 30 West Market street. —This business was established by Mr. Killinger about eight years ago, and has since been carried on by him with marked success and a steady and annual increase in the volume of his trade. His general workshop is located at the corner of Missouri and Court streets and his finishing warerooms at the corner of Mississippi and Potomac streets, the former being 200x100 and the latter 50x60 feet in dimensions. These premises are fitted up with all the conveniences and accessories necessary for the efficient prosecution of the business, and employment is given to a force ranging from fifteen to twenty highly skilled workmen. Mr. Killinger makes a specialty of designing, finishing and fitting up the interior woodwork for bars, banks, offices and stores, and his excellent work has earned for him a large patronage in the city and surrounding country. Much of the finest work in this line to be found in the city is the result of Mr. Killinger's skill and good taste, among other recent jobs executed by him being the fitting up of seven fine restaurants for Mr. W. G. Sherman; fine bars for Gottlieb Wachstetter, J. Christian, Stephen Mattler, and many other prominent ones. Mr. Killinger also imports the finest French mirror plate and manufactures artistic mirror frames, his products in this line being of unsurpassed excellence and in large demand. Mr. Killinger is a practical and experienced man, and carefully supervises all the work of his establishment so as to secure the highest grade of workmanship and to give uniform satisfaction to his patrons. He fills all orders promptly, and the superior facilities he enjoys enable him to do all work in his line at the most reasonable prices.

S. F. Galloway

S. F. Galloway —Dealer in Raw and Manufactured Furs; 200 South Pennsylvania street.—A leading and prominent house engaged in the collection, sale and shipment of raw furs, is that of S. F. Galloway, at the above locality, which was established by him in 1875. He occupies a three-story and basement building, thirty feet front on South Pennsylvania street, and 100 feet deep. The premises are adaptively departmented, and well appointed for the carrying on of the raw fur business, containing every facility for the display and sale of stocks, as also for their storage, preservation and shipment. He buys very largely in the markets of supply, as also from trappers direct, all descriptions of local furs, principally otter, muskrat, skunk, fox, opossum, coon, mink, beaver, etc., which he ships in the raw state to the Eastern markets. In the line of manufactured furs for the local trade, he makes a specialty of ladies' seal garments and appointments, embracing sacques, muffs, gloves, turbans, boas, mufflers, etc., in seal, sable, mink and other furs, especially appropriate to those lines. He also carries large invoices of fancy rugs for the parlor, library and hall-way; also robes in bear, wolf, leopard, fox, and other skins in complete variety. His stocks are of the best material, selected with the greatest care, and sold at prices and upon terms that have commended him to a large and steadily increasing patronage. He does an extensive trade in the city and throughout the State in conjunction with the business of shipping, referred to above, and will soon open a store in the retail district of the city. The house has acquired a wide-spread reputation for its standard worth and reliable and honorable character.

Joseph Haas, V. S.

Joseph Haas, V. S. —Manufacturer of Live Stock Remedies; 56 South Pennsylvania street. The manufacture of specifics and remedial agents generally, for the cure of diseases indigenous to live stock, has become an important line of production within the last twenty-five years, and a leading industry in that special line is owned and managed by Joseph Haas of this city. He began business here in 1877, and from small beginnings has built up a trade annually amounting to nearly $150,000. He occupies a three-story and basement brick building, 25x100 feet in size, containing the laboratory, supplied with all available equipments, office and consultation rooms, packing and storage rooms, with shipping and all other necessary accommodations. His line of manufacture embraces Haas' Hog and Poultry Remedy, and Haas' Alterative, which are specialties, also lung fever, colic and epizootic remedies, and fever drops. These are compounded with care, only the purest and freshest ingredients entering into their composition, and they have been critically tested in America and Europe and found to conform fully to assurances made in their behalf. He employs twenty-five hands and eight travelers, in addition to a large number of resident agents in Great Britain and Continental Europe, from which these countries and Australia, New Zealand and South America are supplied, the travelers here supplying the demand throughout the United States and Canada. His trade is very large; all orders being filled here, the depot of distribution for the world. Mr. Haas is learned in his profession, a scientist and a man of enterprise, whose manufacturing industry has proved a gratifying success.

Indianapolis Basket Factory—Springer & Sperling, Proprietors; Manufacturers of Baskets and Head Linings; 482 East New York street. This firm, of which Messrs. Isaac Springer and E. Sperling are the individual members, was formed in January, 1889, although both of the members of the firm had previously been prominently identified with manufacturing interests. Mr. Springer as a member, for some years, of the box manufacturing firm of Bronson & Springer, and Mr. Sperling as a member of the firm of E. Sperling & Co., basket makers. The works occupy a building 100x100 feet in dimensions, with a most complete equipment of all the necessary machinery and appliances, including a large engine fed by a 9x12 feet boiler, large steam vats for cooking the logs, which are, by the aid of steam-driven veneering machines, shaved into strips out of which baskets are made. Employment is given to a force of twenty hands, in the manufacture of all kinds of baskets, careful supervision being maintained over every detail of the manufacture, and the products of the establishment are all well made and of the best quality in every respect. Although of recent inauguration the factory has already secured a large trade in the city and State and some in Ohio and Illinois, and the firm is prepared to fill orders in the most prompt and satisfactory manner, railroad tracks at the side of the works giving every facility for the receipt of materials and the shipment of products. Both of the members are practical business men and by their reliable business methods commend themselves to the favor and confidence of the trade.

Goth, Coleman & Co. Manufacturers and Dealers in Foreign and Domestic Granite, Marble and Oolitic Limestone Monuments; 157 Massachusetts avenue, and 222, 224 and 226 Michigan street. This firm, which was formed in 1885, is composed of Charles A. Goth, John A. Coleman and John L. Goth, all practical and experienced artists in their lines. Their studio, display and work rooms occupy premises in the form of an irregular parallelogram 60 feet deep, with a frontage of 20 feet on Massachusetts avenue, and 120 feet on Michigan street, and 50 feet wide at the rear limits. They are handsomely appointed and well lighted, furnished with all requisite facilities, and contain an elaborate display of their works of art. They have in stock marble and granite finished and in the rough, and devote their attention principally to the designing and building of a high class of granite monuments, of artistic design and finished workmanship. The house does a large business in granite, and devotes especial attention to that department. They also manufacture rustic monuments from our native stone, and give especial attention to tablets and carved work of every description, also tombs, vaults, sarcophagi, and other enduring memorials of imposing and beautiful design and finish. Among the large and expensive monuments carved and erected by the firm are the Wilkinson Monument at Crown Hill Cemetery, also the Pressly, Sullivan, Sochner, and other monuments, at the same place of sepulture; the Simmons family tomb at Greenfield, this State, and similar work of the same elaborate character elsewhere throughout this and

other States. The firm enjoys a large trade in Kentucky, and the Ware and other monuments at Shelbyville are specimens of their production. They employ a large experience of and competent staff of assistants, and the reputation of the house for finished workmanship and tasteful and elegant designs is unexcelled. Their prices and terms are reasonable and liberal, and they do a steadily increasing business in the city and rapidly extending and becoming established among patrons of art and the public in all portions of this and other States.

L. T. F. Zalser General Engraver and Designer of Seals, Rubber Stamps, Stencils, Etc.; Rooms 1 and 2, 27 and 29 South Meridian street. The business conducted and owned by L. T. F. Zalser, engraver and designer, was established in 1881. He represents an important and valuable industry, and the products of his

manufacture are among the best to be obtained in his special line. The house, which is the foremost of its kind in Indianapolis, occupies rooms 1 and 2, 27 and 29 South Meridian street, furnished with commodious show windows for the display of goods, and equipped with all necessary machinery and appliances of the most approved

pattern and manufacture, together with other facilities and appointments for the sale and shipment of supplies. He is a designer, engraver, and diesinker, also manufacturing steel and rubber stamps, stencils, seals, notarial seals, etc., and deals very extensively in seals and political regalias, badges, buttons and campaign goods generally. His manufactured articles, and all goods carried by him, are of the very best materials, elegant, original and characterized by superior workmanship, while the prices at which they can be purchased by dealers and patrons are inducements exceptional and unrivaled. His trade is large and constantly increasing, heavy sales being made through his agents and commercial travelers in all parts of the country, as also by the house, which issues illustrated catalogues, circulars, and other agencies for the advertisement of his lines of production, in addition to the employment of a force of competent assistants. Mr. Zalser directs the operations of his establishment personally, and has fostered an enterprise that annually increases in importance and prosperity.

Evans Linseed Oil Co.—Manufacturers of Raw and Boiled Linseed Oil; Office, 23 Vance block. This, the only enterprise of its kind in Indianapolis, was founded by J. P. Evans & Co. in 1894. Up to 1887 the enterprise was conducted as a private undertaking, but in that year was duly incorporated, with Joseph R. Evans, President, and William R. Evans, Secretary and Treasurer. Both gentlemen were members of the original firm, and besides having enjoyed a long experience, are familiar with the wants of the trade. The main

formerly located on South Delaware street were destroyed by fire in December, 1883, but rebuilt without delay at their present site. The premises, which it are owned by the company, are occupied with three buildings, severally 75 feet square, 8,000 feet, and 40x75 feet in dimensions, equipped with all requisite machinery and appliances. Their range of production embraces raw and boiled linseed oil and oil cake and meal. The oil is extracted both by pressure and chemical processes, preserving its purity and strength unimpaired, and when placed in stock, is unsurpassed for the uses to which it is designed. The same is true of their oil cake and meal, which are in constant demand for feeding stock and cattle. They employ a force of from twenty-five to thirty hands, and meet the demands of an extensive trade throughout Indiana, Ohio, Illinois, Kentucky, etc. They have unexcelled facilities for the prompt execution of orders at low prices and upon liberal terms.

President; W. H. Perkins as its Vice-President and Secretary; M. A. Potter, Treasurer, and G. W. Atkins, Superintendent of the works. The works occupy the square of ground bounded by Illinois, Eddy and South streets, nearly the entire area of which is occupied by the plant, embracing the factory and warehouse, 192x120 feet in dimensions, the tempering and finishing departments, also the office and salesrooms which occupy a three-story building, 160x85 feet, with additional storage accommodations located in premises 119x120 feet in dimensions. The works are thoroughly equipped with machinery and appliances, unsurpassed in extent or variety, and in many instances the invention of E. C. Atkins, for the manufacture of the specialties of the company. Their specialty is the "Atkins' Celebrated Silver Steel Band Saw," and their range of production includes, in addition, circular, gang, drag and cross-cut saws, hand saw mill specialties, saw mill supplies, such as gummers, sharpeners, swages, filers, indicators, gauges,

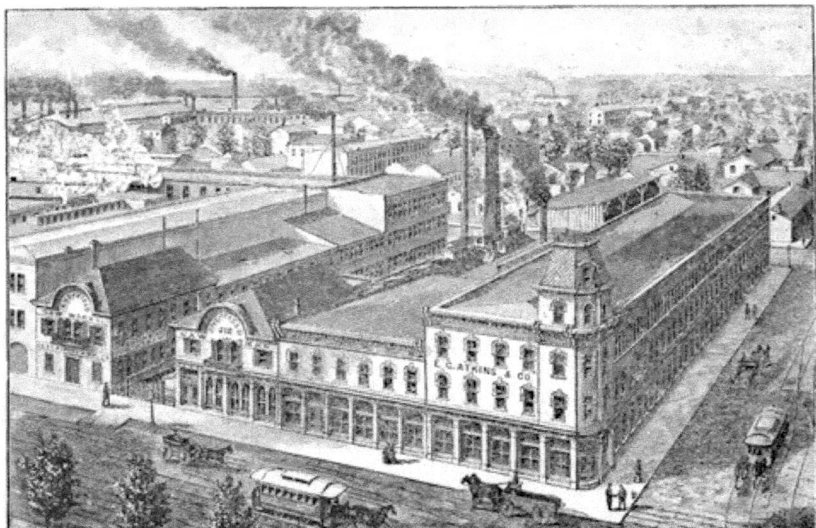

C. F. ATKINS & COMPANY'S BUILDING.

Atlas Engine Works—Manufacturers of Steam Engines and Boilers; Ninth street and Martindale avenue.—This corporation was organized in 1878. The plant consists of a large block of brick buildings, completely equipped for the business. There are also large sheds, storehouses, yards, etc., all covering thirty acres. Natural gas is used as fuel, with the most beneficial results in economy and efficiency. Employment is given to a force ranging from 500 to 600 hands in the manufacture of steam engines and boilers in numerous varieties. The extent of the business may be estimated from the fact that in 1888 they sold over 1,000 complete engine and boiler outfits.

E. C. Atkins & Co.—Manufacturers of the Celebrated Silver Steel Band Saws; Office and Warerooms, 202 to 216 South Illinois street. In 1857, E. C. Atkins, President of E. C. Atkins & Co., began, upon a small scale, the manufacture of saws, and gave birth to a manufacturing industry that thirty years later occupies the foremost position in its lines in the United States, if not in the world. The present company was incorporated in 1885, with Mr. Atkins as its

perfection and excelsior saw tools, and other devices and implements required by the trade. Their saws are made from the finest selected steel, tempered by natural gas, according to the best known methods and by workmen skilled and experienced. They employ from 250 to 275 hands, in addition to eight traveling salesmen, and supply a very large and steadily increasing trade on the Pacific coast, the Northern and Northwestern States, the South and Southwest, the latter sections being furnished from the branch house of the company at Memphis, Tenn. They fill orders promptly and satisfactorily, and their low prices, liberal terms and honorable dealings have given to the company and its individual members an unsurpassed reputation. Catalogues, prices, etc., are furnished upon application.

Indianapolis Art Stained Glass Works—John Black, Proprietor; 119 Massachusetts avenue. Mr. John Black is a native of Glasgow, Scotland, where he served a thorough apprenticeship, and is entirely familiar with the art stained glass business. Locating in Indianapolis during 1886, he embarked in his present enterprise in a small way, and has since devoted his time and talent to its development and promotion, often working sixteen hours a day among the large jobs that have been entrusted to his successful direction. He occupies a two-story and basement building, 25x99 feet, and is about adding a beveling department to his already completely appointed undertaking. The premises are equipped with all necessary machinery and appliances, including four beveling machines, driven by steam. His specialties are private house decoration and ecclesiastical work, to the execution of which, in the most elaborate and artistic manner, his most earnest efforts are directed. Among the many productions of his skill are the memorial and illustrative windows of the First and Seventh Presbyterian churches of this city, the windows of the Soldiers' Orphans' Home at Knightstown, this State, of the German Reformed church at Lima, O., also of churches at Marion, Logansport and other cities of Indiana and adjoining States, in addition to the decoration of residences here and elsewhere. He manufactures and carries in stock heavy and full lines of decorative glass and is prepared to formulate plans and furnish estimates and prices on the shortest notice and in the most satisfactory manner. He employs from six to eight experienced assistants and has built up a large business in the city and State, as also in Illinois, Ohio, and in other western and northwestern States.

Indianapolis Varnish Co.—Elmer, Aldag & Co., Proprietors; Manufacturers of Varnishes; Ohio and Pine streets.—This firm, which began business in 1870, is composed of Messrs. John Elmer, Charles Aldag and August Aldag. From the inception of their business to the present time, they have based their claims to success upon maintaining the quality of their product at the highest standard of excellence, and their business has steadily grown until the demand for their products covers the entire Union. The works of the firm, eligibly located on Ohio and Pine streets, embrace a number of brick buildings covering half a square of ground, and are equipped with every accessory and appliance calculated to add to the effectiveness of the manufacture, including 180 tanks, each of 500 gallons capacity. A force of twenty hands is employed at the works, while a staff of active and competent traveling salesmen represent the firm to the trade. The product of the works includes cabinet makers' and coach varnishes, double elastic coach varnish, piano polish and varnish of all kinds, a leading specialty being made of their substitute shellac, which is a reliable first coating and quick oil finish, and undoubtedly the best shellac substitute offered to the trade. The affairs of the firm are ably managed and conducted, and its dealings with the trade are characterized by uniform fairness and reliability. The firm is not surpassed by any in the country in the quality of its product or the promptness and accuracy with which orders are filled.

The Incandescent Light Co.—Manufacturers of the Welsbach Incandescent Burner; 31 North Illinois street.—The Welsbach Incandescent Burner was invented by Carl Auer von Welsbach, a savant of Vienna, and consists of a modified but very perfect form of the Bunsen burner, the heat from which brings to incandescence a hood or mantle, made by knitting fine cotton thread into a cylinder two inches in diameter by five inches long. This is dipped into nitrates until completely saturated, after which it is subjected to an intense heat, whereby the cotton fibre is consumed, leaving a skeleton of the oxides, perfectly retaining the texture of the woven fabric mentioned above, and forming an extremely fine but coherent and refractory power, capable of covering, in a practical way, a very considerable surface. The burner consumes both natural and artificial gas, produces double the amount of light given by ordinary burners, and is so steady as to render it the perfection of light for reading or fine work by night, producing perfect combustion, without imparting heat or smoke and with but little vitiation of the air of the room. No change is required in brackets or chandeliers by its substitution, and its indestructibility, economy and superior service over all other burners, is rapidly bringing it into almost general adoption. The present company was organized after a thorough investigation of its merits, and owns the controlling rights for its introduction and substitution throughout Marion County, secured from the parent house at

Philadelphia. The officers, H. Jameson, M. D., President; J. B. Musser, Treasurer, and W. De M. Hooper, Secretary, are well known citizens. Dr. Jameson being President also of the Board of School Commissioners, Mr. Musser is a prominent capitalist, and Mr. Hooper is late Superintendent of the Public Library, all gentlemen whose names are guarantees of the value and importance of the undertaking. They occupy a fine suite of offices, 25x80 feet in dimensions, on the main floor of the Young Men's Christian Association building, and give employment to six assistants. Burners will be put in promptly, upon application, at a uniform cost of $2.50 each, and on payments, to responsible parties, at $3 each. Mantles, which will last about 1,000 hours of ordinary use, are renewed for sixty cents each. The company has met with a very flattering success in the city and county, where a steadily increasing business is being conducted.

J. M. Huffer. Manufacturer and Dealer in Harness, Saddles, Etc.; 109 East Washington street.—Mr. J. M. Huffer began operations in this line of business as far back as 1862, and for more than a quarter of a century has been recognized as a valuable exponent of the industry in which he is engaged. He is advantageously and accessibly located at one of the most desirable points in the city's retail trade district, where he occupies a two story and basement building, 30x100 feet in dimensions. The premises are aptly appointed and furnished, provided with all requisite conveniences and appliances and equipped with the necessary facilities for the manufacture, display, sale and shipment of products annually distributed throughout a considerable area of territory in which the trade of the house is located. Mr. Huffer's specialty is fine harness to order, in which he is unsurpassed, making an article the superiority of which is acknowledged. He carries large stocks of light and heavy harness of his own make, also saddles, bridles, collars, robes, horse clothing and equipments, turf goods generally and stable sundries. He also does repairing extensively and warrants all work completed in his establishment. He is amply prepared to ship orders to any point in the State or elsewhere, and his prices and terms, considering the quality of the goods, are low and reasonable. He does a large regular trade in the city and surrounding country, besides responding to requisitions made upon his stocks and services from patrons at a distance.

Peter Routier—Contractor and Builder, and Proprietor of the Capital City Planing Mill; 317 to 327 Massachusetts avenue.—Mr. Peter Routier, who established himself in business in 1860, has since conducted it with continuous success, having earned the favor and confidence of the people of the city by the prompt and faithful execution of all his contracts and by the uniformly superior character of all works turned out under his supervision. He is the oldest established and most extensive builder in Indianapolis, and was the builder of fully half of the best and finest structures in the city. Included among his productions may be enumerated the woodwork on the State House, the new Union Depot, the City Hospital, the Indianapolis High School, the Public Library, the Grand Opera House, English's Hotel and Opera House, the Pan Handle Railroad Car Shops, the Grand Hotel, the Denison House, the Thorpe block, the Conduit block, the Boston block, the Nippenberg block, the Claypool and Talbott blocks, and many other public and business structures, as well as hundreds of fine residences, stores, churches, etc. Mr. Routier is also the proprietor of the Capital City Planing Mill, occupying a four-story brick structure, 100x100 feet in dimensions, and an irregularly shaped two-story building adjoining, covering about as large an area. In addition to these there are large storage sheds, lumber yards, etc., running back to the railroad tracks the entire premises covering about a block of ground. The mill equipment includes a 100 horse power engine, fed by two large boilers, the largest planing machines in the city, and a complete outfit of all the most improved machinery, tools and appliances adapted to the business. The product of the mill is dressed lumber, window and door frames, sash, doors, blinds, etc., is for the greater part utilized in the building of the structures contracted for by Mr. Routier, although outside orders are also filled, and all kinds of mill work are done to order. In the mill, employment is given to a force ranging from forty to fifty hands, while in outside building work, from 150 to gas workmen are employed, according to the season. Mr. Rointer personally supervises all the building operations undertaken by him while the management of the mill is entrusted to his son, Mr. Edward Rointer. The last named gentleman is practically conversant with the business in all its branches, and has himself lately embarked successfully in contracting for residence buildings on his own account. Both of the Messrs. Rointer are capable, business men, and are prompt and reliable in every transaction and justly popular and successful.

Victor Foundry and Machine Works

Ewald Over, Proprietor; Manufacturer of Agricultural Implements, Iron Fences, Castings, Etc.; 240 to 250 South Pennsylvania street. This important manufacturing enterprise was established eighteen years ago, and has been carried on since 1877 by Mr. Ewald Over, who has carried it on with marked success, and has secured for his products a deservedly high reputation for uniform merit. The works embrace a two-story and basement brick building, 100x90 feet in dimensions, in which are located the machine shops, finishing shops, etc., and a completely equipped foundry in the rear, 150x60 feet, with an L 30x50 feet. The works are fitted up with all the most improved tools and machinery adapted to the requirements of the business, and employment is given

to a force ranging from thirty to forty skilled workmen. The products of the works are numerous and varied, embracing a large number of improved agricultural implements, general castings, iron and hardware forces, road making machinery, etc. Among the specialties embraced in the manufacture may be named: Eureka Steam Cookers, Water Filters, Over's Road Plows, Graders and Ditchers, Sawyer's Road Machines, Rowland's Road Machines, Victor One Horse Grain Drills, Preston's Foulter Trucks, Cider Presses, Victor and Smoothing Harrows, Carter's Automatic Gates, Eagle Wagon Bolster Springs, Over's Patent Fence Posts, as well as farm bells, iron fences, and other castings. For many of the special productions the demand covers the entire Union, and includes shipments to Australia, Canada and England, while in the entire line a large trade is enjoyed, covering the States of Indiana, Ohio, Illinois and Kentucky. Mr. Ewald Over, the proprietor of the works, has had a long and practical experience in this department of industry, and has, by his close supervision of every detail of the business, and promptness and accuracy in filling orders, secured for his enterprise a prominent place among the leading manufacturing establishments in this line of production.

E. H. Eldridge & Co.

Lumber, Shingles, Sash, Doors and Blinds; northwest corner of Alabama and Maryland streets. Among the largest and most important operations connected with the lumber interests in Indianapolis, those consummated by E. H. Eldridge & Co. are pre-eminent. The firm, which is composed of E. H. Eldridge and George O. Eldridge, was organized during the year 1878, and has always been leading, influential and successful with dealers and the trade throughout the State. They carry heavy stocks of all qualities and descriptions of lumber, rough and finished, soft and hard, also including in their supplies, shingles, sash, doors, blinds and other lumber products. They are located at the northwest corner of Alabama and Maryland streets, one block south of the Court House, the premises occupied having a frontage of 150 feet on each street, and extending to South street, where an additional area, half a block in extent, is used as piling grounds for hardwood and pine lumber in the rough. The premises also contain commodious sheds for the protection and storage of finished lumber, and adjoin railroad tracks leading to the main lines of railways, diverging from the city in all directions, and affording unsurpassed facilities for shipping to any portion of the surrounding country. They are abundantly provided with conveniences and equipments to fill all orders promptly, and at prices the lowest upon the market. They employ a force of twenty hands, and their annual business aggregates sales of 2,000,000 feet of lumber, 6,000,000 shingles, and large consignments of sash, doors and blinds; the lumber in the city and vicinity and the lumber products to jobbers all over the State. The members of the firm are natives of Massachusetts. They moved to Chicago early in the seventies, thence to Indianapolis, where they have since resided and been identified with the growth and prosperity of the city, to which they have substantially contributed. They are members of the Board of Trade, enterprising, public spirited citizens, and have a large trade that is continually augmenting and expanding.

Geo. A. Richards

Dealer in Natural Gas Supplies; 77 South Illinois street, Telephone No. 364. George A. Richards, after a long experience in the handling of natural gas supplies throughout the oil districts of Pennsylvania and elsewhere, removed to Indianapolis early in 1888, and engaged in the same line of business here. The results of his enterprise have more than exceeded anticipations, a large and steadily increasing trade having responded to his efforts. His location is desirable and adaptive, being at a prominent site on one of the leading avenues of trade, easy of access and convenient in all respects. He occupies premises consisting of the main floor and basement, each 20x120 feet in size, with ample accommodations for the display and storage of stock, and provided with every facility for their display, sale and shipment. He carries full lines of natural gas supplies, tubing, casing and pipe, rig irons, drilling tools and cordage, brass goods and fittings, also plumbers', steam and gas-fitters' tools and implements, materials, supplies and sundries, which he deals in at wholesale and at wholesale prices. They are the products of the leading foundries and machine shops in that line of manufacture, of the best qualities of material, and unsurpassed for the service to which they are designed. He is prepared to respond promptly to all orders submitted for his acceptance either by mail, telephone or in person, and contractors and customers will find large and varied lines of supplies from which to make selections at low prices and upon terms of the most liberal character. His trade is largely local, and his house has also established a high reputation for its reliability and honorable management.

Smith & Plough

Sanitary Plumbers, Steam and Gas-fitters; 106 Massachusetts avenue, and 215 North Alabama street. The firm of Smith & Plough, which began business in November, 1888, is composed of H. M. Smith, formerly foreman with C. W. Meikel, and H. W. Plough. The senior partner gives his personal attention to sanitary plumbing, while Mr. Plough, who has had ten years' experience in all the departments of the business, devotes his personal attention to gas-fitting in all its branches. They occupy the main floor and basement, each 20x60 feet in dimensions, located as above, and are fully equipped and provided with every facility for a prompt and satisfactory service of the trade in all its varied requirements. Their specialty is the piping of houses, halls, hotels, manufacturing and other buildings, for the introduction or substitution of natural gas, and their long experience, perfect knowledge of the art, and first-class workmanship in this particular line makes them invaluable for those who demand efficient and durable service. In the lines of plumbing, steam and gas-fitting, they are equally well prepared to do first-class work only, and though engaged in the business on their own account but a comparatively short time, are in constant requisition for jobs requiring skill, science and mechanical ability for their successful conduct and satisfactory completion. They carry full supplies of piping, fixtures, materials, etc., requisite to every branch of the business, and are not only prepared to fill orders with the least delay and at the lowest prices, but to give their personal supervision to the same, from their inception to their conclusion. Individually, the members of the firm are enterprising and progressive business men, employing from ten to fifteen assistants, and doing a trade in the city and vicinity which is increasing daily.

Sander & Recker—Manufacturers and Dealers in Furniture, 103, 105 and 107 East Washington street.—The furniture establishment of Sander & Recker is old and widely known to the furniture trade, as a depot for the ready procurement of every article in the way of furniture supplies, at the most reasonable rates. The firm, which is made up of Theo. Sander and Gottfried Recker, was organized in 1898, and succeeded to the plant and business of the Western Furniture Company. Their operations have been large, and their management of the business has directed the most substantial rewards to their acceptance. They are most eligibly located, occupying a three-story and basement brick building with a frontage of 66 feet and a depth of 90 feet, including in such dimensions three stores in one, well fitted up and departmented, equipped with every facility and convenience for an adequate display of their lines of manufacture, and the transaction of business operations. They make specialties of bank, office and saloon furniture, filling orders from leading cities in the State for such articles, and extensively engage in the manufacture of parlor suites to order, also of the general lines of furniture adapted to a large and diversified demand. They have unexceptional facilities for turning out first-class work, owning, in addition to their Washington street factory, a controlling interest in the factory of Hulbert Recker & Co., at 209 211 East Washington street, and are prepared to execute orders promptly. They employ thirty skilled operatives, and do a large trade in the city and State. Messrs. Sander and Recker are natives of Germany, the former coming to Indianapolis in 1864, while Mr. Recker has resided here for thirty-four years. Both are leading citizens and merchants, and enjoy the esteem and confidence of the public, as also of the trade to which they minister.

Dewald & Gall—Plumbing and Gas-fitting; 9 Massachusetts avenue, Wyandot block. The plumbing establishment of Dewald & Gall, though started less than two years ago, not only does a large local business, but is steadily extending its field of operations in response to the demands of a steadily increasing trade. The firm is composed of M. Dewald and Peter J. Gall, and was organized in 1887. They occupy a neatly appointed store, 20x50 feet in dimensions, with a very compact workshop in the basement. The premises are equipped with all necessary tools and implements for their lines of work, and provided with requisite facilities and equipments for the display of goods and the transaction of business. Their specialties are the piping of houses for the introduction of natural gas, also sanitary plumbing, gas-fitting and steam-heating work. They are agents for the Archer Fancoast Manufacturing Company, furnished the gas fixtures for the State House and other large contracts, and are prepared to make estimates and undertake contracts in their lines

of endeavor, and employing only the most skilful and experienced workmen and the best materials, beside personally superintending operations, guarantee all work done under their direction. They carry large and varied stocks of gas fixtures, natural gas fittings and supplies, plumbers' materials and sundries, with other articles adequate to their work and trade, of the best qualities and every description, and their prices and terms are low and liberal. They employ from ten to twenty-five men as the demands of the business require, and a large and increasing trade in the city and vicinity is ministered to and supplied.

J. S. Farrell & Co. Constructors of Sanitary Plumbing, Steam and Hot Water Heating Appliances; 84 North Illinois street.—Mr. J. S. Farrell has enjoyed a wide experience in sanitary plumbing, steam and hot water heating, covering a period of over a quarter of a century, during all of which he has been practically engaged in that department of scientific development. The present house was established by Mr. Farrell in 1873, and is one of the leading and representative concerns of its kind in this city. They occupy a two-story and basement building, 25x100 feet in dimensions, divided into display and office departments, also containing a well arranged and fully equipped workshop provided with all necessary facilities and appliances for the rapid and successful production of their varied output. Their specialties are sanitary plumbing, steam and hot water heating and natural gas piping, according to the most approved and correct systems. Their line of manufacture includes steam and hot water heating apparatus, of low and high pressure, direct and indirect radiation, for warming stores, offices, public buildings, private residences and green houses, being also agents for Duplex and other steam heating boilers, the National hot water heater, "Cole" patent syphon pump, Gaskill's patent water lifter or motor, etc., and dealers in iron and lead pipe, steam, sanitary and hydraulic appliances, and plumbers' supplies and sundries generally. Among the firms now using their appliances in this city are: Murphy, Hibben & Co., Pearson & Wetzel, H. Lieber & Co., Ernest L. Hassold, W. L. Elder, Willis G. Sherman and others, being also in use in the State Capitol, Masonic Building, State Reformatory for Women and Girls, Indiana Insane Asylum, Henry Smith's block, etc., all of which are located in Indianapolis, the Indiana State University at Bloomington, Green and Delaware County Court Houses at Bloomfield and Muncie, this State, Montgomery County (Ind.) Poor Farm, McLean County Jail and Sheriff's Residence at Bloomington, Ill., and in public and private buildings throughout the West, in all of which the workmanship is pronounced to be unsurpassed and the materials of a superior quality. They employ from twenty-five to fifty skilled and experienced assistants and do a large and rapidly increasing business throughout the city and State in all directions.

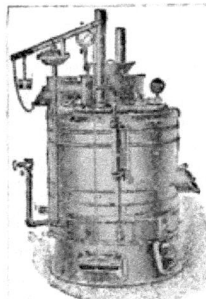

H. Techentin & Co.—Manufacturers and Dealers in Harness, Etc.; 22 South Meridian street.—This house was established in 1881 by Henry Techentin, as successor to H. C. Schulte. The firm carry large stocks of their own manufacture, in addition to full lines of imported and domestic goods, and do a large high-class trade. They occupy a three-story and basement building, 50x80 feet in dimensions, admirably arranged and provided with all requisite facilities and appliances for the manufacture of their finished products. Their specialties are the highest class of coach and carriage harness, made in the latest styles, superbly mounted and adapted to any service, for prices ranging from $100 to $250 per set. They also excel in light buggy and trotting harness, and manufacture race saddles, bridles, lines, traces, bits, riding straps, etc., in great variety, also carrying choice selections of blankets, rugs, horse equipments and stable sundries. Their long experience in the business and complete facilities enable them to fill orders promptly and satisfactorily. They employ from five to ten experienced operatives and meet the demands of their large wholesale and retail trade in the city and throughout the surrounding country. Superior workmanship and honorable enterprise characterize the management and operations of the firm.

Donnan & Off—Dealers in Stoves, Ranges, Etc.; 110 East Washington street.—The well-known and popular house of Donnan & Off, a firm composed of Wallace Donnan and Christian Off, was established in 1875, by Donnan & Wiggins, continuing until 1882, when Mr. Off purchased the Wiggins interest and the present firm was organized. They occupy a three-story and basement building, 25x120 feet in size, well appointed for the display of goods, and with every convenience, including improved telephone service for the purposes of the business. They carry large stocks and full lines of heating and cooking stoves and ranges, also Dangler Vapor Stoves and appurtenances, in addition to tin and copper ware, including tin roofing and spouting. They are agents for Walter's patent tin shingle, and handle the latest improved and best manufacture of natural gas supplies, being also prepared to furnish estimates for piping houses for the introduction of natural gas. Their articles are the products of the best foundries and manufactories, of standard qualities of material, and equipped with the most recent improvements and attachments. Orders receive prompt attention, and all work done under their direction is of a superior character and entirely satisfactory. A force of from ten to fifteen hands is employed, and they respond to the demands of a large trade in the city and throughout the surrounding country.

G. W. Hill & Co.—Manufacturers and Dealers in Regalia and Lodge Goods; 28½ South Illinois street.—The extensive and widely known house of G. W. Hill & Co., engaged in the manufacture of Odd Fellows and other society regalia, was established here by Mr. Hill, in 1872. They are accessibly located in the center of business, occupying the first floor over Roll's carpet store, premises 40x100 feet in dimensions, divided into display and manufacturing departments, each well appointed and provided with all requisite facilities and appliances for the promotion of the objects to which they are severally appropriated. His lines of production embrace special regalia and society equipments and furnishings to order, of the best qualities of material and to designs original and attractive. He also carries large stocks of Odd Fellows, Masonic, Knights Templar, Knights of Pythias, Forester, Patriotic Sons of America, Workingmen, Hibernia, and other society regalia, banners and jewels, lodge paraphernalia, etc., with full lines of materials and trimmings for their manufacture. His supplies include every article known to the craft or handled by any similar concern in the world, and he is prepared to furnish societies, equip lodge rooms, etc., with complete outfits upon the shortest notice, and at the lowest prices compatible with the unsurpassed qualities of his stocks and products. He employs from five to ten experienced assistants, and does a large trade in the city and State, besides filling orders from all parts of the United States.

Irvin Robbins & Co.—Manufacturers of Fine Carriages; 32 East Georgia street. The firm of Irvin Robbins & Co., made up of Irvin Robbins and S. A. Robbins, was organized in 1881, as successor to the Shaw Carriage Company, the latter having been established during 1874, and of which Irvin Robbins was Treasurer. They enjoy a merited reputation for reliability and superior workmanship

throughout the Northwest. They occupy four-story premises for manufacturing and office purposes, having a frontage of 65 feet by a depth of 100 feet, fitted up with every convenience and equipped with all the latest improved machinery and auxiliaries, for first-class production at the least cost of time and labor. Their range of manufacture—which is largely to order—embraces only high class work, in demand by a trade requiring grades of that character, and includes every description of vehicle, such as broughams, rockaways, phaetons, surreys, victorias, dog-carts, buggies of every design and model, and hearses, the latter to order. They keep full lines of their specialties on hand, and are prepared to fill orders at the shortest notice. They also do a fine line of work in repairing, repainting, etc., and direct operations in that department with the skill, taste and finish apparent throughout the entire establishment. They employ a force of forty competent operatives and do a large trade, locally and within a considerable radius of Indianapolis.

Thos. E. Potter—Manufacturer of Straw Goods; 26 and 28 South Tennessee street.—One of the largest industries in the line of manufacturing straw goods for the wholesale and jobbing trade in Indianapolis, is owned and operated by Thos. E. Potter. He has had a long experience in the business, having been similarly engaged in Philadelphia for fifteen years, prior to July, 1888, when he removed to this city and organized his present undertaking. He occupies a three-story and basement building, 50x150 feet, ably and admirably appointed and departmented. The premises are divided into display, stock and work rooms, well equipped with facilities for the manufacture and sale of his products, and for their storage and shipment. His specialties are straw hats, bonnets and children's straw goods in great variety, and his efforts are directed to making their manufacture the leading in their lines in the West. The materials used are the best obtainable in the foreign and domestic markets of supply; the workmen employed are skilled and experienced in their art, and the products always in the latest styles and designs, and of the most superior workmanship. Mr. Potter is prepared to fill orders of any magnitude upon the shortest notice and at the lowest prices consistent with first-class materials and work. Twenty-five sewing machines and all requisite straw working appliances are constantly in operation, which, with the services of from fifty to sixty hands, are required to supply the demands of the trade he has built up among the wholesale and jobbing houses of the city and State. He is a man of enterprise and familiar with the requirements of the business, and his house has acquired a well-merited reputation for liberality and honorable methods of management.

Wright & Wright—Manufacturers and Dealers in Engines, Boilers, Etc.; 113 to 125 South Tennessee street. The establishment of Wright & Wright, which is prominent among the manufacturing industries of Indianapolis, was founded in 1881 by Hadley, Wright & Co., to which the present firm, consisting of H. C. Wright and M. P. Wright, succeeded during 1888. They are located one square west of the Union Depot, where they occupy a three-story and basement building, 120x60 feet, with large boiler shops and storage accommodations in the rear. The main building is devoted to the machine shop, and is completely equipped with extensive machinery, including lathes, drills, punches, planers, presses, etc., and such other mechanical tools and appliances that can be advantageously employed in the service. The boiler shops are equally well supplied and appointed, and the shipping conveniences are complete and efficient. They manufacture engines, boilers, saw mills, heading saws, steam pumps, injectors, brass goods, belting, shafting, pulleys, sheet iron work, hoist rigs, machinery, etc., making a specialty of second-hand power outfits and exchange of goods, and carrying a large stock of boilers, engines and other machinery for immediate shipment. They are also agents for, and carry in stock, Gardner upright engines. They employ from fifteen to twenty skilled mechanics, supplying a steadily increasing trade from Michigan to Texas, and from Pennsylvania to Colorado, but principally throughout Indiana, Ohio, Illinois and Kentucky, in all of which territory their output is considered among the cheapest and best in the markets of the country, and on account of their efficiency and reasonable prices, are in constant demand all over the country. All orders meet with prompt and satisfactory attention, and the interests of patrons are honorably protected and promoted.

Tucker & Dorsey Manufacturing Co.

William H. Tucker, President and Superintendent; Robert L. Dorsey, Secretary and Treasurer; Manufacturers of Wooden Ware Specialties; Office and Works, State avenue and C., L. St. L. & C. Ry. This business had its inception in 1865, when Mr. W. H. Tucker, after serving in the army through the Civil War, began making money-drawers in a retail way. He was shortly afterward joined by Mr. Dorsey (father of the present Secretary and Treasurer, and who died six years ago), the firm of Tucker & Dorsey being established and soon working into an exclusively wholesale trade. Under this style the business was carried on until 1882, when the present corporation was organized. In October, 1887, their works were destroyed by fire, since which the works have been completely rebuilt, the present plant covering three acres. Included in it is the main factory, a two-story brick structure, 120x180 feet in dimensions, a saw mill building 70x80 feet, both completely equipped, and the remainder of the premises is occupied by well-stocked lumber yards and railroad switches, by which their supply of logs is received. A force of from forty-five to fifty workmen is employed in the manufacture of the products, including Tuckers' alarm tills, strongly made of dove-tailed hardwood. This money-drawer has six round cups for coin and compartments for bills of different denominations; is always set, and while as easily opened as a common drawer, it promptly sounds an alarm when tampered with. The mechanism of these drawers is simple, their opening combinations can be changed in a second, and they need no keys and require no repairs. Other specialties are the "Daisy" wrought iron adjustable stove truck, Stone's patent barrel truck (both of which are mounted on Martin's patent casters), the "Hoosier" saw-buck, slaw, vegetable and kraut cutters, towel rollers, folding and iron hook hat and coat racks, towel racks, potato mashers, steak mauls, muddlers, rolling-pins, wood-ball lemon squeezers, knife trays, tinners' mallets, eccentric bench hooks, etc. The trade of the company covers the entire Union and Canada, Mexico, South America, Australia, Great Britain and Europe. Mr. William H. Tucker, the President of this company, and Mr. Robert L. Dorsey, its Secretary and Treasurer, are similarly associated with the Phœnix Caster Co., and the business of both companies is transacted from the same office, under the management of the same officers, although separate and distinct in other respects.

Indiana Electric Service Co.

Controlling the Johnson Heat Regulating Apparatus; Main Office, 216 Fifth street, Louisville, Ky.; Indiana Office, English block, 82 Circle street; J. W. Cheney, Manager.—The advantages derived from the use of steam as an agency for supplying heat to buildings are in a great measure counterbalanced by the inefficiency of the appliances for the regulation of the steam supply ordinarily in use. The room becomes too warm and the valves are closed; it becomes too cold before the change in temperature is noticed. The consequence is a variability of temperature promotive of discomfort and injurious to health. These draw-backs to the effectiveness of steam-heating led to the invention, by Professor W. S. Johnson, of the Johnson Electric Valve. It is simple in mechanism, and by its use a practically invariable temperature is maintained, a great saving in cost to the occupants of rooms in watching the temperature is made, the hygienic condition of the room heated is vastly improved as a result of the equable temperature secured, and an important economy in fuel is made by avoiding the overheating resulting from the use of hand valves. The device can be especially well applied also to the regulation of heat from natural gas, or in fact, any source of heat conveyed by pipes. This electric valve is guaranteed to hold the heat within two degrees of any degree of temperature determined upon. They are used not only in churches, theatres and factories, but also in dwellings. In residences here the apparatus has been applied in those of Dr. O. S. Runnels, W. G. Sherman, the well-known restaurateur, and others. The manufacture of this apparatus was inaugurated in 1885, by the Johnson Electric Service Co., of Milwaukee, Wis., by which the sole manufacture of the apparatus, and its sale in the States of Wisconsin and Minnesota, is still controlled. In 1888, the Indiana Electric Service Co. was organized, and secured the control of this valuable invention for the States of Indiana and Kentucky, the main office of the company being at Louisville, and the Indiana office in the English block in this city. The apparatus has demonstrated its perfect effectiveness by its adoption in a large number of public and private buildings in all the leading cities, and is rapidly becoming popular in this and other cities controlled by the company. To this result Mr. J. W. Cheney, the Manager for Indiana, has largely contributed by the zealous and energetic methods adopted by him in making the merits of the invention known.

Hubert Recker & Co.

Manufacturers of Beer Coolers, Counters, Etc.; 209 and 211 East Washington street. This firm, composed of Hubert Recker, Gottlieb Recker and Theodore Sander, was organized in 1863. The senior member is the active manager of the business, his partners composing the furniture manufacturing firm of Sander & Recker. The firm is located as above, where they occupy premises 50 feet front on East Washington street and running back 200 feet to Pearl street. They are fully equipped for business and manufacturing purposes, having ample accommodations for the display of their artistic productions, and all modern machinery and appliances requisite to the promotion of their lines of output. These include bank and store fixtures, pews and fine interior woodwork for churches, halls, residences, etc., also beer coolers, counters, mirrors, and saloon fixtures generally, with which they have fitted up nearly all the first-class sample rooms in the city, including among them, The Office, Cooper's, Hugole's, The Circle House, and others. They also equipped the Merchants' National and Indianapolis National Banks, and many of the finest stores here, in addition to making the pews and fine woodwork for the Meridian Street church, St. Paul's church, and other ecclesiastical edifices. In the spring of 1888, they fitted up the great furnishing store of Paul Krotz, on West Washington street, with shelving, counters, show cases and other fixtures, a job that has attracted general admiration and the warmest commendation. They use the best qualities of well seasoned hardwoods of imported and American growth, and their products, which are in original and exquisite designs, elaborately carved and finished, are patterns of ornamental and durable workmanship in the highest degree. They employ a force of from fifteen to twenty skilful operatives, and minister to the wants of the trade throughout the city and State.

Munson Lightning Conductor Co. Manufacturer of Lightning Rods: Alvin J. Munson, Proprietor; 94 South Delaware street. The Munson Lightning Conductor Company was established in 1850 by David Munson, father of the present proprietor, Alvin J. Munson. The latter succeeded to the control of the enterprise in 1883, and has since conducted it with prosperous results, in which he has been ably assisted by his brothers, David R. Munson, William G. Munson and Samuel G. Munson. They occupy premises 25x200 feet in dimensions, divided into office and salesrooms, and containing a well equipped and completely appointed workshop. Their range of materials here embraces Munson's new copper tubular and cable lightning conductors, which have been successful in every contest since 1850, being constructed on scientific principles and indorsed by over

500 scientists and college professors as the best conductors ever invented, and the most complete protection against disaster by lightning known. The productions of Mr. Munson have been awarded gold, silver and bronze medals wherever exhibited, and have received the highest indorsements for efficiency and unsurpassed services in all portions of North and South America. They are employed on all the government buildings at Washington City, upon the churches, public edifices and private residences of Indianapolis, also upon the State institutions here, in addition to serving for purposes of protection as conductors and reliably in Baltimore, Philadelphia, Cincinnati, Chicago and other cities located in all sections of the United States. He employs from ten to twenty operatives and assistants, besides two travelers, and in addition to the trade supplied as above stated, ministers to the demands in England and elsewhere in Europe for this line of incalculably valuable productions.

C. B. Cones' Son & Co. Manufacturers of Cones' Boss Pantaloon Overalls, Etc.; 42 North Mississippi street. Though of comparatively recent development, this establishment is unsurpassed in its resources, equipment and superiority of workmanship in all

its lines of production. This industry was started in 1859 by C. B. Cones, Sr., the firm name subsequently becoming C. B. Cones & Co., and, in 1886, C. B. Cones' Son & Co. On the 13th of January, 1888, their place of business on South Meridian street was destroyed by fire, whereupon they purchased their present location, rebuilding and extending the improvements thereon, and completely adapting the premises to the uses for which they are now occupied. They consist of a three-story and basement building, facing the Capitol, having a frontage of fifty feet on North Mississippi street, and a depth of 200 feet. The equipment embraces 200 sewing machines, with a full complement of button hole and cutting machinery, and other labor-saving devices and appliances promotive of the quality and volume of the output, driven by steam. They are also supplied with accommodations for the storage and display of stock, the transaction of business and the prompt filling and shipment of orders of the largest magnitude, and do an annual business amounting to upwards of $350,000 in value. Their range of manufacture includes Cones' Boss pantaloon overalls, pants, shirts, hunting suits, boys' shirts and waists, and duck clothing generally in great variety. All of these lines are specialties of the house, being well known in all parts of the United States for the first-class qualities of the material of which they are composed, their utility and durable wear. The large demand which they annually supply, is expressive of the high degree of confidence they have inspired among dealers and with the public. They employ between 350 and 400 hands, in addition to ten traveling salesmen, and their trade is distributed throughout Indiana, Ohio, Illinois, Michigan, Missouri, Iowa, Kansas, Kentucky, Tennessee, Alabama, Mississippi, Georgia, Texas, and in other portions of the South and Southwest.

Holmes & Co. — Natural Gas and Steam-fitters; 90 East Market street.— E. E. Holmes and George E. Coburn, constituting the firm of Holmes & Co., who have enjoyed a practical experience of years in this field of industry, established themselves in business here during April, 1888, coming originally from Meadville, Pa., where they had been for years in the employ of the Standard Oil Company, piping a large territory for the substitution of natural gas, and completing some of the largest jobs in that specialty at the East, and of late from Uniontown, Scottdale and Connellsville, Pa., where they were in business for themselves. They were accompanied hither by a force of experienced assistants reputed to be superior workmen, and are fully equipped to execute contracts for work. They occupy premises 20x100 feet in size, supplied with machinery and tools necessary to their lines of operation, and carry large stocks of natural gas appliances and steam-heating apparatus, including pipes, fittings and fixtures, and sundries pertaining to the business, including all the latest improvements. They are prepared to do all work, general and special, in their lines, and are enabled to furnish references from clients in Indianapolis who have availed themselves of the facilities and services they tender to the patronage of the public. All orders receive prompt attention and their prices are of the lowest character consistent with the quality of materials used and the high class work rendered. They employ from seventeen to twenty expert operatives, and their trade is steadily increasing in the city and vicinity.

Joseph Gardner—Manufacturer of all kinds of Tin, Copper and Sheet Iron Work, Dealer in Hot Air Furnaces; 39 and 41 Kentucky avenue; Telephone No, 322.— This business was established in 1882 by the present proprietor, who occupies the main floor and basement of premises, 20x60 feet, containing office and display rooms, also a well equipped workshop, provided with ample accommodations and all requisite labor saving devices and mechanical appliances. His specialties are roofing, cornice and spout work for residences, public buildings, etc., in all of which he excels, furnishing the best materials and conducting and completing jobs in either and all of these special departments, in a manner so skilful and efficient as to commend his services to a large and steadily increasing patronage. He also manufactures full lines of tin, sheet iron and copper ware for household use, confection, distilling, brewing and other purposes, for which they are especially adapted, and exercising the same personal supervision and diligence in their composition and production. In addition, he is agent here for the Reynolds, Magee and the Bartlett Sons' Wrought Iron Hot Air Furnaces, which have come into general use, and attained to a large popularity throughout the country. He is prepared to undertake contracts for roofing, adjusting metal skylights, dormer windows, spouts, etc.; and to fill orders, either made personally or over his telephone, No. 322, for general tin, copper and sheet iron work promptly, in the most satisfactory manner, and at the lowest prices. He employs from eight to ten competent assistants, and enjoys a high reputation for experience, enterprise and durable work throughout the city and State, in which he does a large trade in all his lines.

Brower & Love Brothers — Proprietors of the Indiana Warp Mills; Manufacturers of Cotton Warps; Office and Mills on White River, North of Washington street.— This firm, of which Messrs. Abram G. Brower, John R. Love and Hugh M. Love are the individual members, established in business five years ago, succeeding to the business of the Indianapolis Cotton Manufacturing Company, who began operating the mills in 1864. The premises occupied embrace the main mill, a three-story brick structure 100x50 feet in dimensions, with a one-story extension, 140x50 feet, and a new addition now approaching completion, 75x45 feet, as well as spacious boiler and engine houses. The machinery equipment includes a 250-horse power engine, fed by five large boilers, 5,500 spindles, and all the most highly improved machinery adapted to the business. Employment is given to from seventy-five to eighty hands in the manufacture of cotton warp of the best quality, in which a large trade is done in the South and Southwest, a leading market for the product being Louisville, Ky. The operations are extensive, utilizing an average of about 1,500 bales of cotton annually, making over 7,000 warps, each of 1,500 ends and 650 yards in length. Close supervision is maintained, so as to secure in the product the highest standard of merit. All of the members of the firm are business men of a high character and standing. The establishment enjoys a gratifying and steadily growing success.

H. C. Chandler — Designer and Engraver on Wood; 13 East Washington street.—Mr. Chandler began the business here in 1863, and long since established a reputation for beauty and originality of conception and superior excellence of execution. He occupies commodious accommodations, divided into office and operating rooms, provided with every appliance requisite to the prompt service of the trade in every department. His lines of work include the designing and production of fine illustrated catalogues for furniture, fancy goods and other manufactures, cuts of buildings, portraits, fine mechanical work, maps, diagrams, and engraving generally for illustrative and advertising purposes, for which he has secured a well-deserved prominence, his productions being the most perfect embodiments of the latest artistic development in delicacy of coloring, harmonious blending of light and shade, and beauty of effect. Orders are promptly filled. His prices are low, considering the character of the work required by his high class of custom, and his liberal and honorable management commands the confidence of patrons and the public. He employs competent assistants and does a large and increasing trade in the city and State, as also throughout Ohio and Illinois.

C. H. Black Manufacturing Co. — Carriages, Surreys, Phaetons, Etc.; 44 East Maryland street.—The C. H. Black Manufacturing Co., of which H. Z. Beck is President and C. H. Black Secretary and Manager, is a representative establishment engaged in the manufacture of carriages and vehicles. They occupy a three-story and basement building, 25x100 feet in dimensions, with the two upper floors of the premises at 42 East Maryland street, similar in dimensions and arrangement. The main building extends through to East Maryland street, where it connects with a two-story and basement building, 35x30 feet, and numbered 44 on the latter thoroughfare. The premises are equipped with all requisite machinery and appliances, and provided with commodious display and storage accommo-

dations, as also with complete repair and shipping facilities. Their specialty is physicians' phaetons, a conveyance unrivalled for comfort, smooth running and durable materials, with capacity to stand the severest usage. They also manufacture and keep in stock first-class carriages, side-bar and end-spring buggies, business and delivery wagons, road and village carts, and other vehicles of all the leading styles, and harness of equal efficiency and superior workmanship. Their productions are in every feature as comprehensive as they are desirable. They publish an illustrated catalogue and the house is known east and west for its liberal terms and honorable dealings. Their general work finds an extensive demand in the city and State, and their phaetons are shipped to points as far west as California, throughout the South, to New York, Pennsylvania, Connecticut and other Eastern States, also in Canada and other of the British possessions in North America. The services of from twenty to twenty-five experienced operatives are required, and their annual business foots up largely in value.

I. H. Herrington — Manufacturer and Dealer in Light and Heavy Harness; 81 East Market street. Mr. Herrington began business in 1871 and has since been identified with the manufacture of saddlery and harness, each year being required to increase his facilities to comply with the requirements of the steadily augmenting demand. He is located in one of the most bustling and thriving business portions of Indianapolis, where he occupies a three-story and basement building, 35x100 feet in size and apportioned into sales and warerooms, also containing a large and well equipped workshop, provided with every facility and convenience for the manufacture of every article known to the trade. Chief among these are light and heavy harness, adapted to every service, light and heavy saddles for both ladies and gentlemen, bridles, collars, whips, robes, blankets, brushes, stable sundries, horse clothing, etc., complete and full, of the best grades of material and the most finished workmanship. Everything in his line of production is a specialty, the make of which is skilled and superior operatives is under the personal supervision of Mr. Herrington, which fact, combined with other excellencies and the liberal terms offered customers, has served to give to the house the reputation it enjoys among the leading in its lines here and throughout the State. He employs a force of seven assistants and does a large trade in the city and vicinity, in addition to supplying an extensive demand in portions of Indiana, distant from the base of operations.

Arcade Mills — Blanton, Watson & Co., Proprietors; 200 West Maryland street.— The Arcade Mills were established by L. H. Blanton and W. R. Watson in 1879, and though Mr. Blanton has for sometime been sole proprietor, the business has always been conducted under the firm name of Blanton, Watson & Co. The premises occupied cover an area of 60x245 feet, including the mill proper, a four-story and basement brick structure, 60x80 feet in dimensions, with a brick extension used for engine room and boiler house, and an elevator adjoining 60x120 feet in size. The mill is thoroughly equipped with all the latest improved roller process machinery, and turns out 350 barrels of flour daily. The elevator is provided with facilities for the convenient receipt and handling of grain, and has a storage capacity of 18,000 bushels. The lines of production embrace those usual to first-class flouring mills, Mr. Blanton, however, making specialties of "Crown Jewel," "Princess" and other favorite brands of roller process flour, made from the best grades of winter and spring wheat, selected with especial reference to quality, and for purity and absolute intrinsic worth are not surpassed by those of any similar industry in the State. They stand very high with dealers and the trade, either for domestic or bakers' use, and are in constant demand by consumers here and in other portions of the country. Mr. Blanton employs twenty experienced assistants, and supplies the trade throughout the southern and eastern portions of the United States, besides filling extensive orders from Glasgow, Liverpool and other European markets. He is a man of enterprise, and his success is the result of an honorable career and liberal management.

The improved taste for artistic development and production which is apparent in Indianapolis is mainly responsible for the establishment of the designing and engraving house of Charles A. Nicoli, in 1889. He is unselfish in the profession and the delineation of his subjects deserves and commands the high meed of admiration they elicit. He occupies commodious apartments in the Hubbard block, amply arranged and appointed for the business. He makes a specialty of commercial work, and for fine, original designing, neatness and taste is unsurpassed. He also does color work for catalogues of

manufactories and business houses, for show cards and illuminated advertisements. No cheap work is done; only engraving capable of producing the best results is even attempted, and such results are universally conceded to be of a superior order. He is prepared to furnish every description of production in his lines promptly, and his prices are as low as are consistent with the requirements of the service. He employs from six to eight assistants, and does a large trade in the city and throughout Indiana, Illinois, Ohio, Minnesota and elsewhere.

Hoosier Woolen Factory C. E. Giesendorf & Co., Proprietors; 401 West Washington street.—This establishment, the pioneer of its kind in Indianapolis, was founded by C. E. Giesendorf and Christian Giesendorf, brothers, in 1846, and was equipped with what was then the latest improved machinery, carted from Dayton, O., there being no railway facilities available. Since that date all the best patterns of machinery and appliances have been added as fast as they were obtainable, until it is to-day conceded to be perfect in all its appointments and appliances. The brothers operated the factory for some years, and upon the death of G. W. Giesendorf the present firm, consisting of C. E. Giesendorf and Isaac Thalman, was organized. The woolen mill and warehouse occupy a three-story and basement building, 50x250 feet in dimensions. Their range of manufacture embraces ten-quarter wide skirting, flannels that are warranted not to shrink, and tinted with colors guaranteed to be safe and healthy; plaid and flannel blankets in all colors, and of pure wool; Scotch novelty suitings, tweeds, jeans, warranted pure wool filling and fast colors; stocking yarn free from all poisonous colors, satinets, etc., which are carried in large invoices and sold to the trade at the lowest prices consistent with their superiority in respect to materials and workmanship. They also deal heavily in wool, carrying selected fleeces, first-class in all respects, and having a high reputation with the trade. They employ from fifty to sixty hands, in addition to five traveling salesmen, and their trade extends throughout the East, West, North and Northwest in every direction, also being equally extensive in New York City, Philadelphia, and other large depots of manufacture and supply in different parts of the United States.

Spiegel, Thoms & Co.—Manufacturers and Dealers in Furniture and Chairs; 71 and 73 West Washington street.—The firm

of Spiegel, Thoms & Co., composed of Augustus Spiegel, Frederick Thoms and Henry Frank, was organized during 1855, since which date the firm name has remained unchanged, though Christian Spiegel, one of the original founders, retired from the business about 1873. They occupy as salesrooms a massive iron front building, five stories high, fronting 40 feet on West Washington street, and extending 500 feet in depth to a like frontage on Kentucky avenue. Their factory, extending from 50 to 74 East street, consists of a double five-story and basement building, 50x106 feet in dimensions, equipped with all modern machinery and appliances, and provided with complete facilities for handling the products. The salesrooms are furnished with elevator service and finely departmented. The main floor is devoted to the display of rattan goods and fancy furniture, the second floor to parlor, library and upholstered furniture, the third to furniture for chamber and dining room equipments, the fourth to surplus stock, and the fifth to the upholstering departments. The floors in this building are built independent of the walls, being separately supported from the foundations up. Their special lines of manufacture are fine parlor tables, extension dining tables, hall stands and racks, ladies' fancy desks, escritoires, etc. They are also sole proprietors of Wotch's patent machine for destroying moths in furniture and carpets. Only the best materials are employed in every line, and their facilities are so complete and effective that they insure to customers and the trade cheapness in price, superior workmanship and unsurpassed durability. A force of 130 operatives, from ten to twenty salesmen and seven travelers are kept constantly in the service, and their trade is distributed in all parts of the United States, from Maine to California. The affairs of the concern are managed with liberality and enterprise and the concern itself occupies a front rank among the manufacturing and commercial undertakings of the West.

Comstock & Coonse — Manufacturers of Wooden Chain and Wooden Force Pumps; 199 South Meridian street. This business was originally established by R. A. Durban in 1850, the firm subsequently becoming Durban & Douglas, and in 1871 A. S. Durban & Co., being composed of A. S. Durban and A. S. Comstock, head of the present firm. In 1876 the latter succeeded to the sole ownership and in 1880, upon the admission of G. W. Coonse as a partner, the firm of Comstock & Coonse was organized. They occupy a two-story and basement building, 50x100 feet in dimensions, completely equipped with all the latest improved machinery and appliances, and also occupy the two-story and basement building, 25x100 feet in dimensions, at 34 East South street, for warehouse purposes. They carry heavy lines of stock of their own manufacture, including the Coonse Force Pump, a superior article in its line; also wood, chain and wooden force pumps, iron pumps, pitcher spout pumps, tubing, iron and lead pipe, rubber hose, hose connections, nozzles, pipe wrenches, drive well points and cylinders, plumbers' sinks and other articles connected with their lines in chief. The greatest pains are taken in their manufacture, the lumber being subjected to the most critical inspection, and the selection and finishing of the working parts of the pumps, buckets, leathers, valves, etc., receiving especial attention. Their facilities for promptly and satisfactorily filling and shipping orders are complete, goods leaving the city always on the day of shipment, and being pushed to their destination with all possible speed, and every effort is made to meet the demand with the least trouble or expense. They employ from twenty-five to thirty assistants, besides two travelers, and do a large and constantly augmenting trade throughout Indiana, Ohio, Illinois, Minnesota, Kentucky, New York, New Jersey and in other portions of the South and East, in all of which territory the house exerts a wide-spread influence and enjoys a distinguished reputation.

William Wiegel—Manufacturer of Fine Show Cases; 6 West Louisiana street.—The Capital City Show Case Works was established by Mr. Wiegel in conjunction with Mr. Ruehl during 1877, and operated until 1887 under the firm name of Wiegel & Ruehl, when the senior partner succeeded to the sole ownership of the enterprise. He occupies a four-story and basement building.

sixteen feet in dimensions, equipped with all requisite machinery and appliances for speedy and finished production, also containing ample accommodations for storage and display purposes, in addition to very available shipping facilities. His specialty is the manufacture of the celebrated celluloid cases, which, with nearly all his lines, are made to order. His range of production embraces plain, square, round front, upright, circle, mansard, single and double monitor cases for ordinary use, also for special purposes, such as prescription, cigars, perfumeries, fancy articles, nick-nacks, etc., for counter, side wall and center of stores. They are made of bird's-eye maple, mahogany, rosewood, cherry, walnut, and other hardwoods, with improved hardwood sliding doors, the silver mouldings being the very best 18 per cent. German silver, and the product in every way first-class. No cheap or shoddy work is turned out by Mr. Wiegel, who is himself a practical mechanic and personally attends to the business, employing none but experienced workmen familiar with their trade. All orders receive prompt attention, and all sales are made at prices as low as is consistent with good workmanship and honest material. He carries large stocks of cases, iron show-case stands, spring hinges, alarm money tills, etc., giving employment to from eight to ten hands, and does a large trade throughout Indiana, Ohio and Illinois.

Indianapolis Manufacturers' and Carpenters' Union— Manufacturers of Sash, Doors, Blinds, Etc.; 38, 40 and 42 South New Jersey street. This company was incorporated in 1874, as successor to Warren Tate, who established the business in 1864. The present officers are Val. Schaaf, President and Superintendent, with Fred Schmid, Secretary and Treasurer, and their management of the company's affairs is characterized by methods that materially contribute to the prosperity of the corporation. They occupy a three-story structure, 60x200 feet, with large and fully stocked lumber yards yards adjoining. The mechanical equipment embraces all the latest improved machinery and appliances, including, planers, edgers, cutters,

trimmers, grooving machines, etc., replacing old machinery with that of more recent patterns as soon as the improvements proposed are perfected, the whole driven by an engine of 150-horse power, with steam furnished from a battery of two five-flue boilers. Their range of manufacture is large and varied, including doors, sash and blinds, door and window frames, brackets, moulding, etc., flooring, ceiling, rough and dressed pine, poplar and ash lumber. They also dress lumber and work flooring to order, deal in frame lumber, shingles and lath, newels and balusters, and extensively engage in job turning. They employ from seventy-five to one hundred hands, and supply the demands of a large and constantly increasing trade among builders and contractors in the city and throughout the surrounding country.

Wm. H. Armstrong & Co.—Manufacturers and Importers of Surgical Instruments; 93 South Illinois street. The firm of Wm. H. Armstrong & Co., are a recent accession to Indianapolis commercial circles. It is composed of W. H. Armstrong and Emil Willbrandt, the latter being admitted to the firm on January 1, 1889. The business was established some years ago removing from Terre Haute to this city January 1, 1889, since which date they have continued

here the manufacture and importation of surgical instruments which they had carried on at Terre Haute. They occupy a handsomely fitted up store 25x100 feet, well equipped with machinery of a special character for the work to which they are devoted, and provided with conveniences and facilities for display and trade purposes. They carry heavy stocks of goods in their lines, of European and American make and reputation, also of their own manufacture of the best quality of material and effective and serviceable for the uses to which they are applied. Their supplies are made up of surgical instruments, deformity apparatus, trusses, elastic hosiery, splints, crutches, rubber and cotton webbing, shoulder and spine braces, adjustable hip extension and ankle braces etc. The composition of the instruments and appliances handled is of standard worth and well known reliability, and they are sold at the regular market prices and terms. The firm, though in operation here but a short time, have made an excellent reputation for skill in their specialties, and for the variety and quality of their goods, which are in extensive use as far east as New York and Pennsylvania, as also in the North, Northwest, Southwest and South. They employ a large number of operatives, including three salesmen, and are prepared to promptly fill and ship orders to customers in any portion of the United States.

J. M. Bohmie Carriage Manufacturer; 223 and 225 East Washington street. The oldest and among the most experienced practical carriage makers here is J. M. Bohmie. He located at Indianapolis at the close of the war, having served through that trying period as a member of an Illinois regiment, and entered the service of the Shaw Carriage Company, with which he remained in the capacity of foreman for a period of fifteen years. Upon the retirement from business of the company, in 1876, Mr. Bohmie embarked in the same line on his own account, opening an establishment on New Jersey street, where he remained until 1887, when he removed to his present site. He owns and occupies commodious premises, 35x200 feet in dimensions, provided with all necessary machinery and implements for building, equipping and furnishing the finest grades of vehicles, from a light road wagon to the most substantial and elaborate coaches and hearses. He makes only to order, and has the reputation of manufacturing the handsomest proportioned and smoothest running buggies and carriages to be found in the city. He uses only the best materials, the woodwork being second-growth, thoroughly seasoned hickory, and the iron and steel included in the running gear are of equal excellence and tested worth. His works are in constant operation in the filling of orders from the city and all parts of the State, giving employment to a force of twenty-five skilled operatives, and he does an annual trade aggregating between $40,000 and $50,000 in value. The superior product turned out, low prices and honorable business methods are known and esteemed by the trade in all directions.

Indianapolis Moulding and Picture Frame Co.—Manufacturers of Hardwood Mouldings; 606 to 630 Madison avenue. This business was established in 1874, and the gentlemen composing the firm are Messrs. John F. Mayer, H. Lieber and W. Wellmann, all of whom are gentlemen of experience and ability, devoting their energies to the details of the business and fully cognizant of the requirements of the trade. They occupy a three-story and basement brick building, 50x150 feet in dimensions, a large addition to the factory having been built last Fall, and have spacious lumber yards, commodious storage sheds, and every convenience and facility as well for the receipt of materials and shipment of their products as for the successful prosecution of the manufacturing operations. The machinery equipment includes a 75-horse power engine, two large boilers, five large moulding machines, planers, lathes, saws of various descriptions, and all other appliances adapted to aid or expedite the operations of the business. A force ranging from fifty to sixty hands is employed in the manufacture of all kinds of hardwood mouldings, both plain and ornamental, which they make a specialty of. Indianapolis being a particularly favorable location for the prosecution of such an enterprise, on account of its superior shipping facilities, and the wood used being all grown in the State. The firm enjoys a deservedly high reputation for the superiority of its products, which has secured for them a demand not only covering the entire Union and Canada, but also including a considerable export trade to England and Australia. A large stock is constantly carried, which enables them to fill orders in a prompt and satisfactory manner. The firm maintains a New York office, at 43 West Broadway, Mr. A. Muehsam, agent, is a gentleman of first-class business abilities, with a large acquaintance among the picture-frame dealers in the large Eastern cities, and the fact that he has represented the firm for the last ten years, and in that long period succeeding in not only keeping almost all his old customers but yearly adding a large number of new ones, speaks very highly for him. The sagacity of the proprietors in conducting their business, and the reliability of their methods, have combined to give to their enterprise its present foremost standing and to secure a steady and continuous expansion in the volume of their trade.

Emrich, Paulini & Co.—Manufacturers of Furniture; 100 to 200 West Morris street. This prominent manufacturing firm, of which Messrs. H. Emrich, O. B. Paulini and S. P. Porter are the individual members, was established seven years ago, and has since built up a large and steadily growing business in all parts of the Union, and especially in the leading Eastern cities. The plant is an extensive one, covering over one and one-half acres of ground, and including, in addition to extensive lumber yards, a two-story factory, 50x220 feet in dimensions, and a two-story warehouse, 50x150 feet. The factory has a complete equipment of the latest and most improved woodworking machinery, a 70-horse power engine and large boilers, and employment is given to a force ranging from eighty to ninety hands in the manufacture of imitation walnut bedsteads, of which this firm makes an exclusive specialty. The bedsteads, which are made of fine hickory, are finished in such an exact imitation of the finest walnut as to defy the scrutiny of the closest observer, retaining their appearance throughout their terms of service, and are equally as durable as the genuine walnut goods. They are made in the most attractive and stylish designs, and supply the need of the public for a handsome and serviceable bedstead, at a moderate price. The firm enjoys the most superior facilities for the production of these goods, and orders are filled in a prompt and satisfactory manner. The members of the firm are all practically conversant with the details of the business and have secured, by their uniformly accurate and reliable methods of dealing, a firmly established place in the confidence of the trade.

American Paper Box Co.—Manufacturers of Paper Boxes; corner of New York and Alabama streets. The American Paper Box Company was established in this city during 1884, by W. A. Ford, being then located on South Meridian street, whence they removed to their present site in 1886, where they have built up a large and prosperous business, which is continually increasing and extending. The premises occupied are 50x100 feet in dimensions. The first floor is devoted to the storage and stock rooms, and the second floor, which is lofty, well lighted and ventilated, is occupied for manufacturing purposes and equipped with all modern facilities and appliances, requisite to the economical production of superior stocks. The factory is soon to be remodeled and will be the largest in the State. Their make includes paper boxes of every character and description, for dry goods houses, hatters, milliners, confectioners, druggists, dealers in fancy articles, physicians, and for other lines of professional, commercial and manufacturing business, in every size and in great variety. They carry large and full lines of these articles of utility and ornament, also of the best quality of straw board, and orders by mail, telegraph or in person will be promptly and satisfactorily filled. Mr. Ford, the Superintendent, who has been identified with this enterprise from its inception, is a master mechanic in every branch of the business, and personally supervises the business in all its details. He has invented a machine for cutting paper boxes which is far superior to any now in use. The affairs of the company are managed on liberal and honorable principles, and the excellent quality of their goods, combined with the cheapest prices in the State, command them a large and steadily growing trade in the city and

throughout the State. From ten to twenty-five hands, according to the season, are employed, and the company invites everybody to visit them and see them manufacture paper boxes. They are prepared to make every article in the paper box line, also to print labels in any style. By patronizing home industry employment is given to our own citizens, the city is built up and a home market is established, and no local enterprise is more worthy of encouragement than that of the American Paper Box Co.

Thompson Brothers Manufacturers of Tables, Hat Racks, Etc.; Dimension Stock Cut to Order; 293 and 295 Christian avenue.— This firm, of which Messrs. R. W. and L. C. Thompson are the individual members, was formed in November, 1888. Mr. R. W. Thompson resides at Burlington, Ia., where he is engaged as Cashier of the Burlington Insurance Company, and the business here is under the supervision of his brother, Mr. L. C. Thompson, who brings to the enterprise the benefit of a long and practical experience, having been for seven years superintendent of the works of D. E. Stone & Co., in the same line, which were destroyed by fire in 1888. The works operated by the firm embrace a two-story mill, 70x100 feet in dimensions, a large brick boiler house and a steaming and drying house. The equipment includes a 60-horse power engine, a 60x14 boiler, a large patent steamer for steaming lumber before going to the dry house, and a full outfit of the best modern woodworking machinery. A force ranging from forty-five to fifty hands is employed, and a large business is done in cutting dimension stock in walnut and other hardwoods to order, principally for Eastern organ builders, sewing machine and furniture manufacturers, etc.; and the firm also manufactures furniture for local cabinet makers to order, and all the products are of the best quality. All of the operations of the works are conducted under the immediate personal supervision of Mr. L. C. Thompson. Although of recent inauguration the enterprise has already been attended by a notable and gratifying success, the volume of orders filled being steadily on the increase, and the establishment has already secured a substantial place in the favor and confidence of the trade.

W. H. Short—Paper Box Manufacturer; 27 South Meridian street.—The factory of W. H. Short was established by that gentleman in 1876 to supply the wants of a local trade in paper boxes, and during his experience he has several times been compelled to increase his facilities and enlarge his accommodations to keep pace with the requirements of the service. Located in the midst of the commercial and jobbing interests, to whose wants he specially ministers, he occupies premises 40x80 feet in dimensions, and completely equipped and appointed in every department for the prompt filling of orders. His products include boxes of every description, and for every purpose, from the delicate artistic article used for the choicest lines of bon-bons and French candies, to the more substantial grades of boxes adapted to goods of a more cumbersome character. They are made of the best and most approved materials, in any form, shape or design, furnished in the latest style, and plain or ornamented, as the taste or necessity of the trade demands. He employs from twelve to fifteen hands, and his trade is in the city and surrounding country. Mr. Short is experienced in his range of manufacture, doing superior work and selling at low prices, inducements which are appreciated by the public and the trade.

Central Chair Co.—Manufacturers of Cane and Upholstered Chairs and Rockers; corner Georgia and Missouri streets.—The Central Chair Company, which occupies a leading position in its line of industry, was incorporated in 1884, as successor to A. D. Streight, who established the business in 1880, and under its present management has been successful from its inception. The present officers are: T. L. Thompson, President; C. F. Woerner, Vice-President, and B. F. Schmid, Secretary; gentlemen of large capital, long experience, and thoroughly familiar with the requirements of a large trade handling their lines exclusively. They occupy a four-story and basement brick building, 50x180 feet in dimensions, for factory purposes, with a two-story warehouse 50x100 feet in size, and a commodious lumber-yard containing drying kilns, storage sheds, and other premises adjoining. The factory proper is completely equipped with all the requisite carving, turning, planing, and other furniture machinery of the latest improved pattern, driven by a powerful engine fed from a battery of boilers of the most modern design. They manufacture an almost endless variety of cane chairs and rockers, while their designs in upholstered furniture are fully as complete and comprehensive, made of the best grades of mahogany, antique oak, cherry, walnut, imitation walnut and mahogany, and other hardwoods susceptible of the highest polish, and finished in silk, satin, velvet, brocatelle and rep. They are in all respects the most perfect in their lines offered to the trade, products of superior workmanship and durability, and both for use and ornament challenge successful competition. The company is prepared to fill and ship orders of any magnitude to any point in the United States, at low prices and upon the most liberal terms; and the high standard of work in which they have been so pre-eminently successful has secured a very large and

early years of the business, two partners, who subsequently retired, and he continued alone until January 1, 1888, when Mr. Albert Sahm, who had begun with the house in 1872 as apprentice, and later became successively bookkeeper and financial manager, was admitted to the firm. The warehouse premises comprise a four-story and basement building, 19x90 feet in dimensions, at 451 and 455 North Alabama street. In the rear of this building the firm had a four-story and basement factory, running back to 128, 130 and 132 Fort Wayne avenue, which was burned February 22, 1889, with a loss of $25,000, only met by insurance to the amount of $15,000. They at once secured temporary manufacturing quarters, and started to rebuild the burned premises, to be used in the future as upholstering and finishing shape, which will be comprised in a two-story building, 60x130 feet in area. At Hanway street, on the L. M. & I. Railroad, they have erected a large factory, under the personal supervision of Mr. Stechhan, which is completely equipped with the most modern and improved machinery, and affords the far better facilities than

OTTO STECHHAN & COMPANY'S BUILDINGS.

profitable trade within the territory between Philadelphia and the Mississippi River. They employ 100 operatives and assistants, besides four traveling salesmen, and the house has achieved a success and reputation enjoyed by very few of its contemporaries in the West.

Otto Stechhan & Co.—Manufacturers of Lounges, Parlor Suites and Reclining Chairs for the Trade Only; Office and Ware-room, 451, 453 and 455 North Alabama street. This important manufacturing establishment affords a striking example of the rewards which attend patient industry when directed by sagacious methods and sound business management. It was started by Mr. Otto Stechhan, who began in 1874 in a retail way, afterward adding the manufacturing department and himself doing a large portion of the work. The production of a superior quality of goods soon secured for him a steady expansion of trade which necessitated constant additions to the facilities for manufacture. Mr. Stechhan had, in the

ever before for carrying on the business upon an extensive scale. Employment is given to a force ranging from 125 to 150 hands in the manufacture of lounges, parlor suites and reclining chairs, and a large business is also done in the production of frames for other manufacturers. The firm is favorably known and largely patronized by the trade in all parts of the United States and Canada, and a staff of four active and competent traveling salesmen is constantly employed. Mr. Stechhan is an experienced manufacturer, whose thorough and practical knowledge of the business has been a leading factor in the success attained by the house, and Mr. Sahm, his partner, is a business man of superior attainments who efficiently looks after the office and financial affairs of the house.

R. R. Miles—Manufacturer of Jeans and Cassimere Pants; 70 South Illinois street. Mr. Miles engaged in his present line of operations during 1884, having, for a period of four years previously, been engaged in the dry goods business. In the spring of 1888, the increase of trade demanding more commodious accommodations, he removed from 29 and 33 South Meridian street to his present location, where he occupies premises complete and available in every particular. They consist of a three-story and basement building, 20x125 feet, equipped with all requisite machinery and appliances and furnished with every facility for the exposition of the choice lines of goods carried in stock. His specialty is the manufacture to order of jeans and cassimere pants at prices cheaper than are demanded for the same description of materials and articles ready made, and a large patronage attests the superior excellence of his output. He also manufactures overalls, shirts, drawers, etc., and is prepared to promptly fill all orders for these commodities in all sizes and patterns, cheaper than they can be obtained elsewhere. In addition to the above he handles gents' furnishing goods of every description, including underwear and socks in silk, woolen, flannel, and of lighter materials, linen and muslin shirts, neckwear and novelties, imported and domestic, in great variety and of the choicest qualities. He employs from forty to fifty hands, and does a large trade throughout the city and State, in addition to jobbing extensively among retail clothiers.

William Langsenkamp — Manufacturer of Brew Kettles, Soda Fountains, Etc.; 100 South Delaware, corner Georgia street.

Mr. Langsenkamp has been engaged in business as a coppersmith for a period of twenty-one years, having established himself here in 1867, since which he has conducted a large and prosperous business, and acquired an established reputation for superior workmanship and liberal dealing. He occupies the main floor and basement of premises 25x125 feet in size, including workshops, office and salesrooms, each well equipped with all necessary appliances adapted to the business. His lines of production embrace brew kettles, soda fountains, false bottoms, beer coolers, alcohol stills, columns, gas generators, candy kettles, dyers' cylinders, vulcanizers, etc., of the best qualities of material, and made and finished in the best manner. He also engages extensively in the fitting of steam and natural gas pipe in private residences and public buildings, in which he is equally successful, and carries full lines of sheet copper and brass, copper and brass tubing, and other supplies incidental to his lines in chief. He employs a force of from five to eight competent operatives and does a large trade in the city and State, in addition to filling orders from portions of Ohio and Illinois, and his annual business foots up largely in volume and value.

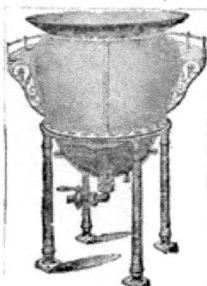

John Guedelhoefer — Wagon and Carriage Builder; corner Kentucky avenue and Georgia street.

Mr. Guedelhoefer began business here during 1875, in a shop but twelve feet square, with limited facilities and still more limited resources, but through the exercise of industry, enterprise and honorable dealings, his equipment has been steadily increased, his field of operations been steadily extended, and his line of productions augmented in volume and value. He now occupies a triangular piece of ground, upon which has been erected a blacksmith shop 30x60 feet in dimensions, a wagon factory 30x80 feet, and a building 40x100 feet in dimensions, occupied by the woodworking, painting and finishing departments, also for the storage of stock. He purposes still further increasing his facilities, having recently purchased property opposite his present site, 40 feet front on Georgia street and 125 feet deep, whereon he will immediately erect a fully equipped and completely appointed manufactory, provided with all requisite machinery for supplying the demand of his large and constantly increasing patronage. He builds

every description of vehicles, including carriages, buggies, light road and delivery wagons, heavy and platform wagons, the finest laundry wagons, and the cheapest and best patented butcher wagons in the city, as well as heavy, the running gear for threshing machinery, and other conveyances adapted to the wants of purchasers, of every character and description. Only the best materials are employed in their construction and finish, and when completed, they are models of design, durability and skilled workmanship. In addition to his manufacture, he does general blacksmithing and horse-shoeing work, also job work in painting, repairing and trimming, and executes all contracts in these lines, promptly and at the lowest rates. He employs a force of twenty experienced hands to keep pace with the demands of his large trade in the city and vicinity, and his establishment is managed so liberally and with such honorable enterprise as to secure for him an invaluable and influential reputation. He manufactures the cheapest and best patented butcher wagons in the city.

Thos. J. Hamilton — Manufacturer of Fine Cigars; 52 and 54 Kentucky avenue.

Mr. Hamilton established his business here in 1877 and has secured a reputation for pure production, reasonable prices, liberal terms and honorable methods as invaluable as it is influential and established. He conducts his business prudently, keeping his rents and expenses at a low figure, so as to put money in goods, but his premises are equipped with all requisite appliances for the speedy and economical manufacture of his lines, all of which are favorites and in large demand with the trade. His specialties are "La Blonde," "Hambletonian" and "Flora," 10 cent cigars; "Chance," "Board of Trade," "Little Habana," "Marion County," "Indiana Belle," "Home Rule" and other favorite and celebrated brands. These are made of the best growth of imported and domestic tobaccos, possessing in a marked degree purity, flavor and other qualities so indispensable to the requirements of a patronage that is both exacting and critical, and are to be obtained in quantities to suit, at reasonable prices and upon liberal terms. He also manufactures special brands to order for a large trade, employing the same care and exercising the greatest degree of protection for the interests of his patrons. From thirteen to sixteen assistants and operatives are retained in the service by Mr. Hamilton, who is a practical cigar manufacturer himself, and does a large trade in the city and surrounding country, throughout both of which his house is regarded as a depot of supply, offering unsurpassed inducements to the trade in every particular.

Indianapolis Planing Mill Co. — Manufacturers of Doors, Window Frames, Etc.; corner Meridian and Wilkins streets.

This company was incorporated in January, 1889, as successors to the business theretofore conducted by the firm of Knickerbocker & Novial, proprietors of the old South Meridian street planing mill, the site of which is occupied by the present corporation. The management of the establishment and its operations are directed by an executive board, of which William Kraas is President, D. Mussmann, Treasurer, and C. Haupt, Secretary, with Louis F. Burtin, Manager. They are men of experience in the business, enterprising in the promotion of its magnitude and importance, and liberal in their dealings with the trade. The planing mill occupies a two-story building, 50x100 feet in dimensions, and is amply equipped with every facility and mechanical appliance for rapid and economical production, including planers, edgers, trimmers, re-sawers, tongue and grooving machines, etc., driven by an engine of 50-horse power, fed from a battery of boilers, 4x16 feet in size. The lumber yard, warehouse for the storage of finished materials, dry kilns and other appurtenances adjoin the mill, and are adequately provided with conveniences and facilities. From thirty to thirty-five hands are employed, and the lines of manufacture embrace door and window frames, interior wood work, mouldings of every description, also doing scroll and band sawing, and dealing extensively in hard and soft wood lumber, rough and finished, lath, shingles, etc., with other supplies and sundries for building purposes. Their stocks and products are unsurpassed in respect to quality and material, specially adapted to the uses for which they are designed, and in all respects meeting the requirements of the most exacting patronage. They do a large established trade in the city and vicinity, principally with contractors and builders, and all orders are promptly filled.

Architectural Iron Works Frederick Noelke, Proprietor; 212 to 224 South Pennsylvania street. This manufacturing establishment was founded by Noelke & Co., in 1872, the firm becoming Noelke, Smallwood & Co. in 1876, but in the year following, Mr. Frederick Noelke became sole owner, and has since continued in that capacity. He owns and occupies extensive premises, the foundry

being two stories high, 188x80 feet in size, and amply equipped with the machinery and appliances adapted to his varied lines of production, with other conveniences and appointments for the transaction of business and the shipment of orders. His line of manufacture embraces jail and court house work, iron trusses, girders, columns and lintels, iron beams, stairs, doors and gratings, bridge and roof bolts, and all kinds of iron building material. He did the iron work on the City Hall and Market House, Catholic Hospital, Schmidt's Brewery, and many other public and private buildings in Indianapolis and other cities in this and the adjoining States. In all of these, and in all other contracts executed by Mr. Noelke, the best qualities of wrought iron are used, and the prices and workmanship are such as to increase the value of the establishment as a productive enterprise, and Indianapolis as a manufacturing center. He employs a force of twenty-five hands, and his trade is in the State in all directions.

L. W. Ott Manufacturing Co. W. F. Kuhn, President; F. P. Bailey, Vice-President; A. Kuhn, Secretary and Treasurer; Manufacturers of Patent Bed and Single Lounges, Etc.; 109 to 115 West Morris street. Among the numerous furniture manufacturers of Indianapolis, that of the L. W. Ott Manufacturing Co. has a leading prominence, earned by the superior quality of its products and the extent of its trade. The business was originally established in 1876 by the firm of L. W. Ott & Co., of which Mr. W. F. Kuhn was a member, and was continued under that style until early in 1884, when the present company was incorporated, with officers as named in the headlines of this article. The premises occupied are nearly a block in extent, and include the main factory, a two-story brick building, 100x30 feet in dimensions, a large warehouse, three stories high, 130x30 feet, lumber yards, etc. The factory premises have a complete equipment of the latest and most improved woodworking machinery, propelled by a 75 horse power engine, fed by two large boilers. A force of from 100 to 125 workmen is employed under competent supervision, and the products include patent bed and single lounges, reclining chairs and rockers, and the greatest care is taken in the selection of materials, and in all the details of manufacture. As a consequence, the goods manufactured by this company are unsurpassed in beauty of design, elegance of finish, durability and excellence of workmanship, and are in large and steadily growing demand in all parts of the Union, and especially in the leading East ern cities. The company is one of ample resources and the most superior facilities for the prosecution of its business, and the experienced direction of its affairs by competent business men has commended it to the favor and confidence of the trade.

Ballweg & Co.—Manufacturers of Wooden Boxes, Etc.; Wilkins street and Pogue's Run.—This firm, which is composed of Messrs. F. W. Ballweg and William Blizard, established in business about seven years ago, and have since actively conducted it with a gratifying and continually increasing success. They have built up a large demand for their products in packing boxes, crates and shooks,

which they sell in large quantities to pork packers, egg and poultry shippers, and to manufacturers of soap and other articles, numbering among their customers many of the leading manufacturers and shippers of the city and its vicinity. They make boxes to order of any desired size, and to suit the requirements of any character of business, and their goods are always acceptable, being made in a workmanlike manner and promptly delivered. For the prosecution of the business, the firm has every convenience and facility, having an extensive plant, covering two and one-half acres of ground, upon which is located their extensive lumber yards and their mill, the latter a two-story building 70x175 feet in dimensions. The mill is equipped with a complete outfit of machinery, including a 60 horse power engine, two large boilers, a large Sturtevant blower, large planers, resaws and all the necessary machinery and appliances for the efficient prosecution of the business, in which a force of from fifty to sixty workmen are engaged. The members of the firm are thoroughly practical and experienced men, who by close attention to every detail of the business and reliability in all their transactions have steadily added to their trade from year to year.

Thos. H. Gage. Electrician; Dealer in Electric Bells, Burglar Alarms, Etc.; 27 Circle street. Thos. H. Gage, a practical electrician, experienced and expert in the application of that science, established himself in Indianapolis during June, 1888. He occupies premises divided into office and salesroom, with accommodations also for workroom purposes, and his output embraces electrical instruments and appointments of every character and description, such as electric bells, burglar alarms, electric gas lighting, electric tube speaking systems, etc., also promptly and neatly repairing all work in his line, but making new work a specialty. Among his latest professional success was the equipment of the Terre Haute House, of Terre Haute, this State, with bells, annunciators, and other electric apparatus, a work that has received the highest commendation. In addition to this, he has furnished residences and public buildings here and elsewhere with appliances in his lines, with equal satisfaction to those who availed themselves of his services.

T. B. Laycock & Co. Manufacturers of Spring Beds, Cots, Etc.; corner of First street and Canal. This firm, which is composed of Thomas B. Laycock, W. H. Laycock and Irwin M. Dean, was organized in 1885, and their operations have grown in magnitude and importance from their inception. They occupy a three-story and basement building, 130x50 feet in dimensions, with an annex, used for engine and boiler house purposes, also brick dry house, lumber yard, etc. The premises are well fitted up and arranged for business, and equipped with the latest machinery and appliances. During October, 1887, the plant was destroyed by fire, and the present structure immediately erected upon the ruins of that previously occupied, and was completed with special reference to the business in its furnishings and appointments, with results apparent in its arrangements and outfit. Their lines of manufacture embrace spring beds of all kinds, woven

wire mattresses, cots and children's folding cribs, bed, lounge and machine springs, also springs for upholstering, cots, etc., of the best qualities of material, in all respects adequate to the requirements of the service for which they are designed, and enjoying a reputation for handsome finish, wonderful durability, etc., not surpassed by competing houses in the country. They are prepared to fill orders promptly and satisfactorily, and to ship consignments securely packed against danger of damage in transit. A force of from thirty-five to forty experienced hands are employed, and a large and steadily increasing trade is served throughout Indiana, Illinois, Ohio and Kentucky, as also in the southern States to New Orleans, and the southeastern States to Baltimore. The members of the firm manage their establishment with characteristic enterprise and liberality, and no kindred industry in the country has pursued a more honorable and successful career.

Klee & Coleman — Manufacturers of Mineral Waters; 227 and 229 South Delaware street. The largest establishment for the manufacture of soft drinks in Indianapolis is owned by the firm of Klee & Coleman, and managed by W. H. Miller. The firm is composed of J. Klee and H. Coleman, and was organized in 1879. Both members are residents of Dayton, O., where Mr. Klee is similarly

engaged and Mr. Coleman conducts extensive operations in lumber and lumber products. They occupy premises erected by them and under their personal direction at a large outlay, and into which they moved January 1, 1888, from the building they had for eight years previously occupied, on Delaware street, opposite their present site. They are of brick, three stories in height, 43x129 feet in dimensions, and equipped with generators for making carbonic acid gas, and other mechanical appliances, driven by a steam engine of 25-horse power. The building is also furnished with all modern conveniences and facilities for storage and shipping purposes, and is one of the most completely appointed establishments of its kind in the Northwest. They employ seventeen hands, and their annual output embraces 25,000 boxes of soda water, 69,000 dozen bottles of ginger ale and 12,000 dozen bottles of sparkling champagne cider, which are disposed of to the trade in the city and throughout the State. They are also prepared to charge portable fountains and have fountains to lease during the season. W. H. Miller has entire control of the business here, having been with the company for many years.

J. C. Hirschman & Co. — Manufacturers of Mattresses and Comforts; 173 East Washington street. This business, established by Mr. Hirschman in 1876, has achieved success as the result of enterprise and first-class work, and is continually augmenting in extent and value. Their retail department is located in the most convenient portion of the city, the factory being at the southwest corner of New Jersey and Wabash streets. The former is 25x100 feet in dimensions, and the latter sufficiently commodious for the

purposes to which it is appropriated. Both are equipped with all modern conveniences and appliances requisite to the service, and provided with facilities adapted to their several needs. Their range of manufacture embraces spring, hair and moss mattresses, pillows, comforts and other articles appertaining to each of these special lines. None but the best and most durable materials are employed, and only the most skillful and experienced workmen are employed. The result is an article promotive of comfort and embodying the highest class of workmanship. They also deal in feathers, perfectly cured and ready for immediate use, and bedding of attractive pattern and reliable quality. The firm owns and operates the Electric Feather Renovating Machine, the latest invention of its kind, and by far the best machine in the country for its purpose. They do a very large retail trade in the city and surrounding country, besides jobbing extensively throughout Indiana, Illinois and Ohio, and the house is well known and esteemed for the value of its products and its equitable business methods.

Frederick Dietz — Indianapolis Box Factory; Manufacturer of All Kinds of Wooden Boxes to Order; Madison avenue, south end of Delaware street. This enterprise was established in 1869 by Mr. Frederick Dietz, who two years later built his present works. The plant covers three and one-half acres, the factory being a three-story and basement brick building, 100x60 feet in dimensions, equipped with a 100-horse power engine, three large boilers, and a complete equipment of the latest and most highly improved woodworking machinery. Employment is given to a force ranging from sixty to seventy hands, and every description of wooden boxes for all purposes and in all sizes are made. Mr. Dietz enjoys a large trade with the manufacturing and shipping firms of the city and the State of Indiana. The boxes made at this factory are justly celebrated for their superior quality of materials and workmanship, and their durability, and the first-class facilities enjoyed enable Mr. Dietz to fill orders in a prompt and satisfactory manner. He is a thoroughly practical and experienced man, carefully selects all materials, maintains a close supervision over all of the operations of his factory, and has by uniformly fair and accurate dealings earned the favor and confidence of all with whom he has business transactions.

F. M. Rottler — Manufacturer Harness, Saddlery and Turf Goods; 13 North Delaware street. Mr. F. M. Rottler has been engaged in the manufacture of fine harness and turf goods in this city for the past eleven years, having commenced operations here in 1878. He occupies a three-story and basement building, 25x100 feet, and carries the largest and most complete stock in his lines of any house in Indianapolis. The premises are handsomely fitted up with fine walnut wall cases and other facilities for a comprehensive display of his products, also containing a well equipped workshop, office and salesrooms. His specialties are fine hand-made turf goods of every description. They embrace light driving harness, racing saddles and bridles, horse boots and clothing generally, for which he receives orders from turfmen in all parts of the United States. They are made of the best qualities of material in the most secure and substantial manner. He also carries good stocks of fine carriage and buggy harness, saddles, bridles, whips, blankets, robes, and stable sundries in great variety. He employs from seven to ten experienced and competent assistants, and does a large trade throughout the city and surrounding country, the demands for his specialties, however, proceeding from all the leading cities in the Union.

Healy & O'Brien — Dealers in Plumbers', Gas and Steamfitters' Supplies; 57 West Maryland street. This firm, consisting of James M. Healy and Michael O'Brien, was organized in March, 1888, as successors to James M. Healy, the senior partner, who established the business during 1874. They are desirably located, and occupy a two-story and basement building 25x100 feet in dimensions, and amply equipped with room for the sale display and storage of their large lines of stock. They are contractors, on an extensive scale, for all kinds of steam heating, natural and artificial gas-fitting, fine sanitary plumbing and sewerage work. In these branches of their trade they are experienced, proficient and thoroughly familiar with the scientific principles necessary to first-class and successful work, without which no job can stand the test of time or survive. They have none but competent workmen, guaranteeing satisfaction in all particulars, also furnishing estimates and soliciting orders, with assurances of their speedy and substantial completion. They also carry full lines of gas fixtures in original and artistic designs, and gas fitters' supplies and specialties connected with the adaptation of residences and public buildings to the utilization of natural gas for lighting, heating and domestic purposes. Their stocks are composed of the best quality of materials, and their facilities are such that all orders will receive immediate attention. They have done the plumbing, steam and gas-fitting in many of the largest establishments in Indianapolis, notably the new St. Vincent Infirmary, and elsewhere in the State, displaying in all of these a quality of skill and familiarity with the requirements of the service that has commended them to an increased patronage and extended reputation. They employ a force of twenty skilled workmen and respond to a large demand in the city and throughout the surrounding country.

A. A. McKain—Granite Dealer, 32 Massachusetts avenue. The illustration on this page of the Colfax monument shows one of the handsomest ornaments of the city. The monument was erected by the I. O. O. F. and The Daughters of Rebekah. The designer and contractor, A. A. McKain, 32 Massachusetts avenue, is the builder of many fine monuments throughout the middle Western States. It is not too much to say that no other man has built so many large and excellent monuments in the State of Indiana. The character of the work done by him is shown by the fact that the well-known New England Granite Company has given Mr. McKain exclusive control of their celebrated white Westerly granite in his territory. Those who are acquainted with this granite will need no further recommendation of any one who supplies it.

Gem Steam Laundry—The Pioneer Laundry of Indianapolis; Main Office, 13 North Illinois street; Steam Works, 38 and 40 Kentucky avenue; W. H. Reed, Proprietor. Cleanliness being the companion of godliness, Indianapolis is well provided with agencies tending to not only maintain, but to confirm and strengthen that relation. Among those leading in such behalf is the Gem Steam Laundry, established in 1877 by the present proprietor, who started it originally as a necessary adjunct to his custom shirt factory. It has become one of the largest steam laundries in the State, employing steadily twenty-five to thirty hands. The appointments of the laundry are all of a superior kind, including all the latest and most approved machinery, and in this respect unsurpassed. The Gem Steam Laundry is the only laundry in the city or State which can claim for the benefit of its patrons the use of soft filtered rain water, having three large cisterns, with an aggregate capacity of 800 barrels, the most assuring thing of good work, and especially in washing flannels it is essential. It is this fact which has given the Gem Laundry its high and merited reputation throughout the city for the highest order of laundry work. Connected with the establishment is a department devoted exclusively to the doing up of lace curtains, under the superintendence of an experienced lady dresser of lace curtains.

The Palace Shirt Factory—Walsman & Roll, Proprietors, 13 North Illinois street, opposite Bates House. The firm of Walsman & Roll, composed of E. F. Walsman and E. P. Roll, proprietors of the Palace Shirt Factory, was organized in January, 1889, and succeeded to the business formerly carried on by Willoughby H. Reed, with whom Mr. Walsman had been engaged for sixteen years previous. The house is one of the most select in every respect in its lines in the city. They are located as above, an unsurpassed site, being on one of the leading retail thoroughfares, directly opposite the Bates House, and otherwise advantageous and available. The premises occupied are most attractively arranged and appointed for the handsome and complete display of their choice lines of goods, being light, roomy and neatly finished. Their specialty is the manufacture of fine dress shirts exclusively to order, in which they employ the finest materials and turn out a line of products that for fit, finish, appearance and superior workmanship are unrivaled. They carry full lines of the same character, also gents' furnishing goods in great variety, made up of underwear in silk, balbriggan, woolen, flannel, lisle thread and linen, hose of imported and domestic manufacture, collars, cuffs, neck-wear, gloves, canes, umbrellas, foreign novelties, etc., in the latest styles, adapted to any service, social or ordinary. All in all, they are exceptionally prepared to meet the demands of the high class patronage to which they cater, and their prices are so reasonable and satisfactory, that they furnish inducements of a superior character to customers. They do a steadily increasing local and transient trade, and the house is rapidly acquiring a reputation resting upon a basis of absolute merit.

POSTAL STATISTICS.

THE net revenue of the Indianapolis postoffice for the year 1888 was $16,000; the receipts for the first quarter of 1889 were $50,000 in round numbers. Forty-six carriers were employed during 1888, a total of 152 collection and 117 delivery trips were made daily and 11,040,000 pieces of mail matter handled. The money order business amounted to $4,316,343.44; of which $278,303.03 was received for orders issued, and $1,038,040.41 was paid out on orders received. There are 244 letter-boxes distributed throughout the city and among the hotels, and four delivery and collection trips are made daily in the business centers, and two each in the outskirts.

WINDSOR BLOCK, OWNED BY M. N. SPADES.

SOCIAL ATTRACTIONS.

INDIANAPOLIS is eminently a city of social attractions. Education, refinement and intelligence rather than wealth or lineage are made the conditions precedent to recognition, and the observance of this rule has been attended with the most gratifying results. Though cosmopolitan, Indianapolis is not a city of clubs, and beyond a limited number of social organizations of an exclusively private character there are none to speak of except the Athletic, Caledonian and Chess clubs, each of which includes a large membership upon its rolls. Social amenities universally prevail, however, among all classes, both of American and foreign nationality, and the opportunities for social hospitality are available throughout the year. Aside from these the secret, military and benevolent organizations, musical associations and other societies for purposes of intellectual and social development are numerously represented and well sustained. The Masonic fraternity is represented by eight Blue lodges, two lodges of Royal Arch Masons, one council of Royal and Select Masters, one consistory, one commandery, one lodge of Perfection, one chapter of Rose Croix and one council of the Prince of Jerusalem. In addition to these there are seven lodges of colored Masons. There are eleven lodges and three encampments of Odd Fellows, also six colored lodges; of the Order of Chosen Friends there are eleven councils, one supreme council, one grand council and one benefit league; three divisions of the Ancient Order of Hibernians; four lodges of the United Workmen; one of Elks; six of Druids; one council and four tribes of Red Men; three castles of the Knights and Ladies of the Golden Rule; one supreme lodge and four subordinate lodges of the Knights of Honor; one supreme and ten subordinate lodges of Knights and Ladies of Honor; fifteen lodges of Knights of Pythias; three commanderies of the Knights and Ladies of Universal Brotherhood; one lodge each of the order of Golden Chain and Golden Shore; eight branches of the Iron Hall; one lodge of the Order of Pente; one grand council and four subordinate councils of the Royal Arcanum; one supreme lodge and five subordinate lodges of the Secret League; nine lodges, one of which is colored, of the United Brothers of Friendship; one camp of the Grand Army of Fraternity; eight posts of the Grand Army of the Republic; fifty-one labor organizations; four Hebrew societies; nine medical societies; nine musical societies; eight bands of music; eight military companies and seventy-eight miscellaneous societies.

INDIANAPOLIS BOARD OF TRADE.

THE business community of Indianapolis has recognized the influence exerted by organized effort in the promotion of facilities for commerce and the expansion of the trade of the city. This recognition has been evinced in the creation, from time to time, of numerous organizations, some of them intended to regulate or benefit specified industries, while others have occupied a more extended field, and devoted themselves to the augmentation of the business interests of the city. Some of the earlier efforts in this direction were weakly sustained, but they served to emphasize the needs of the business world, and have culminated in the successful and influential association known as the Indianapolis Board of Trade.

The origin of this business organization dates back to 1804, when, after preliminary meetings, T. B. Elliott, now deceased, was elected the first President, serving in that capacity for three years. Under that organization the Chamber of Commerce building was erected in 1874, a description of which will be found elsewhere in this volume. On June 9, 1882, the Board of Trade was re-organized, Mr. F. P. Rush becoming the first President under the new charter, and at that time all the commercial organizations then existing in the city were consolidated with it. The membership of the board, which is limited to 500 persons, is made up of leading men of all the commercial, manufacturing, professional and business pursuits of the city, and also includes a number of business men residents of other places in the State of Indiana. The objects of the organization include not only the ordinary features of a Board of Trade proper, but also embrace the general promotion of the commercial and manufacturing interests of the city of Indianapolis, and the dissemination of information as to resources and conditions which may tend to exhibit and make prominent the business advantages of the city.

Mortuary benefits are paid to the heirs of deceased members of the Board, each member paying $2.00 on each death, and the membership is confined to active, healthy business men under sixty years of age. The membership fee is $15.00 per year.

All inquiries in reference to the advantages afforded to new manufacturing establishments seeking a location, addressed to "The Indianapolis Board of Trade, Indianapolis, Ind.," are referred to the committee appointed for that purpose, and receive prompt attention.

The Board, in its endeavors to promote the business interests of the city, has pursued measures of the utmost importance toward securing an augmentation of the productive industries of the city. It has given cordial support to the project for assuring to manufacturing enterprises the benefit of free gas for fuel, and otherwise promoted organized measures in behalf of Indianapolis.

The organization publishes reports showing the volume and growth of the business of the city, which contain valuable information in regard to the advantages of the city as a place of business or residence.

The following is a list, corrected to date, of the officers, Board of Governors and members of the Board of Trade:

BOARD OF TRADE BUILDING.

OFFICERS.

WM. SCOTT, President; GEO. G. TANNER, Vice-President; D. A. RICHARDSON, Treasurer; ARTHUR GILLET, Secretary.

BOARD OF GOVERNORS.

W. D. Wiles,	J. A. Wildman,	J. B. Connor,	Geo. F. Townley,	Geo. S. Brecount,	J. M. Shaw,
W. H. Cooper,	J. F. Pratt,	E. C. Atkins,	C. E. Coffin,	J. W. Murphy,	C. C. Foster,
S. F. Gray,	Geo. F. Branham,	V. K. Hendricks,	N. S. Byram,	Geo. C. Webster, Jr.,	I. R. Ross,
J. T. Wallick,	A. H. Schwinge,	R. S. Foster,	Geo. W. Sloan,	Arthur Jordan,	J. H. Holliday,
W. F. Piel, Jr.,	C. W. Blackmore,	W. L. Elder,	S. F. Robinson,	Jno. W. Schmidt,	Eli Lilly,
A. A. Barnes,	E. B. Martindale,	Albert Baker,	S. T. Bowen,	M. A. Woollen,	D. P. Erwin.
Chas. E. Hall,	S. K. Fletcher,	P. F. Bryce,	E. H. Eldridge.		

LIST OF MEMBERS OF BOARD OF TRADE.

Adams, H. C.
Adams, J. C.
Alexander, J. D.
Andrews, L. N.
Appel, J. J.
Applegate, Berg
Atkins, E. C.
Ayres, L. S.
Bachman, V.
Baker, Albert
Baker, A. R.
Baggs, Frederick
Baird, William
Baldwin, Siles
Ballard, Addison
Bals, H. C. G.
Barnes, A. A.
Barrows, W. F.
Bassett, Thomas M.
Bates, Hervey
Bates, Hervey Jr.
Beck, George C.
Becker, Jacob
Bennett, M. H.
Bennett, Wm. H.
Berner, Frederick
Bieler, Jacob L.
Bird, Frank
Blackmore, C. W.
Blackmore, D.
Blake, John G.
Blanchard, F. A.
Blanton, L. H.
Blessing, John
Bond, James M.
Bowen, Silas T.
Boyd, John M.
Bradbury, D. M.
Bradshaw, J. M.
Branch, E. F.
Branham, G. F.
Brecount, G. S.
Brink, Christian A.
Brown, James D.
Bruner, August
Brush, George E.
Brush, John T.
Bryan, D. C.
Bryan, J. W.
Bruce, Peter F.
Buddenbaum, J. A.
Buchl, Salmon A.
Burford, Wm. B.
Burris, A. H.
Busby, Addison
Byram, Norman S.
Callender, C. W.
Carey, H. C.
Carey, S. B.
Carnahan, J. R.
Carr, Bruce
Carriger, John J.
Carter, John
Colwart, K. W.
Caven, John
Charlton, T. J.
Cherry, Andrew O.
Christman, F.
Cilley, Henry
Coburn, Henry
Coclin, Charles F.
Collin, David W.
Colgan, C. J.
Combe, Henry T.
Comegys, C. G.
Comer, C. S.
Connor, John B.
Cook, Ralph J.
Cooper, W. E.
Cooper, W. H.
Cooper, John J.

Cornelius, E. G.
Couch, R. D.
Cullen, Terry J.
Culpepper, C. E.
Cunningham, N. T.
Cunsinger, Edward
Cutter, Charles L.
Daggett, William
Daily, Milton
Davidson, J. M.
Davis, F. A. W.
Day, Samuel D.
Day, Thomas C.
Dean, John C.
Denny, Caleb S.
Dewar, Lewis
Dietz, Frederick
Donough, D. R.
Drelson, Matthias
Drew, L. W.
Dunn, Edward
Duy, George C.
Dyer, Sidney M.
Engle, John G.
Eagle, John H.
Eagle, Wm. O.
Eastman, W. N.
Eden, Charlton
Edel, H.
Egan, Edward C.
Eiler, Wm. G.
Eldridge, E. H.
Eldridge, G. O.
Elliott, E. C.
Elliott, N. K.
Erdelmeyer, F.
Ervin, Rice
Erwin, D. P.
Evans, George T.
Evans, J.
Evans, Joseph R.
Evans, John O.
Falnley, F.
Fahreen, J. G.
Ferger, Chas.
Finney, Jasper
Fishback, W. P.
Flanner, Frank W.
Fletcher, Allen M.
Fletcher, S. A.
Fletcher, S. J.
Fletcher, S. K.
Folsom, David K.
Foltz, Howard M.
Foster, Chapin C.
Foster, Robert S.
Fox, Jacob
Frank, Henry
Fraser, Henry S.
Fraser, S. D.
Frenzel, John P.
Frenzel, Otto N.
Friedgen, C.
Fugate, James L.
Gable, L. A.
Gall, Albert
Gall, Edmund F.
Gallup, W. P.
Gardner, A. J.
Gates, Alfred B.
Gates, Austin B.
Gent, J. F.
Gilbreath, John S.
Gillet, Arthur
Gott, W. F.
Goodhart, B. F.
Gordon, Irving S.
Gruhling, Peter
Gray, Samuel F.
Gregory, Fred A.

Griffith, T. E.
Griffith, W. H.
Griffith, W. C.
Guild, David
Hagen, Andrew
Halford, A. J.
Hall, Charles F.
Hall, Will C.
Hanna, H. H.
Harris, J. E.
Harris, P. O.
Hasselman, O. B.
Hasselman, W. J.
Hasson, James
Hauschild, R. F.
Hawkins, Edward
Hawkins, R. G.
Hayes, Thomas
Haynes, G. V.
Hays, F. W.
Hays, Hamilton
Hendy, Charles W.
Hedges, Isaac
Hendricks, V. K.
Henderson, C. E.
Henderson, W.
Hereth, Asl.
Hendricks, J. B.
Hetherington, B. F.
Heywood, J. B.
Hibbard, H. W.
Hickman, Clark
Higgins, John
Higgins, W. L.
Hildebrand, J. S.
Hinsdale, D. C.
Hogle, A. F.
Hollenbeck, C. F.
Holliday, F. T.
Holliday, John H.
Holliday, Wm. J.
Hollweg, Louis
Holman, John A.
Holton, W. B.
Hopkins, L. C.
Howard, Geo. F.
Howlen, E. C.
Huey, M. S.
Hunt, P. G. C.
Hunter, W. G.
Hutchins, H. H.
Isams, William P.
Irwin, Robert H.
Janes, Frank E.
Jeger, Rodney
Johnston, H. W.
Johnston, John F.
Johnston, W. W., Sr.
Jones, John W.
Jordan, Arthur
Judson, F. K.
Kennedy, Geo. W.
Kerr, C. B.
Kienmeyer, William
Kingsbury, J. G.
Kinney, Horace F.
Kipp, Nathan H.
Kipp, Robert
Koerner, C. C.
Krauss, Paul H.
Kuntz, William E.
Laird, William H.
Lamb, Robert N.
Landers, Franklin
Landis, Milton W.
Laverman, James T.
Lazarus, John S.
Lee, H. H.
Leiter, William J.
Leonard, John R.

Lewis, William H.
Lewis, Charles S.
Lieber, Herman
Lieber, Peter
Lilly, Eli
Lilly, George
Lilly, James W.
Lindeman, Frank
Lynn, William C.
Lyon, William W.
MacCurdy, W. W. H.
Maguire, Charles
Mabel, Volney T.
Marx, Wm. F.
Martindale, E. B.
Maus, Frank A.
Mayer, Charles
Mayfield, G. E.
Mefla, Gustav
Mendenhall, J. F.
Merritt, Worth
Metz, Fred
Metzger, A.
Metzger, Jacob
Meyer, August B.
Meyer, Adolph J.
Meyer, Charles F.
Middlesworth, W.
Miller, Enrique C.
Miner, Willis R.
Minor, B. H.
Mooney, Edmund
Mooney, Thomas
Mooney, W. A.
Moore, Geo. W.
Moore, John
Moore, John L.
Moore, Joseph A.
Morris, Nathan
Morris, S. H.
Morrison, A. F.
Morrison, J. A.
Morrison, Wm. H.
Mulkrney, P. J.
Mummenhoff, F.
Munson, E. A.
Murphy, John W.
Murphy, A. W.
Myers, J. D.
McBride, F. A.
McCarty, Nicholas
McCleary, A. M.
McCormack, A. F.
McCrea, Wm. W.
McCrea, Rollin H.
McCutcheon, J. C.
McGaughey, J. F.
McGettingan, J. E.
McIntyre, T. A.
McKain, Arthur A.
McKee, Jas. R.
McLain, Moses G.
McLeod, A. D.
McLeod, A. H.
Newcomer, F. S.
Nickum, John K.
Nordyke, A. H.
Oakrinne, John
Oter, Ewald
Parmelee, Wm. H.
Parnott, Horace
Pattison, A. E.
Peelle, Stanton J.
Pendleton, A. D.
Pendleton, R. C. J.
Perkins, J. A.
Perry, John C.
Phillips, Samuel C.
Pickens, Samuel O.
Piel, Henry W.
Piel, Wm. F. Jr.

Pierce, Charles C.
Plowman, E. L.
Porter, E. B.
Potter, M. A.
Poulhaser, Leu
Potts, Alfred F.
Pratt, Julius F.
Pray, Enos E.
Pray, Samuel D.
Pray, William
Ranck, David H.
Randolph, F.
Ransdell, J. M.
Rawling, C. M.
Ray, John W.
Reasoner, Wm. F.
Reasoner, John A.
Reeker, G. J.
Reeves, Edward
Rehm, George H.
Reynolds, Frank
Rhodes, Wm. A.
Richards, Wm. J.
Richardson, D. A.
Richardson, J. B.
Richardson, W. P.
Rivers, Walter
Robbins, Irvin
Robinson, Samuel
Robinson, S. F.
Root, G. R.
Root, O. H.
Ross, James R.
Rouse, R. K.
Rouse, Thos.
Routier, P.
Rowe, S. P.
Rusmels, O. S.
Rush, Fred. P.
Ryan, H. H.
Ryan, J. R.
Sander, Theodore
Sanders, J. E.
Sayles, C. F.
Schaffner, John
Schleicher, A.
Schmalfhols, C.
Schmidt, J. W.
Schmitt, Lorenz
Schmidt, Wm. H.
Schmuck, G.
Schnull, J.
Schnull, G. A.
Scholl, Charles
Schrader, C.
Schurmann, Edw.
Schwabacher, J.
Schwinge, A. H.
Scott, Robert F.
Scott, Wm.
Sellers, Daniel
Sells, Michael
Schaffer, J. C.
Sharble, Ellis V.
Shaw, John M.
Sheerin, S. P.
Shepard, C. F.
Shepard, S. M.
Sherman, W. G.
Shideler, D. B.
Shideler, J. E.
Shiel, Roger R.
Shotwell, C. A.
Shreve, J. H.
Sklower, H. E.
Slam, George W.
Sloan, E. W.
Small, W. H.
Smith, Azra
Smith, A. H.
Smith, H. B.

Smith, J. W.
Smiley, Z. T.
Smythe, Wm. H.
Snider, Geo. W.
Snyder, D. E.
Sohl, Alfred J.
Sohl, Levi
Spahr, F. L.
Spotts, Wm.
Stalnaker, E. D.
Stanberry, J. V.
Stewart, B.
Stewart, J. H.
Stiles, H. G.
Stone, Thos. B.
Story, J. M.
Stout, G. W.
Sullivan, W. A.
Sullivan, G. R.
Swain, David
Sweet, F. B.
Syfers, Rufus K.
Sweeny, Charles
Taggart, Thos.
Talbot, R. L.
Tanner, G. G.
Taylor, Major
Thale, Henry H.
Thoman, Isaac
Thomas, Richard
Thompson, G. S.
Thompson, L. M.
Thompson, J. W.
Thomas, Fred.
Thomson, A. W.
Thomson, J.
Townley, G. F.
Treat, A. J.
Van Camp, C.
Van Camp, F.
Van Camp, G. C.
Van Deinse, A. J.
Van Tillongh, J. B.
Van Winkle, J. Q.
Walcott, C. H.
Walk, J. C.
Walker, L. C.
Wallick, J. F.
Walton, A. G.
Ward, Boswell
Wardwell, H. L.
Warman, F.
Warren, G. S.
Wasson, H. P.
Wasson, W. G.
Watson, M. D.
Weaver, O. D.
Webster, G. C.
Webster, S. C., Jr.
Wells, Andrew J.
Wells, Merrit
Whistler, J. M.
Whitcomb, D. F.
White, A. R.
White, Thos.
Wishman, J. A.
Wiles, Wm. D.
Williams, Wm.
Wilkinson, F. N.
Williams, E. L.
Wilson, S. B.
Winslow, W. W.
Witt, B. F.
Woerher, John Jr.
Wood, Ford
Woodward, V. W.
Woollen, M. A.
Wright, John C.
Zimmerman, C.
Zimmerman, J.

Wm. Scott & Co.—Grain Dealers; Board of Trade building. —One of the leading and representative houses in this city engaged in the purchase of grain for shipment to the Eastern and European markets is that of William Scott & Co. It was established by William Scott in 1879, and by him directed until 1883, when he was joined by Robert F. Scott, his brother, and the present firm was organized. They have every facility for the conduct of their business upon the largest scale. Their range of operation includes the purchase in large, round car-load lots, throughout Indiana, Illinois, Minnesota, and other western and northwestern States, of wheat, rye, oats, corn, barley, clover and timothy seed, and other cereals for direct shipment to the seaboard. They own and manage an elevator of considerable capacity at Monon, the crossing of the Louisville, New Albany & Chicago, Indianapolis & Chicago, and other important railways. They have direct wire connection with the leading markets of the United States; also correspondents in all prominent cities, and are everywhere known as representatives of a house of established reliability and prestige. The members of the firm are also members of the Board of Trade, of which Mr. William Scott, the senior partner, is President.

Chas. A. Shotwell—Shipping Grain, Flour and Feed and Brokerage; Room 18, Board of Trade. Chas. A. Shotwell, extensively engaged in the purchase of grain, flour and feed for shipment, and doing an equally extensive line of operations in the capacity of broker, became established here in 1879, and has built up a large and steadily increasing trade. He occupies a commodious and well equipped office, and being a member of the Board of Trade, also having important connections at all the leading depots of supply to which he makes consignments, enjoys unusual facilities for the successful and profitable conduct of his lines of business. He purchases grain, flour, feed, etc., throughout the West, also on the Board here, shipping east and south in car-load lots, and the resources of the house are such that he is enabled to fill the largest orders with promptness and accuracy. He also buys and sells on account of customers in large quantities and is prepared to do a general brokerage business, and makes advances on consignments. Mr. Shotwell gives his personal attention to the business, and has achieved success as the result of honorable methods and liberal management.

Minor & Cooper—Grain Dealers and Commission Merchants; Room 17, Chamber of Commerce.—This firm, organized in 1885, is composed of B. B. Minor and W. H. Cooper. Both members have had large and extended experience. Mr. Minor having been a prominent grain merchant at Effingham, Ill., for nearly twenty years, and Mr. Cooper was similarly engaged for about the same length of time in this city. They occupy spacious offices, handsomely fitted up and provided with every facility and accommodation for the transaction of business, as also with every appointment to enable them to keep pace with the fluctuations of the markets and the movements of grain, feed and other commodities, to the purchase and sale of which they devote their attention. They buy very largely on their own account and to order, securing their stocks in Indiana and throughout other States in the West and Northwest, in car-load lots exclusively, and shipping in bulk only, to the depots of supply for the Eastern and Southern markets. Messrs. Minor & Cooper are members of the Board of Trade, and are prepared to give immediate attention to the execution of orders. Their house is prominent for the honorable methods which characterize its operations.

Fred P. Rush & Co.—Grain Dealers and Brokers, Proprietors of Elevator "B"; 10, 12 and 14 Chamber of Commerce.—A leading firm, doing a very heavy business, not only as dealers in grain for personal account, but as brokers for account of others, is that of Fred P. Rush & Co., organized in 1863, and composed of Fred P. Rush, Geo. E. Townley and E. G. Gail. They are members of the Board of Trade, familiar with the requirements of the business and noted for their honorable methods, Mr. Rush having been thus engaged for thirty-three years, and Messrs. Townley & Gail a proportionate length of time. Their offices are provided with every

facility and convenience, including telegraph, telephone and other service for the information of their patrons in respect to the fluctuations in prices and the conditions of the markets generally. They also own and operate elevator "B," erected in 1874, on the line of the Vandalia Railroad tracks in this city, complete in its equipment, furnished with all the latest machinery and appliances for handling and cleaning grain and with a total capacity of 300,000 bushels. They are heavy purchasers in large lots in the grain producing regions of the North and Northwest and equally heavy shippers of the same commodity in car-load lots to the Eastern and Southern markets, also buying and selling for cash and future delivery to the order of customers. They employ a full staff of clerks with from ten to twelve assistants at elevator "B," and are prepared to execute orders promptly.

D. Blackmore & Co.—General Commission Merchants; Room 20, Chamber of Commerce. This firm, composed of Dawson Blackmore and C. W. Blackmore, was organized in 1873. This business has steadily increased in volume and value from its inception, in keeping with the enterprise and liberal management which have characterized their operations. They are prepared to promptly execute all commissions entrusted to them, and purchase grain and flour heavily in Indiana, Illinois and elsewhere, shipping the former to the Eastern markets and the latter to the South, and north into Canada, and in which latter section they have a large trade. Both members of the firm are also members of the Board of Trade of this city, and in addition to their large business as dealers in flour, grain and millfeed, do a heavy commission business in all these lines, for cash and future delivery. They solicit consignments upon which they make liberal cash advances, and their opportunities for the disposition of goods sent them to the best advantage, render them very valuable agents, through whom either to make deals or transact business in connection with the purchase and sale for account of consigners, of the articles referred to. Remittances are made immediately after sales are completed, and no house in the city is more thoroughly equipped for the advantageous disposition of consignments.

O. D. Weaver—Provision Broker; 4 Board of Trade.—Mr. Weaver established business in 1889, and has since conducted it with the most pronounced and gratifying success. He has enjoyed a long experience, rendering him thoroughly familiar with the requirements of the trade, and a valuable agent through whom to conduct operations in his lines. He occupies offices, 25x80 feet in dimensions, in the Board of Trade building, and is furnished with every facility to execute orders promptly, as also to furnish the trade with accurate and reliable data as to the fluctuations in prices and the movements and conditions of the markets. He buys and sells on his own account and to order, limiting his operations to deals in provisions and purchasing only in large round lots, hams and meats by the car-load, and lard in lots of 250 tierces each. These are obtained here, as also in the Chicago, Omaha, Kansas City, and other Western markets, and shipped, the pickled meats to New York, Philadelphia, and other Eastern depots of supply, the sides to points in the Southern States, and the lard principally to New York City and Chicago. He makes a leading specialty of these lines, in the handling of which he has attained to prominence, and does a large and constantly increasing trade. He enjoys the confidence of the public and the trade, and is one of the most active and enterprising brokers in this city.

Mutchner & Higgins—Buyers and Shippers of Western Grain; 32 Board of Trade building. The firm of Mutchner & Higgins was organized in 1885, and is composed of P. E. Mutchner and Wm. L. Higgins. They occupy commodious offices provided with every facility for prosecuting their business successfully and upon a large scale. They also owned elevator "D," a very extensive and exceptionally well equipped establishment, which was destroyed by fire February 12, 1889, entailing a loss of $50,000 and causing a temporary suspension of operations in those departments. They are now rebuilding the elevator, and it will shortly be completed, with better facilities than before its destruction. They are large purchasers of wheat, corn, oats, rye, etc., upon the markets of Indianapolis and throughout the grain producing States of the West and Northwest, for personal account and to order, for cash, or future delivery, and no similar house in the city bears a more enviable reputation or is better prepared to meet the demands of customers and the trade. They purchase in large round lots only, shipping almost entirely to the Eastern markets, and are prepared to make purchases, sales and shipments at the shortest notice and upon the most reasonable terms. They enjoy a reputation among commercial circles in all portions of the country in harmony with the honorable methods and sterling probity which characterize their operations.

W. B. Overman Commission Broker, Grain and Provisions, 12 and 14 Chamber of Commerce building. Among the most prominent and representative grain and provision brokers, operating on the Indianapolis markets, is W. B. Overman, located as above in the Chamber of Commerce. He began his present enterprise in 1886, having been for three years previous to that date a prominent pork packer here, and has since directed and managed large deals in his

special lines for a correspondingly large and steadily increasing clientage. He occupies a suite of handsome offices, and is provided with every facility for the transaction of business, including ticker, telephone and telegraph facilities; also advertising upon a large display board the latest quotations, fluctuations in prices, movements of crops, state of the market, etc., in all the principal cities of the country, announced at brief intervals, through business hours, daily. Orders for the purchase or sale of grain and produce for cash or future delivery, are promptly executed, and being a member of the Chicago and Indianapolis Boards of Trade, he is able to furnish his clients with special advantages in placing their commissions either here or in Chicago, where most of the deals passing through his hands are made. Orders either by mail or wire are as carefully attended to as if made in person, and at the lowest rates. He does a large and constantly augmenting business, and is known as a man of great executive ability and enterprise, as also the head of a house, the operations and management of which are characterized by honorable and liberal methods.

HOTELS.

HE hotels of Indianapolis enjoy a reputation for superiority widespread and substantial. They have served to extend the fame of the city throughout every State in the Union, as also to all portions of Europe. In respect to size, equipment, appointments and elegant service, they are surpassed by those of no city in the country. They are commodious, luxuriously furnished, provided with gas, electric lights, passenger elevators and all modern conveniences, while their tables are supplied with all the solids and delicacies that can tempt the appetite of the most fastidious of guests. The Denison House has accommodations for 500 guests, also the Bates House and the Grand Hotel; the Occidental and Spencer for 300 each; the Hotel English for 200; the Brunswick and Circle 150 each; the St. Charles for 125; the Weddell for 100. There are also other caravansaries with more limited facilities. In addition to those mentioned, there are a number of first-class family and European hotels which are handsomely maintained, and still further add to the reputation of the city as a home for travelers, and where they are made the recipients of the most hospitable entertainment.

New Denison Hotel George O. Taylor & Co., Proprietors, corner of Pennsylvania and Ohio streets. The judgment formed in regard to the merits of a city by the visiting stranger is in a large measure founded upon the qualities of its hotels, and as modern standards of excellence in hotel accommodation are very high, the possession of a first-class house, modern and progressive in its appointments, and adequate to the requirements of the most exacting visitor, is an important acquisition. Indianapolis is especially favored in this regard, having in the New Denison Hotel, as now conducted, a house which is admitted to possess few equals and no rival. The house was erected in 1879 upon plans embracing all the architectural requirements for a first-class hotel structure. It passed through several changes of management prior to 1886, in which year the building was purchased by Judge E. B. Martindale, and the proprietorship and management of the hotel business passed into the hands of Geo. O. Taylor & Co., composed of Messrs. George O. Taylor and Lynn B. Martindale, the latter gentleman being a son of Judge Martindale. These gentlemen have thoroughly refurnished and refitted the house in the most elegant and artistic manner, and sparing neither pains nor expense, have succeeded in making it in its equipment and appointments the leading hotel in the State, and one of the finest in the entire country. The building, a handsome and imposing four-story and basement structure, with a front of dressed stone on Pennsylvania street, covers a quarter of a block of ground, and is a solid building of 200x202½ feet in dimensions. The location is one admirably adapted to the purpose, being in the heart of the business portion of the city, and convenient to the banks, postoffice, public library, theatres, etc., and accessible to all transportation lines. The hotel has 150 large guests' rooms, many of them en suite and with bath attachments, as well as fifty sample rooms for commercial travelers. On occasion the house can afford accommodation for over 500 guests. On the ground floor of the hotel are the handsome general and ladies' entrances, elegant and spacious offices, rotunda and reading room, as well as the hotel bar, barber shops, etc., while the handsomely equipped bath-rooms,

lavatory, etc., are located in the basement. On the first floor are the parlors and reception rooms, the furnishings and appointments of which are models of elegance and good taste, and on this floor are also located the lofty, spacious and conveniently arranged dining room, with a seating capacity for over 300 guests; the ladies' ordinary, affording accommodations for 50 guests, etc. On the upper floors the sleeping rooms are located. The hotel is heated by steam, with natural gas in the grates, and is lighted by the new system of large incandescent electric lamps, as well as with both natural and artificial gas. The electric lights are supplied from the proprietors' own plant, which, with the engine and boiler rooms, are located at a remote distance in the rear of the building; and the kitchens, etc., are so located in rear buildings as to preclude the possibility of any odor reaching the residence portion of the hotel. The broad and handsome stairways; the halls, fifteen feet in width, running at right angles through each floor; the exterior fire escapes, built upon the most approved modern design; the perfect hydraulic guest and baggage elevators, and the numberless other conveniences and accessories provided by the management contribute to the comfort of guests and the completeness of the accommodations of this modern hotel. The staff of clerks, including Mr. W. W. Browning, chief day clerk, Mr. Chat. Cunningham, chief night clerk, and their assistants are experienced and efficient; and over 100 trained attendants are employed to look after the wants of the guests of the house. The cuisine is not surpassed in excellence anywhere in the country, and the service and attendance is all that can be desired. The owner of the building, Hon. E. B. Martindale, is a large property holder and capitalist, a prominent, respected and enterprising citizen, an active and influential member of the Board of Trade, and an enthusiastic supporter of all measures tending to promote the material interests of Indianapolis. Mr. George O. Taylor, the senior of the proprietary firm, is a popular hotel man of long experience and extensive acquaintance, whose accurate knowledge of the needs of the traveling public constantly fits him for the management of the house; and Mr. Lynn B. Martindale, his partner, although his present connection has been his only experience in hotel management, has already become very popular with, and widely known among, the traveling public. As now controlled and managed, the New Denison Hotel is not only a credit to Indianapolis, but is also a worthy representative of the highest class of modern American hotels.

The Bates House Louis Kedeski, Proprietor, northeast corner of Washington and Illinois streets. The location of this well-known house is adjacent to the Union Depot, the State House, and other places of public resort. The premises occupied consist of a four-story and basement brick building, with 220 feet front on Illinois street and an additional frontage of 230 feet on Washington street, substantially constructed and provided with every modern equipment and convenience. The main floor contains offices, reading-rooms, lavatories, barber-shop, etc., fronting on Illinois street, and the bar-

room, billiard rooms, and a number of fine stores, occupy the Washington street front. The second floor contains drawing and reception rooms, grand parlor, and a dining room with capacity for the accommodation of 300 guests. The remaining upper floors contain 300 guest chambers, commercial travelers' sample rooms, etc. The entire hotel is handsomely furnished and provided with all the modern conveniences usually found in first-class hotels.

Hotel English and English's Opera House — Hon. William H. English, Proprietor; James W. Duncan, Manager of Hotel; Northwest side Circle Park. The Hotel English was erected in 1884, and occupies a four-story and basement stone front building, 250x100 feet in dimensions, with a lofty and spacious rotunda, elegantly appointed offices and reading rooms, etc., on the ground

floor, over one hundred guest rooms, spacious dining rooms, and commodious halls and stairways throughout. The house is under the management of Mr. James W. Duncan, a hotel man of long and practical experience. English's Opera House, in the same block, has a seating capacity of 2,000 and presents to its patrons the leading and most popular attractions. The proprietor of the hotel and opera house, Hon. William H. English, is a prominent citizen of Indiana and was the Democratic nominee for Vice-President of the United States in 1880.

Grand Hotel George F. Pingst, Proprietor; corner of Illinois and Maryland streets. This hotel, which was completed and opened to the public in 1875, occupies an imposing five-story structure, having a frontage of 250 feet on Illinois street by 200 feet on Maryland street, and is an architectural ornament to the city. It is provided with all modern conveniences for the entertainment of guests in a first-class manner, and is elegantly furnished throughout. The billiard and bar-room, barber shop and Turkish and other bath conveniences, are in the basement. The  main floor is devoted to the office, reading and writing rooms, rotunda, etc., and has forty sample rooms for commercial travelers. The dining room, with capacity to comfortably accommodate 500 guests, the ladies' ordinary, for 50 guests, grand parlor, reception rooms, etc., occupy the second floor. The upper stories are used for guest chambers, of which there are 212. The house is provided with ample fire escape facilities, and is practically fire-proof. The cuisine is unsurpassed, and the service completely in harmony with the most exacting requirements. The location is most central, being but two blocks from the Union Depot, adjacent to the banks, places of public resort, in the business heart of the city, etc., and the terms are from $3 to $5 per diem. This hotel is a favorite resort for commercial travelers, tourists, etc., and is always full. Mr. Pingst, the proprietor, is one of the oldest and best known hotel men in the country, and his management of his present enterprise has been of a character that explains its high reputation and pronounced popularity. T. J. Cullen, the chief clerk, with his assistants, W. G. Elliott, A. W. Updegraff and W. F. Hinerling, have been with the house since its establishment, and are favorites with the traveling public, and the house enjoys a large and high-class trade.

Weddell House Major A. W. Hanson, Proprietor; 107 South Illinois street, one-half square north from Union Depot. Major A. W. Hanson, proprietor and host of the Weddell House, is the pioneer hotel man of Indianapolis, having been born and bred to the business and identified with the ownership and management of hotels almost from boyhood. His present undertaking, the Weddell House, was thrown open to the public in 1875, and under Major Hanson's administration, covering a period of more than thirteen years, has annually grown in popularity with travelers and the public. It is admirably located at the above site, adjacent to the Union Depot, accessible to all street car lines, as also to the postoffice, banks, commercial and amusement centers; the premises, consisting of a three-story brick building 100 feet square, containing accommodations for 100 guests. The main floor is occupied with the office, reading room, dining hall and ladies' ordinary; the second floor with the parlor and reception rooms, also containing large, fine commercial sample rooms, superior to those generally used for that purpose, and bed room suites, while the third floor is devoted to sleeping accommodations. The house is handsomely fitted up, furnished and decorated, supplied with all the latest modern conveniences, and provided with every precaution against fire, as also with ample means of escape. The sleeping chambers are single and en suite, light, airy, thoroughly ventilated, handsomely finished and contain everything that will promote the comfort of patrons, while the cuisine includes all the substantials and delicacies of the season, prepared under the supervision of experienced chefs, and the service in every department is not surpassed by that of any similar establishment in the city. The terms are $2 per diem, and the trade, which is mainly transient, consisting of tourists and commercial travelers, is very large and steadily increasing.

St. Charles Hotel—John Murray, Proprietor; 26 to 28 North Illinois street, next to Bates House. The St. Charles Hotel has been a home for transients and an old established custom for many years. The proprietor, Mr. John Murray, entered upon the control and management of the house in 1884, and his administration has been of a character to commend the St. Charles to a large, continued and steadily increasing patronage. Located on one of the principal streets of the city, adjoining the Bates House, within easy distance of the Union Depot, near to the commercial and financial centers of the city, the house offers unsurpassed inducements in the way of delightful accommodations at low prices, to tourists or permanent residents. The premises are four stories high, 100 feet front on North Illinois street and 100 feet deep, and have a capacity for 125 guests. The office, sample, reading and dining rooms occupy the first floor, the parlor, drawing and reception rooms monopolizing the second story, and the sleeping apartments the two remaining upper floors. The interior is handsomely decorated and furnished in the latest and most modern style, appointed with every facility for the comfort and convenience of guests and supplied with every equipment calculated to promote their security. Natural gas is employed for heating and lighting purposes, a new and improved pattern of fire escape descends from each room to the street, and the service generally, including the cuisine, is all that the most fastidious of patrons could suggest. No expense or pains are spared to contribute to all the requirements of customers in the minutest detail, and the house enjoys the reputation of being one of the most desirable and hospitable establishments of its kind in the city or State. It is also provided with a restaurant, open day and night, telegraph and telephone service, is in immediate proximity to railway ticket offices, and is managed according to the most liberal and honorable methods. A force of fifteen courteous assistants are employed, and the regular rates are $1.50 per diem. Mr. Murray will make special rates to the profession. The St. Charles caters to a large trade throughout Indiana and the States adjoining.

Sherman's—Sherman's Cafe, 59 South Illinois street, Horace C. Keever, Manager; Sherman's Exchange Restaurant, 62 North Pennsylvania street, Charles E. Kershner, Manager; Sherman's Dairy Kitchen, 46 East Washington street, Thomas L. Brannon, Manager.—Mr. W. G. Sherman came to this city twelve years ago from Chicago, and has since resided in Indianapolis. For a few years he engaged in hotel management, and in that capacity was connected with the Grand Hotel and the Bates House. In 1882 he opened his first restaurant, afterward acquiring the other two, and now his establishments hold deserved recognition as the most complete and popular restaurants in the city. Meals are served on the American plan, at 25 cents per meal, or on the European plan, excellent meals being provided at from twenty cents upward, the best meal in the city being served for $1.00. Each of the establishments is provided with lunch counters for the convenience of the business public. For variety and quality the bills of fare of these restaurants are unsurpassed, and the cuisine and service are all that can be desired. Their patronage is very large, and Mr. Sherman has, with the aid of his efficient managers, achieved a deserved and notable success.

Circle House—15 North Meridian street, three squares north of Union Depot; H. Ackelow, Proprietor. The Circle House was opened some years ago, and has been since 1882 owned and managed by H. Ackelow, who at that date succeeded F. R. Welz. It is conveniently located in the city's business center, within three squares of the Union Depot, and adjacent to the postoffice, banks, places of public resort, and the wholesale and retail trade districts. The premises consist of a four-story and basement brick building, 100x200 feet in dimensions, with facilities to accommodate 150 guests. The main floor is occupied with office, reading, reception rooms, etc., also with an elegantly equipped and well stocked sample room. The dining room is finely finished and furnished and will seat eighty patrons. Broad stairways lead to the upper floors, which contain the parlors, drawing room and commercial travelers' display rooms. The two upper stories are devoted to sleeping chambers, single and en suite. They are all commodious, well ventilated and provided with every convenience or luxury that will contribute to the comfort of occupants. The cuisine is unsurpassed, the tables being supplied with all the substantials and delicacies to be found in the markets, and the service in this important branch of the establishment is of the best order. The house is heated and lighted by natural gas, and every precaution against fire has been enlisted in the equipment. The house is a model in its line, employing a force of fifteen assistants, and does a large transient trade. Its established rates are $2 per diem, with special prices for families and regular customers.

RELIGIOUS.

THE cause of religion found expression in the earliest days of the city's development, and the religious character of the people, as also their liberality, is attested by the number of churches identified with it and the large membership which contributes to their support and maintenance. Services were first held here in 1821, and denominational associations were organized soon after: The Methodists in 1822, the Baptists and Presbyterians in 1823, the Christians during 1833, Episcopalians in 1837, Catholics in 1840, Congregationalists in 1857 and the Hebrews in 1855. The various sects are at present represented by a total membership of about 32,000, and own property aggregating $5,000,000 in value. These establish one society of Adventists, nineteen Baptist, seven Catholic, seven Christian, two Congregational, five Episcopal societies and two Missions, one Evangelical and one Evangelical association, one Friends', one German Reformed, four Lutheran, two Hebrew, twenty-six Methodist Episcopal, one colored Methodist Episcopal; also one Union Sunday school, one Methodist Protestant, thirteen Presbyterian societies and four Missions, one each of the Swedenborgian, United Brethren, United Presbyterian, and the Exposition Sunday School, which is a branch of the Second Presbyterian church, or ninety-nine religious organizations regularly established, seven missions and two Sabbath schools. The church edifices are models of architectural beauty and substantial construction and services held regularly are attended by large and appreciative congregations. Besides the church organizations proper there are a number of societies more or less connected with the churches and working in connection with them in the promotion of Christianity, benevolence and charity, embracing the Young Men's Christian Association, the German Orphans' Home, the Home for Aged Poor, St. Vincent's Infirmary and others.

REAL ESTATE AND INSURANCE.

THE real estate available in Indianapolis for residence or business purposes, for factory sites or investments, offers the most substantial inducements to purchasers, by reason of low prices, reasonable terms and a steady appreciation in values. The markets in these commodities began to show signs of activity at an early day in the history of the city. During 1860 real estate houses, which at that date were limited to those owned and operated by William Y. Wylie, McKernan & Pierce, and John S. Spann, did a large business. Through the years of the war the market prices fluctuated, but upon the close of hostilities became active. This activity increased in volume until the panic of 1873, when the boom was at its height. During that and the year preceding there were 106 real estate offices in the city, and their daily transactions involved from half to three-quarters of a million of dollars in value. The effect of the panic precipitated the sale of a very large number of holdings, demoralizing prices and creating an absence of demand from which the market did not recover for several years. In the latter part of 1878 a mild reaction occurred, which was maintained throughout 1879, and continued throughout 1880. The year following investments began to be made; these have been continued, and while the transfers of property during 1888 were less in value than in 1887, the falling off was owing to the excitement incident to the elections, National and State. Since the conclusion of the campaign, however, the markets have revived and the sales of improved and unimproved property have steadily grown in number. The introduction of natural gas resulting in an increase of sales and an advance of prices in 1887, produced a similar result in 1888. Another notable feature was the number of lots sold to mechanics and others, upon which to erect homes for themselves; the records of building permits showing a large proportion to have been issued for cottages. The statistics as to the value of property sold in this city from 1882 to 1889, as per the following table, indicate a steady increase, except in 1888, when, for the reasons above stated, there was a perceptible falling off. In 1884 the value of property transferred aggregated $6,624,276; 1885, $6,005,756; 1886, $6,956,054; 1887, $13,110,729.52, and in 1888, $7,318,220.75. In 1884 permits were issued for the erection of buildings, the total cost of which was $467,835; 1885, $835,100; 1886, $1,213,000; 1887, $1,252,574, and in 1888, $1,357,000. The prospects for 1889 are very promising. Large investments of foreign capital it is believed will be made, and the indications for improvements are equally encouraging.

RESIDENCE PROPERTY.

Residence property is valued in proportion to desirableness of location, surroundings and accessibility to the business centers. Lots for this purpose can be purchased at reasonable rates, and upon easy terms. On Meridian, Delaware and some other of the leading thoroughfares, residence property commands from $100 to $150 per front foot; on Pennsylvania, Illinois and streets of equal prominence, from $75 to $100; on the side streets at a lower figure, and in the recent additions at from $5.00 to $15.00. On the outskirts, a comfortable home, with pure water, gas, street railroad facilities, and other accessories, houses can be built, ready for occupancy, for $1,600. For $5,000 one can put up or purchase a substantial residence in a genteel portion of the city, in the midst of a cultivated society, and for $10,000 a handsome brick residence, equipped with all modern improvements. Frame residences are to be had at a cost twenty per cent. less than brick or stone. Rents are cheap.

BUSINESS PROPERTY.

The most valuable business property in the city is located on Washington street between Pennsylvania and Illinois. Improved real estate in that square commands from $2,000 to $2,500 per foot. At a recent sale the Wasson property brought $65,000 cash, or $2,500 per foot. Unimproved property in the same locality is held at $1,800, and improved realty along Washington street, on the squares west of Illinois or east of Pennsylvania, at $1,000, the price diminishing as the distance from the latter streets increases. On Maryland, Georgia and other side streets immediately off the main thoroughfares, but in the business centers, sales have been made at from $300 to $500 per foot frontage. On Illinois, Pennsylvania and other highways of trade, from Washington street to the Union Depot, property has doubled in value within a short time, and dealers report none on the market. A commodious and well appointed brick store building, equipped with the latest improvements, can be erected and finished for $10,000. Store rents also range in price according to location. The Ayers building is held at $12,000; Wasson's building at $5,500, and the Benton Store at $4,000 per annum. These are located on Washington street, also between Illinois and Pennsylvania, where single stores readily bring an annual rental of $2,500. On South Meridian street from $1,500 to $3,000 per year is paid; on South Pennsylvania from $50.00 to $75.00 per month, and on South Illinois street from $75.00 to $125.00. Rents of stores at a distance from these points are cheaper, and double stores, with complete accommodations, are available at reasonable rates. Office rentals are low.

FACTORY SITES.

No city in the United States offers more flattering inducements for factory sites than Indianapolis. The complete railroad facilities available, cheap fuel—natural gas, vicinity of the city to coal and iron fields, and other advantages, combine to render Indianapolis almost unapproachable in this respect. Factory property can be purchased in the city limits within easy reach of the fire department and contiguous to railway lines, at prices within the range of modest pretensions. Along the Belt Line Road property for manufacturing occupation is in extensive demand. Citizens have encouraged investments of this character, and will not only welcome the advent of manufacturing enterprises, but will substantially aid all ventures proposed in such connection by the donation of land and by other means at their disposal. Indianapolis affords an attractive field for capitalists and others in the premises, and even a casual investigation will convince the most incredulous. Evidence of the rapid increase in the value of city property is afforded by the sale on April 13, 1889, of the former property of the Franklin Insurance Company, corner of Kentucky avenue and Illinois street, for $72,500. In the Fall of 1888, the Franklin Insurance Company's holding sold for $33,000; the present sale, however, includes land not included in the original property, and in its entirety brought about $61,000. It fronts 190 feet on Illinois street and 196 feet on Kentucky avenue, and the purchasers, New York and Cincinnati capitalists, will immediately begin the erection of a six-story office building of pressed brick, to cost $150,000, and to cover the entire space.

INSURANCE.

Insurance companies organized in the State have been in operation in Indianapolis for upward of fifty years. They are of approved financial strength and integrity, their stockholders and managers representing millions of dollars of private fortune, and being among the wealthiest and most prominent citizens of Indiana. Among the companies originating in the State, and for a very considerable period identified with Indianapolis business, is the Citizens' of Evansville, chartered in 1842; the Franklin, organized at Franklin in 1851, but removing to this city during 1884; the Indiana of Indianapolis, also chartered in 1843; the German Mutual Fire, incorporated in 1854; the National Benefit Association of Indianapolis, chartered in 1881, insuring against accidents; the Old Wayne, a mutual life association, organized in this city in 1885; the Indianapolis Mutual Fire, in 1884; the Manufacturers' Mutual Fire, in 1886; the Iron Hall, etc., with other associations for the protection of members, nearly all of which are free from debt and have a reserve fund in bank. Their management has been characterized by liberality and good judgment, and their prompt adjustment of claims according to the letter of their contracts of insurance, has secured for them an immense business and a national reputation.

The leading companies of the United States and Europe, fire, life and accident, long since established agencies in this city, and do a large business, which is steadily increasing and expanding with the city's growth and development. They represent a total capital approximating $200,000,000, with correspondingly large assets and surplus, and enjoy a well earned reputation for the prompt and equitable adjustment of losses, as also for low rates.

Charles F. Sayles — Insurance, Loans, Real Estate and Rental Agent; 75 and 77 East Market street; Telephone No. 176. The demand for Indianapolis real estate is steadily on the increase. The constant additions to the population, and the absorption of property for manufacturing and other interests, has necessarily given the market strength, and created what seems to be a boom. It is not, however, the continuous withdrawal of property for immediate improvement is the cause of advancing values. A live and pushing house, heavily interested in real estate, loan, rental and insurance operations is that of Charles F. Sayles, which was formed in 1873 by the firm of Barnard & Sayles, to which the present proprietor, who was the junior partner of that firm, succeeded in 1887. He occupies a well appointed suite of offices, and is furnished with every convenience, including telephone service, that will aid in the transaction of business. His deals in real estate are generally limited to improved city property, which he buys on his own account or to order, and involve annually large amounts of money. He also conducts an extensive business in the rental of the same class of property for residence and business purposes, and constantly has from four to five hundred tenants on his list. In addition to these, he places very large sums of local and foreign capital, the same being loaned upon first mortgage or other valuable securities, and does other business connected with these departments, such as taking care of estates, placing insurance, for which he is provided with superior facilities, the discharge of incumbrances, etc. In his capacity of underwriter, he is the local agent here for the Home, Citizens', Fidelity and Casualty, and Liberty, of New York; Phoenix and Ætna, of Hartford; London Assurance Corporation, and Norwich Union, of England; Traders' of Chicago, and other reliable corporations, representing a total cash capital of $84,248,325; assets amounting to $39,021,133.75; and surplus aggregating $26,764,555. All of these companies are of standard worth, furnishing insurance at low rates and adjusting losses with commendable promptness and liberality. Mr. Sayles is familiar with the details of every department of his business, and personally directs their conduct and operations. He does a large and annually increasing trade in the city and vicinity, and his house enjoys the confidence of commercial, financial and insurance circles in all parts of the State.

Ohio Farmers' Insurance Co. — Headquarters at LeRoy, O.; O. S. Wells, State Agent for Indiana; C. W. Oakes, Indianapolis Agent; 94 East Washington street. — Among the insurance corporations of the country the Ohio Farmers' Insurance Co. has an exceptionally excellent reputation for its conservative methods and for the thorough reliability which has characterized its entire corporate

history. It was established in 1848, and it confines its risks to farm property and dwellings, taking no manufacturing or business risks and limiting the amount of insurance carried upon any single risk to $6,000. The great care taken in the selection of risks has secured for this company a standing among the most substantial of American insurance corporations, and at the beginning of the present year it had assets amounting to $1,476,527.14; a reinsurance fund of $1,031,454.13, and a net surplus over all liabilities of $425,104.66. The business of the company is confined to the States west of the Ohio River, and in Indiana it does an active business, its premium receipts in this State for 1888 having been $102,791, while in the same year it paid out on Indiana losses $59,332. The company has maintained a branch office in this city for the past ten years, and its business for Indiana is in the hands of Mr. O. S. Wells, an insurance man of experience and marked ability, who ably represents the interests of the company in this State and exercises intelligent supervision over the 125 agents of the company in his territory. Mr. C. W. Oakes, the Indianapolis agent of the company, has had its local interests in charge for the past ten years, and is also agent for the well known and substantial Teutonia Insurance Co., of Dayton, O. He is a capable and efficient underwriter, and carries a large number of the most desirable risks in the city.

Abromet & Monroe — General Insurance, Real Estate, Loans, etc., Rooms 3 and 4, 24½ N. Pennsylvania street. — This agency was established in 1861 by A. Abromet, who conducted it until May, 1888, when he was joined by Mr. A. R. Monroe in the formation of the present firm. Both members are experienced in the several departments of business to which they devote their attention, and hold a high rank for the care they exercise in the management of the enterprise. They occupy an available suite of offices, and represent a large number of the strongest insurance companies in the world. Among these are the Lancashire, of Manchester, England, capital, $15,000,000.00, net surplus in United States, $671,941.00; Scottish Union and National, of England, capital, $10,000,000.00, net surplus in United States, $1,073,252.00; Lion Fire, of London, England, capital, $4,504,155.00, net surplus in United States, $236,225.00; Anglo-Nevada, of San Francisco, Cal., capital, $2,000,000.00, policy holders' surplus, $2,053,551.74; Commercial Union, of London, England, capital, $12,500,000, net surplus in United States, $930,355.00; British America, of Toronto, Canada, capital, $2,000,000.00, surplus in United States, $388,367.05; California Insurance Co., of San Francisco, Cal., capital, $600,000.00, policy holders' surplus, $805,091.00; Phoenix (Tornado) Insurance Co., of Brooklyn, N. Y., capital, $1,000,000.00, policy holders' surplus, $1,153,687.00; Fidelity and Casualty Accident Insurance Co., of New York, capital, $250,000.00, policy holders' surplus, $900,359.70; and the Ætna Life, of Hartford, Conn., cash assets, over $13,000,000.00, which has paid to policy holders over $24,000,000.00. In the department of real estate and rentals they are prepared to execute orders for the sale, purchase or lease of city and suburban property, and otherwise to supply the demands of customers promptly and satisfactorily. Mr. Abromet also represents a syndicate for the purchase of old Mexican bonds. The house is one of the best known in the State for its reliability and honorable career, and the firm enjoys a superior reputation for energy and integrity in the prosecution of their business.

Henry Coe — General Insurance; 13 Martindale block. — This prominent agency was established by Mr. Coe in 1873, and until January 1, 1886, he was senior member of the firm of Henry Coe & Co., his partner being A. M. De Souchet. He is president of the Indianapolis Board of Underwriters and is an insurance man of acknowledged ability, managing one of the strongest, if not the strongest, agency in the city. He represents a number of the leading insurance companies of America, including, among others, the America, of Philadelphia; Hartford and Connecticut, of Hartford, Conn.; The Farmers', of York, Pa.; The American Central, of St. Louis, Mo.; The German, of Peoria, and other companies, representing a total capital of over $6,000,000; assets aggregating $23,104,868, and surplus amounting to $4,468,000, a showing conclusive of solvency, business success, and unsurpassed management. Through these, Mr. Coe is prepared to offer the most favorable inducements to those seeking insurance at the lowest rates, consistent with the risk assumed, the inducements of security against loss or damage by their prompt and equitable adjustment, and corporations with almost unlimited resources and absolutely reliable. Prior to 1888, he carried on a real estate, loan and renting agency, in conjunction with his present business, but since that date he has relinquished those departments to devote his entire attention to insurance, and is doing a large and prosperous line of operations in the city and throughout the surrounding suburbs. He is also district agent of the American Surety Co., of New York, for the counties of Boone, Hamilton, Hancock, Hendricks, Johnson, Madison, Marion, Morgan and Shelby. The American is the *largest surety company* in the world, and its bonds are accepted by all of the Courts of Indiana.

Alexander Metzger—Insurance, Real Estate, Loans and Steamship Agent, Odd Fellows' Hall, Pennsylvania and Washington streets. Among the many extensive, important and successful insurance, real estate, etc., houses in this city, that of Alexander Metzger is prominent, standing high in the public estimation and fully deserving the confidence and prosperity that has attended its career. The business was established by Mr. Metzger in 1863. He occupies a handsome suite of offices in the Odd Fellows' Hall and is provided with every convenience for the successful conduct of his important lines of business. In the department of insurance he is State agent for the Metropolitan Plate Glass company, organized under the casualty laws of New York to do an exclusively plate glass insurance against accidental breakage. It has a capital and surplus of $281,500 and $100,000 in government bonds deposited with the insurance department of the State of New York for the protection of policy holders. He is also the local agent of the Hartford Steam Boiler Inspection and Insurance Company, and the following corporations taking risks against fire only: The Queen, of Liverpool, Guardian, of London, Buffalo German of New York, and Williamsburg City, of Brooklyn, representing an aggregate capital of $6,400,000, aggregate assets of $12,781,843.20 and an aggregate surplus of $4,276,751.84, all which have attained to a pre-eminent success, and their management is characterized by energy and enterprise though safe and conservative. His real estate operations are large, consisting chiefly of city property, also making large investments of city capital and doing an extensive business in leasing properties here, having, at the opening of 1889, over six hundred tenants on his rent roll. In addition, he makes collections in all European countries, buys and sells foreign exchange, etc., and is agent for the Cunard, Inman, Guion, National, Anchor, North German Lloyds, White Star, Red Star, American, Dominion, Hamburg and Bremen, Royal Netherlands, Baltimore Bremen, French and Italian steamship lines, also for the United States and Brazil Steamship Co. and other South American and inland navigation companies. His business in all its departments is very large in the city and State. Mr. Metzger has had a long experience and enjoys many advantages valuable to all seeking superior inducements in his lines, and employs honorable methods in its management.

Robert Martindale—Real Estate and Loans; Martindale block, 62 East Market street. Mr. Robert Martindale, who established himself in business about eleven years ago, has attained a prominent position in connection with real estate operations and the marketing of superior residence properties. He formerly carried on a general real estate, insurance and rental business, but has disposed of the insurance and rental branches and now confines his energies to dealing in and platting real estate, chiefly on his own account, and to the negotiation of loans on real estate security. He platted and successfully sold the Hall, the Stilz and Hill's subdivisions, and he is now rapidly disposing of the first section of Lincoln Park addition, of which he is the owner, and which is divided into 642 lots, beginning at North Meridian and Fourteenth streets, running across Pennsylvania street, Talbott avenue, Delaware, Alabama and New Jersey streets, to Central avenue. This is one of the most eligibly located, and desirable additions to the city, and the lots in it are in great request for residence purposes. Mr. Martindale has been prominent in many

enterprises for the benefit of the city, and is one of the most active workers in the organization formed for supplying free gas to manufacturers. He was the originator of the second mortgage plan, by which the purchaser of a lot may raise moneys from building societies or others for building purposes, giving a first mortgage for same, while Mr. Martindale accepts a second mortgage for the land. He is a son of Judge E. B. Martindale, one of the most prominent real estate owners of the city, and long a leader in its business community. Mr. Robert Martindale is a zealous advocate of the material interests of Indianapolis and a representative of American energy and business progress.

Richardson & McCrea—Insurance, Loans, Real Estate and Rents; 14 Talbott block; Telephone No. 182. This business was established in 1874 by B. A. Richardson, head of the present firm, becoming Richardson & Kothe in 1877. During 1887, Frank F. McCrea became a third partner, and in November, 1888, Mr. Kothe retiring to embark in the wholesale grocery business the firm name was changed to its present style. They occupy handsomely appointed offices and are agents for a large number of prominent companies in fire, life, accident, steam boiler, plate glass, tornado and live stock insurance, placing a majority of the risks in manufacturing lines here, and doing a large business in the line of steam boiler insurance. Among the companies the firm represent are the Phenix of Brooklyn; Detroit Fire and Marine; Michigan Fire and Marine; Hamburg Bremen of Germany; Western Assurance of Toronto; Mutual Life; New York; Central Live Stock of Indianapolis; Phenix of London; Continental of New York; Firemen's of Dayton, O.; Niagara of New York; Insurance Company of North America. These companies combine all the requisites of stability, superior management and honorable methods. The firm also buy and sell for their own account and to order large blocks of city and suburban real estate, and manage the collection of rents and the care of property subject to lease. In addition, they negotiate loans, placing local capital chiefly, make investments for patrons, place insurance and execute other commissions connected with their principal lines of business, promptly and in the most satisfactory manner. They transact a large and steadily increasing business, and their intelligent and enterprising management has given to the house the confidence of the community in all portions of the State.

Northwestern Mutual Life Insurance Co., David F. Swain, General Agent; 60 East Market street. The universal effort of all provident men, either in mercantile or mechanical pursuits, is to add to their estates from year to year, so that in the event of death they may leave to those whom they loved, and for whom they have labored, a sufficiency enabling them to at least be equal to the "battle of life" to those with whom they may have to contend. No medium is known by which such a result can be so surely accomplished as through a policy of life insurance, and this medium is approved by the example of the most prominent and successful financiers of the day. Most of the financial institutions issuing life insurance contracts, if not all of them, are good and worthy of confidence, but particularly conspicuous among the many is the Northwestern Mutual Life Insurance Company, of Milwaukee, Wis., pre-eminently a western institution, which began business in November, 1858. Since its organization the company has paid to the representatives of deceased policy holders, for death losses, $17,015,761.04; to living policy holders for dividends, matured endowments, surrendered and lapsed policies, $28,388,572.12; a total of $45,331,312.31 paid to benefaciaries, and adding to this sum the present assets of $32,672,811.36, it is shown that the total amount paid to policy holders and held for them is $78,007,123.67. During the same period the total premium receipts have been $68,284,832.26, and the company has, therefore, paid to policy holders and invested for them, $9,317,321.41 in excess of the entire premium receipts. The company invests its funds upon improved real estate security at Western rates of interest, and has now thus placed over $27,000,000.00. Its location enables it to select the choicest securities, commanding the highest rates of interest, and no loans are made by the company on stocks, collaterals, or any kind of fluctuating or doubtful securities. While thus guarding the safety of its investments, it has always been able to secure profitable rates of interest, the interest receipts since organization having been $23,277,433.88, or $9,731,364.01 in excess of the death losses paid during the same period. The organization of the company is purely mutual. It has no capital stock, and all profits are divided among its policy holders, who are full partners, with liabilities limited only to the extent of annual premiums while the policy is in force. Every policy holder has a vote in the management of the company for each $1,000 of insurance. The abuse of the proxy system has been carefully guarded against in the charter. Proxies can be used but once; only within sixty days after execution. No officer, trustee, agent, clerk or employe of the company can cast a proxy vote, and no one person can cast over one hundred proxy votes at any one election. The company confines its business to the Northern United States, and risks are carefully selected — many occupations debarring from insurance. This scrutiny of risks has secured a remarkably favorable death rate—less, for the past ten years, than any other large company. For 1884 the death losses were but .695 per cent. of the mean amount insured; for 1885, but .696 per cent.; in 1886, but .682 per cent.; 1.01 per cent. in 1887, and .689 per cent. in 1888, or an average of .691 per cent. for five years—the lowest rate of mortality ever experienced in America by a company of the age and size of the Northwestern. Thus combining the lowest mortality with the highest interest income, the Northwestern offers the cheapest, best and safest policies. The company established an agency here about twenty-five years ago. Mr. David F. Swain, who has been a citizen of Indianapolis for over twenty years, is now in charge, and has been the general agent for over eight years, and does a large business, issuing, in some years, as much as $2,250,000 in policies (residents of the State). He has a handsome suite of offices, and directs the business of the company in Indiana, employing from fifteen to twenty sub-agents. The company also conducts a loan department in this city, managed by Mr. Frank Taylor, who charge no commission for procuring loans, and this department is carried on in a manner alike advantageous to the corporation and to the citizens of Indianapolis. Messrs. Swain and Taylor are both experienced business men, and worthily represent the great corporation whose interests in this State they have in charge.

Thomas C. Day & Co.

Thomas C. Day & Co. Financial Agents, Mortgage Loans, Etc.; 72 East Market street.—The investment of capital in a way which combines safety with security is a problem of the utmost importance, and the selection of a trustworthy and efficient agent through whom to make such investments an important matter. In this line of usefulness there is no firm which has a higher standing than that of Thomas C. Day & Co. The business was established about twenty-two years ago by Mr. Thomas C. Day, who was joined in 1879 by Mr. W. C. Griffith in the formation of the present firm. They occupy a handsome suite of offices at 72 East Market street, where they carry on an active and extensive business in investments of all kinds, placing mortgage loans on city and farm property, and buying and selling city, county and other bonds on their own account and as agents for others. They have among their clients many of the largest local capitalists, and also are the representatives of some of the most prominent of Eastern monetary institutions. The firm combines all the qualifications of practical experience in investment matters and accurate knowledge of values and of the markets, and their advice upon financial questions is justly regarded as sound and reliable. The uniformly satisfactory relations with investors, maintained by this house for so many years, are the result of sagacious and honorable methods, and the firm is regarded as a representative one in its line.

William E. Stevenson & Co.

William E. Stevenson & Co. — Real Estate, Loan and Rental Agents; 84 East Market street, Hartford block. Mr. W. E. Stevenson came to this city from Greencastle, this State, in the spring of 1888. He was one of the leading and successful merchants of Greencastle, having been engaged in the hardware business for about eighteen years as a member of the firm of J. D. Stevenson & Son, and also of the firm of W. E. Stevenson & Co. In the spring of 1885, he disposed of his interest in the hardware business, and for the following three years engaged in the real estate and banking business. He served as a Director of the Central National Bank, and also as Cashier of the Putnam County Bank. He was one of the prime movers in securing to Greencastle the splendid system of water works and gas works, in both companies serving as Secretary and Director. Mr. Stevenson was also among the first of Greencastle citizens in organizing the building and loan associations which have been so beneficial in building up his former home. He was also a member of the City School Board, serving as Secretary and Treasurer, and only resigned his position when leaving his native city to enter into business at Indianapolis. The firm occupy the ground floor of the Hartford block, well adapted with every convenience for the transaction of the business to which they give their entire service and personal attention. Mr. Stevenson's means are ample, and any business entrusted to the firm will be handled with care and dispatch. Satisfaction is guaranteed to all who entrust their business with them, and all who have property to sell, exchange or rent, and those who would have their property looked after, as to collecting of rents, placing of insurance, and all other details, whether local or non-residents, can make no mistake in confiding in this firm and placing their business with them.

Berkshire Life Insurance Co.

Berkshire Life Insurance Co. Indiana State Agency; James Green, General Agent, No. 8 Martindale block.—This company was organized under a perpetual charter granted by the Legislature of Massachusetts in 1851. The home office is at Pittsfield in that commonwealth, with agencies located in many States of the Union. The charter provides that all securities in which the assets of the company are invested shall be of the highest character of first funds, and the investments are consequently made upon the basis of security and rates of income. The business is conducted upon the mutual plan, by which the policy holders receive the entire benefit arising from their payments into the treasury. The company issues life policies, upon which the premiums are paid as long as the assured may live; limited payment life policies, upon which premiums are paid for a limited number of years; and endowment policies, upon which premiums are paid during the full terms for which they are issued. In the selection of risks great care is exercised, none but sound lives being taken, and in addition to the certainty of payment of policies at maturity, none of them are forfeited in the event that the holders are unable to pay the premiums when the same become due. In such cases after two full annual premiums have been paid, the policy holder is furnished with insurance for a proportionate amount payable the same as if no lapse had occurred. The solvency of the company is indisputable. The Treasurer's annual report for the year ending December 31, 1888, shows total receipts during the year of $1,014,607.73, the issue of 831 policies for $2,243,165, and disbursements amounting to $804,075.31. The total number of policies then in force was 9,275, covering $21,191,228 of insurance. The assets were $4,122,542.83 and the surplus, Massachusetts standard, was $491,578.38. The company, as indicated from this exhibit, is entitled to the confidence it now enjoys among the insuring public, and such confidence is further emphasized by the low rates it charges for the quality of insurance furnished, as also for its characteristic promptness in the adjustment of claims. The agent of the company for Indiana is Mr. James Green, who has filled that important position for nearly 20 years. He occupies a suite of offices in the Martindale block, and by his enterprise and management has enhanced the value of the company's influence, and promoted the company's prosperity in the city and State, throughout which he does a large annual business.

Clinton M. Thompson

Clinton M. Thompson —Fire and Accident Insurance and Rents; 62 East Market street. Clinton M. Thompson has been a prominent and enterprising underwriter in Indiana for more than twenty years, residing principally at Bowling Green, where he was sole agent for a number of insurance companies of acknowledged reliability, including the Phoenix and Ætna, of Hartford, etc. From Bowling Green he removed to Terre Haute, where he was Secretary of the Board of Trade, and from thence he came to Indianapolis in 1888.

During November of that year he purchased the fire and accident insurance and rental departments theretofore owned by Robert Martindale & Co., an old house established at an early day by Judge Martindale, and continued their operation. He is local agent for the Germania Fire, of New York; the Phœnix, of Hartford, and the Merchants', of Newark, N.J., all of which are fire insurance companies, with a total cash capital of $3,200,000, total assets amounting to $8,112,662.81, and an aggregate surplus of $2,116,686.07. He is also agent for the Equitable Accident, of Cincinnati, the special object of which is expressed in its corporate title, and possessed of large resources. He is well equipped for the business and able to offer patrons seeking protection from loss by fire or accident, the inducements of low rates and prompt settlement of claims for loss or damages. His department of realty and rents is equally well provided for the execution of commissions in these lines promptly, and he gives particular attention to the leasing of city and suburban property, the collection of rents, and the general supervision of the same, and his business, which has already reached large proportions, is steadily increasing in volume and value, as the result of the enterprise and honourable dealings which have characterized his operations.

McGilliard & Dark—General Insurance Agents, Etc.; 64 East Market street.—The most extensive, enterprising and influential insurance firm in the State is McGilliard & Dark, composed of M. V. McGilliard and Charles E. Dark. Their agency was established by McGilliard & Brown in 1866, the firm changing to its present style in 1883. Both members are experienced and popular underwriters, making insurance their specialty for years, with results that have found expression in constantly increasing business and prosperity. They occupy an advantageously located and handsomely appointed suite of offices, and are provided with every facility for the service of their large clientage. They represent the leading companies in America, being general agents and managers of the Indiana Insurance Company of this city, of which Mr. Dark is also Vice-President and Mr. McGilliard is Secretary, a corporation having a capital stock of $200,000, with assets amounting to over $172,000 and less than $50,000 liabilities; also general agents of the Citizens', of Evansville, this State, which, on January 1, 1889, had a paid-up capital of $200,000, with $219,469.93 assets, and only $19,934.61 liabilities, including reinsurance and reserve funds; local agents for the German Fire, of Pittsburgh, and the People's Insurance Company, also of Pittsburgh, reprcsenting a total capital of $400,000, total assets aggregating $770,429.51, and a total surplus of $562,227.63, in addition to which they do a brokerage business through some thirty first-class companies in all parts of the country. The premium receipts of their business are over $350,000 per annum. The exhibits here made indicate a quality of responsibility that must recommend the firm to the patronage of all seeking reliable insurance at favorable rates, and such recommendation is further emphasized by the character of the patronage which avails itself of such substantial inducements as they are prepared to offer. They do a very large business in the city and State, also writing special lines of policies for customers in every section of the Northern, Southern and Western States, into which remote territory the reputation of the firm for reliability, liberal terms and honorable dealings has been extended and is firmly established.

Wm. & H. M. Hadley—Life and Fire Insurance and Real Estate; Basement 70 East Market street, opposite Postoffice.—The insurance agency of Wm. & H. M. Hadley was established by the senior member of the present firm in 1876, the junior member, his son, being admitted into the business as a partner during 1888. They occupy a handsome suite of offices and are prepared to offer customers reliable insurance at low rates. Their field of operations embraces fire and life insurance, in both of which branches they represent a list of companies of the most valuable and substantial character, including The Insurance Company of North America, the oldest company in its line in America, with assets amounting in round numbers to $10,000,000, and $6,000,000 surplus; The Pennsylvania Fire, established in 1825, with present assets aggregating $2,890,817.51, and a surplus of $1,682,929.27; The Orient Insurance Company, of

Hartford, Conn., with a capital of $1,000,000, and $1,143,125 surplus; The President Life and Trust Co., of Philadelphia, and other companies long established and equally responsible. In the department of real estate, their attention is largely devoted to the sale or lease of improved city property, and property along the Belt Line Railway. They have large lists of property for sale or lease, adapted to occupation for residence, commercial or manufacturing purposes, and parties desiring to buy or sell will do well to consult these gentlemen. They are also prepared to loan money, having the command of Eastern capital to any amount, to negotiate loans in behalf of clients, etc., and do a large business in all their departments. The members of the firm are experienced and influential operators in their several lines, and their house enjoys a distinguished reputation for reliability, liberality and correct business methods.

Connecticut Mutual Life Insurance Co.—No. 32 Vance block. This company, noted as one of the oldest, largest and most prosperous life insurance enterprises in the world, was organized in 1846 at Hartford, Conn., and has, through a long and active career, maintained its reputation for solvency, liberality, and fidelity to the interests and protection of policy holders. During the company's history, now covering nearly half a century, it has disbursed upward of $12,000,000 per year for death claims alone, returned a surplus of over $45,000,000, and transacted its entire business at a total expense of a trifle more than $17,000,000. Of their receipts during the same period, 62.09 per cent. have gone to policy holders and their beneficiaries, 26.57 per cent. to swell the volume of net assets, 8.39 per cent. for expenses, and 2.17 per cent. for taxes, a record that challenges comparison in the history of life insurance. The year 1888 was prosperous for the company. Its expenses were decreased and the number of its policies was increased, making the total number in force greater than 79,000. Its assets on December 31, 1888, amounted to $57,360,640.20, and its surplus, by the Connecticut standard of 4 per cent., was $4,362,037.59. Their policies are judiciously managed, their contracts of insurance are conservative, and the character of the assets which protect them, the volume and margin of the surplus, and the methods adopted and enforced, conclusively demonstrate that no company in the world furnishes more substantial security for the protection of those for whose benefit life insurance was originated and is supported. The company has agencies at every city in the United States. The agency was established at Indianapolis about 1846, and has been in operation for 42 years. Charles P. Greene has been the representative for the State of Indiana since 1882. He is a man of long experience in life insurance, and patrons of the company and the public can rely upon prompt service and the most honorable treatment at his hands. His office is at No. 32 Vance block, of which building the Connecticut Mutual are the owners.

Equitable Life Assurance Society of the United States—J. R. Shideler, Manager; J. C. Shideler, Cashier; southeast corner Washington and Meridian streets. This society, from its organization in New York in 1859 to the present time, has enjoyed of an uninterruptedly prosperous and successful career, with its paid-up capital of $100,000 untouched, and a phenomenally large and annually increasing surplus. The association is mutual in the broadest sense, and its plans embrace the ordinary life, endowment, term, semi and free tontine and others, the rate being determined by the plan selected and the age of the applicant. Policies are written for male applicants between the ages of from 25 to 70, and for applicants younger than the minimum age cited, upon certain conditions. Great care is exercised in the selection of risks and the death rate is less than 75 per cent. of the regular mortality tables, thereby increasing the surplus and producing a corresponding profit to members. The financial condition of the society, as shown by its statement, dated December 31, 1888, exhibits an outstanding assurance of $539,516,136, assets amounting to $95,042,272,96, and liabilities aggregating $71,228,207.81, with net assets of $95,042,022.96, representing the grandest results ever achieved by any insurance company in the world's history. During 1888 there was $145,043,435 new assurance written. The company is noted for able management, prompt adjustment of claims and unswerving fidelity to the interests of patrons. The Indianapolis agency has been a feature of this city for many years. Since 1872 it has been under the management of D. B. Shideler. He occupies handsome offices in the Blackford block, and directs the society's business throughout the State, with local agents at all the leading cities and towns within the territory, in addition to five travelers and a force of office assistants. His constant supervision has materially contributed to the company's success. He is assisted in his conduct of affairs by J. E. Shideler, Cashier of the agency, and the house enjoys the implicit confidence of the insuring public in all directions.

The Germania Life Insurance Co.

Life Insurance; Chas. Kahlo, Manager for Indiana; Fletcher Bank building. This company, which commenced business in 1860, has its home office at No. 20 Nassau street, New York City, with State agencies in all the large cities of the United States and the German Empire. On January 1, 1889, the Germania had assets amounting to $13,961,109.83, and a total surplus as regards policy holders of $1,888,521.33, with a total insurance in force of $40,032,179.00. During 1888, the total income was $2,344,588.89, and from the date of its organization up to the close of that year, a period of 28 years, had paid to its policy holders for death claims, endowments, annuities, dividends and surrenders a total of $21,316,201.00. It issues policies according to the ordinary life and endowment plans, also "dividend notine" and "absolute bond" policies, in which the amount assured becomes payable at the end of specified periods or at previous death. Premiums are payable in semi-annual or quarterly installments, and by careful selection of risks, the company's losses are naturally light, and their rates correspondingly low. The company has done business here for many years. In November, 1888, Charles Kahlo was appointed manager for the State of Indiana. He is a man of enterprise and broad views, who served as American Consul to Sydney, Australia, for about four years, being appointed to that station by President Garfield, and is especially qualified to promote the interests and success of the Germania in this section of the country. His business is large throughout the city and State.

John R. Leonard.

Fire Insurance, Real Estate and Loans; Ætna Building, North Pennsylvania street. Mr. Leonard, who established this business in 1886, is a representative citizen who had for four years, prior to embarking in his present operations, served as the collector of customs for the port of Indianapolis, upon retiring from which he accepted the local agency of the Ætna, of Hartford, Conn., and the North British and Mercantile, of London, with a large scope of territory under his management. Both companies are exclusively fire, the first named having a capital of $4,000,000, assets amounting to $9,438,388, and a surplus of $5,348,058, while the latter has $3,125,000 capital, $1,857,217 assets and $109,874,286 surplus. In the domain of real estate, he buys and sells city property, improved and unimproved upon the most favorable terms, on his own account and to order, and is a valuable agency through which to effect transactions. He also negotiates loans, invests money upon mortgage and other first-class securities, and executes commissions promptly and satisfactorily. His business in all its departments is conducted upon the most liberal and honorable basis. Losses are adjusted and paid as soon as the same are legitimately determined, property is bought and sold to the best advantage, and the money of capitalists and interests of his clients are most scrupulously cared for. He employs a staff of competent assistants and does a steadily increasing business.

Pacific Mutual Life Insurance Co.

Charles A. Holland, District Agent; W. H. Herrick, General Agent, Grand Rapids, Mich.; 92 East Market street. This company, organized in 1867, has from that date paid over $4,500,000 to policy holders, and to-day has actual cash assets aggregating upward of $1,950,000. It does a life, endowment and accident insurance business upon all plans, making a leading feature of its plan of insurance against accident, by which those injured in railroad or other accidents receive a weekly indemnity during the period of their detention from labor, and if total disability or death follows, the payment to them or their heirs of the amount of

the policy. The latter are non-forfeitable, contain no restrictions on travel or place of destination, and expressly stipulate that no deductions are made at death, for amounts of indemnity paid previously. The risks assumed are limited in amount in respect to those engaged in occupations, the pursuit of which is accompanied by more than ordinary danger, and in no event is the payment of claims delayed after they become due. The affairs of the company, throughout its history, have been managed with such fidelity, and exhibited this particular inducement so often and so manifestly, as to not only challenge public acknowledgement, but to enhance its reputation and advance its prosperity to its present high standard. The average time between filing of death proofs and payment of death claims, during 1888, was one and one-half days. The firm of Holland & Glazier took charge of the company's affairs here in the spring of 1888. During December of the same year, Charles A. Holland, the senior member of the firm, succeeded to the business. Prior to embarking in his present enterprise, he was a railroad engineer, but becoming disabled in an accident, and having a large acquaintance among railroad men, with whom the company does its chief business, accepted the agency. The company issues accident tickets and policies to travelers, with an insurance not to exceed $6,000, and a weekly indemnity of $30, in addition to its regular operations above mentioned. This office is tributary to the general agency at Grand Rapids, Mich., in charge of W. H. Herrick. Mr. Holland includes within his territory the States of Indiana, Illinois and Ohio; employs a force of five solicitors and is doing a prosperous business.

Powell & Rhodes

Real Estate, Rentals and Insurance; 72 East Market street.—The real estate and insurance firm of Powell & Rhodes, organized in 1888, is composed of W. A. Rhodes and Geo. W. Powell. Mr. Rhodes is secretary of the Franklin Building Association, of the Indianapolis Building and Loan Association, and of the Mutual Home and Savings Association, three of the most reliable and substantial corporations of their kind in the country, having a total capital of $2,300,000, and total assets in round numbers approximating $490,000. He also owns large coal interests here, having extensive yards at the corner of Delaware and Merrill streets, fully equipped for the business and handling heavy stocks of anthracite and bituminous coal. Mr. Powell was for many years of the real estate house of John S. Spann & Co., and subsequently for a period of five years partner in the firm of Fitzgerald & Powell. The firm are accessibly located, and buy, sell, exchange and lease city and suburban property on their own account, and possesses advantages in their knowledge of values, perfect titles and other important information connected with real estate here and in the vicinity that renders their services specially desirable. They have a large list of choice holdings for sale or rent, and all commissions to purchase, sell or lease, entrusted to their direction are faithfully and satisfactorily carried out. They are also sole agents for the Agricultural Insurance Company of Watertown, N. Y., the strongest and largest company doing an exclusively dwelling business in the United States. It has been in operation 36 years, now issues over 75,000 policies per annum, and has paid for losses since its organization the sum of $5,981,002.22. Upon January 1, 1889, its capital was $500,000, its net assets for the protection of policy holders were $1,058,105.52, and its net surplus over capital, reserve and all liabilities, was $393,191.00. The company's rates are low, and all losses are promptly paid immediately they are as certained. They also represent several others of the most substantial fire companies. Messrs. Powell & Rhodes attend personally to the various departments of their undertaking, and under their careful and honorable management, the business, which has grown steadily in its dimensions from the start, is increasing in importance and prosperity.

The Mutual Life Insurance Co. of New York.

Ferguson & Grant, General Agents, Detroit, Mich.; J. J. Price, Local Agent, Indianapolis; 14 Talbott block.—This company was incorporated in 1843 upon the mutual plan and without a dollar of capital. Every dollar of its assets is the property of the policy holders; every dollar of profit is divided among those whose contributions were the means by which it was produced, and the management and control of the business, with the business itself, is owned by and held solely for the benefit of the policy holders. The advantages thus offered by the Mutual Life, of New York, are so plainly apparent that even the most inexperienced will readily comprehend their importance and value. It issues policies upon the life and endowment plans at the lowest rates compatible with the quality of insurance furnished and the risks assumed, and all policies issued are non-forfeitable as to premium payment after three annual premiums have been paid, and the 15 and 20 year distribution policies are by far the most liberal insurance plan ever offered by any company. On January 1, 1889, the total assets of the company amounted to $149,608,333.06, and its total surplus to $7,049,696,163. During 1889, the number of policies in force was increased 37,436, making the total number in force at the close of that year 138,360, and $14,722,559.22 were returned to policy holders; the cash receipts for the same period aggregating $26,215,932.52. The company has been represented here for many years, Indiana being included in the department of which Michigan is a portion, with headquarters at Detroit, in charge of Ferguson & Grant. The local agent for Indianapolis and Marion County is J. J. Price, who has managed the business since 1884. He is an able, energetic, enterprising representative of insurance interests and his management has inspired confidence in behalf of the company.

The Howard Aid Association

Berry Self, President; Lew Replogle, Secretary and Treasurer; 10 and 11 Masonic Temple. The propriety of life insurance is no longer questioned by prudent men, but the great objection that is generally made to old-line companies of recognized solidity is that insurance, as furnished by them, is a dear investment, the premium charges being out of all just proportion to the amount necessary to pay losses and expenses; and an insurance contract, combining safety with economy, has long been much desired by the insuring public. To efficiently meet this want the Howard Aid Association was formed in 1878, and was after reincorporated in accordance with the provisions of the act of March 9, 1883. The plans of insurance of the old-line companies, and at the same time are not dependent upon uncertain contributions, as are the purely cooperative associations. Every member who enters the company makes a payment to his individual credit fund, and a percentage of each future assessment is also placed to this fund, which is ample to reimburse the persistent member in case of his lapse, and insures a payment from each member, whether he responds to the assessment call or not, and also serves the purpose of keeping his policy in force. The company is also strengthened by a security fund, limited to $50,000. This fund, which is invested in the name of the association, belongs to its members, and the interest upon it is applied to the payment of

assessments of all members who have been in good standing for five years. The practical operations of these plans have proved their sagacity, and the net result of the company's experience shows that it affords safe insurance at a remarkably low rate of premium, affording a maximum of benefit with a minimum of burden. Its practical beneficence is demonstrated by the fact that it has paid out over $130,000 to the widows and heirs of its members. The association has members in twenty-seven States and Territories, and its business is steadily and annually increasing. The management of the company is in the hands of gentlemen of the highest character and standing, and its Board of Directors is composed of prominent business men of the city. The association is recognized as one of the strongest in the country, while none presents to the policy holder a greater amount of benefit from an insurance standpoint.

H. H. Beville — Factory Site and General Real Estate and Investment Broker; Rooms 4, 5 and 6, 28½ West Washington street; Telephone 304. One of the influential real estate brokers in this city is H. H. Beville, who established the business in 1879, and through the exercise of enterprise has steadily increased his operations in volume and importance. His specialty, and one to which he devotes very particular attention, is the securing of large tracts of land at the most available points on the Belt Line Road, as also in the city for subdivision, sale and donation, as the location of factory sites, manufacturing industries, and for other improvements of a public or private character. The result of his endeavors in this direction is that he controls nearly every parcel of land of value for the purposes indicated along that great public highway of trade. Among these are 160 acres bounded by East Washington street, the Belt Line Road, English avenue, and the new Pan Handle shops, a large tract adjoining the above, platted into lots; 43 acres on the Belt Line Road, between the city and Haughville; 22 acres at Haughville; 55 acres between the city and

LEW REPLOGLE.

Haughville, through which the Belt Line tracks have been laid; two tracts of 66 and 55 acres respectively on the Belt Road, in the southeastern part of the city; 73 acres within the city limits on the northeast; 30 acres in the northern part of the city, and 55 additional acres in the same section, all traversed by the Belt Line Road, with many other parcels of large dimensions and values, from which he is empowered to donate from three to five acres and upwards to desirable parties for factory sites. He donated the land on which is located the works of the Ragsdale Manufacturing Company from Baltimore. This company, which has a cash capital of $150,000, employs a force of 100 hands, and when under full headway will put on 100 more. It is located on land near the Belt Line Road, and Mr. Beville is negotiating for the location here of several other establishments that will be sources of supply in their lines of immense value to the city's prosperity. In addition to the above, he has large plats of improved and unimproved city and suburban property for sale or rent, and does a general real estate business, besides caring for the property of non-residents, making investments for local and foreign capitalists, negotiating loans, loaning money, placing insurance, and performing other acts of a fiduciary character for clients. He is located as above, where he occupies commodious offices, and does a very large annual business. He is prepared to execute commissions without delay, to escort parties desirous of locating or making investments to view his various properties, in his own conveyance, and all orders left personally at his office, or transmitted over his telephones, No. 305 and No. 457, will receive prompt attention. Mr. Deville enjoys a reputation as an enterprising operator and public-spirited citizen, and persons having property for sale or to rent, or wishing to make purchase of Indianapolis property, will find him an invaluable agency through whom to conduct such transactions.

Indianapolis German Mutual Fire Insurance Co.—

113½ East Washington street.—This company was organized July 15, 1864, and incorporated on the 5th of August following. The present membership numbers upward of 1,700, and the company is carrying nearly $2,000,000 of risks. Its losses for thirteen months ending February 28, 1889, were but $250. The company's organization is strictly mutual in its design and operations, the members participating in the accruing profits and being guaranteed first-class protection at the lowest rates consistent with the risks assumed. A very large and steadily increasing business is annually done, the risks taken embracing those insuring (in this and other reliable companies), the Western Furniture Association's property, some fifty policies; the property of the Cabinet Makers' Union, of the Krause lounge factory, of Severan, Oysterman & Co., Frank A. Maus, William Pälin and many others among the largest property owners of the city. On the 16th day of January, 1889, the date of the last annual report, there were 1,641 policies in force for $1,762,010, being an increase of 334 policies and $348,870.00 insurance since the report rendered for the previous year, and total assets amounting to $119,02,090, with less than $20 total liabilities. The present officers are Friedrich Ostermeyer, President; E. F. Knodel, Vice-President; Hermann Sicholdt, who has been with the company since its organization in his present capacity of Secretary; August Ahlag, Treasurer, who, with J. H. Scharn, Henry Bauer, Franklin Vonnegut, Henry Spielholf, Christ Renner, Gustav Stark, Christ Gompf, Albert Sahm, Gottlieb C. Krug, Christ Watermann, Frank A. Maus and Henry Pauli, constitute the Board of Directors.

John S. Spann & Co.—

Insurance, Real Estate, Rents and Loans; 80 East Market street, Hartford block.—This house was founded in 1859, and the present firm, composed of John S. Spann and Thomas H. Spann, was organized in 1868. Their lines of operation include the buying and selling of real estate as agents only, the rental of property for account of the owner or lessor, the negotiating of loans and a general insurance business. The senior member of the firm is the oldest underwriter in the city, having embarked in that field of usefulness here at an early day. They are eligibly located, and occupy a handsome suite of offices, amply provided with conveniences and facilities for the business. In the department of insurance the business is mainly local and is prosperous and well managed. They are agents for the Liverpool and London and Globe Insurance Company, with United States assets amounting to $646,381,091, and $3,000,427.28 surplus, also of the Rochester German, of Rochester, N. Y., and the New Hampshire, of Manchester, N. H., representing a total capital of $1,128,200, assets of $8,945,735.96, and a surplus of $3,074,030.03. On January 29, 1884, they were appointed agents for the Connecticut Mutual Life, a corporation of national celebrity, treated at length in this book. Through these companies the firm is enabled to offer reliable insurance at the lowest rates. In the department of real estate they are agents for the purchase and sale of improved and unimproved property in the city and State, giving owners the full value of the market price, excepting only regular commissions, which are of course measured by the amount of the purchase money, also attending to the lease of properties and at present having over 700 tenants upon their lists. In addition, they invest money, negotiate loans,

place insurance, etc., acting in these connections on behalf of a large constituency of local and Eastern capitalists. Their long experience renders their advice and services in all matters pertaining to real estate and investments of the greatest value. They do a large local business, and the house, managed with judicious liberality, is not excelled by any similar undertaking in its line in the State.

Gregory & Appel

Insurance, Loans, Real Estate and Rents; 96 East Market street; Telephone No. 994.—This firm, which is composed of Fred. A. Gregory and John J. Appel, was organized in 1884. They are eligibly and advantageously located, and represent some of the oldest and most reliable insurance corporations in America, with well-established records for solvency, fair rates and equitable dealings; embracing among others, the Citizens', of St. Louis, Mo., organized in 1857; the Westchester Fire, of New York, established the same year; the New York Bowery, also of New York; the Northwestern National, of Milwaukee, Wis., and the Manufacturers' Mutual, of this city, all companies of financial responsibility and liberal management. In real estate and rentals they represent equally extensive interests, their holdings of realty in the city and suburbs, for sale, rent or exchange, improved and unimproved, being exceptionally large, and offering unsurpassed inducements to purchasers and lessees in location, price and terms. Their rental list embraces upward of 300 tenants. In addition, they care for the estates of non-residents and other properties, attending to the keeping of same in condition, the payment of taxes and insurance, etc. They negotiate loans on first mortgages and other solvent securities, mainly for capitalists in the city and vicinity, in which also their trade now is. The members of the firm give their personal attention to the business, which they have developed into large proportions, and their house deservedly occupies a high and representative position.

W. H. Hobbs—

Insurance and Real Estate, Rents and Loans; 74 East Market street.—The insurance and real estate agency of W. H. Hobbs occupies a prominent place in Indianapolis and is a significant factor in the total of the city's business in that line. It was established by Mr. Hobbs in 1874, and has rapidly grown in value and importance to the insuring public of the city and State. He is located at 74 East Market street, where he occupies a suite of commodious offices well appointed for business, and provided with all requisite accommodations for the prompt execution of orders for services. He is the local agent for the Sun, Fire and Marine, of San Francisco, and for the United Firemen's, of Philadelphia. His long experience in the real estate business has given him a good judgment as to values of property. He is the agent for the sale of some of the most desirable real estate in the city. Indianapolis, like a number of other cities, has a large number of property owners who reside in different parts of the Union, who must depend on the agents for the collection of their rents and for the sale and management of their property. Mr. Hobbs has always given this branch of the business prompt and careful attention. Those who have had business with him have had no occasion for complaint. He also loans on improved property, first mortgage, money sent him by parties in the East, and collects and remits the interest. Indianapolis being a prosperous city, a large amount of money is loaned on desirable real estate, and parties looking for those to attend to this branch of their business, naturally go to the more experienced and well known agents. Mr. Hobbs gives his individual attention to the business and his agency is recognized for its intrinsic worth and reliability.

The Old Wayne Mutual Life Insurance Co. of

Indianapolis.—77½ East Market street.—This company was chartered March 6, 1884, as a life insurance association upon a plan by which the funds for beneficiaries are derived from assessments made upon members monthly, according to the table of rates adopted by the association, and which is just for all ages. The membership fee is $10.00 for the first $1,000 of insurance, and $5.00 for each additional $1,000 up to $2,000, which is the highest amount issued upon the life of any applicant. Any person, male or female, in good health and habits, between the ages of 21 and 85 years, inclusive, may become members, and each applicant is subjected to a rigid medical examination. In addition to such precaution, the charter provides that if the insured die within six months from the date of the policy, the beneficiary shall not receive more than double the amount of the assessment paid thereon; if within a year, the benefits shall be paid not to exceed one-half the amount of the policy. After a year, if death occurs, the full claim is paid at the home office within sixty days from the date of approval of death proof. By a careful computation it has been ascertained that the largest amount of assessments individual members can be called upon to pay in one year, under any circumstances, on each $1,000 of insurance carried, is but $12.00 for a person 60 years of age, and $7.00 for a person 85 years old. Women are entitled to certificates at the same cost as men. There can be but one assessment per month. The mortuary fund can only be applied to the payment of death losses, and the plans of the company embrace many other advantages for the benefit of members. The company has grown in strength and popularity since its organization, and has agents constantly employed in all portions of the State, throughout which it is doing a large and steadily increasing business, the income from premiums, etc., being over $5,000 per month. The company's office is located as above. The present officers are as follows: Dr. L. C. Stewart, who succeeded Dr. Harman, President; C. C. Gilmore, Secretary; John Finnas was Secretary until 1888, when he became Treasurer; P. W. Bartholomew, Legal Adviser; and L. C. Stewart, M. D., Medical Examiner; all men of position and prominence, and enjoying public confidence in the highest degree.

John Wocher General Insurance Agency; Franklin building, Circle and Market streets.— The general insurance agency of John Wocher was established by that gentleman in 1887. He is an old and enterprising citizen of Indianapolis, formerly head of the wholesale millinery house of Wocher, Rich & Hanford, and the present President of the Franklin Insurance Company of Indianapolis. He occupies a handsome suite of commodious and nicely appointed offices, and represents a number of the leading insurance corporations of America and Europe. Mr. Wocher is thoroughly familiar with the insurance business, and represents the Detroit Fire and Marine, the capital of which has been increased from $300,000 to $550,000 since March 3, 1866, and which, during the same period, has paid a total of $2,271,293.20 in losses; The London & Lancashire of Liverpool, the German-American of New York, the Franklin of Indianapolis, and other corporations of acknowledged worth and reliability, representing a total capital of $2,276,000; assets amounting to $9,550,366, and surplus aggregating $4,500,695.19. The Franklin Insurance Company, of which, as already stated, Mr. Wocher is President, with its resources and advantages, are set forth in detail in another part of this volume. He is prepared to write policies for fire and other lines of insurance at all times, and possesses the best facilities, and is enabled to offer superior inducements to the public and his large patronage. He is assisted by a staff of experienced underwriters, and his business is largely in the city and vicinity.

The Franklin Insurance Co., of Indiana— Franklin building, Circle street, corner of Market. This company was organized at Franklin, Ind., during 1851. In 1875 the headquarters of the company were removed to Indianapolis, and in 1875, they erected the handsome four-story and basement brick building, now occupied by their offices. The premises are substantially constructed and are

architecturally an ornament to the city; front the Circle Park, opposite the Soldiers' Monument, and are equipped with all modern conveniences. The capital of the company is $500,000, and its affairs are managed according to the soundest principles of insurance policy, and its condition is one of unquestioned solvency and impregnable integrity. All losses are promptly adjusted upon the most equitable basis immediately they are determined. The company's annual statement, at the close of the year 1888, showed the assets to be $862,551.23, total liabilities, including the capital stock and re-insurance reserves, $323,012.97, and the surplus $538,538.97. John Wocher was elected President in August, 1887, J. M. Neuburger being at the same time elected Secretary. The former is a retired merchant, and Mr. Neuburger was one of the founders of the company and its Vice-President until that office was abolished. He is one of the oldest and most experienced insurance men in the State. The Board of Directors is composed of John Wocher, A. L. Roche, Morris Hennoch, J. M. Neuburger and William L. Kizer. Their business is large and principally in the city and State.

The United States Life Insurance Co.— J. W. Lanktree, Manager for Indiana; 25 East Market street.—The United States Life Insurance Company was organized in 1850, with headquarters in New York City. The executive officers, Board of Directors and subordinate committees are made up of leading merchants and capitalists of the Empire State. Policies are issued according to all approved plans of insurance, in addition to which the company has a specially desirable plan of term insurance, peculiar to itself, and known as the "continuable term plan." Its advantages include bona fide insurance for a definite amount, upon a liberal contract and an incontestable policy, at the lowest cost, affording the maximum of insurance at the minimum of cash outlay. Policies under this plan are issued for 10, 15 or 20 year terms, and are renewable at the end of the term upon payment of the premium called for by the increased age. They are non-forfeitable after three years to the extent of their legal reserve value, which is used to purchase extended insurance; and they participate in profits at the end of each term. The company is conducted for the mutual benefit of members, to whom all profits belong. Ten days' absolute grace is allowed in the payment of premiums and all policy claims are paid as soon as satisfactory proofs are submitted, without waiting any specified number of days, and without discount. During the four years ending December 31, 1888, the company paid 301 death claims amounting to $1,404,894, in none of which was payment delayed beyond 30 days after proof of loss was received, a record that challenges comparison in the history of life insurance. At the close of the year 1888, the company possessed assets amounting to $5,976,299.82, and a surplus, as regards policy holders, of $968,023.68, but which, on the former basis of valuation (i.e., American table and 4% per cent. interest), is $1,016,629.82. During 1888, there was $6,333,663.30 of new insurance written and $527,413.98 paid policy holders, leaving the total amount of insurance in force on the 31st of December of that year $25,455,249. The company has maintained an agency in this State for many years. In 1889, Mr. J. W. Lanktree, the present manager, succeeded to the direction of affairs here. He had been for the previous four years agent in this territory of the Equitable Life, also of New York, and is specially equipped for the business. He occupies handsome and commodious offices, employing a large force of agents throughout the city and State and doing large and perceptibly increasing operations in his line. The company's pronounced success in Indianapolis and Indiana has been and is due to his liberal and honorable management of the trust.

Hamlin & Co.— Real Estate, Rental and Loan Agents; 36 North Delaware street. This firm, composed of Levi H. Hamlin and Samuel E. Hamlin, established their present business during 1861. They occupy commodious and handsomely appointed offices, and do a large business in the purchase and sale of improved and unimproved city and suburban real estate, the collection of rents, the renting of tenements for account of proprietors, the latter collecting the rents themselves but paying the firm a commission for their services in the first instance; payment of taxes, placing of insurance, contesting of unjust assessments, care of estates for non-residents, and other operations connected with the transfer of real estate. They make a specialty of buying and selling all kinds of merchandise and established business property, farming lands, etc., and enjoy such facilities in this department for superior service that their office is the recognized bureau in these lines in this city. They also negotiate and place loans upon first-class securities and execute other trusts for clients of a confidential character in the most satisfactory manner, and upon the most reasonable terms. Their long experience gives their opinions in respect to titles, values, etc., great weight, and their honorable career of more than a quarter of a century has obtained for them the fullest confidence of investors, capitalists and the general public.

The New England Mutual Life Insurance Company, of Boston, Mass.

—D. F. Appel, General Agent; 10 When block.—The "New England Mutual" was chartered by the State of Massachusetts April 1st, 1835, and commenced business in December, 1843. Since organization it has received from members in premiums the sum of $53,198,000, and has paid in death claims, endowments, surrender values and dividends, $44,251,030. The assets of the company on January 1st, 1889, amounted to $19,724,538, with a surplus over all liabilities of $2,436,184. The payments heretofore made to policy holders, together with the present assets, amount to $16,728,468 more than all the premiums paid by members, in addition to which the expenses of conducting the business for more than 45 years have been paid. The investments of the company are of the most reliable character, which is proven by the fact that on the first of this year not one dollar of interest was due and unpaid. Distributions of surplus (commonly called dividends) are made each year upon every policy in force. All policies issued are subject to the provisions of the world-renowned "Massachusetts non-forfeiture laws," which define and protect the rights of members in every particular. Cash surrender and paid-up insurance values are plainly written in every policy, so that the holder may know its precise value for the entire term for which it is issued. The special feature of the company is the life rate endowment policy written for the same rates formerly charged for policies payable at death only. Since the organization of the company, only four claims have been decided by verdicts of juries. Forty-five years of honorable dealing with its members have placed the New England Mutual in the very front rank of the life insurance companies of the country. The Indiana agency was first established in 1853. D. F. Appel, the present general agent, was appointed March 1st, 1883, after having been special agent for the Western States of several life insurance companies. The agency under his management has been a success, and the growth of the business has been very satisfactory to the company.

Phœnix Mutual Life Insurance Co.

— E. S. Folsom, Manager; Talbott block.—This company was incorporated in 1851 under the name of the American Temperance Life Insurance Company, the idea being to insure only men of total abstinence habits, the same to be taken at lower rates than those established by ordinary life companies. Ten years later the temperance feature was abandoned and the name of the company was changed to that by which it is now known. Its management is liberal but conservative, characterized by ability and fidelity to the interests of members, and it has grown in strength, influence and importance year by year. The company issues all forms of insurance offered by contemporaries, making specialties of policies, however, including endowments at 80 at life rates; life, endowment, and annuity policies (copyrighted), with valuable options at 65, and indorsed guaranteed cash values at stated periods; stated paid-up insurance values after three years; non-forfeitable and incontestable, and paid-up insurance, good without surrender or any formality or attention being required from the insured. These specialties are original with the company, and afford inducements to the insuring public irresistibly conclusive of their advantages. On the 1st of January, 1888, the company's gross assets amounted to $10,501.53,974, and the surplus, estimated at the

Connecticut and Massachusetts standard of 4 per cent. to $1,210,013.39, but estimated at the 4½ per cent. standard fixed by many of the States, $8,760,000.00. The Indiana branch was established in this city late in the fifties. For the past twenty-two years it has been under the direction of E. S. Folsom, under whom its career here has been remarkably successful, and in the highest degree prosperous, notwithstanding adverse action by the Indiana Legislature toward foreign insurance interests. Since then many of the foreign life companies established here ceased writing policies, devoting their attention to the care of the large business established throughout the State previous to 1885, when such obnoxious legislation was inaugurated. The company, however, will resume operations in the territory, it is expected, within a brief period. Mr. Folsom, who occupies a handsomely appointed suite of offices in the Talbott block, is active and enterprising, and his honorable dealings and prompt recognition and protection of the rights and interests of patrons, have earned for himself an enviable reputation, and for the company an extensive clientage.

C. E. Coffin & Co.

— Investment Bankers, Real Estate, Loans, Insurance, Etc.; 90 East Market street. This firm, composed of Charles E. Coffin and Charles F. Holloway, was organized in 1873 as successor to the real estate firm of Wiley & Martin, established in 1845, and with whom Mr. Coffin had been associated since 1867. They occupy commodious and handsomely appointed offices in their own building on East Market street, and are gentlemen of more than ordinary prominence in real estate, financial and insurance circles. In their real estate department they operate extensively in the purchase, sale and lease of city and country properties, and have the largest rent roll here, over 1,000 tenants being embraced thereon. They are thoroughly familiar with the values of improved and unimproved realty in Indianapolis and vicinity, also with titles to holdings here, and are otherwise valuable agents through whom to transact business. They also negotiate loans and make investments of local and Eastern capital, besides managing other business incident to and connected with all of these. Their facilities for placing insurance are equally comprehensive, being well known and popular underwriters and the managing representatives of many of the most prominent and reliable corporations of the world, including among others The London Assurance of England, British America of Toronto, Milwaukee Mechanics' of Milwaukee, People's of New Hampshire, Franklin of Philadelphia, Glens Falls of New York, and Firemen's of Newark. The firm of C. E. Coffin & Co. has grown to be one of the strongest,

financially, in the city, and enjoys the confidence of the business community in a marked degree. Their success has not been due to risky speculations with fortunate terminations, but is the result of hard labor, good judgment and persistent effort in a legitimate field. The senior member of the firm is the Chairman of the Real Estate Committee of the Board of Trade, and is prominently connected with many of the public enterprises of the city.

Mutual Benefit Life Insurance Co.

Newark, N. J.; Capt. B. B. Peck, State Agent; 13 Martindale block. This company is one of the oldest, most substantial, liberal and equitable in its dealings with patrons of any enterprise in the United States similarly engaged. It was organized in 1845, and has headquarters at Newark, with branches in every State of the Union. They issue policies upon all healthy male lives between the ages of 14 and 70 years, according to all approved plans, for any amount from $500 to $20,000—though $15,000 is the limit, except upon specially favorable risks—the premiums upon which may be paid annually, semi-annually or quarterly. All policies, after payment of two years' premiums, are absolutely non-forfeitable; all surplus is returned to policy holders in the form of dividends, and lapsed policies are re-instated upon compliance with regulations, the equity and good conscience of which none can dispute. These are some of the inducements the company offers the public. In addition to the regular forms of policy, the company issues convertible policies, including all the exceptionally liberal features of the regular policy, with the addition of a guaranteed cash surrender value, which will be paid on demand at any time after ten years' premiums have been paid, upon surrender of the policy fully receipted, while in force or within three months from date of lapse. According to the last annual report, issued January 1, 1889, there were 57,054 policies in force, representing in insurance of $153,428,592.00, the total assets at the same date being $42,289,607.71; and the actual surplus, $3,762,523.21 (by Massachusetts standard). Actuaries 4 per cent. reserve and market values. During the year, death claims approximating $400,000 were paid to beneficiaries in this State. The branch office was established here many years ago, and in 1885 Capt. B. B. Peck succeeded to the management. Beside directing the operations of three sub-agencies in Indiana, he has entire charge of the business throughout the State, requiring the services of a large number of special agents for its successful conduct. He is an enterprising and honorable representative of insurance interests, and his efforts have materially appreciated the company's business in volume and value. The record of the company, and its honorable career of nearly half a century, is conclusive that the Mutual furnishes the best insurance at the lowest cost price.

German Mutual Insurance Co. of Indiana

37 South Delaware street.—This company, organized in 1854, is the oldest home fire insurance corporation of Indiana, and also one of the most substantial and best managed. The annual report of its condition at the close of 1888, showed total assets of $384,227.31, with liabilities amounting to less than $20,000, and a surplus of $364,227.31. The total losses which occurred and were adjusted during that year represented $9,025,508, and the total number of policies extant and in force were 3,087, for a total of $3,389,50,050 insurance. The headquarters of the company are located in this city, and occupy a handsome and commodious suite of offices, and contracts of insurance are executed at the lowest rates consistent with the risks assumed. They issue policies upon properties in the city and State, having agents at all the chief points, and its officers are in a position to personally investigate the character of every obligation undertaken or concluded. Mr. A. Seidensticker is President and Lorenzo Schmidt is Secretary, with a Board of Directors consisting of G. Schmuck, Frederick Schmid, A. Hagen, Peter Spitzfaden, Frederick Dietz, Edward Mueller, Geo. Fingst and Louis H. Mueller, leading business men and capitalists who have been connected with the company for years. President Seidensticker has been associated with the German Mutual since its organization and Mr. Schmidt has filled the position of Secretary since 1873. Both are experienced insurance men, the latter being also local agent here for the Springfield Fire and Marine,

of Springfield, Mass., with a capital of $1,250,000, assets of a par value of $1,836,400, and a surplus over all liabilities of $647,092.98. Great care is taken by the German Mutual in the acceptance of risks, and all losses are promptly and satisfactorily adjusted upon the most equitable basis.

Prather & Hanckel

Real Estate, Rentals, Fire Insurance and Loans; 66 East Market street.—This firm, composed of Austin B. Prather and Henry S. Hanckel, was organized in 1886, and has done a large and successful business from the start, the members being experienced in each department, and enterprising, public spirited men. Their dealings in city and suburban property are very large. They purchase, for their own account and to order, their knowledge of values, present and prospective, and other requisites to a successful conduct of the business, making their services especially desirable and in constant demand. They also collect rents—their present rent roll numbering some 600 tenants—probably the largest in the city—care for estates, pay taxes, place insurance, attend to the repair of premises, contest illegal and inequitable assessments, and discharge other duties connected with these lines promptly and satisfactorily, and at the lowest prices. In addition, they are prepared to consider applications for loans, and to negotiate loans of local capital, being provided with facilities that enable them to transact the business expeditiously and in the most reliable and accurate manner. Upon embarking in business, they succeeded to the insurance department of the well known house of William L. Mick & Co., in whose employ Mr. Prather had been for years. They now represent the Commercial Union Assurance Company, of London, England, exhibiting assets in the United States of $2,716,026.62, a net surplus of $630,355.53; and surplus income of $353,370.12; also of the New Hampshire Fire Insurance Company, of Manchester, N. H., having a capital of $600,000, total assets amounting to $1,505,101.00, and $304,351.79 surplus. Both of these companies have enjoyed an established reputation for substantiality since their organization, and by steady and conservative methods have secured general public confidence. The firm are prepared to issue policies at liberal rates, and to guarantee complete protection and the immediate adjustment of claims for losses sustained. The members of the firm attend personally to all business intrusted to them, and refer by permission to the Indianapolis National Bank, John S. Spann & Co., and others.

Provident Savings Life Assurance Society, of New York

Sudlow & Marsh, Managers for Indiana, Southern and Central Ohio, Kentucky, Tennessee and West Virginia; 90½ East Market street.—This company, which was organized in February, 1875, with a capital of $100,000, has made the guiding principle of its policy the providing of the largest amount of insurance at the lowest possible cost. It offers every plan to its patrons that experience has shown to be desirable, including the endowment, the limited payment, the twenty-year limited term with level premium, and other plans, making a specialty, however, of the yearly renewable term plan, which is fast becoming the most popular form of insurance. One of the closest thinkers and ablest writers on life insurance—the insurance commissioner of Massachusetts—says: "That insurance that does not insure is dear at any price. Insurance that costs beyond the needs of safety is an unjust burden. That system is best which combines safety with minimum cost." The principles thus enunciated are fully carried out by the Provident Savings. It provides a policy furnishing pure life insurance unmixed with banking or investment, the expenses being definitely fixed by the policy contract, and averaging about one-third those of level premium companies. As an additional safeguard against sudden and excessive mortality, it provides a guaranty fund, of which the share contributed by each persistent policy holder—if not so needed—is returned at stated times. Its plans have received the unqualified endorsement of the leading actuaries and insurance commissioners, and its popularity is attested by nearly $70,000,000 of insurance written in six years. It applies to life insurance the same principles as those that govern fire insurance, premiums being for insurance purely, and not for banking purposes. To illustrate: At the age of 45 years the premium charged is $190.40

for a policy of $10,000, or $1.00 per $1,000, which sum may be paid as a level rate during the expectation of life, and which payments may be realized by the savings from mortality from year to year. An analysis of this premium shows its component parts to be $9.00 for expenses of management, $10.5.60 for death losses, and $44.90 for guarantee fund. Compare this with other companies which, combining banking with insurance, charge at age 45 a premium of $37.930 for $10,000 of insurance, divided as follows: Expenses, $108.50, death claims, $105.50, and $115.70 deposited with the company as a banking liability which cannot be used to pay current death losses. The society also issues a new form of renewable term policy, upon which dividends are applied to maintain uniform premiums, the society, after deducting the expense charge, limited to $4.00 annually on each $1,000 insured, agreeing to appropriate the residue of each renewal premium paid upon this and upon other similar policies as follows: So much as is necessary for its share of death losses is deposited in bank as a death fund, to be used solely in settlement of death claims. The remainder is deposited in trust as a surplus and guaranty fund, in the

annual interest-bearing coupon bonds, in amounts of $500 and over, at six per cent. interest, payable at the Mercantile Trust Company, New York; secondly, 4% per cent. compound interest bearing installment savings bonds of $1,000, due in twenty years, the holders paying $30.30 each year during that term, these payments, although aggregating but $600 actually paid, securing to the investor, with the interest, $1,600, and larger amounts in proportion. The result of yearly saving is thus directly seen and realized by the holder of the bond. These and other denominations can be obtained maturing in ten, fifteen, twenty, twenty-five, thirty or thirty-five years, with installments payable weekly, monthly, quarterly, semi-annually or annually, at the convenience of investors. The security is unsurpassed, the Jarvis-Conklin Mortgage Trust Company having a fully paid-up capital of $1,500,000, and its entire assets being pledged to secure owners of bonds and securities of this company, in addition to a special guarantee fund of $100,000 in United States Government bonds which have been set aside and to which additions will be made from time to time. Should the investor be unable to continue the

HUBBARD BLOCK, SOUTHWEST CORNER OF MERIDIAN AND WASHINGTON STREETS.

Farmers' Loan and Trust Co., or other depository, and is applied to offset increase in the rates of premium on account of advancing age. In case of death, the unused surplus in the guaranty fund is paid as an addition to the sum insured. Should the policy, after five full years' premiums have been paid, be terminated solely by the non-payment of any stated premium when due, said unused surplus may be applied to purchase paid-up insurance, provided application be made therefor while this policy is in full force and effect, otherwise said surplus will be applied as a single premium to renew and extend the full amount of this insurance for so long a time as said surplus so used will purchase. This is the simplest and most equitable life policy issued, its terms securing the return to policy holders of every dollar paid for insurance, and not used for actual mortality, in addition to the face of the policy.

Messrs. Sudlow & Marsh are also sole agents for the Jarvis-Conklin Mortgage Trust Co. in the same territory. The object of this company is to separate the investment from the insurance, and provide the public what they have long been wanting: First, semi-

installments, the contract can be terminated at any time at the option of the owner of the bond, he drawing the money paid, with interest. No better opportunity is offered for the investment of capital, while to those of small means equal benefits are offered by payment in installments as low as $1.00 a week. The firm of Sudlow & Marsh, from its connection with these two companies, is enabled to offer the public protection against every emergency of life or death. Thus, by the payment to them of one dollar per week, a man at the age of 35 can secure a policy of $1,000 of insurance in the Provident Savings Life, and a $1,000 bond from the Jarvis-Conklin Mortgage Trust Company, payable to him in full in twenty years. If living, he gets back all the money he has paid in, and has had his insurance during the entire period. If he dies, his heirs will have the insurance of $1,000 paid to them by the Provident Savings and in addition will receive from the Jarvis-Conklin Mortgage Trust Company all the money paid in on the bond with 4% per cent. compound interest thereon. Thus, a man of small means need not accept such low rates of interest as 3 or 3½ per cent., when larger can be obtained with equal, if not better, security; and, again, there is no other place where he can invest such a small sum as one dollar per week and get such large interest for it. Should necessity require, the cash value of the bond can be obtained at any time, without notice, before the termination of the contract, and other advantages of this bond are, in addition to the benefit of compound interest, that it can be easily transferred or assigned to others. The Jarvis-Conklin Mortgage Trust Co. also issues debenture bonds in denominations of $300, $500, $1,000 and $5,000, or larger amounts if required, bearing 6 per cent, interest, payable half-yearly, running for ten years, and having interest coupons payable at the offices of the Mercantile Trust Co., of New York, or which may be cashed or collected through any bank. These debentures are most desirable securities, each debenture in a series being secured by the entire deposit of first mortgage liens in that series. They are based upon real estate security of from two to three times their value, secured by mortgages carefully selected. They are a direct obligation of the company, can be used, if needed, for collateral, and can be held in convenient sums within the reach of small as well as large investors, without the expense or trouble necessary to the care of a mortgage and its accompanying papers. Any further information will be gladly given upon application personally or by letter to Sudlow & Marsh, Managers, 90½ East Market street, Indianapolis.

Robert Zener & Co.

Robert Zener & Co.—Fire, Life, Accident, Plate Glass, Etc., Insurance Agents; 31-33 North Pennsylvania street.—This house was founded in 1877 by Cleveland & Co. The establishment has since passed through several changes of management, and in 1888 the present firm was organized and succeeded to the ownership of the enterprise. They are the duly authorized State agents for Lloyd's Plate Glass Insurance Company, for the insurance of plate glass in stores and residences; general agents for the Employers' Liability Assurance Corporation, of London, England, with a paid-up capital of $5,000,000, and $200,000 deposited in the United States for the payment of claims maturing in this country. The operations of this company are described in a special article following this one, Messrs. Zener & Co. are also general agents for the Hartford Life and Annuity Company, of Hartford, Conn., for which, and the Employers' Liability, of London, they do business all over the State, having sub-agents at all the principal points. In addition to these, they are the local agents here for the St. Paul Fire and Marine Insurance Company, of St. Paul, Minn.; the Springfield Fire and Marine, of Massachusetts; the Girard Fire, of Philadelphia; the Union, of California; the Royal Insurance Company, of Liverpool, and the Northern Assurance Company, of London, England; representing a total capital of $6,247,475.00, assets amounting to $39,568,714.67, and an aggregate surplus of $12,664,714.62. These companies are all of the highest character, honorable in their dealings, liberal in their rates, and prompt in the adjustment of claims made against them for losses or damages protected in their contracts of insurance. The firm is prepared to offer unsurpassed inducements to the public, and the business done by them in the city and State is very large and steadily increasing.

The Employers' Liability Assurance Corporation, Limited, of London

The Employers' Liability Assurance Corporation, Limited, of London—Robert Zener & Co., General Agents for Indiana.—A new plan of insurance introduced into Indiana by Messrs. Robert Zener & Co., who represent the Employers' Liability Assurance Corporation (Limited) of London, is deservedly meeting with success and receiving a large and growing patronage from manufacturers and others. Among other forms of insurance the company makes a specialty of protecting employers against any liability incurred as a result of accidents happening to their employees. The corporation issues to the employer a policy based upon the amount paid out by him in wages. The employer estimates the amount of money he expects to pay his workmen for the ensuing year, and receives from the corporation a policy covering the estimated amount of the pay-roll, and to this amount the corporation is liable, indemnifying the insured against any compensation or damages for injuries sustained by his employees, including all law costs which may accrue as the result of

any legal proceedings based upon such injuries, the employer being relieved of all trouble or expense beyond the payment of the premium. The manufacturer or contractor thus protected is enabled to compute almost exactly every year what his expenses for injuries to his employees may amount to. The policy covers any and all workmen in the employ of the insured, and the names of workmen are not required. They may be changed as often as is necessary without notice to the corporation. The company began business in England in 1880, and has written nearly 15,000 policies. Two years ago they began operation in the United States and have already placed about 2,500 policies with manufacturers in this country, including several large firms in Indianapolis. The corporation also insures the owners or lessees of a building containing an elevator, against any accident to any person whatever that may be injured by the elevator. Mr. H. L. Segur has associated with Robert Zener & Co. in the Employers' Liability department of the above corporation. He is meeting with gratifying success, and this protection, though new to the people of Indiana, is rapidly recommending itself to favor in this city and State.

W. E. Mick & Co.

W. E. Mick & Co.—Real Estate and Loans; 68 East Market street. This firm, which is identified in a prominent way with the real estate interests of the city and surrounding country, is composed of Mr. W. E. Mick and his son, Mr. Edward L. Mick. The business was established in 1866 by the senior member, who conducted it alone for several years prior to admitting his son to the firm, when the present style was assumed. They occupy an elegant suite of offices, occupying the main floor, 25x100 feet in dimensions, of the building at 68 East Market street. They carry on an active and extensive business, covering all sorts of real estate transactions, buying, selling and renting city, suburban and farm properties, placing money on mortgages, and generally attending to all matters connected with real estate management and investment. Both of the members of the firm are natives of Indianapolis, members of the Board of Trade, and active and progressive business men. Their valuable experience in connection with important dealings has made them accurate judges of the values, present and prospective, of city and suburban property, and enables them to make investments on terms most advantageous to those placing business in their hands. The close and tireless attention paid to every interest confided to them, their promptness and accurate methods of dealing have earned for the firm a leading place among the real estate houses of the city.

Railway Officials' and Conductors' Accident Association

Railway Officials' and Conductors' Accident Association—Lafayette D. Hibbard, President; Chalmers Brown, George J. Johnson and Charles L. Nelson, Vice-Presidents; William K. Bellis, Secretary and Treasurer; 36½ West Washington street.—Organized five years ago, the Railway Officials' and Conductors' Accident Association, having its principal office in this city, has since presented a most remarkable promptness and fidelity in the administration of its business. The association was formed for the purpose of providing insurance against accidents to railway officials, conductors and employees, and by its honorable course has commended itself to a large clientage of persons engaged in the railway service in all parts of the Union, Canada and Mexico. The cost of insurance in this association is low, while the rates of payment for injuries are most liberal. The association has paid every claim proved against it, from its organization to the present time, without one moment's delay in any case; has never contested, compromised or discounted a claim, and has conducted itself, in its dealings with its members, upon the highest and most honorable principles of justice. Since its organization over $50,000,000 worth of insurance has been written; and yet the business has, notwithstanding its great volume, been uniformly carried on upon methods which have commended the management of the association to the favor and confidence of its members. The perfect protection afforded by the policies of the association has secured for it the largest membership among railway officials and conductors than any other accident company. The affairs of the company are ably administered by the officers named in the head-lines of this article, and its Board of Directors is made up of prominent railroad officials, including Messrs. L. D. Hibbard, Vandalia Line; Chalmers Brown, C., I. St. L. & C. Railway; Austin Putnam, O. I. & W. Railway; D. B. Earhart, C., I. St. L. & C. Railway, and William K. Bellis, Secretary and Treasurer of this association.

The Order of The Iron Hall—Circle Square.—The Order of The Iron Hall is an Indianapolis organization, incorporated in this city during 1881. From the headquarters here the executive board direct the operation of 1,600 local branches distributed throughout thirty-eight States, with a total membership stated at 47,000. It is a fraternal and assessment organization, embodying in its plan of operation a system of benefits, based upon the most equitable principles, that gives the most money to members at the least possible cost. Any white person between the ages of eighteen and sixty-five years, of moral character, steady habits, reputable calling, competent to earn a livelihood, and believing in the existence of a Supreme Intelligent Being, is eligible to membership, upon passing a satisfactory medical examination and the payment of an initiation fee of not less than three dollars. The assessments in this order are payable, upon thirty days' notice, by members of the several branches, eighty per cent. of which is forwarded to the Supreme Cashier in this city for sick benefits, the balance of twenty per cent. remaining in the hands of the officers of the branch, to be loaned at interest compounded semi-annually, or otherwise, and used in the payment of maturing certificates. Members who pay for seven years the full assessment of $2.50 receive a stated sum, not to exceed $1,000, from the income of the order, on the maturing year of their certificate. In case of sickness or accident they will be entitled to receive, under certain conditions, from $5 to $25 per week, but in no case to exceed the sum

of $500 during the seven years, which sum or sums are deducted from the amount due on the maturity of certificates. They also pay, after two years' membership, one-half face of certificate. The maximum liability of the order on each certificate is limited to $1,000, to meet which they have the receipts of the regular assessments, the profits from lapses and the reserve derived from the setting aside of the twenty per cent. above referred to. The Iron Hall admits women to membership, the benefit certificates to sisterhood branches, however, never exceeding $600. All local branches are under the control of the Supreme Sitting, a representative body made up of delegates from local branches, holding biennial sessions and issuing semi-annual reports of the condition of the order. The headquarters in this city are located on Circle Square, where they own and occupy a fine three-story and basement brick building 33x125 feet in dimensions, well appointed and equipped for business, and where a force of twenty clerks and assistants are constantly employed. Up to March 1, 1889, this fraternal order had levied 112 assessments, the proceeds

of which amounted to $2,200,000, which amount was paid to members in benefits during the time of sickness and disability, besides accumulating a reserve fund of $539,000. Their monthly disbursements average $142,000; and at a meeting of the Philadelphia branches, convened in that city January 22, 1889, there was $76,942.50 paid to the eighty-two holders of matured seven year certificates, in sums ranging from $250 to $1,000. As similar certificates are maturing daily, the amounts which pass through the banks here are not only very heavy but form an important item in the monetary transactions of the city. The present officers of the Supreme Sitting are F. D. Somerby, Supreme Justice, Indianapolis; P. C. Perkins, Supreme Vice-Justice, Baltimore, Md.; W. F. Lauder, Supreme Accountant, and M. C. Davis, Supreme Cashier, both of Indianapolis, with subordinate officers, residents in other portions of the city and country. The Order of the Iron Hall occupies a field original to itself, and during its career has faithfully and honorably executed the trust committed to its care.

Hiram Plummer Real Estate, Rents and Mortgage Loans; 93 East Market street.—A recent addition to the substantial houses engaged in the real estate, rental and mortgage loan business of Indianapolis, is that of Hiram Plummer, a well known ex-official of Marion County. He became established in the spring of 1888, and has built up a large trade in the disposal of property in subdivisions, for which he is the agent, in all parts of the city and county. He buys and sells city and suburban properties, his list at all times including superior attractions. His subdivisions embrace the Springdale and Brookside additions, also the subdivision of Square 2, Lincoln Park. The latter extends from Fourteenth to Fifteenth streets, and from Pennsylvania street to Talbott avenue. It is divided into 32 lots, each being 105 by 140.98 feet in dimensions, within one square of the proposed cable road, provided for gas and water supplies and otherwise desirable. He also controls three other additions, comprising 16 acres on the line of the Belt Railroad. These lots are for sale by Mr. Plummer at low rates and upon liberal terms. His list of tenants is upward of two hundred, and is daily receiving accessions. He also effects leases for long terms, cares for properties, pays taxes, buys and sells mortgage notes, negotiates loans, invests capital, places insurance, and generally attends to every department connected with real estate and loans. He is equipped with every convenience and facility for the prompt execution of orders at the lowest prices compatible with the valuable services rendered.

National Benefit Association of Indianapolis—Accident Indemnity; Talbott block, Pennsylvania and Market streets.—This association is a home organization, having been incorporated in this city during 1881. The objects of the association are for the payment of sums ranging from $4,000 to $5,000 for permanent disability or death, by accident, and the payment of an indemnity of from $5 to $25 per week to the assured permanently or temporarily incapacitated. No medical examination is required for admission to membership, the only expense incurred being the expense fee and assessments for the indemnity fund, the latter remaining the exclusive property of members for their protection, while the former goes to paying the expenses of the association. The association is managed by a board, the duties, responsibilities and powers of which are clearly defined and limited by the provisions of the charter. Among the powers limited is the retention of funds paid for assessments to that use exclusively—the prohibition placed upon the board's creating a liability against the indemnity fund, or to create a liability for the expense of management beyond the amount of the expense fund to meet. In short, no money can be appropriated from either the expense or indemnity funds for the payment of liabilities other than those expressly provided for in the creation of the funds themselves. The company has enjoyed a career signally successful under a management so skillful, equitable and at the same time liberal as to commend its advantages to an annually increasing patronage from among all classes of citizens. The headquarters of the association are located in the Talbott block, where they occupy a handsome suite of offices and employ a large force of assistants, in addition to several hundred agents operating in all portions of Indiana, Ohio, Illinois, Missouri, Michigan, Tennessee, Pennsylvania and elsewhere. It is free from debt, has assets amounting to $107,764, and a reserve fund of $50,000 on deposit in the First National Bank of Cleveland, O. It has paid $478,036,38 in claims, $463,1175 of which was received by the employes of the Indianapolis, Bloomington & Western Road at a saving to the latter of $28,362,08, which additional amount any other accident company would have charged for the insurance. The present board of management, besides the members of the executive board, consist of John C. New, James Bachman and John A. Wilkens, Indianapolis; Gen. Jas, Barnett, President First National Bank, Solon Burgess, wholesale grocer, Stiles C. Smith, wholesale grocer, George W. Stockley, President Brush Electric Light Co., and N. F. Wood, Superintendent N. Y., L. E. & W. R. R., all of Cleveland, O. Matthew Henning, of Evansville, Ind., is President; Ralph Worthington, of Cleveland, Vice-President, and John A. Wilkens, of this city, Secretary and Comptroller. All claims are paid without delay or discount on receipt of satisfactory proof, and the business is steadily increasing in volume and value.

The Travelers' Insurance Co. Life and Accident Insurance; H. M. Hagg, Local Agent, Vance block. The Travelers' Insurance Company, the only successful life insurance company in the United States conducted on the stock plan, with low premiums instead of promises of dividends, was incorporated in 1863, as an accident company. Business was commenced in 1864 and, in 1896, the charter was amended, providing for the transaction of life insur-

ance in addition. During its career, the company has annually increased the volume and value of benefits it confers, extending the influence exerted, and promoting the objects which is its organization was sought to conserve. It now pays out annually over $4,000,000 for accidents alone, in addition to large sums paid to life insurance beneficiaries. The company's headquarters are at Hartford, Conn., but its branches and agencies are located in all the principal cities of the United States. The State of Indiana is within the territory of which the State of Michigan is part, with the main office at Detroit, in charge of J. W. Thompson, H. M. Hag being the local agent in Indianapolis, a position he has honorably filled since 1886. He is prepared to issue life policies on the ordinary limited payment, endowment or coupon annuity endowment plans, also policies of accident insurance. On the first of January the company's assets amounted to $10,582,984,04, and its surplus to $2,908,210,41. At that date there had been a total of $2,880 life and 1,525,220 accident policies written, and the total losses paid in both departments, since their organization, footed up the enormous sum of $15,809,770,20. The company also issue accident tickets for 25 cents per diem, that are on sale at all local agencies and at all leading railroad stations. The advantages offered by Mr. Hag are low rates and the absolute payment of all damages sustained, immediately they are brought to his knowledge, without question; life policies, upon proof of death being furnished. His business is very large and to his efforts and enterprise the discharge of his trust, The Travelers enjoys a substantial and established reputation here, and throughout the territory within his jurisdiction.

UNION STOCK YARDS.

THE Belt Railroad and Stock Yards Company was organized in 1876, and began operations on November 12, 1877. The company's yards are located on a plat of ground containing 105 acres, situated two miles southwest from the center of the city. The plant consists of seven sheds averaging 450x250 feet in extent, with one intermediate section, same size, not covered; all subdivided into sections and pens arranged in the most convenient manner for the feeding, watering and handling of any class of stock offered for sale or in transit. The sheds were constructed in the most substantial manner, the best cedar poles being used to support the roofs, which are gravel, of first quality. The fences separating pens, etc., are of oak. All the structural work is in apparently as good condition as when erected, it having been the policy of the management to maintain the property in first-class condition. In addition to the sheds covering the pens, there are chutes, with platforms, etc., for unloading and loading stock, extending 1,200 feet on both east and west sides of the Stock Yards; a sawdust bin, 400 feet in length, located conveniently for bedding cars to be loaded with stock; a hay barn, 200x60 feet; corn cribs, 220x70 feet, capacity

UNION STOCK YARDS.

90,000 bushels ear corn; horse and mule sales stables, 220x60 feet, with auxiliary stables, one 124x50 feet and one 350x50 feet; also stable and house for fire department (to gallons hose) and hose reel; 26x38 feet, all in good condition, and covered with good shingle and gravel roofs. The yards are thoroughly equipped with scales and all necessary appliances for prompt handling of stock. The water supply is derived from driven wells, pumped by the company's pumps into tanks, elevated sufficiently to afford pressure to force the water into any part of the yards. The water mains extend through each alley, connecting with fire hydrants at convenient and numerous places, as well as with the small hydrants, located in each pen for the watering of stock. The hotel and exchange, a two-story brick building, with stone foundation and trimmings, slate roof, complete throughout, 220x87 feet, with a wing 114x87 feet, all in excellent condition. From January 1st to December 31, 1888, there were 875,946 head of hogs, 87,180 cattle, 84,094 sheep, and 24,661 horses, of which 147,201 hogs, 63,501 cattle, 70,144 sheep, and 19,038 horses were shipped to other points, the balance being retained for Indianapolis delivery. During the year the transactions amounted to $23,000,000 in value.

Fort, Johnston & Co.—General Commission Salesmen of Live Stock; Exchange building, Union Stock Yards. Messrs. J. W. Fort and W. M. Johnston, of this firm, have been identified with the live stock business in this city ever since the establishment of the Union Stock Yards. Mr. Fort was a member of the firm of Fort, Dye & Co., and Mr. Johnston of W. W. Johnson & Co., up to seven years ago, when these gentlemen associated themselves and formed the present firm. They have since built up a large and active business, and the firm holds a prominent position as one of the leading live stock commission firms operating at the Union Stock Yards. They give their personal attention to all stock consigned to them, and do a heavy business. They sell to buyers for eastern houses, on order, as well as to local packers, butchers, etc., handling about $1,500,000 worth of business annually. Their business is entirely on commission, and the faithful manner in which they attend to all business entrusted to them and the promptness of their returns, has established for them a first-class standing as a representative firm in their line.

A. Baber & Co.—Live Stock Commission Dealers; Exchange building, Union Stock Yards.—This firm, which is composed of Messrs. Adin Baber, J. B. Sedgwick and E. Nichols, was formed ten years ago, and has since enjoyed an active and constantly increasing business, commending itself to favor and patronage by the close care and attention paid to all transactions entrusted to them, and the promptness with which returns are made. They have every convenience and facility for prompt and efficient execution of orders, and they sell on commission only, their sales amounting to over $2,500,000 annually. They have a prosperous branch at the New York Central Stock Yards, at East Buffalo, N. Y. All of the members are practical and experienced men, conversant with every detail of the business, and the firm has a standing second to none in the trade.

M. Sells & Co.—Live Stock Commission Merchants; Exchange building, Union Stock Yards.—The oldest house at the Union Stock Yards engaged in the purchase and sale of live stock is that of M. Sells & Co., of which Messrs. Mike Sells and Smith Graves are the individual members. The business was originally established fifteen years ago by Sells & McKee, the firm changing to its present style and membership in 1881. Both of the members of the firm are thoroughly conversant with every detail of the business and possess an intimate acquaintance with the live stock markets of the country and with the principal stockmen who have transactions at the Union Stock Yards. They buy and sell and ship on order all kinds of live stock, and also have an extensive business with local packers and butchers. Mr. Mike Sells, the senior member of the firm, is the cattle salesman, Mr. Smith Graves, his partner, is the hog salesman, and Mr. Joel Slunn is employed as sheep salesman. They receive consignments from all sections, and do a large business, their transactions aggregating about $3,000,000 yearly. The firm is deservedly a favorite with raisers and shippers of stock, having earned their confidence by the close attention given to all commissions placed in their hands.

R. R. Shiel & Co.—Live Stock Purchasing Agents; Union Stock Yards.—This firm, of which Messrs. R. R. Shiel and R. R. Reeves are the individual members, was formed in 1884. Both of the members of the firm brought to it a long and practical experience, Mr. Shiel having been connected with transactions in live stock for the past twenty years, and Mr. Reeves having also carried on business in the same line for several years prior to forming this partnership. The firm makes a specialty of the business of purchasing stock on order only, and have a large connection with eastern customers for whom they buy on an average about 250,000 hogs and 6,000 head of cattle, besides other stock, per annum; their purchases amounting to about $4,500,000 yearly; and they buy in this market and ship east. Their cattle buyer is Mr. Abraham Kahn, and their sheep buyer, Mr. H. C. Farrow, both gentlemen of extensive acquaintance and practical experience. The members of the firm personally attend to filling orders, and their uniform promptness and accuracy have steadily increased their business until this is now the largest live stock purchasing house in Indianapolis.

G. F. Herriott—Live Stock Purchasing Agent; Exchange building, Union Stock Yards.—Mr. Herriott has had a long and practical experience in live stock transactions in this market, having established in business ten years ago, originally as a selling commission merchant, and for the past seven years has been engaged as a purchasing agent, buying on order only for houses in New York, Baltimore, Cleveland, Buffalo and other eastern points. Mr. Herriott possesses an intimate acquaintance with the local live stock market which gives to his services recognized value, and enables him to fill the orders of the trade to the best advantage. As a consequence he has secured an extensive patronage, his purchases amounting to about $1,500,000 yearly. Mr. Herriott pays close personal attention to all matters placed in his hands and is uniformly prompt and accurate. He refers by permission to Fletcher's Bank, to Coffin, Greenstreet & Fletcher, pork packers, and to W. P. Ijams, Manager of the Union Stock Yards.

OTHER BUSINESS LINES.

ACTIVITIES of Indianapolis embrace every department of endeavor, both in productive and distributive lines. In appropriate groupings a number of these have been specially referred to in this book, but among the avocations pursued there are many which do not properly come under the classifications made in those chapters, but which are nevertheless so important as to merit special mention. In order to properly represent these branches of business, reference will be made, in the succeeding paragraphs, to representative establishments engaged in them.

The Mercantile Agency—R. G. Dun & Co.—No. 2 Old *Sentinel* building.—The present enterprise owned and managed by R. G. Dun & Co. was established in New York City by Judge Lewis Tappan during 1841, for the promotion and protection of trade in the procurement and dissemination of information respecting the financial standing of merchants, bankers, manufacturers, capitalists and traders generally. The property and franchise of the enterprise was acquired by the present firm some time after its establishment, and under their management has become one of the most prominent agencies in its line in the world. The headquarters are in New York City, with over 130 branch and associate offices distributed throughout the United States and Canada. These offices are in charge of capable and experienced officers, possessing complete and comprehensive facilities for the adequate rendition of services, and the conduct and operation of this chain of agencies entails an expense of more than three millions of dollars annually. The most perfect system prevails in every department, a large force of reporters being employed whose duty includes a personal investigation of the status and condition of members of commercial, financial and other circles engaged in trading, and the reports made are of guaranteed accuracy and reliability, thus insuring to patrons an absolutely safe guide for operations involving credit and accommodation. The agency also includes law and collection departments among its facilities, employing able attorneys in the transaction of their legal business, and giving prompt attention to the collection of claims in any part of the

United States or Canada. The Indianapolis branch was located here in 1871, and has become an invaluable source of information to patrons, as also one of the most important of any directed by the company. A. F. McCormick has been in charge as manager since 1886, the city department being under the immediate direction of Daniel Boote, whose connection with the mercantile agency extends over nineteen years. The administration of Mr. McCormick has been characterized by an ability and honorable enterprise that has commended the agency to the patronage of the leading bankers, merchants, and others throughout the city and State, and the services rendered to an extensive and extended constituency have been acceptable, reliable and received with a confidence that becomes more implicit with succeeding years. All information as to terms of membership, etc., is cheerfully furnished upon application, and all commissions are promptly and satisfactorily executed. Their office is in the Old *Sentinel* building.

The Bradstreet Mercantile Agency — Henry Eitel, Superintendent for Indiana; northwest corner Washington and Meridian streets. — The Bradstreet Company was founded in 1849 and incorporated in 1876. Its career during the thirty years of its existence has been honorable and successful and its present capital and surplus exceed $1,500,000. The objects of the company are, in brief, to furnish subscribers with information of a commercial character in respect to the condition of trade, that will enable the latter to discriminate with approximate accuracy between a safe and an unsafe transaction, also with specific information for their protection against fraudulent dealers, undue risks, etc., in their various transactions involving the granting of credit. The company's facilities to promote such objects are most complete, comprehensive and reliable, embracing in addition to its large corps of skilled employes located in all portions of the United States and Canada, as also in Great Britain, France, Austria, Germany and Australia, over 100,000 correspondents who contribute the result of their investigations and opinions at brief intervals. These reports are disseminated among subscribers as soon as rendered, and no commercial center is more fully alive to their reliability, importance and value than Indianapolis. An evidence of this is to be found in their recent reports of mercantile failures in the United States and Canada for 1888, which amounted to 12,317, an increase of 11.5 per cent. over those of 1887. Of the failures for the latter year, the proportion of those failing which had only a moderate or fair credit, or which were not assigned any credit, was 94.8 per cent., against 91 per cent. in 1887. Of the total failures in the latter year, but 141 were given a first class rating and but 155 in 1887. These figures conclusively demonstrate the efficiency of the Bradstreet Agency, and must be the means of guiding merchants to the adoption of a policy limiting their credit to firms with moderate credit or having no credit whatever. The company also makes special mercantile reports, furnish books of reference, letters of introduction, recommend representatives or agents for manufacturers or others desiring to establish new business relations, and publish a weekly journal — *Bradstreet's* — in which are presented the results of their investigations into the material advancement of business interests, the prospects, etc., in an acceptable and comprehensive manner. The company is the largest institution of its kind in the world, and its value to mercantile interests is augmenting daily. The present officers of the company are: Chas. F. Clark, President; Edward F. Randolph, Treasurer, and Henry C. Young, Secretary, with headquarters in New York City. The Indianapolis agency was established here in 1878 by Henry Eitel, the present manager, who had for five years previous been similarly connected with the McKillop Agency in this city. He occupies a handsome suite of offices located as above, employing from ten to twelve clerks and has charge of the company's business throughout Indiana. He is prepared to execute commissions, furnish information and transact all operations promptly and satisfactorily. His long experience and intimate knowledge of the requirements of the service make him an invaluable representative of the company, whose success and prosperity he has so substantially promoted as also of subscribers whose interests he has so honorably protected and prospered.

ARCHITECTS.

D. A. Bohlen & Son — Architects, 95 East Washington street, Rooms 16 and 17. — One of the oldest architects in the city or State is D. A. Bohlen, head of the firm of D. A. Bohlen & Son, located as above. He began his professional career in this city in 1853, and is the author of designs after which some of the most prominent and strikingly attractive ecclesiastical structures and public buildings of the city and State were erected under his personal superintendence. In 1884, Oscar D. Bohlen, who had meanwhile become an expert and accomplished artist in the same line, was received into partnership and the present firm was organized. They occupy a handsome suite of offices conveniently appointed and furnished with every facility requisite to the business. They employ a force of skillful draughtsmen and are prepared to furnish plans and estimates for architectural work, also to supervise and personally manage the erection of improvements, enlisting in that department long practical experience and an intimate familiarity with all the requirements in that behalf. Among their more recent designs furnished are the St. Mary's Roman Catholic Church and Convent, St. Vincent's Hospital, and a number of private residences, the Roman Catholic Church at Oldenburg, residences at Shelbyville and other public and private buildings. The St. Paul's Evangelical Lutheran Church, the German Church of the Evangelical Alliance, St. John's Roman Catholic Cathedral, St. Joseph's Roman Catholic Church, the Robert Park M. E. Church, Fletcher's Bank building, Talbott block, Hubbard block, etc., all of this city, were built after their designs and under their direction. They do a large business in the city and State, exerting a widespread influence in promoting a high standard of excellence, and enhancing in value the reputation of the same territory for the superiority of its architectural possessions.

Charles G. Mueller — Architect and Superintendent; 31 and 32 Talbott block. — Mr. Mueller is a practical architect of talent, experience and skill, and his designs are universally conceded to be of the highest order. The business was founded during 1880, by the firm of Huebner & Mueller, and continued under their joint management until 1883, when Mr. Mueller succeeded to the sole ownership, and has since remained in that relation to the enterprise. He occupies a handsome suite of offices in the Talbott block, divided into designing, conference and business departments, and has a large line of operations in the various branches of the profession, and for all of which he is exceptionally well equipped and appointed. He devotes his personal attention to making designs of residences, public buildings, manufactories, churches, State institutions, etc., formulating and preparing plans for their interior arrangements, furnishing estimates, superintending their construction and completion, and otherwise promoting the interests of clients, and faithfully discharging the duties of the trust committed to his discretion and execution. Among the handsome improvements in this city made according to his designs are: The City Hospital, the German Catholic Hall, on South Delaware street, Smith's block, on North Illinois street; the Rodius' block, adjoining the *Sentinel* office; Dwyer's block, at the South End; the addition to C. Maus & Co.'s malt house, and to Birdsall's warehouse, etc.; the Hancock County Poor Asylum; the Putnam County Poor Asylum; the postmaster's residence, and two churches at Greencastle, this State, large business blocks at Logansport, and other edifices in this and the States adjoining. All orders receive prompt attention, and his personal supervision, and his superior excellence has created a constant demand for his services throughout the city and State.

R. P. Daggett & Co. — Architects; 18 When block. — This business was established by Mr. Daggett in 1868, and the present firm organized in 1875, when James B. Lucas became his partner. They occupy a handsome suite of offices, divided into draughting, designing and business departments, and provided with every accommodation and facility for the formulating of plans and the execution of commissions in their line. During the past few years, their operations have extended into almost every city, town and village of Indiana, besides being extensive in the adjoining States, while during the past twenty years, the value of work which has passed through their hands approximates $6,000,000. Among the improvements erected since 1885, according to plans and specifications prepared by the firm, are the St. Patrick, Hall's Place M. E. and the English Lutheran Churches; the headquarters of the fire department and eight fire engine houses; the two High School buildings, the Girl's Classical School and a number of the public school buildings, including public school No. 5, the design for which received the first premium at the Centennial Exposition, Philadelphia, and leading business houses and private residences, all of this city. Also the Court House of Shelby County; Court House and Jail, Warren County; First Presbyterian Church, Franklin; Cumberland Church, Danville; the school buildings of Shelbyville, New Palestine, Mexico, Fairland, Morristown, Freedom, Arcadia and elsewhere in this State; the Hartford City Bank, Indiana Starch Company's Works, at Franklin, the Exchange, Halcyon, Sterling, Stewart, Scottish Rite, and Bank of Commerce blocks, at Indianapolis, in addition to bank, factory and residence buildings at Lafayette, Logansport, Terre Haute, Kokomo, Greencastle, Crawfordsville, and elsewhere in Indiana; at Chicago and Jacksonville, Ill., and at various points in Ohio, Kentucky, and other States. During 1888, their designs were used for the business blocks of R. S. McKee, J. B. Mansur, William Hearle, etc., in this city, also for the remodeling of the Park Theatre, and the residences of Dr. O. S. Runnels, John C. Dean, W. G. Sherman, Albert D. Thomas and others, and for public buildings, factories, etc., in Muncie, Marion, Anderson, Huntington, Wabash, Warsaw and other Indiana towns. Their work demonstrates the superior ability of the firm, as practitioners of the profession in which they are engaged. Their terms are as low as are consistent with first-class service, and the firm fully merits the large and prosperous business of which they are the recipients.

J. H. Stem—Architect; Suite No. 51, Fletcher & Sharpe' block. J. H. Stem is one of the prominent and leading architects of the city. He has devoted many years to the study of the art as applied to public and private buildings, and also to ecclesiastical architecture. He has been established here since 1873. For a number of years his brother, A. H. Stem, was associated with him in his professional practice, but in 1886 the firm was dissolved, A. H. Stem removing to St. Paul, Minn., the present partner since conducting the business alone. He occupies a suite of offices in the Fletcher & Sharpe block, divided into office, display and draughting departments, and is well provided with conveniences and appointments for the designing of plans and specifications, as also for the estimates of buildings of the most ornate or substantial character. Among the prominent buildings that in beauty of design, interior arrangements, and in all other respects have commended themselves to public admiration, recently completed by Mr. Stem, are the Cyclorama Building, the business blocks of George Stout and Dr. Jameson on South Meridian street, the Soldiers' and Sailors' Orphans' Home at Knightstown, the University and several business blocks at Vincennes, with private residences here and throughout the State, as also in the States adjoining. His work in all particulars has demonstrated his natural aptitude for the profession, and his services are in constant requisition in all portions of the country. During the early part of 1889 he was engaged in the construction of improvements in New York. He employs a corps of experienced draughtsmen and supplies a large demand in Indiana, Ohio and Illinois principally, and also provides plans and superintends their execution in all sections of the Union.

BUSINESS UNIVERSITY.

Indianapolis Business University William M. Kedman, Emmet J. Heeb, and Elisha B. Osborn, Principals and Proprietors; 24 to 40 North Pennsylvania street.—The advantages of Indianapolis as a center in which a business education can be effectively acquired are of the best character; for here, in addition to the moderate cost

of living and the excellence of the social environments, is to be found, in the Indianapolis Business University, an institution having no equals in the country, in the experience and efficiency of its faculty, the thoroughness of its methods of instruction or the completeness of its course. In this university practical instruction is given in book-keeping, commercial arithmetic, business penmanship, commercial law, business correspondence, political economy, practical grammar, orthography, business papers, methods of actual business (office practice), and lectures upon various subjects connected with business education. In addition, there is a short-hand course comprising the study of the principles of phonography and their application, with drills in dictation and amanuensis work, type-

LOCATION OF THE BUSINESS UNIVERSITY—WHEN BLOCK, NORTH PENNSYLVANIA STREET, OPPOSITE POSTOFFICE.

writer practice, penmanship, correspondence, English grammar and spelling; and the various departments are in charge of competent and experienced instructors. The thorough, practical, and progressive principles upon which the university is conducted have commended it to favor, and an average of 500 pupils per annum receive instruction in the institution, pupils coming from Indiana and the surrounding States. The strongest endorsement of the university, however, is found in its home patronage, which is, at all times, large, many of the leading business men of Indianapolis and their sons having received their business education in this institution. Numerous applications are received from business men for assistants, and over 100 students have recently secured responsible positions with business firms in the city and State, and the university is considered by the business world to be a valuable medium for securing commercial help. The university was originally established in 1850 by W. McKee Scott, afterward becoming one of the Bryant & Stratton Colleges. In January, 1888, the entire interests of the various commercial colleges of the city, including the original Bryant & Stratton College and Indianapolis Business College, were purchased by the present proprietors and consolidated under the existing title of the Indianapolis Business University. The principals and proprietors who now have its destinies in charge are experienced educators, who have so managed the affairs of the university as to give it a leading place among the most thorough and reliable business colleges in the United States.

LIVERY STABLES.

Booth's Stables—Jno. L. Booth, Proprietor; Fine Carriages and Light Livery; 422 East Walbash street.—Booth's Stables, owned and occupied by John L. Booth, for the conduct of a high class livery business, centrally located, elegantly equipped and amply provided with commodious accommodations and appointments, is a favorite depot of supply for admirers of fine horseflesh and livery establishments. Mr. Booth began operations in his present line here during 1887, as senior partner of the firm of Booth & Crary, successors to W. J. Ripley. In July, 1888, Mr. Booth purchased the interest of Crary, and since that date has carried on the business under the name and style of Booth's Stables. The premises occupied consist of a handsome and spacious two-story brick building, 120x100 feet in dimensions, admirably situated for the convenience of a large trade, substantially constructed, well lighted and ventilated, and furnished with every facility for the care of stock, as also for the ready escape of the horses in case of fire. The stable proper occupies the basement of the building. It is fitted up with roomy stalls, ordinary and box, containing all the latest improvements designed for the health, comfort and safety of occupants, and is specially noted for cleanliness and perfect sanitary regulations. On the main floor are commodious carriage rooms, wash rooms, harness and toilet rooms, also a handsome suite of offices, provided and equipped with telephone service and other conveniences. The upper floor is used for storage purposes. He operates a perfectly systematized hack service for the public accommodation, employing seven large handsome carriages, reliable horses and careful and experienced drivers; also a regular livery business, for which he is supplied with the latest pattern of coupes, phaetons, buggies, light road wagons and other conveyances, turning out only first class vehicles for weddings, funerals, receptions, parties and other occasions, public and private, and at the most reasonable prices. He employs fifteen assistants and twenty five horses, and does a large and steadily increasing local business. Mr. Booth has

the exclusive franchise of the district telegraph calls for carriages to any part of the city. They also place in the residence of patrons who place their outfits in the care and board of the stable, a private call box, which will summon at any time their vehicles, etc. They have a private telephone with the A. M. D. T. office, also a telephone separate for general exchange business.

PATENT ATTORNEYS.

C. & E. W. Bradford—Patent Attorneys; 16 and 18 Hubbard block, corner Washington and Meridian streets. The spirit of invention is greatly aided by the advantages afforded inventors by the governments of civilized nations in protecting them by means of patents. These have become so numerous that questions of patentability, of infringement, etc., form a special branch of study which renders the aid of experienced and expert counsel a necessity. In this line, Indianapolis is the possessor of a firm known to inventors in all parts of the country as composed of gentlemen of superior knowledge and a successful record. The business was established in 1876, by Mr. Chester Bradford, who was joined, seven years ago, by his brother, Mr. Ernest W. Bradford, in the formation of the present firm. These gentlemen combine a practical knowledge both of mechanics and patent law with the technical experience in the patent department of the United States and other governments, necessary to insure prompt and efficient action, and they do a large business in securing patents, trade marks, designs, copyrights, and all forms of governmental protection; act as counsel and experts in litigated cases, or in cases where litigation is threatened; make investigations as to the validity or scope of existing patents for the protection of purchasers or others interested, and attend to all other business connected with patents. A member of the firm spends a large portion of the time in Washington, and the firm enjoys facilities for the prosecution of the business which are unsurpassed. Their charges are reasonable, and their services in every instance satisfactory.

AS A NEWS CENTER.

NO agency has contributed more effectively to the building up of Indianapolis and the promulgation of the city's advantages than the city press. From the birth of the *Gazette*, in January, 1822, to that of the *Sun*, less than one year ago, journalistic effort has proved to be the most powerful instrumentality enlisted in the behalf mentioned. The history of the Indianapolis press dates back to the *Gazette*, now the *Sentinel*, first issued on the 22d of January, sixty-seven years ago, and includes within its pages an account of the founding, on March 7, 1833, of the *Western Censor and Emigrant's Guide*, now the Indianapolis *Journal*. Many papers have appeared upon the stage of action in this city within the past fifty years, like Pallas armed for the fray, but few survive. They strutted their brief hour and were heard of no more. The press of Indianapolis to-day is considered the equal of that of any city of the same population in the United States. It is made up of the *Sentinel* and the *Journal*, daily morning papers, and the *News* and *Sun*, published in the afternoon; the *Daily Telegraph* and the *Indiana Tribune*, also daily, the two latter being published in the

German language. In addition to these there are twenty-eight weekly and twenty-eight monthly publications, one semi-monthly paper and one quarterly. The dailies above mentioned also issue Sunday and weekly editions. All of these are ably edited and occupy a front rank among their contemporaries. The dailies furnish their subscribers with a complete transcript of the local news morning and evening, while the facilities of the Western Union and Postal Telegraph systems are taxed to furnish complete and interesting accounts of happenings at a distance. The weeklies, semi-weeklies and monthlies handle every variety of subjects in a manner that commends them to the consideration and reflection of large and growing constituencies.

BREWERIES.

THE increase in the consumption of malt liquors, in preference to the stronger stimulants formerly in almost universal use, is an industrial fact the truth of which is borne out by the growth in number and size of the establishments engaged in brewing in various sections of the country. In Indianapolis the brewing business was established in 1835 by John L. Young, who carried it on until 1843, when other owners succeeded, the enterprise afterward being abandoned and the buildings torn down. Several later ventures were made in the business, the oldest and largest of those now in existence being that of C. F. Schmidt, who established it about thirty years ago. Since that time there has been a marked improvement in the facilities for manufacture, owing to the invention and introduction of labor-saving machinery, and a steady increase in the product and in the

There are now three large breweries in operation here—those of C. F. Schmidt, the P. Lieber Brewing Co., and C. Maus, and another and smaller one is conducted by A. Hitzelberger. The quality of Indianapolis beer is of recognized excellence, the water supply being peculiarly adapted to this manufacture, while the processes employed are of the most improved character.

C. F. Schmidt—Brewer and Bottler of Lager Beer.—One of the manufacturing establishments of Indianapolis which is specially prominent by reason of the completeness of its plant and the extent of its trade, is the brewery of C. F. Schmidt. This celebrated brewery, which had its foundation in 1859, has grown into a commanding position as the result of industry, honorable conduct and commendable enterprise. It was founded by Messrs. C. F. Schmidt and Charles

BREWERY AND WAREHOUSES OF C. F. SCHMIDT.

importance of the industry as an employer of labor. The statistics of the industry fully exemplify this growth, the beer product of the city having been shown by a Board of Trade report to have amounted to $317,000 in 1873, with an investment of $125,000 capital, and forty-five hands being employed in the industry. In 1880 the value of the product had increased to $477,000, and the number of those employed to seventy-four. Since then an important growth has been exhibited in the industry, the production of the breweries having amounted to $2,000,000 in value in 1898, and the capital now invested in the business amounts to $1,200,000, while 210 hands are employed, and an average of about $15,000 per month is paid in internal revenue taxes. The growth has not been achieved by an increase in the number of establishments, but in the enlargement of the capacity of the existing ones,

Jaeger, the latter retiring in 1861, and Mr. Schmidt becoming sole proprietor and conducting it until his death in 1872. Mr. William Fieber managed the business from that time until 1874, when he also died, and Mrs. C. F. Schmidt, widow of the original proprietor, took charge until her decease in 1877. From that time the business was managed by the executors, Messrs. William Kothe and John W. Schmidt until March, 1882, when Messrs. John W. Schmidt and Edward Schmidt, sons of the founder, became the proprietors of the business, and still carry it on under its original name. Great improvements have been made from time to time in the brewery premises, which now consist of a number of large and elegant brick buildings, covering five acres of ground, including brew house, ice houses, bottling department, storage houses, boiler houses, stable, malt and hop warehouses, etc., while the machinery equipment includes two engines, each of 150 horse power, five steel tubular boilers, 13½x16 feet, brew kettles having a capacity of 300 barrels, two large Linde ice machines, and all the latest and most efficient machinery and appliances for the production of beer in accordance with the most approved processes. The cellarage facilities of the brewery are unsurpassed, consisting of "home dry" cellars, thirty-five feet deep, with cement floors, iron and cement ceilings, etc., and fitted with cylinder vats of large capacity. Employment is given to a force ranging from ninety to one hundred hands, while sixty-two fine horses are utilized in the delivery of beer and other necessary hauling. The brewery has a capacity for the production of 150,000 barrels of beer annually, and a large trade is enjoyed in the city and throughout the State of Indiana, as well as to many points in Illinois. The products of the brewery are in high favor with consumers, in consequence of their purity and superior flavor, and include the Standard Lager Beer, for which the brewery has so long been noted; the Weiner Beer, a pale, amber-colored beer, brewed from Canada malt and Bohemian hops, mild in taste and with a fine hop flavor, and which is sold in kegs and bottled; and the Export Beer, specially brewed for bottling, and which will keep in any climate. Messrs. John W. and Edward Schmidt, the proprietors of the brewery, are thoroughly conversant with the business in all its details, and are regarded as enterprising business men who have greatly extended the business built up by its founder.

C. Maus—Brewer of Lager Beer; Frank A. Maus, Manager; northwest corner of New York and Agnes streets. Among the brewing establishments of the State of Indiana, none has a better reputation than that of C. Maus. It was established in 1868 by Mr. Casper Maus, whose practical knowledge of the business built it up to a successful condition. In 1876 he died, and the business is now owned by his widow, Mrs. Magdalena Maus, and managed by her son, Mr. Frank A. Maus, under whose direction the business has steadily grown. The brewery premises comprise a three-story brick building, equipped with a 40-horse power engine, three large boilers and the latest and most highly improved brewing and refrigerating machinery, the premises covering half a block of ground. The brewery has a capacity for the production of 50,000 barrels of beer annually, and employment is given to a force of thirty-five men, while ten teams are utilized in the city delivery. The product of the brewery is a healthy and nutritious family beverage, made exclusively from the best quality of malt and hops, and the popularity of the beer steadily increases from year to year, with a corresponding expansion of the

trade of the brewery. The processes of manufacture employed are of the most improved character, and the quality of the beer brewed is steadily maintained at the high standard for which the brewery is noted. The business is conducted upon reliable and progressive principles, which have secured for the brewery an important stand-

ing with the trade, and its affairs are administered in an efficient manner by Mr. Frank A. Maus, who, in addition to his position as manager of this brewery, is also Secretary and Treasurer of the Broad Ripple Gas Co., and otherwise prominent in important business enterprises. The record of the establishment, covering a period of thirty years, is one of sustained merit in its product and uniform propriety in business dealings.

The P. Lieber Brewing Co. Peter Lieber, President; William Shrieves, Secretary; Albert Lieber, Treasurer; City Brewery; Brewers of Lager Beer; South Madison street. The large and complete brewery establishment conducted by the P. Lieber Brewing Co., and known as the City Brewery, was originally established twenty-six years ago by the firm of P. Lieber & Co., changing to the present corporation in 1888. This company, organized with a capital of $500,000, is under the executive management of Mr. Peter Lieber, who has been at

THE P. LIEBER BREWING CO.'S BREWERY.

the head of the enterprise from its inception, and whose practical ability has been the leading factor in building up the business to its present gratifying position of prominence. The premises occupied by the company, and upon which their brewery, barns, etc., are located, cover an area of two and one half acres. The brewery occupies a handsome brick block, two stories above and two stories below ground, the last two affording cellarage to a depth of 42 feet, and the equipment includes a 75-horse power engine; three large 15½x16 feet boilers, run by natural gas; large brewing kettles, with a capacity of 250 barrels per day, and all the most modern machinery for brewing purposes, including a new and highly improved refrigerating machine for producing refrigeration by the De la Vergne process, recently added to their plant, and increasing the capacity of the brewery from 40,000 to 100,000 barrels per annum. By this addition, also, they are relieved of the necessity of gathering ice in winter, and enabled to turn their ice houses into store houses. They give employment to a force ranging from fifty-five to sixty hands, and they have thirty-five horses, which they utilize in delivering their product to their customers in the city and its surroundings. The beer brewed by the company is in high favor with consumers, and in a consequently large and growing demand by the trade. This popularity has been secured by the use of the best and purest materials and the adoption of the most approved brewing processes. The officers of the company are gentlemen of practical business experience and thoroughly conversant with the brewing industry, and all the operations of the brewery are conducted under competent supervision, and their methods of dealing are of a character which commends them to the favor of the trade and the public.

THE RETAIL TRADE.

THE advantages possessed by Indianapolis as a center for mercantile enterprises contemplating the sale of goods to consumers, are numerous and favorable. The large population of the city, which is steadily increasing at a rate more rapid than at any previous period of local history, affords in itself an important source of custom, added to which is the constant influx of visitors from all parts of the State, who find the Capital City one specially prepared to supply their needs in all the articles of necessity and luxury. The retail stores of the city cover every line of mercantile business, and many of them, in size and completeness of equipment, compare favorably with the most extensive and pretentious establishments of a similar character in the country. These facts are well known to the people of Indianapolis, and neighboring cities and country districts, and it is appreciated by them that it is no longer necessary to go to distant places to do shopping. The railroad connections of the city act as feeders to its trade, bringing not only large numbers who come expressly for the purpose of buying, but also gathering here, in conventions and important meetings, people from all parts of the State, who furnish custom to the stores. Among the leading retail establishments of the city many of the most prominent are noticed in the succeeding paragraphs of this chapter.

H. P. Wasson & Co.—Retailers of Dry Goods; 12 and 14 West Washington street.—One of the foremost of the retail dry goods emporiums in the city or State, carrying the most extensive and choicest lines all through, is that of H. P. Wasson & Co. at the above location on the most fashionable retail highway of Indianapolis. It was established in 1883 by Mr. Wasson, who is President of the Cleveland Dry Goods Company, of Cleveland, O., in which city he passes much of his time, the business here being in charge of John Daglish, who attends also to the selection and purchase of the stocks, visiting the eastern markets two or three times a year for that especial purpose. The premises occupied consist of an elegant three-story and basement building, 40x150 feet in dimensions and handsomely appointed and equipped. Every facility for the display of the superb lines of goods carried, and the convenience and accommodation of the high class trade to which the firm ministers, has been provided, including improved elevator and telephone service. Their stocks, which are selected with special reference to the wants of customers here, embrace foreign and domestic silks, satins, velvets, dress goods, laces, embroideries, shawls, wraps, hosiery, gloves, linens, domestic cottons, ladies' and gents' furnishings, nick-nacks, notions, novelties, etc., imported and of American make, in great variety and of the best description. A dressmaking department is included in the equipment of the establishment, in charge of an experienced *modiste*, and supplied with every auxiliary that can in any way contribute to meet the demand for prompt or superior workmanship. The house is in all respects a model of enterprise, elegance and liberal management, commanding the confidence and patronage of the best class of customers in the city and vicinity, as also among transients, giving employment to a force of one hundred clerks and doing an annual business very large, and steadily increasing in volume and value.

Egan & Treat—Drapers and Tailors; 24 North Pennsylvania street.—One of the leading and most fashionable draper and tailoring firms in Indianapolis or the State, is that of Egan & Treat, composed of E. C. Egan and A. J. Treat, which was organized and began operations during 1868, and since that period has conducted a large trade of the highest character. They are located at one of the most eligible sites on North Pennsylvania street, and occupy handsome premises, 20x125 feet in dimensions. They are attractively furnished, supplied with every available convenience that will facilitate the promotion and dispatch of business, or the accommodation of a large and exacting patronage. They are also equipped and appointed for an adequate display of their varied lines of stocks and for the successful handling of the trade. Their supplies are as diversified as they are select, embracing the choicest qualities of imported English, Scotch, French and German fabrics; also the products of the most celebrated American looms, in addition to trimmings, novelties, etc., included in the stock of a prominent high class establishment, such as Messrs. Egan & Treat own and manage. They make to order exclusively and by careful measurement, and the garments are always in the latest fashionable styles, cut and fitted by artists in these departments and trimmed and finished in a manner to challenge the criticism of the most fastidious patron or purveyor. They employ from thirty to thirty-five expert and accomplished assistants and supply a large and increasing local demand, also from regular customers throughout the country from Maine to California, in addition to that of customers residing in equally remote sections who send in their measures and orders, prompted thereto by the high reputation enjoyed by the house for superior production and honorable business methods, wherever it is known.

Eastman, Schleicher & Lee—Carpets, Draperies and Wall Paper; 5, 7 and 9 East Washington street.—This firm, which was organized in 1885, is composed of Walter H. Eastman, Adolph Schleicher and Fielding T. Lee, and is leading and representative in every respect. They occupy a four-story and basement building, 22x120 feet, also two floors, each 30x135 feet in dimensions, in the building adjoining to the east, and the premises in their entirety are exceptionally equipped and provided with conveniences for an elaborate display of their stocks, as also for their facilities for shipments and the transaction of business. The seven floors occupied by the firm are appropriated to several departments, being connected by the celebrated Crane elevator. One is used for the display of draperies and ingrain carpets, another for Brussels and finer grades of carpets, a third for wall paper and decorations, the fourth for mattings; the fifth for handkums and oil cloths, and their lace curtain and portiere stock is a feature of Indianapolis. An original feature of the establishment is what is known as the "Oriental Room," of which a recent newspaper article says: "It has a vestibule which might be termed a royal Japanese arch, constructed with characteristic Japanese roof, supported with square columns, adorned with fantastic figures in relief and inclosed with fretwork of marvelous pattern and ornamentation. Double curtains of richest texture divide the porch from the interior, which is as intensely Turkish as the entrance is Japanese. If admiration kindles at sight of the entrance, silent wonder is stirred or escapes in exclamations when the visitor stands within. The eye wanders from Turkish rugs, which softly cushion the feet, to walls and ceilings hung in drapery done in all the exquisite forms of beauty and grace. The stately mirror with its Turkish columns, the superb mantel cabinet with its precious burden of bric-a-brac and ornaments beyond enumeration, the carved Turkish vases with their rank growth of exotic plants, the circular divan with high back, inclosing a basin and playing fountain, sending off a perfumed spray; the overhanging Turkish lamps giving forth light as if from a sentimental moon; the soft notes of a musical box and a yet more musical bird, floating out upon the air of the place, inviting Turkish couches, soft as down, to recline upon there are some of the features of the Oriental room within which one may easily fancy the languid dalliance of an Oriental harem. A dusky lad, Abdul by name, of slight form and bedecked in full Turkish costume, waits on the place, carrying out the thought. Nothing could be said in exaggeration or in peril of raising expectation beyond the point of realization." The firm carry the most complete lines, imported direct from the European markets and selected with care from the products of the most famous American manufactories. Their specialty is the equipment of residences, halls, public buildings, etc., ready for furnishing, personally attending to the fitting of carpets, arrangement of draperies, etc. They employ a competent force of assistants, and supply the wants of a large trade in the city and throughout the State. The members of the firm have enjoyed a long experience in the business, and their success the recognition of deserving merit.

W. H. Messenger—Dealer in Furniture, Carpets and Stoves; 101 East Washington street, and 13 to 17 South Delaware street. From 1878 to 1884 Mr. Messenger held a controlling interest in the house of Born & Co. During the latter year, however, he embarked in the present enterprise of which he has since remained the sole proprietor. He occupies a commodious four-story and basement building, 25x100 feet in dimensions, at the rear of which is a two-story building 60x100 feet, and fronting on Delaware street, the warehouse for the storage of surplus stock being 25x100 feet, and located at 186 South Meridian street. The premises are conveniently appointed and equipped for the special uses for which they are severally occupied, such being particularly the case with the Washington street store, which is provided with the finest elevator service in the State, made expressly to Mr. Messenger's order. He deals in furniture, carpets, stoves, mattresses and household furnishings generally. The store on Washington street is departmented and supplied with every accommodation for the rare and comprehensive displays of stock. The basement is devoted to stoves and mattresses, the main floor to office purposes and the exposition of chamber suits, china and glassware, the second floor to rattan goods and fancy furniture, the third to side-boards, library suites, chiffoniers, folding beds, etc., and the fourth floor to the display of parlor and drawing-room suites, upholstered in the richest fabrics and latest designs. The carpet warerooms occupy the second floor of the building on Delaware street, the main floor of the same premises being utilized for shipping purposes. The stocks throughout are of the best manufacture, thoroughly classified and arranged, and are in every particular unsurpassed in style, attractive finish and substantial durability. The services of twenty-five assistants and three wagons are required in the business, and a very large local trade is supplied, as also an extensive and steadily increasing demand throughout the country from New York to Minnesota.

Emil Wulschner—Wholesale and Retail Dealer in Pianos and Organs; 42 and 44 North Pennsylvania street. Emil Wulschner has been engaged as wholesale and retail dealer in musical instruments and publications in Indianapolis since 1877, when he began the business, and now conducts one of the leading establishments in that line in the Northwest. He occupies the main floor and basement, each 40x100 feet in dimensions, well supplied with all requisite facilities for the purposes of display, sale and shipment of stock. One portion of the premises is devoted to band instruments, sheet and book music, and musical novelties, the other portion to pianos and organs. He also occupies a commodious four-story warehouse to the rear of the Indianapolis News office. He carries pianos of the Steinway & Son, H. F. Miller, Vose & Sons, New England, Wheelock, Chickering and other celebrated manufacture, which are warranted for five years, and may be exchanged at any time. He handles organs of the Burdett pattern, and an excellent organ of his own make, also brass and reed instruments, and deals largely in guitars, mandolins, harps, banjos and small instruments in great variety, also book and sheet music, music stands, racks and stools and issues large editions of his illustrated catalogues of musical supplies quarterly, which are distributed throughout the country. He imports steadily through the

Indianapolis custom house an average of 200 brass instruments per month, and does the largest trade in that line in the city, selling an average of four band sets of twelve instruments each every week. This department, with that devoted to small goods and musical publications, is in charge of Frank J. Carlen, Jr., who also attends to their importation and sale. His stocks are of the best description in the market, and purchasers can rely upon the instruments and supplies being exactly as represented. He employs twenty-five assistants and seven traveling salesmen, and ships an average of half a dozen pianos daily to patrons residing in Indiana, Ohio, Illinois and in States more remote. His trade in band instruments is distributed throughout the Union, and his annual business foots up largely in value.

C. E. Kregelo—Undertaker and Funeral Director; 123 and 125 North Delaware street. The undertaking house of C. E. Kregelo was established in 1855 by David Kregelo, father of the present proprietor, the latter succeeding to the business upon the former's retirement, some years ago. He brings to his aid in the discharge of the solemn duties which devolve upon him, experience and the characteristics in harmony with a profession of a nature so delicate, and at the same time so responsible. During 1888, Mr. Kregelo contributed to the architectural finish of one of the leading business thoroughfares of Indianapolis, by erecting at the above locality a handsome and elegantly appointed brick edifice three stories high and 40x225 feet in dimensions. The building contains, beside offices, display and reception rooms, a mortuary chapel in which the sacred services preceding the interment of the deceased may be solemnized amid surroundings as impressive as attend those conducted beneath cathedral dome, with the pomp and circumstance of religious formality and observance. The upper stories, accessible by means of elevators, are occupied with the embalming and trimming departments, and to the rear of the chapel is the morgue, opposite which, and separated by a court-yard, are the carriage repository and stables. His equipment for funerals embraces the most elegant caskets, coffins, burial robes, shrouds, trimmings and appointments that cultured taste and skillful workmanship can design or complete, together with three funeral cars and sixteen black horses; also the fullest complement of carriages, horses and other accessories. He employs a staff of the most accomplished embalmers in the country, and is prepared to respond to requisitions made upon his services day or night, either here or at a distance. Mr. Kregelo's facilities are so complete, that he is able to take charge of all ceremonies incident to the demands of his profession, and is beyond question the leading funeral director in the State.

Albert Gall—Importer and Dealer in Carpets, Etc.; 17 and 19 West Washington street. The oldest, most extensive and popular carpet house in the State is that of Albert Gall. It was established in 1863, and since 1869 has been exclusively owned and managed by the present proprietor. During its career of more than a quarter of a century its annual business has grown in volume and influence. He is located in the heart of the trade district, and occupies a handsome four-story and basement stone front building, 36x200 feet in dimensions, specially erected for Mr. Gall to accommodate the demands of the business, and provided with all the modern facilities and conveniences, including hydraulic passenger and freight elevators, with other appurtenances calculated to promote the display of stock and the satisfactory handling of the trade. He carries large and comprehensive lines of Moquet, Axminster, Velvet, Brussels, Tapestry and Imperial carpets, in the latest and richest designs; oriental and other styles of rugs, portieres, hangings, etc., oil cloths, linoleums, druggets, mattings, also importing the finest Nottingham and other famous makes of European lace curtains of the most delicate texture, and carrying large invoices of curtain goods in silk, velvet, satin and rep, with full supplies of wall papers and goods for interior decoration purposes, of American and foreign manufacture, in great variety and profusion. There is no house in the West so entirely prepared to respond to demands made upon its stocks and services, and the many orders executed annually for the papering and interior decoration of residences, public and society halls, banks, etc., throughout the State, emphasize the esteem in which it is held by a high class of patronage. A staff of fifteen or more assistants is kept constantly in the service, and during the busy season from thirty to fifty artistic decorators and paper hangers, with their helpers, are required. Mr. Gall employs only the most experienced workmen, and does a large and steadily augmenting trade in the city and State. He is a practical business man, and his establishment enjoys advantages that enable him to offer the most substantial inducements to patrons and the public.

Model Clothing Co. — Clothiers, Hatters and Furnishers; corner of Washington and Pennsylvania streets. The Model Clothing Co., a pattern establishment, as its name would indicate, in every particular, was opened here in 1883, by B. Rothschild, I. M. Hays and S. Hays, composing the firm of Rothschild, Hays & Co., of Rochester, N. Y., where the headquarters and factories of the concern are located, and where Messrs. Rothschild and I. M. Hays reside; the business here being in charge of S. Hays, the junior partner, and is exclusively retail, that at Rochester being exclusively wholesale. The Indianapolis houses is located at the leading business corner in the city, where they occupy premises fronting 89 feet on East Washington street and 189 feet on Pennsylvania street. The interior is handsomely appointed and equipped, furnished with all requisite conveniences, including telephone service and the latest improved electric light plant, the latter driven by an engine owned and operated by the firm. The store is departmented and the manage-

ment of affairs is characterized by a policy so liberal and judicious, as to inspire deserved confidence and commendation. They handle very large and complete invoices of clothing for men and boys, including overcoats, ulsters, dress suits, and suits for the counting room, hats, caps, furs, and equally extensive and desirable supplies of furnishing goods, ties, scarfs, mufflers, etc., imported and of domestic manufacture. The clothing is made in accordance with the latest and most select fashions, and in material, fit and workmanship, is unexcelled. It is the product of their Rochester factories, where only experienced and accomplished operatives are retained in the service, and is noted for its elegant appearance and perfect for durable wear. They are prepared to promptly fill and ship orders to any portion of the country, and customers can always rely upon receiving the best articles at the lowest prices. They employ a staff of forty clerks, and supply a very large local and transient demand, in addition to an equally large trade in all parts of Indiana and adjoining States. The house is representative in every sense of the word, and its value to Indianapolis as a factor of commercial enterprise, is daily becoming more and more apparent.

Cunningham & Zimmer — Wall-paper, Oil-cloths, Mattings and Window Shades; 62 North Illinois street. The firm of Cunningham & Zimmer is composed of William T. Cunningham and Henry W. Zimmer, and was organized and began operations during 1887. They occupy a building two stories high, with basement underneath, having a frontage of 25 feet and a depth of 100 feet, well supplied with all necessary conveniences and modern appointments for the business. Their stocks are full and complete in all lines of imported and domestic goods. They embrace wall-papers, interior decorations, mattings, window shades, lambrequins, ornaments, decorations, etc., in great variety. They are also prepared to furnish Lincrusta Walton to those who desire it. This favorite decorative goods comes in over 1,000 different designs, a full and complete catalogue of which may be seen at any time at their store. They will furnish special designs if desired, and are prepared to make contracts with owners for the decoration of their premises. They formerly carried carpets and other furnishings of that description, but relinquished that department in order to devote more room and closer attention to their present business. Their goods are of the best European and American manufacture, obtained direct from first hands, fashionable in style, artistic in design, elegant in finish, and sold at the lowest prices at which such goods can be profitably put. They do a large business in wall-papering and interior decoration of stores, residences, public buildings, halls, lodge rooms, churches, etc., their work in this line being unsurpassed. From ten to fifteen assistants are steadily employed, and a large business is done in the city and surrounding country. The house is in every respect a reliable and representative one.

Wm. Terrell — Wood and Slate Mantels; 60 North Pennsylvania street. This business was established by Mr. Terrell in 1881, and has been successful from its inception. He occupies the basement and main floor, each 30x30 feet in size, in one of the handsomest blocks on one of the most fashionable business thoroughfares in the city, and caters to a high class of trade here and elsewhere. Previous to locating in this city, Mr. Terrell had been for many years associated with the United States Encaustic and Majolica Tile Works, where he acquired a valuable knowledge of the business, and entire familiarity with the demands of the trade. His specialty is the placing of mantels, grates, marble and encaustic floor tiling, parquetry, wood carpentry, etc., in fine private residences, banks, theatres, halls and other expensively constructed buildings, for which he carries full lines of goods of the best material and most durable manufacture. During the past year he directed the equipment and interior decoration of the Citizens' National Bank, at Peru, Ind.; Menger Hotel, San Antonio, Tex.; Phœnix Hotel, Lexington, Ky.; Churchill House, Alpena, Mich.; Indiana Hospital for Insane; Soldiers' Orphans' Home, Knightstown, Ind.; City Hall, Indianapolis, Ind.; Kirby House, Muncie, Ind., and does a business extending into the southern States as far as Texas, west to Salt Lake City, with some on the Pacific coast, and is large in Indiana and the bordering States, an evidence of the importance and value of his enterprise in building up the reputation and importance of Indianapolis as a commercial center.

J. George Mueller, Ph. G. — Dispensing Pharmacist; southwest corner Washington and East streets.—A notable and enterprising drug house of this city, with an experience here of nearly twenty years, is that of J. George Mueller, Ph. G. It was established early in the sixties, passing into the hands of R. H. Mueller in 1861, with whom the present proprietor, though in no way related, served for many years, and whom he finally succeeded during 1887. He is a practical and accomplished chemist and pharmacist (graduate of Cincinnati College of Pharmacy), peculiarly qualified for the successful professional career he is pursuing and entirely familiar with the requirements of the select patronage to which he ministers. His place of business at the above prominent and accessible corner in the commercial center of Indianapolis, occupies the main floor and basement, each 20x100 feet in dimensions, attractively appointed, handsomely fitted up, and furnished with all requisite facilities that can in any way contribute to the convenience of the trade or the efficiency of the service. His specialties include a number of preparations which he puts up exclusively for patrons of his establishment, pure drugs and accuracy in the compounding of prescriptions of all schools of medicine. His stocks in every department are always full and of the most select descriptions, embracing in addition to staple articles, proprietary medicines, of imported and American origin and make, fluid extracts, physicians' supplies, surgical instruments and appliances, pure wines and cordials for medicinal use, soaps, perfumeries, toilet articles and sundries, fancy lines and other commodities general to the business in great variety and of established worth. He employs a staff of five experienced pharmacists and assistants, and in catering to the wants of a large retail trade in the city and vicinity, has acquired a well-earned reputation for superior stocks, reasonable prices and honorable dealings.

A. P. Garrison—Dealer in Light-Running "Domestic" Sewing Machines; 11 Massachusetts avenue, Wyandot block. The Indianapolis branch of the Domestic Sewing Machine Co. is supervised by A. P. Garrison, who assumed direction of its operations in 1884. He has been in the company's service for fourteen years, and is intimately familiar with the requirements of the trade and the superior excellence of the "Domestic" for manufacturing and domestic purposes. His policy is to purchase the machines direct from the factory, obtaining them at greatly reduced prices, and he is thereby enabled to sell them to the trade at rates and upon terms more liberal than the same can be had of competing companies or agents engaged in the same line of operations. The territory assigned to

his special occupation and supply includes Indianapolis and Marion County. He is located at 11 Massachusetts avenue, a valuable and prominent site, where he occupies the basement and main floor, each 20 x 125 feet in their dimensions, running through to Ohio street. These are divided into sale, display, and storage rooms, being fully equipped and well appointed for their several purposes, as also for the transaction of business. He carries full lines of the "Domestic," with all the latest improved attachments and appliances; the machines encased in rosewood, mahogany, oak, walnut, maple, and other hardwoods, plain and in elaborate designs, and for sale at the most moderate prices consistent with their intrinsic worth, and upon the most advantageous terms. He employs from twelve to fifteen assistants and is constantly engaged in responding to the demands of the trade, established and increasing, throughout the territory within his jurisdiction to supply. The "Domestic" of to-day is, as it has always been, the leader in progress, and the one and only perfect sewing machine made, and is justly entitled to its familiar trade-mark, "The star that leads them all."

Original Eagle Clothing Co.—Leaders in Fine Clothing, Gents' Furnishings, Hats and Caps, Etc.; 5 and 7 West Washington street.—The Eagle Clothing Company is a pioneer in the ready-made clothing trade of Indianapolis, the house having been for nearly thirty years a prominent and popular depot of supplies, not only for customers in the city but throughout the State. It was founded in 1853, by Max Danham, who was succeeded later by M. Gnesheimer. In 1872, Mr. L. Strauss, the present proprietor, became a partner in the enterprise and finally sole owner, in which latter capacity he has since remained. He is located at the most available point in the retail district, and carries large and varied stocks. The premises occupied consist of a four-story and basement building, 40x100 feet in

dimensions, provided with all modern facilities and equipments for the business. The house is everywhere recognized as one of the leading men's and boys' furnishing houses in the State, a reputation sustained and confirmed by honorable dealings and superb goods. The latter embrace large and select invoices of men's, youths' and boys' clothing, made of the finest and medium grades of the leading products of European and American houses in the latest patterns, and according to the most recent styles of the prevailing fashion. In furnishing goods the stocks are equally choice, comprehensive and complete, including silk, woolen, ballbriggan, etc., hose and underwear, shirts, collars, cuffs, ties, scarfs, umbrellas, canes, novelties, hats and caps, etc., of the best foreign and domestic make, in almost endless styles and profusion. All the goods carried by the house are sold at prices that insure the continued patronage of customers. Mr. Strauss is a merchant and citizen eminent for his enterprise, who has developed for his house a constantly growing success. He employs a force of fifteen clerks and does a large city and country retail trade, besides jobbing extensively in certain lines throughout Indiana and the States adjoining.

Norbert Landgraf—Merchant Tailor; 38 North Illinois street.—Norbert Landgraf, an experienced merchant tailor, located as above indicated in the building of the Young Men's Christian Association, began business in 1886. The premises occupied for parlors are neat and attractive, furnished with every facility that will promote a comprehensive display of his goods or the expeditious transaction of business, and equipped with all modern facilities and conveniences for the accommodation of the trade. He gives his personal attention to the management of the house, and, although having in his service

the most experienced and artistic assistants, personally supervises the cut, make, finish, style and fit of his choice lines of production. He carries very select stocks of English, German, Scotch, Austrian, Belgian and French fabrics, also those of the best American manufacture, in cloth, diagonal, cassimere, tweed, etc., with the usual supplies of vestings and trimmings, also imported novelties in the way of gentlemen's wear. He makes only to order, and his workmanship and the style and finish of his products are conceded to be unsurpassed. He employs from twenty-five to thirty hands, and beside the large high-class demands he supplies in the city and vicinity, does a large trade among tailors in fine imported trimmings and specialties.

Wilson & Rupert—Dealers in Furniture, Carpets, Stoves and House Furnishing Goods; 50 West Washington street. This well-known house was established by O. E. Wilson, in 1886, on East Washington street. He removed to his present location and, admitting F. H. Rupert as a partner, the present firm was organized. They occupy the basement and two floors of premises 20x120 feet in dimensions, conveniently and adequately equipped for the display of their stocks and the transaction of business, and carry full lines of goods. They embrace oil cloths, rugs, carpets, mattings, brackets, shades, album stands, pictures, mirrors, plain and easy chairs and rockers, parlor, dining-room and bedroom suites, bed springs, mattresses, pillows, comforts, blankets, toilet sets, stand lamps, kitchen safes, extension tables, stationary and hanging lamps, lace curtains, store and kitchen furniture, with notions and novelties in general assortment adapted to household service. The stocks all around are complete and of the best descriptions, the products of leading manufactories devoted to that line of specialties, and purchased in such amount and upon such terms that they are able to offer the most substantial inducements in respect to prices to customers and the trade. They employ a staff of competent assistants, also operating two wagons for the free delivery of goods, and do a large business in the city and vicinity. The members of the firm are thoroughly practical men who give their personal attention to the business, and their success and the success their house has met with is an honest acknowledgement of low prices, liberal terms and honorable methods by the trade they supply.

The Singer Manufacturing Co.—Headquarters for the State of Indiana, 72 and 74 West Washington street, near Illinois street. The Singer Manufacturing Company is by far the largest and most influential enterprise of its kind in the world. The home office of the company, the "Singer Building," is situated on Union Square, New York City, and its main factory at Elizabethport, with two woodworking establishments, at South Bend, Ind., and Cairo, Ill., and factories of immense proportions at Glasgow, Scotland, Vienna, Austria and Montreal, Canada, for the supply of foreign trade. The Indianapolis agency was established more than thirty years ago, and now controls some thirty-five branches, representing one hundred sub-agencies within the State of Indiana. A large force is employed and large interests are represented in these sub-agencies, and the headquarters here consist of the main floor and basement, each 20x150 feet in dimensions, handsomely appointed and furnished, and containing accommodations for the large stocks required to be carried at a distributing point of such importance as Indianapolis. The lines include all the latest improved machines, prominent among which are the new "Singer Automatic," the new "Singer Vibrator," and the "Singer Oscillator," made expressly for family sewing, and other patterns adapted to all classes of work, in addition to which they are manufacturing special machines for boot and shoe, clothing, and for other lines of manufacturing requiring the use of sewing machines, and are prepared to completely fit up factories requiring the use of sewing machines to be run by power. A force of thirty operatives and assistants are employed here, whose services are devoted to the trade in the city, in which it is steadily augmenting in volume and value, as it also is in all portions of the State, a substantial acknowledgement of the worth of the "Singer" as an article of public necessity and economy, and of the capable and efficient administration of affairs by the company's representatives.

Carl Moller—Dealer in Wall-paper, Decorations, Etc.; 161 East Washington street.—Carl Moller, an artistic decorator and dealer in wall-paper, and ornamentations for the interior adornment of private residences, public buildings, theatres, churches, etc., began business here in the year 1876, and has, during his residence in this city, executed work in his special lines, than which there is none more elaborate and finished in the State. His location is most desirable and available, as above indicated, where he occupies premises 20x120 feet in dimensions, and admirably furnished and appointed, being provided with every facility and equipment for the display of his rich and showy lines of goods, as also for the transaction of business, and the shipment of consignments. He imports direct from the leading depots of supply in Europe, and handles the choicest lines of American production in wall-papers, decorative art work, blinds, lace and other patterns of curtains, and furnishings in general. His goods are unsurpassed in material, style and finish, and his house enjoys a widespread and entirely deserved reputation for the originality and elegance of its supplies, as also for the superiority of its workmanship. During the decorating season he gives employment to a force of skilled and experienced assistants, ranging in number from twenty-five to thirty, and does a large business in the city and throughout the surrounding country, besides filling orders for the finest description of work, and personally superintending same, at distant points.

F. P. Smith & Co.—Wholesale and Retail China, Glassware, Lamps, Etc.; 21 and 23 North Illinois street.—This business was established in 1878 by H. B. Smith & Co., to whom the present firm succeeded January 1, 1884. Up to November, 1888, they were located at 37 South Meridian street. During the latter month, however, they removed to their present site, one of the most eligible and accessible in the business portion of the city. The premises consist of a handsome new three-story and basement brick building, 25x130 feet in dimensions, admirably arranged and appointed, and provided with every facility and convenience adapted to the requirements of the trade or the conduct of the business. They carry large and full stocks of everything in their lines handled by a first-class house of the kind. They embrace fine French and English china, English granite ware, American white and decorated ware, including the famous decorated chamber ware made at Trenton, N. J., the patterns

and shapes of which have been attempted to be copied by old European potteries, French, English, Bohemian, Belgian and American glassware in great variety, fine electro-plated ware, table cutlery and other articles of household utility and ornament. They also deal in chandeliers, library and student lamps, lanterns, brackets, oil stoves, lubricating, fluid, headlight, signal and carbon oils, improved burners and lamp trimmings generally, gasoline, etc. The several departments of the house are filled with the choicest stocks adapted to each, complete and comprehensive, of the most varied descriptions and sold at low prices. They are abundantly prepared to fill and ship orders promptly, and in all respects to meet the demands of customers everywhere. They do a large retail trade in the city, as also an equally extensive wholesale and jobbing trade throughout the State, and the house in every way merits the confidence and patronage it receives.

J. T. Power—Washington Market; 78 and 80 North Pennsylvania street.—Probably the largest, and certainly the most prominent, fancy grocery house in the State is the Washington Market, owned and managed by J. T. Power. It was established in 1878 by the present proprietor, and has attained to reputation and prominence as a base of the choicest supplies of edibles, etc., not rivaled by that of any establishment of a similar character in the Northwest. The premises occupied consist of the main floor and basement of a double store, conveniently and accessibly located, directly opposite the New Denison House, with a total frontage of 50 feet, and a depth of 150 feet; also the rear portion of the floor above affording additional space, 50x100 feet in dimensions. A completely equipped meat market has been erected in the center of the main store, provided with refrigerator facilities for the storage and preservation of meats, fruits, and dairy products. His stocks of fancy groceries and delicacies embrace imported fruits and preserves, canned and bottled sauces and condiments, nuts, raisins and novelties, as well as the finest brands exclusively of champagne, sherry, Rhine and French wines and brandies; also carrying large lines of fruits and wines of American growth and production. All articles are of selected grades, models of purity, freshness, flavor and absolute worth in their several departments, such as are handled only by leading concerns of the same character, and serving a high class trade. Mr. Power is prepared to fill orders promptly and to ship consignments to any portion of the State, securely packed against damage in transit. He does a large business in the city and throughout the surrounding country, also a large family trade within a considerable radius of Indianapolis, and supplies grocers in adjacent cities and towns with delicacies, wines, etc., very extensively.

William T. Marcy—Dealer in Fine Diamonds, Watches, Jewelry, Spectacles and Opera Glasses; 38 West Washington street.— The trade supplied by William T. Marcy is the acquisition of years of enterprising industry by the present proprietor and his predecessors, Messrs. McLean & Northrup, who established the "Old Bates House Jewelry Store" in 1853, whom Mr. Marcy succeeded in 1876, and has since managed and directed the business with annually increasing prosperity. He occupies the main floor and basement of a building at the above locality, each 25x150 feet in dimensions, admirably appointed, attractively furnished and supplied with all requisite conveniences and facilities. He carries large and carefully selected assortments of stocks of every description, including imported and American make of watches, in solid gold and filled cases, stem and key winders; diamonds, rubies, pearls, opals, emeralds, garnets, sapphires, topaz, turquoise, and other precious gems, loose and mounted, or mounted to order in showy designs; genuine Rogers Bros.' knives and forks, silverware, with solid silver and electroplated ware of the best make, in addition to clocks in bronze, china and marble, solid gold jewelry, gold and silver charms and ornaments, opera glasses, bric-a-brac, and other articles of virtu only handled by first-class dealers, and his specialty is spectacles, eye-glasses and opera-glasses, of which he carries the largest and best stocks in the West in every variety. Prescriptions of oculists are filled and glasses adjusted to the vision by expert workmen. He also manufactures gold jewelry to order, does the general repairing of watches, jewelry and music boxes, designs and executes engraving, etc., a fully equipped workshop being one of the special departments of his establishment, and guarantees satisfaction in every instance. His stocks and lines of production are the best available to purchase or manufacture, unsurpassed in qualities, materials, design and finish, and sold at prices consistent with their intrinsic worth. Mr. Marcy is an enterprising, experienced merchant and does a large trade in the city as also within a radius of one hundred miles of Indianapolis, besides jobbing extensively in certain lines and filling the orders of jewelers and families for goods, only carried by an establishment of the prominence and character of that which he conducts. A special feature of this house is its watch repairing department and fine engraving by expert workmen. The location of the house, opposite the transfer car, is easily accessible from all parts of the city.

Major Taylor—Men's Furnisher; 38 East Washington street. —Major Taylor began business in this city in 1884, on Illinois street, whence he removed to his present site during January, 1887. He is handsomely and prominently located, occupying commodious and well appointed premises 20x80 feet in dimensions, the interior handsomely fitted up and equipped with all facilities and improvements for displaying his stocks to the best advantage, and the transaction of business incident to his large and rapidly increasing trade, operating in conjunction with his retail business the Excelsior Laundry, in which line he has had an experience extended over twenty-seven years. His specialty is the manufacture of gentlemen's dress shirts to order, in which he employs the best qualities of linen and muslin and the most skilled workmen, and furnishes an article for the gentleman's wardrobe as indispensable as it is superior in materials and workmanship. He also handles gents' furnishing goods in great variety and of the most approved make in silk, woolen, flannel, lawn and gossamer for light and heavy wear, imported direct from Europe and obtained from the leading factories and haberdashers of America, also cuffs, collars, gloves, hose, handkerchiefs, ties, scarfs, canes, umbrellas, notions and novelties of foreign and domestic make in great profusion. He deals only in first-class commodities of the finest texture and caters to a high class patronage. He employs a large corps of assistants in his factory and laundry, also a full staff of clerks and does a large trade in the city and vicinity, also a trade with transients of very considerable proportions.

Tutewiler—Undertaker and Funeral Director; 72 West Market street, Cyclorama Place; Telephone No. 216.—Although but recently established in the profession here, Henry W. Tutewiler had four years experience as manager of an undertaking house on Pennsylvania street, in this city, prior to embarking for himself. He began business upon his own account in November, 1888, enlisting in its conduct, in addition to his personal services, the fullest complement of facilities and requisite appointments. He is availably located, occupying a suite of apartments, 25x100 feet in dimensions, in the Cyclorama building, arranged with regard to the appropriate and decorous formalities incident to a business, in such particulars, so delicate and exacting. The premises are divided into display, office and finishing departments, and communicate with a morgue and embalming rooms, where remains can be retained and preserved pending interment. He carries the usual lines of goods pertaining to occasions for which they are designed, embracing caskets, burial cases, robes, shrouds, society and religious symbols, and is prepared to furnish floral emblems, designs and offerings of cut flowers, when required. His equipment includes hearses, for children and adults, carriages—horses handled by careful drivers—etc., and gives his personal attention to the details of funeral pageants at the most reasonable prices. He responds to orders, day or night, taking charge of all arrangements from death to burial, and displays that quality of tender respect which has led to a demand for his services. He employs five experienced assistants, and his trade is among all classes of the community. Mr. Tutewiler, a few years ago, was City Treasurer, and covered back into the treasury the interest on the public money, and conducted his office in the interest of the tax payers. He was born and raised in the city, and has lived here continuously, excepting three years of service in the late war as a member of 17th Indiana Volunteer Mounted Infantry, Wilder's Brigade.

L. H. Renkert—The Granger Drug Store; Dealer in Drugs and Medicines; 164 West Washington street.—The Granger Drug Store, established by L. H. Renkert in 1877, enjoys a wide-spread reputation for superiority in the lines of goods handled, prompt service and reasonable prices. He removed to his present site in 1879, occupying a most eligible and available location. The premises have 25 feet front on West Washington street, and are attractively furnished and appointed. His specialties are pure drugs and chemicals and the preparation of prescriptions. In the latter department he is especially successful, employing only expert pharmacists and the purest of ingredients. He carries, in addition to standard supplies, full stocks of extracts and elixirs, proprietary medicines, physicians' supplies, hospital sundries and appliances, pure wines and liquors for medicinal purposes, surgical instruments, perfumeries, fancy soaps, toilet waters and articles, paints, oils and varnishes, window glass and general sundries in great profusion and of the best qualities. His arrangements and facilities to meet the public demand are complete, enabling him to promptly fill all orders at prices compatible with a first-class service, and the perfect management which characterizes the business has acquired for the house an enviable record and reputation. He does a large and increasing trade in the city and among the farming interests of the surrounding country, and his annual business represents a correspondingly large valuation.

Dedert & Sudbrock—Dealers in Dry Goods, Notions, Etc.; 158 and 160 East Washington street.—The dry goods house of Dedert & Sudbrock is a well appointed and managed concern, carrying large and varied lines, and supplying a large and constantly increasing demand. The firm is made up of William Dedert and Frank H. Sudbrock, and was organized during 1889. They are located at one of the most available and desirable points for their business in the city, occupying a three-story and basement building, 40 feet front on East Washington street, and 100 feet deep. The premises are admirably equipped and provided with a full complement of conveniences for the adequate and attractive display of their goods, as also for their sale and the transaction of business. They handle staple and fancy dry goods, embracing everything in their line of foreign and domestic manufacture, ladies' and gentlemen's furnishing goods, notions in great variety, and all else that goes to make the supplies carried by a first-class establishment of the type owned and conducted by the firm. Their invoices are of a superior quality in material, texture and finish, and sold at prices that offer substantial inducements to purchasers. They employ a force of trusty, courteous and experienced clerks, and their trade, which is steadily augmenting in value and volume, is throughout the city and surrounding country. The house has already acquired a valuable reputation, and the pronounced success that has attended its career in the past, assures its prosperity in the future.

W. C. Van Arsdel & Co.—Wholesale and Retail Dry Goods and Furnishing Goods; 109 and 111 South Illinois street. A prominent and steadily patronized dry goods, notions and furnishing goods house, located in the center of trade near the new Union Depot, is owned and managed by W. C. Van Arsdel and James Ostrander, composing the firm of W. C. Van Arsdel & Co. It was organized in 1885 and began business in the Bates House block, on Washington street. The increase in business was so large, however, that they were compelled to increase their facilities, to accommodate which they removed to their present site during 1888. They occupy a commodious three-story and basement brick building, 35x100 feet in dimensions, and though furnished with every auxiliary for the convenience of customers, the premises are severely taxed by the constantly augmenting volume of their trade, and they contemplate doubling their capacity. They carry full lines of fancy and staple dry goods of imported and American manufacture, including dress goods in all textures, white goods, linens, cottons, blankets, flannels, hosiery, underwear, furnishing goods, gloves, laces, ribbons, embroideries, shawls, wraps, fancy articles, carpets, notions and novelties in great variety and profusion, and are prepared to supply all demands made upon their stock resources promptly and at the most reasonable cost. Their lines are select, comprehensive and complete and the business is conducted according to a policy both liberal and equitable. This is the only house in the State that carries a full line of high and medium grades of cloaks at wholesale. They employ from twelve to fifteen courteous and experienced assistants and do a heavy retail trade in the city and with transients, besides an extensive and valuable jobbing trade throughout the State, in all portions of which the house enjoys a well merited reputation as a representative of Indianapolis commercial industries.

Marceau & Power—Fotografers; 36 and 38 North Illinois street; Gallery on ground floor.—The largest, finest and in every way the best appointed establishment in the State devoted to the promotion of photographic art, is that of Marceau & Power. The firm is composed of Theo. C. Marceau and Luke W. Power, and was organized in September, 1888. Both members are men of practical experience, Mr. Marceau being also head of the firm of Marceau & Bellsmith, the leading photographers of Cincinnati, O., where he resides, and Mr. Power having been connected with a fashionable gallery in New York City for many years prior to establishing himself in Indianapolis. Their gallery occupies the main floor of the building at the above site, on North Illinois street, the same being 25x130 feet in dimensions, handsomely appointed, and, besides the gallery proper, contains elegantly furnished parlors, reception, toilet and operating rooms, artistically fitted up and finished. The work rooms and retouching departments are located in the basement, commodious in its proportions, well lighted and equipped with all the latest modern apparatus and appliances requisite to the service. Their printing department on Meridian street is supplied with all improved facilities and connected with the gallery by means of telephone. Their specialties are fine large photo and crayon work, cabinets enlarged to any size, panel portraits, vignettes, also the collateral branches of the re-productive art in its highest development, and evidencing in their production the skill and taste inseparable from genius, promoted and made perfect by years of experience and study. The instantaneous process is used exclusively in the taking of pictures, and, though cloudy weather is preferred for sittings, they are prepared to execute work at all times. Their establishment is most attractive in all particulars, a force of eighteen experienced operatives is employed, and nothing has been left wanting to maintain the well established reputation already enjoyed with admirers of artistic designs and superior workmanship, here and elsewhere. Since locating in this city, the firm has been constantly occupied upon work for an exacting and high-class of patrons, not only in Indianapolis, but among transients, and for customers throughout the surrounding country. There is a steady increase in the demand for their services, and the verdict of approval and admiration, attests the high estimate placed upon the same, as also upon the products of their camera.

Indianapolis Hardware Co.—Hardware, Doors, Sash, Blinds and Frames; 249 West Washington street, corner of West street. This company was incorporated in July, 1888, with E. H. Eldridge, head of the extensive lumber firm of E. H. Eldridge & Co., as President, and O. W. Gladden, Secretary. The latter has been for many years in the same line of business, having, during a portion of that period, been with the old hardware house of Hildebrandt & Fugate in a responsible capacity, and well qualified by experience for a successful conduct of operations. They occupy a three-story and basement building, 20x100 feet in dimensions, well apportioned and provided with accommodations and facilities for the display of goods and the transaction of business. They carry a large and complete stock of builders' hardware, including doors, sash, blinds, frames, etc., and mechanical tools, in both of which departments their stocks are as complete as a comprehensive knowledge of the requirements of the trade can contribute to make them. They make a

SEW MEXICO FOUNTAIN.

specialty of E. C. Simmons' "Keen Kutter" edge tools, files, saws, etc., all fully warranted to be the best of the kind, of which they carry all sizes and varieties. They also carry equally select and full lines of hardware of every character and description, embracing farmers and household hardware, table and pocket cutlery in great variety and profusion, the products of the most celebrated European and American manufacture, and unsurpassed in respect to assortment and quality. Their aim is to furnish the best articles at the most reasonable rates to customers, and by purchasing in large invoices from producers direct, they are enabled to offer the best inducements to their customers. They employ a full staff of assistants, and by prompt filling of orders and honorable methods they have built up a local business that is daily increasing in importance and value.

Bertermann Bros.—Florists; 37 to 43 Massachusetts avenue; Telephone 840.—The gardens and greenhouses of Bertermann Bros., leading florists and plant propagators of this vicinity, present an appearance of beauty and attractions as indescribable almost as they are frequented and admired. The firm, consisting of John Bertermann and William Bertermann, was organized in 1878, and they have achieved success upon the basis of merit. They are located as above, having a frontage of one hundred feet on Massachusetts avenue, with a depth of seventy feet, upon which have been erected commodious conservatories supplied with every facility and convenience for the maintainance of an equable temperature throughout all seasons. Their office is also here, but their main collection of greenhouses are located on the East National road, two miles from the Court House. Telephone 198. They are very extensive, employing over 20,000 feet of glass in their construction, and unsurpassed in

their appointment and equipments. Their main business consists of raising cut flowers to supply their city store, and in this way are able to furnish any and every large order on the shortest possible notice. Their places are connected by telephone. All telegrams are delivered day or night. The brothers' specialties are artistic floral designs and cut flowers, for the supplying of which they are amply provided with facilities, and prepared to promptly respond to orders for designs for decorative purposes, as also for funerals, weddings, receptions, parties and other occasions at which flowers are indispensable. They employ a force of ten to twelve skillful assistants and do a large trade in the city and State, throughout which their undertaking enjoys a long continued and wide-spread reputation for its honorable dealings, reasonable prices and fidelity to the interests of its patrons.

George W. Sloan & Co.—Apothecaries; 22 West Washington street.—Mr. Sloan has been continuously in the drug business in this city since 1848, and his establishment has long been known to

the medical profession in all portions of the State as one of exceptional value in its lines. The premises occupied are located at the best site on the most fashionable retail thoroughfare of the city, and in the heart of the trade district. They consist of a two-story and basement building, 20x150 feet in dimensions, attractively fitted up and equipped with every convenience for the purposes of the business. Very large stocks and full lines of goods are carried, embracing pure and fresh drugs and chemicals, compounds, preparations, extracts, elixirs, patent medicines, trusses, etc., physicians' and hospital supplies, druggists' sundries, perfumeries, toilet articles, fancy goods, cigars, wines and liquors for medicinal purposes, and novelties appertaining to all these lines. In the compounding of prescriptions experienced chemists are employed and only the best quality of medicaments are used, an important feature of the house that has given additional prestige to its long continued career. A large local and transient trade is supplied in addition to an extensive demand from physicians and dealers throughout Indiana. Mr. Sloan is an enterprising public-spirited citizen and an experienced apothecary, and his establishment has contributed to develop and elevate the retail drug trade in this section of the country.

W. C. Gramling—Merchant Tailor; 42 North Illinois street. This house was founded in 1886 by the present proprietor, who has since continued to enlarge his trade and extend his reputation. He gives the closest attention to the business and from a long and valuable experience is specially qualified for its successful and prosperous conduct. He occupies attractive premises, having a frontage of 25x100 feet in dimensions, handsomely furnished, conveniently arranged, and provided with all modern facilities for an ample display of his carefully selected stocks. He imports from the leading depots of supply, handling the choicest lines of English, Scotch, French and Austrian cloths, suitings, vestings, linings, trimmings, etc., and also carries the products of the best American looms. He makes exclusively to order; everything in the latest style and of the best material, neither cheap goods nor inexperienced assistants being used or employed. Every garment produced is up to the highest standard, and unsurpassed in respect to fit, finish and capacity for durable service. The house is representative of its kind, offering to customers the inducements of reasonable prices for first-class articles, and other advantages both exceptional and valuable. Mr. Gramling employs a force of competent journeymen, from thirty to forty in number, and does a large trade in the city, as also with transients, and patrons residing throughout the surrounding country.

Horace F. Wood—Boarding, Livery and Sale Stables; 23 and 25 Circle street.—This extensive livery business was established in 1834 by John M. Wood, father of the present proprietor, and from 1849 to 1879, was operated under the direction of Wood & Foundry. In the latter year, upon the death of Mr. Foundry, the surviving partner managed the concern until 1883, when Horace F. Wood succeeded to the business, and has since continued its conduct. His stables, carriage houses, etc., occupy nearly one-half a block in the city's business center, adjacent to the hotels, Union Depot, and other points advantageous as sources of patronage, and are in all respects completely equipped and appointed. The premises contain over one hundred stalls, many of them large box stalls for the stabling of valuable stock, and in the arrangement and construction of this department, due regard has been paid to sanitary requirements, as also to the removal of animals in case of fire. The coach house, harness rooms, etc., are upon the same scale of superior excellence in their lines, and fully as meritorious in every particular. His specialties include first-class livery service, the sale of fine bred stock, and the boarding of private horses and establishments. He owns, for public service, twenty-five head of horses, embracing roadsters, driving and riding horses, etc., together with a superb line of coaches, carriages, coupes, road wagons, buggies, etc., and is prepared to furnish conveyances at the shortest notice and lowest rates for weddings, receptions, funerals and other private and public occasions. The sales department of the establishment is an important feature, being devoted to the purchase and sale of fine carriage, buggy and saddle horses for his own account and to order, and his boarding department is occupied with some seventy-five horses belonging to private owners and families, which are assured the maximum of care at the minimum of cost, and risk of loss or damage by fire or other causes. The property and equipments, among the most valuable in the city, are owned by Mr. Wood, who devotes his personal attention to their management with annually increasing prosperity.

Tucker's Glove Store—H. S. Tucker, Proprietor, 10 East Washington street. This favorite establishment is located on the fashionable highway of trade of Indianapolis. Mr. H. S. Tucker engaged in this business in 1882, and has since conducted it successfully and prosperously. He occupies premises 25x125 feet in dimensions, handsomely furnished and provided with every convenience and facility for an attractive display of goods, and admirably departmented for the accommodations of customers and dispatch of business. His specialties are gloves and fine qualities of furnishing goods. He is sole agent for the famous Foster and Alexandre kid gloves for ladies and gentlemen. The unsurpassed worth of which is constantly demonstrated by the increased demand made for these brands. He also carries moustquetaire, misses', ladies', driving and shopping gloves, men's fur and heavy lined gloves, fabric gloves, fur and woolen mittens and heavy working gloves and mittens of all kinds and sizes, and at all prices. The gloves are fitted to the hand before purchasing, and all gloves sent by mail can be exchanged if not injured. His stocks of underwear, hosiery and furnishing goods are equally select and varied, the products of the leading European and American manufacture in silk, woolen, balbriggan and other textures, in large assortment and of unrivaled workmanship. He is prepared to fill orders from patrons at a distance, and packs and ships the most delicate articles secure from damage in transit. He does a large trade in the city and surrounding country, beside supplying an extensive demand from all parts of the State.

Chas. June—Wholesale and Retail Dealer in Oysters, Fish and Game, 61 North Illinois street. Since 1884, when Mr. June embarked in business, he has met with the fullest success, his trade annually increasing in volume, requiring constant attention, and, on account of its rapid expansion, necessitating his relinquishment of stalls in the East Market building, that he might be enabled to devote his entire services to its promotion and supply. He occupies the main floor and basement, each 25x80 feet in dimensions, at the above location, with an extension 25x80 feet containing the oyster and fish departments. The premises are provided with all modern equipments for the preservation and storage of his commodities, and with ample accommodations for the prompt execution and shipment of orders. He receives very large consignments of oysters, fish and game, crabs, lobsters, frogs' legs, shrimps, etc., also of butter and eggs, of the best qualities all around, pure, fresh and sweet and in steady demand by a class of customers with whom inferior grades in these lines are unknown. Mr. June also handles the finest grades of butterine in this market, from two of the best factories in the State. Long experience, coupled with reliability, low prices and honorable management, have secured to him a widely established reputation. He employs from eight to ten assistants, and utilizes three wagons for the free delivery

of purchases and does a large business among private families, hotels restaurants, etc., in the city and vicinity. All orders in person, over telephone No. 593, and by mail meet with immediate acknowledgment, and customers can rely upon the most satisfactory service in every particular. Mr. June also runs an extensive poultry farm in connection, carrying generally 1,000 chickens and turkeys, thereby being enabled to supply fresh and fine fowls at all times.

S. D. Crane—Dealer in Diamonds, Watches, Etc.; 98 East Washington street.—A nicely fitted up and well stocked jewelry store is that of S. D. Crane, who established it in 1874, and has since conducted it with annually increasing prosperity. He occupies well appointed and tastefully furnished premises, 20x75 feet in dimensions, located on the leading and fashionable thoroughfare of Indianapolis. The stock carried is full and complete in all the lines handled, embracing diamonds, loose and mounted, in the most elaborate styles of the latest fashion; pearls, rubies, sapphires and other choice gems; watches, imported, also of American make, in solid gold and silver cases; solid gold jewelry, solid silver and electro-plated ware; clocks in bronze, marble and china; choice patterns of the ceramic art, bric-a-brac, charms and novelties in great variety and profusion; precious stones and fine jewelry, and his patronage embraces the better class of trade. He also attends to the repairing of fine watches and jewelry, and being a finished workman himself, and employing none but competent assistants, he not only gives the fullest satisfaction to patrons, but enjoys a wide-spread and well merited reputation for superior skill and workmanship. His prices are reasonable, and he does a large local trade among those who appreciate and will accept none but the best and most desirable of articles in the lines of goods such as are dealt in at this old established house. Mr. Crane, whose portrait accompanies this article, has been a resident of Indianapolis all his life, having been born in the immediate vicinity.

William Haerle—Dealer in Ladies' and Children's Furnishings; 4 West Washington street. This is one of the oldest and most representative depots of supply in its special departments in the city. It was established by the present proprietor in 1862, and has been a successful enterprise from its inception. He occupies the elegant store and basement fronting 25 feet on West Washington street, with a depth of 120 feet, and an "L" extending into North Meridian street, used for office purposes. The premises are handsomely furnished and attractively appointed, equipped with all requisite conveniences and provided with every modern facility for the business. He carries a very large and select stocks, importing special features and buying in the Eastern markets on a scale so extensive that purchasers secure advantages in variety, quality and prices unexcelled and invaluable. His supplies embrace underwear, corsets, hosiery, gloves, handkerchiefs, real and imitation laces, ribbons, buttons, dress trimmings, notions, fancy goods, zephyrs, Germantown and Saxony wools, stamped goods and novelties in general. Mr. Haerle gives special attention to his art department (stamping and fine needlework), and does a very extensive business in ladies' art work, embroideries, embroidery supplies and materials, and all his goods, in every department, are first-class in every particular. He is amply prepared to promptly fill and ship orders to distant points, and in all respects protect and consult the interests of patrons.

C. F. & G. J. Lay—Druggists and Pharmacists; 174 West Washington street.—The drug house now owned and operated by C. F. & G. J. Lay, was established in 1874 by G. J. Frebert. The latter died during September, 1888, when C. F. Lay, who had been for many years prescription and general clerk under Mr. Frebert's administration, became associated with G. J. Lay, his brother, in the purchase of the enterprise, and organized the present firm. They occupy the main floor at the above site, 20x100 feet in dimensions, provided with ample accommodations for the display and sale of their select stocks of drugs and chemicals, proprietary medicines, physicians' supplies and sundries, medicinal compounds, pure wines and liquors for medicinal use, toilet articles, perfumeries, novelties and notions, in the several lines composing a first-class stock in a first-class drug house. They also handle Piso's Consumption Cure and Catarrh Remedy extensively, and exercise extraordinary care in the preparation of prescriptions. They do a large local and farmers' trade, and enjoy a well-merited reputation for the purity of their goods, low prices and the liberal and honorable character of their management and dealings.

H. T. Hearsey Bicycles, Repairing and Nickel-plating; 147 North Delaware street.—H. T. Hearsey, one of the leading dealers in bicycles in the State, having the exclusive sale of the Columbia bicycles and tricycles, and Gormully & Jeffery Manufacturing Co.'s full lines of machines, the New Mail bicycles and safeties, and other leading patterns of cycles in Indiana, began business here during 1885 coming from Boston. He occupies premises 30x100 feet in dimensions, divided into office, display and salesrooms, also containing a well equipped and appointed repair shop. In addition to the sole agency for the make of the Pope Manufacturing Company, of Boston, embracing the Columbia bicycles, safeties and tricycles, and the World typewriters, he manufactures spade handles, handle bars and spoke wrenches, and carries a full line of supplies and sundries for repairs, which are made at the shortest notice. He also carries full

stocks of cheap bicycles and safeties for men and boys, second-hand bicycles, which are taken in exchange for new ones, etc. His repair department is prepared with all necessary machinery and appliances for repairing, nickel-plating and enameling, in first-class style and at lower figures than factory prices. Having had ten years' experience, and employing only skillful and competent operatives, his work in this department is specially noticeable for its superior excellence and durability. Estimates on work are furnished upon application and illustrated catalogues of all the machines kept in stock are mailed upon request. On the receipt of a small amount, to guarantee freight charges, he will send any wheel on his list for examination, and fills all orders for anything in his line with commendable promptness. He does a large trade throughout the State, in which he has over 1,000 customers, who act as agents among their friends, and his low prices, honorable methods and unsurpassed facilities, have made the house a famous resort for a steadily increasing patronage. Mr. Hearsey is popular throughout the State, and is esteemed in all circles for his eminent social and business qualities.

August C. Smith—Merchant Tailor; 27 Virginia avenue.—Mr. Smith, who established himself in the merchant tailoring business during February, 1889, had been for sixteen years previous head cutter for the house of Rupp & Co., similarly engaged in this city,

and brings to his aid not only a long and exacting experience but a quality of taste, that especially qualifies him to meet all the requirements of a high-class trade. He occupies a store 22 feet front on Virginia avenue, irregular in shape, and extending back 100 feet to Maryland street. The premises are handsome in appearance, attractively arranged and appointed, and furnished with every facility for a comprehensive display of his selected lines of goods, embracing all the latest imported and American novelties in the latest designs and patterns, including the best qualities of English, Scotch, French and German cloths, cassimeres, vestings, tweeds, diagonals, etc., with all the leading grades of production from domestic looms. He makes to order heavy and light overcoats, suits and garments for weddings, receptions and other social occasions; also for business purposes, in the most recent approved fashion, in style and at unrivaled, models of elegance and finished workmanship. He is prepared to execute orders promptly and satisfactorily, and his prices and terms are low and liberal. He employs from fifteen to twenty experienced assistants, and his trade in the city and vicinity is steadily increasing and extending.

The White Sewing Machine Co.—A. W. Hilliker, Manager; 64 North Pennsylvania street.—The White Sewing Machine Company, which has its headquarters and factories at Cleveland, O., has branch offices in all the leading cities of America and Europe. The celebrated White Sewing Machine, manufactured by them, is a favorite in the households of America, and its simplicity of construction, durability of parts, adaptability of adjustment, light and quiet running, make it the best machine for family use. In short, all that constitutes a perfect family sewing machine, "The White is King." At the Cincinnati Centennial Exposition the first, highest, and only award on sewing machines, was given to the "White" as "the best family sewing machine." The Indianapolis branch was established in December, 1886. Previous to that year the company had been represented here by a purchasing agent, that is, an agent who purchased the machines and sold them for his own account. The office and warehouse in this city occupy premises 50x150 feet in dimensions. They are admirably adapted to the purposes of the business, also furnished with every facility for the storage, sale and shipment of goods. Large lines of stock are carried, embracing every pattern of this most complete and invaluable implement of household economy, finished in the most artistic and attractive designs, equipped with all the latest improved appliances, and sold at prices and upon terms that place them within reach of every class of customers. From Indianapolis the trade in the city and throughout Marion County is supplied. From twelve to fifteen solicitors are constantly employed, and the volume of business has steadily increased each year, an exhibit of successful management, and an evidence of the high appreciation in which the "White" is held by a discriminating public.

E. M. Van Pelt—Dealer in Flour and Feed; 62 North Delaware street.—Mr. E. M. Van Pelt began operations here in 1885, and his career has been that of a prosperous and honorable merchant from its inception. He occupies a two-story and basement building, 20x75 feet in size, eligibly and advantageously located as above, directly opposite the City Hall. The premises are well arranged and equipped with all the necessary conveniences for the successful conduct of the business. He carries large stocks and full lines of standard brands of high grade spring and winter wheat, family and bakers' flour, buckwheat flour, corn and oatmeal, graham flour, and other productions of the same description, noted for their superior excellence and in great demand by a high class of consumers. He also carries equally extensive and complete supplies of hay, straw, corn, oats, middlings, chopped feed, granulated oil cake, etc., for stock, all of the best quality and description. His lines all around are exceptionally comprehensive and are sold at the lowest market quotations. He is amply prepared to supply all demands at the lowest prices and delivers goods at the residences of purchasers or at the depot free of charge, and does a large local trade in addition to ministering to the wants of customers within a considerable radius of the city.

Brosnan Bros. & Co.—Dry Goods and Notions; 37 and 39 South Illinois street.—This substantial and reliable dry goods house was started here during the year 1881. The firm is composed of Daniel D. Brosnan and John Brosnan, both gentlemen of long experience in the business. They occupy a two-story and basement building, 50x75 feet in dimensions, and though the large and increasing business taxes their capacity to the utmost, they are furnished with every modern convenience and facility that will promote its uninterrupted and successful operation. They carry large stocks of dry goods and notions, embracing silks, satins, dress goods, woolens, flannels, linens, domestics, hosiery, underwear, ladies' and gent's furnishings generally, laces, embroideries, parasols, prints, novelties, and these goods, both imported and domestic, are carefully selected from the best manufactories. They are purchased in large supplies and the firm is prepared to offer to customers substantial and exceptional inducements, in quality and prices. The house employs from thirty to forty competent assistants, and supplies a large local and transient demand, besides doing an equally extensive and growing trade with dealers and farmers throughout the surrounding country.

D. H. Baldwin & Co.—Pianos and Organs; 95 and 99 North Pennsylvania street.—The firm of D. H. Baldwin & Co. is in all respects the most prominent and influential in its line in the West and South. The Indianapolis house was established in 1873, and they occupy splendidly appointed premises at 95-97-99 North Pennsylvania street, 60x100 feet, with varnishing and repair rooms 25x60 feet in dimensions, where they carry large and complete assorted stocks of goods in this line. The house enjoys an established reputation, commercially and professionally, as extended as it is influential.

John A. Reaume—Shirts, Furnishings, and Laundry; 32 West Washington street, and 72 and 74 South Illinois street.—One of the oldest dealers in shirts and gentlemen's furnishing goods in the city or vicinity is John A. Reaume, who also owns and directs the operations of the New York Laundry. The gents' furnishings business was established by Mr. Reaume in 1866, and has annually increased in volume and value. He is prominently located in the building of the Indianapolis News, occupying the basement and main floor, each 20x100 feet in size, where he carries large stocks of shirts, collars, cuffs, underwear, hose, ties, cravats, scarfs, umbrellas, canes, European novelties, etc., of the best makes and materials, and in styles and at prices beyond successful competition. About 1883 he opened the New York Laundry, at 72 and 74 South Illinois street, which is now the largest and best equipped enterprise of its kind in the State, doing the finest work promptly and satisfactorily. This department is supplied with the latest improved laundry machinery, also having large accommodations for drying purposes and every facility adapted to the service. One of his specialties in this department is delicate work, in which the laundry excels. No chemicals are ever employed, and the same care is exercised in the processes incident to operations as in the best regulated households. His trade in both lines of business is very large in the city and surrounding country, requiring the services of between fifty and sixty hands and two wagons, and is extending and increasing throughout the State in all directions.

W. P. Maine—Dealer in Stoves, Slate and Iron Mantels, Etc.; 61 and 63 West Washington street.—The stove and tinware house owned and managed by W. P. Maine is one of the oldest and most prominent in its line in the city. It was established by R. L. McOat about 1830, the firm later becoming R. L. & A. W. McOat, and finally Geo. McOat, whom Mr. Maine succeeded in December, 1888. He is

from New York, experienced in the business, and is fully equipped to meet all the requirements of the trade. He occupies an eligibly located four-story and basement building, 50x100 feet in dimensions, and with the improvements he has recently completed and the equipments he has recently added, enjoys facilities unsurpassed in every particular by any similar undertaking in the State. His lines of manufacture include that of tinware and roofing materials, in which experienced hands are employed, and only the best class of workmanship turned out. His stocks embrace heating, cooking, gasoline and oil stoves, slate and iron mantels, refrigerators, kitchen furnishing goods and hollow iron and tinware in great variety, and complete lines of shelf hardware, all of these goods being of the best quality and from the leading factories and foundries of the country. He employs ten experienced workmen and a competent force of salesmen, and does a large trade in Indianapolis and throughout the surrounding country.

G. W. Barnes & Co.—Instalment Dealers; 64 East Market street.—Selling fine lines of household goods and other articles of established utility upon the instalment plan has become universally popular and proportionately prosperous. Among the leading houses thus engaged in this city is that of G. W. Barnes & Co., a firm organized and established during 1887. They occupy the basement and main floor of premises 25x100 feet in dimensions, attractively furnished and completely appointed, where they carry full and complete lines of goods of the best qualities, which are sold at low prices and upon the most liberal terms to customers or the trade. They handle all articles and novelties of merit as soon as they appear, their stocks embracing Smyrna rugs, lace curtains blankets in season, carpet sweepers, ladies' plush toilet sets, pictures, mirrors, easels, lamps, clocks, opera glasses, wall pockets, albums, dictionaries, bibles, and other books, Rogers' best flatware, silver-plated hollow ware, watches and jewelry, ladies' dress goods, wraps, etc. Also novelties, together with the Colby wringer, which latter they warrant for two years. These goods are sold at the firm's store, or through agents, upon small payments. The system is heartily indorsed. The house, by its enterprise and honorable methods, has acquired an enviable reputation and an extensive patronage. They employ a large force of salesmen, and supply a large and increasing demand in the city and throughout the State.

C. E. Carter—Manufacturing Confectioner, Caterer, Etc.; 91 North Illinois street.—One of the oldest and the most prominent caterer and manufacturer of fancy confections in the city is Mr. Carter, who established this business in 1867, and has since then occupied the leading position in his line of business in Indianapolis and Indiana. He is eligibly located as above, where he occupies a two-story and basement building, 25x100 feet in dimensions, completely fitted up and furnished for the business. His range of manufacture embraces candy, confections, cake, ice cream, cake ornaments and other articles for use at weddings, receptions, dinners, teas, parties and other social occasions equally formal and distinguished, and at the shortest notice. The edibles, conserves, delicacies, fruits, ices, and other articles included upon the menu served are of the choicest qualities, and the service itself is unsurpassed in respect to completeness and elegance. He employs a force of from eight to ten competent assistants, and a retinue of courteous and acceptable aids during the social season to meet the demands of a high class patronage in the city and vicinity.

Foster & Son—Merchant Tailors; Bates House, 20 North Illinois street.—This prominent merchant tailoring firm is composed of Messrs. Edward Foster and Thomas J. Foster. The business was first established here by Mr. Foster, Sr., in 1875, when he located on The Circle, coming to Indianapolis from Rushville, this State, after an experience in that city of twenty years. In 1882 the present firm was organized. Their present quarters at 20 North Illinois street, Bates House block, consist of commodious and handsomely furnished tailoring parlors, equipped and appointed in the latest styles, appropriate to the display of the fine lines of goods carried. They include the finest imported English, Scotch, Austrian, French and German fabrics of the choicest designs and most durable finish, with the products of the leading American looms, and the usual complement of trimmings, vestings, etc., only included in the invoices of first-class dealers. They make, specially to order, gentlemen's garments, according to the most modern fashion, and which, in cut, fit and appearance, are unsurpassed. They employ the most capable operatives, and are prepared to fill orders from any portion of the country upon the shortest notice and at the most reasonable prices. From fifteen to twenty hands are required in the business, and their trade is in the city and throughout the surrounding country. The senior member of the firm learned his trade in Ireland, and after fifteen years' service at Manchester, England, immigrated to America, locating as above stated. The junior member is equally finished in the details of the business, and their house enjoys a well merited reputation in all respects.

Edward B. Smith Steam and Chemical Dye Works; 57 North Pennsylvania street.—The oldest and largest steam and chemical dyeing establishment in Indianapolis is that of Edward B. Smith. He began operations along in 1868, and has built up a trade that is only measured by his capacity to supply, in all parts of the State, as also in territory more remote. He occupies premises 25x100 feet in dimensions, handsomely furnished and supplied with all requisite facilities for the business, and his dye works on Valle street are

equipped with all necessary machinery and appliances. His specialty is the dyeing of delicate fabrics, such as crape, broche and cashmere shawls, laces and embroideries, silks and merinos, feathers and kid gloves, also paying careful attention to ladies' and gentlemen's woolen garments and woolen and cotton goods of every description. He gives his personal supervision to every department of the business and executes work in his lines, than which there is none superior done in the West. He employs a force of twelve competent and experienced operatives, and supplies a large and growing demand for his services in the city and State.

Geo. Mannfeld Clothier, Merchant Tailor and Gents' Furnishings; 17 East Washington street.—This house was established during 1854, by the firm of Bauer & Goepper, the present proprietor being in their employ. Four years later the concern passed into the control of F. Goepper, and, in 1862, Mr. Mannfeld became a partner, the firm name being F. Goepper & Co.; changed to Goepper & Mannfeld in 1876, and so remained until 1882, when the former died and Mr. Mannfeld succeeded to the sole ownership. He occupies, at the site where the business has been located for thirty-five years, a handsome three story and basement building, 20x120 feet in dimensions, well appointed and provided with all requisite facilities and conveniences. The business is about equally divided between merchant tailoring and the handling of ready-made clothing. His range of manufacture includes garments for gentlemen, made to order in the latest styles of fashion, of the very best patterns and qualities and in price and superior workmanship unsurpassed. He carries large stocks of imported goods from which to make selections, and is prepared to fill orders for suits and garments adapted to every requirement. His stocks of ready-made clothing are equally competen-

sive and select, the products of the very best Eastern manufacture and his lines of gents' furnishing goods, hats, caps, notions, novelties, etc., can not be excelled for variety, quality or durability. Mr. Mannfeld is a prominent representative of commercial enterprise, and a reputable and popular business man.

C. Friedgen Manufacturer and Dealer in Boots and Shoes; 21 North Pennsylvania street. Among the well known and prosperous establishments in Indianapolis engaged in the manufacture and sale of boots and shoes, the house of C. Friedgen occupies a leading position. It was established by Mr. Friedgen in 1862, and for over a quarter of a century has been in successful operation. He occupies premises in the Etna building, 20x120 feet in size, admirably appointed and neatly fitted up. He carries the best Eastern make of boots and shoes manufactured to his order and for this market exclusively, composed of the choicest grades of French calf, kangaroo, kid and patent leather in the latest fashions, and warranted as represented. He carries no pegged or wire fastened work, and handles no cheap goods. He also manufactures a very fine class of boots and shoes to order, in which the best materials are employed and the products are most perfect samples of style, fit and superior workmanship. In this line he caters to a high class trade in the city and throughout the State, also in States adjoining, his trade in other lines being large in the city and vicinity. His relations with eastern producers are such that he is enabled to offer superior inducements in quality and prices to his patrons. Mr. Friedgen's long experience in the business and thorough knowledge of its details and requirements, entitle the house to the enviable position it holds in the commercial and manufacturing circles of Indianapolis.

J. E. Whelden Gents' Furnishing Goods, Laundry, Etc.; 85 West Pennsylvania street.—Mr. Whelden became established here in 1884, and has from the start conducted a large and successful business, handling only the leading and best lines of goods, and conserving a demand among the leading and best classes of customers. The premises occupied for store purposes, located in the New Denison House block, are commodious and handsomely appointed, entrance being obtained on Pennsylvania street, and from the hotel lobby. He handles shirts in stock, and the choicest lines of silk, woolen, balbriggan and other grades of underwear and hosiery, besides gloves, ties, scarfs, mufflers, silk goods, gold and silver headed umbrellas, notions, novelties, and the better class of furnishings and furnishing goods generally, and his laundry facilities are very complete for superior and expeditious work. His supplies are selected with special reference to the requirements of this market and the demands of an exacting patronage, and are imported direct or purchased from first hands. Mr. Whelden is prepared to offer the inducements of reasonable prices and liberal terms to customers and the public. A large local and transient trade is supplied, and the house enjoys a well merited reputation for its enterprise and honorable business methods.

Craig Confectionery 20 East Washington street.—One of the best known and most popular houses in the city, engaged in the manufacture of fine confections, is that of J. A. Craig, who established his present enterprise here in 1873, previous to which he conducted a similar industry in Chicago. His place of business fronts 20 feet on East Washington street, with a depth of 64 feet, where it communicates with the manufacturing department, 20x70 feet in dimensions. The premises are attractively and handsomely fitted up, and equipped with all requisite conveniences and appliances for the business. His products embrace everything in confections of the best grades, such as bon-bons, creams, caramels, chocolates, fruit tablets, French nougat, fancy confections etc., in general assortment. Purity of materials and products is Mr. Craig's specialty. Only the best grades of sugar, fruits and nuts, and other essentials are used, and the consequence is that his candies and articles generally obtain a preference with the trade. These are put up in handsome packages, artistic boxes, baskets, etc., available for presents, mailing or shipment, and are in great demand throughout the city and vicinity, as also among transient visitors. He is prepared to fill orders promptly, and at satisfactory prices, and the house enjoys a reputation as established as it is extended and influential.

Ballard & Brundage—Dealers in Men's Fine Furnishings; 37 North Illinois street. A valuable addition to the business interests of Indianapolis was made in 1886, by the establishment of the gent's furnishing house of Ballard & Brundage, the firm being composed of G. C. Ballard and S. M. Brundage. They occupy a handsomely fitted up store, 20x75 feet in size, well appointed for the business, and provided with every facility for responding to the demands of the trade. Their specialty is men's fine dress shirts to order, in the making of which skilled operatives and the very best qualities of goods only are employed. In this particular they are conceded to be unrivalled. They also carry large and well-selected lines of gentlemen's shirts and furnishing goods, including underwear, hosiery, collars, cuffs, ties, scarfs, mufflers, gloves, canes, gold and silver headed umbrellas, European novelties, etc., in great variety and of the choicest selection. The concern is in every respect a leading emporium of its kind, and the firm offers inducements in regard to materials, prices and lines from which to make selections, unsurpassed in this market. They do a large and steadily increasing trade in the city and throughout the surrounding country.

P. J. Kelleher—Hatter, Furrier and Gent's Furnishings; 23 West Washington street. Mr. Kelleher, who established this business in 1881, occupies an attractive store located at one of the most convenient and accessible sites on the leading retail thoroughfare of Indianapolis. The premises are 20x150 feet in dimensions and equipped with every facility for the display of the diversified stocks carried, and all conveniences for the efficient conduct of the business. Large invoices of hats of the most approved fashionable make are kept in stock, also caps and straw goods, in addition to fur caps, gloves and collars in seal, otter, lynx, beaver, etc. The lines of gent's furnishings embrace shirts, collars, cuffs, gloves, underwear, hose, silk goods, scarfs, mufflers, ties, umbrellas, canes, the most recent European novelties, and notions of the choicest qualities and latest patterns. The lists, in short, include everything that can be useful or valuable to a gentleman's wardrobe. Mr. Kelleher imports direct and purchases from first hands, thereby insuring to patrons the "pick of the market," and guaranteeing the best articles at the lowest prices. He supplies a large and high class local demand, and his house possesses the confidence and patronage of an extensive constituency within a considerable radius of Indianapolis.

Chas. J. Kuhn—Fine Groceries; 47 and 49 North Illinois street; Telephone No. 602.—This enterprise was established by Albert C. Kuhn, brother of the present proprietor, many years ago, the latter, who had been associated in the management of the concern for some nine years prior to January, 1888, at that date succeeding to the ownership. He occupies premises 25x100 feet in their dimensions, availably located and furnished with every modern convenience and appointment that can facilitate the accommodation of customers or the expeditious transaction of business. His specialties are coffees, teas, sugars, spices, etc., pure and fresh, the finest grades in the market, and which are carried in large supply; also handling equally extensive stocks of fine fancy groceries. The latter embrace delicacies, bottled and canned fruits, foreign and domestic preserves, sauces and condiments, imported Swiss, Gruyere and other foreign cheeses, imported fruits and vegetables, also vegetables indigenous to this climate in

their season, and other articles, making up an assortment of the most varied and attractive character. He is provided with telephone service and other mediums for the prompt service of patrons, and with the lowest market prices, offers substantial inducements to the public. He employs ten assistants, also operating three wagons and making no charges for delivering goods at the depots, throughout the city or in the suburbs, where he does a large retail trade, having also a fine family trade, and jobbing specialties to grocers in all portions of the State. The house is representative in all respects and of prominent importance in its line.

William Kotteman—Dealer in Furniture, Etc.; 89 and 91 East Washington street.—Prior to embarking in business on his own account in 1882, Mr. Kotteman had been for years in the employ of leading firms in the same line in this city, and acquired a thorough knowledge of the service in all its departments and equal familiarity with the requirements of a trade that made Indianapolis its base of supplies. His location is specially adapted to the convenience of his large and growing patronage, and the premises occupied specially attractive and adequate. They consist of a three-story brick building, 20x165 feet in dimensions, neatly appointed and completely equipped, and contain full lines of his diversified stock of elegant and medium grades of furniture. They embrace sets for parlor, dining and reception rooms, library, bed chamber and kitchen, in rosewood, mahogany, oak, maple, cherry and other hardwoods, made according to the most recent designs, and decorated in prevailing styles. He also carries equally complete lines of carpets, crockery, glass and queensware, table cutlery, stoves, ranges, tinware and other articles of utility and ornamentation. The three stores, into which the premises are divided, contain everything in the way of household furnishings that can be required by the most exacting of patrons. He employs a full staff of assistants, and does a large trade in the city and vicinity.

Paul H. Kraus—Shirt Manufacturer and Men's Furnisher; 44 and 46 East Washington street.—This extensive shirt manufactory was established in 1873 by the firm of Eddy & West. Mr. Kraus began life as a messenger boy in the Indiana National Bank of this city, when Mr. Eddy was Cashier. When the latter embarked in the present business Mr. Kraus accompanied him, and in 1882 succeeded to his interest, becoming sole proprietor upon the death of Mr. West, which occurred during the same year. He occupies a very attractive store consisting of a three-story and basement building, 30x100 feet in size, handsomely furnished and fitted up. The third floor is used as a laundry, the second floor for shirt manufacturing, the main floor for salesrooms and the basement for storage. His specialty is the making of men's fine shirts to order, giving his personal attention to the measure of patrons and the cutting and finishing of the garment, and turning out an article that for style, fit and durability, as also for material, is not surpassed in the Indianapolis market. He is amply prepared to fill orders from a distance, and to make prompt shipments, and in every way to minister to the requirements of the trade. He also carries large and select stocks of men's fine furnishing goods, imported through the custom house here, embracing the famous underwear of Welsh, Margotson & Co., and Virgoe, Middleton & Co., of London, as also the latest English and other European novelties in collars, cuffs, ties, scarfs, gloves, canes, umbrellas, etc. He employs a force of fifty girls in his manufacturing department, with three travelers and a staff of clerks in the sales department, and supplies the trade generally in the city and State.

Wm. Schoppenhorst—Merchant Tailor; Vance Block Point.—This business was established over twenty years ago by Jacob Huber. In 1876, Mr. Schoppenhorst became a partner in the establishment, the firm name remaining Jacob Huber, however, and so continuing until January 1, 1888, at which date Mr. Schoppenhorst purchased the Huber interest and has since been sole owner of the enterprise. He occupies a commodious and handsomely appointed store, triangular in shape, at the junction of Pennsylvania and Washington streets and Virginia avenue, in one of the most prominent and architecturally attractive business blocks of the city. His specialty is order work to measure, in which he excels, making it a point to render entire satisfaction to the high class of customers who are his exclusive patrons. His cutters and fitters are men who combine skill, experience and natural aptitude for the special departments, and whose products are models of elegance and finish. He carries full lines and large stocks of imported English, Scotch, French and Austrian cloths, cassimeres, suitings and vestings, also the products of the leading American looms, in broadcloth, diagonal, tweed and other patterns of goods of the finest texture, in the latest styles, and of the most durable qualities. His products, considering their value, can be purchased at low rates and upon reasonable terms. He gives employment to from twenty-five to thirty expert hands, and does a very large business in the city and throughout the surrounding country.

Konz—The American Tailor; 9 South Illinois street.—Situated in the center of the retail trade district of this city, the house of H. Konz, draper and tailor, has, in a short time, become prominently identified with a high class trade, by whom he is recognized as a purveyor of unsurpassed taste and artistic originality. He is known as "The American Tailor," commencing business in 1885, in the Vance block, whence he moved to his present site, in the Occidental Hotel block, during the spring of 1888. He occupies premises 20x60 feet in dimensions, tastefully arranged and admirably appointed, and his specialties are fine tailoring and moderate prices, and he carries full lines of imported and domestic cloths, cassimeres and vestings, also trimmings, etc., of the latest patterns and best qualities. He makes only to order, his lines of production embracing overcoats, ulsters, suits and single garments, adapted to weddings and other social occasions, as also for business purposes, displaying the truest expression of taste and refinement in appearance, and skilled and cultivated talent in their make-up and finishings. He employs from fifteen to twenty experienced and competent tailors, and does a large local trade, also among transients, with all of whom he enjoys an established reputation for superior articles of dress at the most reasonable prices.

Lilly & Stalnaker—Wholesale and Retail Hardware; 64 East Washington street.—The representative and leading hardware firm of Lilly & Stalnaker is composed of J. W. Lilly and Frank D. Stalnaker. The business was established in 1863, under the firm name of Vajin, New & Co., by whom it was conducted for many years, the present firm succeeding in 1887, and continuing operations with increased facilities and increased results. They are eligibly located at 64 East Washington street, where they occupy a four-story building, 25x100 feet in size, containing all modern improvements, and equipped with every device and appointment that can contribute to the successful handling of their large lines of stock, and the shipment of orders. They carry very complete and comprehensive invoices of hardware, embracing builders' hardware, house furnishing goods, cutlery, mechanical tools and appliances, both domestic and imported, in all grades and designs. They obtain these from first hands and import direct, and the qualities of their stock, together with reasonable prices and liberal terms, have acquired for the firm a well deserved and firmly established reputation, wherever they are known. They employ twelve competent assistants, and do a large retail trade in the city, as also a wholesale trade, extending to the furthest limits of the State in every direction.

W. J. Eisele—Dealer in Watches, Diamonds and Jewelry; 24 East Washington street.—This extensive and popular emporium in its line was established in 1856 by Craft & Co., with whom Mr. Eisele was associated for many years, succeeding to the sole ownership of the establishment in 1884. He is prominently located on the most fashionable promenade in the city, occupying the main floor and basement of premises 20x100 feet in dimensions, finished in walnut, furnished with artistic silver mounted display cases, and supplied with every convenience that will add to the attractions or accommodation of the trade. His stock embraces imported and American watches, in gold, silver and filled cases, diamonds, sapphires, pearls,

rubies, emeralds and other rare gems, mounted to order and in stock, gold and rolled jewelry, silver and plated ware, opera glasses, spectacles and optical goods, clocks and bijouterie generally, of the best make and in the latest fashionable styles. The manufacture of jewelry is a specialty of Mr. Eisele's, and his knowledge of the art, taste and originality and delicate workmanship are in constant requisition for fine work for bridal presents and other testimonials of an appropriate character. He also does repairing extensively, and his work meets universal commendation. His trade is large, and augmenting in volume in the city and among transients.

L. Mueller—Fashionable Merchant Tailor; 40 South Illinois street.—Mr. Mueller established his business in 1878, and has acquired a reputation and high class trade, not surpassed by that of any similar undertaking in this city. He occupies a three-story and basement building, 25x100 feet in dimensions, located on one of the leading highways of trade, and furnished and finished in a manner exceptionally complete and attractive. His stocks are select and complete, embracing the finest grades of imported English, Scotch, French and German fabrics, and the higher quality of products of American looms, with trimmings, linings, vestings, etc., in great variety and assortment. His garments are patterns of elegance and merit in material, make, finish and appearance. He makes to order exclusively, his son, Louis Mueller, Jr., having charge of the cutting and fitting departments, furnishing wedding outfits, business suits, overcoats, and single garments generally, when required, and gives employment to from twenty to twenty-five expert and artistic tailors. He does a large local trade, also supplying the demands of customers residing elsewhere in the State, the house having commended itself to favor by reasonable prices and honorable business methods.

P. Gramling & Son—Merchant Tailors, and Dealers in Clothing, Etc.; 35 East Washington street.—Mr. P. Gramling established this business in 1854, and just thirty years later, or in 1884, Eugene Gramling, his son, was admitted as a partner, and the present firm was organized. They are eligibly located as above, where they occupy premises 20x160 feet in size, handsomely appointed and provided with complete facilities for the business. Their line of manufacture embraces gentlemen's clothing to order, this department being according to the latest designs of the prevailing fashions and patterns of fit, materials, and first-class workmanship. The firm carry large stocks of foreign and domestic cloths, trimmings, etc., in great variety and of the finest qualities. In the ready-made clothing department they handle selected lines, made to their order by the most famous eastern houses and for this market, in the most recent styles, and unexcelled for comfort and durable wear. Their stocks of furnishing goods are equally choice and comprehensive, including imported and American manufacture, in silk, balbriggan, woolen, flannel and lighter grades of material of standard worth and substantial character. The establishment enjoys a highly deserved and influential reputation all over Indiana, as also in more distant sections, as a representative in the highest sense of the commercial interests of Indianapolis. The firm employ a large force of clerks, journeymen, etc., and do a large trade in the city and vicinity; also filling orders extensively from customers throughout the State.

Bates House Pharmacy; 51 West Washington street, Bates House block.—This is a very handsomely equipped, admirably located and neatly appointed drug store, with entrances from Washington street and the hotel rotunda. The appointments are first-class in every particular, including very handsome show cases, marble top counters, tile flooring, etc., also a very handsome soda fountain. The proprietor, Mr. F. Will Pantzer, is a graduate of the renowned Philadelphia College of Pharmacy and has had several years' practical experience in the best prescription drug stores of Philadelphia and New York. For the past two years he has been the junior partner of the firm of C. H. Broich & Co., at the corner of Morris and South Meridian streets, this city, and has materially contributed toward making that the best appointed drug store in the southern part of the city. He

-specialties are the handling of pure drugs and chemicals, and the compounding of physicians' prescriptions. He carries selected stocks of everything appertaining to the drug business, embracing all of the new and latest discovered remedies, alkaloids, elixirs, fluid extracts, surgical dressings, perfumes, toilet and medicinal soaps, mineral waters, wines and liquors for medicinal purposes, domestic and imported cigars, novelties, etc. His goods are all of standard purity, fresh from the most celebrated dispensaries of the world, and always reliable. In the compounding of prescriptions he employs only competent pharmacists, and enjoys the highest reputation for skill and superiority in that department. He does a large and increasing city and transient trade.

James N. Mayhew Practical and Expert Optician, 13 North Meridian street. A practical and accomplished optician, educated to the profession and possessing a thorough and extensive experience, a comprehensive and accurate knowledge of the principles of optics and their application to the aid of defective vision, is Mr. James N. Mayhew. He has been thus engaged in this city for over twenty years. For a period of fifteen years, he was associated with Moses, the well-known spectacle man, subsequently in the jewelry and optical business on his own account, being then located on West Washington street, and continuing until 1886, when he abandoned the jewelry department that he might devote himself exclusively to his present line, and removed to the premises now occupied by his business, at 13 North Meridian street. They are handsomely arranged and appointed, and contain every appliance requisite to the successful prosecution of the service. He carries full lines of optical goods and supplies, embracing spectacles and eye-glasses, magnifying glasses, lorgnettes, etc., of the best manufacture, in the latest design and at the lowest prices consistent with their valuable properties. His particular specialty is the filling of oculists' prescriptions with exceptional care, making repairs neatly and promptly and attends to the details of the business and the acknowledgement of orders in the most satisfactory manner. Persons who appreciate the importance of having frames and lenses properly fitted or reset, are recommended to Mr. Mayhew with the assurance of honorable treatment. He does a large trade in the city and has acquired the patronage of the most distinguished oculists throughout the State, by whom and the public generally, his establishment is regarded as the leading and most reliable of its kind in Indiana.

Geo. A. Van Pelt Flour, Meal, Feed, Breakfast Cereals, Etc., 121 North Delaware street. Mr. G. A. Van Pelt established himself in Indianapolis as a grain and flour dealer in 1877, and conducts the largest and most complete establishment of the kind in Indiana. He occupies a two-story building, 20 feet front by 200 feet deep, and also owns and controls a branch store at the corner of Massachusetts avenue and Ash street, and aims to have every known cereal preparation represented in stock, and to this end will cheerfully procure from any part of the United States, any article called for, not already in store. A partial list of his manufactured cereals, and other health foods, includes wheat foods: whole wheat, rolled wheat, wheatlet, wheat meal, cracked wheat, wheat flakes, wheat germ meal, parched wheat farinose, wheat grits, wheat gluten, wheat farina, etc.; fine graham flour, medium graham flour, coarse graham flour, Akron and home ground. Oat foods: oat meal, fine, medium and coarse; oat groats, rolled oats, oat flour, shredded oats, avoine, avdavena flakes, Schumacher's rolled avena. Aunt Abbey's cooked rolled oats, and all other kinds. Barley foods: barley groats, barley flour, crushed barley, pearl barley, barley flakes. Rye foods: rye graham, rye grain, rye farina, rye meal. Corn foods: corn meal, standard white, clear cream, fine pearl, medium pearl, coarse pearl, yellow bolted, yellow fancy, yellow granulated, hominy granulated, breakfast hominy, coarse hominy. Miscellaneous: gluten flour, granula, rice flour, Lockport fine flour of the entire wheat, hop yeast cakes, all kinds of rice, samp, cerealine, punited molds, A, B, C, food for the little ones, etc.; and in flour and feed his stock embraces some twenty-five different brands of flour from eighteen mills, in Indiana, Ohio, St. Louis and Minneapolis; rye flour (selected brands), eastern and Indiana buckwheat flour, and all kinds of grain and feed, including hay and straw; bird foods, poultry foods and cures, ground oyster shells, bone meal, egg producers, and everything for poultry keepers; horse and cattle condition powders, flax seed, oil cake and oil meal, etc. Many articles are kept in stock, not enumerated above, and he has many goods in his line never before sold in Indianapolis, and goods are delivered free to any part of the city and freight depots.

L. A. Catt Wholesale and Retail Dealer in Flour, Etc., 175 West Washington street. This business was founded in 1876 by Mr. Catt, who is a native of this State, a man of long and active experience in the business and familiar with the wants of the trade, and in all respects prominent in mercantile and financial circles. He occupies a three-story and basement building, at the above site, 20x200 feet in dimensions, provided with every convenience and facility, including telephone service, for the successful conduct of operations and the accommodation of his stocks and consignments. He deals in the choicest brands of flour, for family and general use, embracing the products of the leading mills of the West and Northwest, of unsurpassed quality, and otherwise known for its superior excellence. He also carries full lines and complete stocks of prairie and timothy hay, corn, bran, oats, shorts, middlings, meal, etc., fresh, pure and sweet, and sold in quantities or in car-load lots at the lowest market rates. Fresh supplies are received daily, thereby enabling Mr. Catt to fill orders promptly and to offer the most liberal inducements to his patrons and the public. He does a large local wholesale and retail trade, and the house has acquired an extended reputation in harmony with the enterprise and honorable methods which characterize its management and operations.

E. W. Vance & Co. Fancy Dry Goods, Millinery, Etc., 96 East Washington street. One of the most handsomely fitted up, centrally located and completely equipped dry goods stores in the city, is that of E. W. Vance & Co., established by Mr. Vance in 1883. It is described as "the ladies' store par excellence of the city," and the description is fully confirmed by the facts. The premises occupied are 20x150 feet in dimensions, and the stocks are very full and complete in all lines, imported and domestic, embracing fancy dry goods in great variety, sewing, knitting, embroidering and floss silk of every description, silk underwear and mittens, hose in silk and woolen, ladies' furnishings, buttons, embroideries, gloves, millinery and millinery goods and ornaments, plumes and feathers, ribbons and laces, novelties and bijouterie of the latest Parisian, European and eastern make and most fashionable styles. His invoices are selected with great care, and, as above indicated, are of the choicest character and qualities, adapted to the wants of a refined taste and the requirements of an exacting constituency, which are fully met and provided for. He employs a force of from fifteen to twenty competent and obliging assistants, and does a large trade in the city and surrounding country, as also with transient visitors.

R. W. Furnas Plain and Fancy Ice Cream and Fruit Ices, Etc.; 112 and 114 North Pennsylvania street. The well known and reliable establishment of R. W. Furnas, devoted to the manufacture of ice cream, fruit ices, and butter, also dealing in milk and cream, has been the leading establishment in its line in Indianapolis since it was started by the present proprietor in 1876. He occupies premises 40x50 feet, in the Rink building, the ice cream parlors being handsomely decorated, appointed and furnished. To the rear of these, and extending to an alley, is the manufacturing department, 30x150 feet in dimensions, supplied with all modern equipments, including ice cream freezers with a total capacity of forty gallons of ice cream per hour, and ice shaving machinery, etc., driven by steam. His specialties are plain and fancy ice creams, sherbets, fruit ices, sweet cream, creamery butter and milk. The raw material is mostly obtained at Bridgeport and Friendswood, both in this State, Mr. Furnas owning a creamery at the former, whence milk and cream are brought to the city daily, the supplies in summer averaging nearly 1,600 gallons of milk and cream per diem. The heaviest output of ice cream ever made by this house was in the summer of 1888, when a daily average of 200 gallons was made for thirty consecutive days. He supplies hotels, confectioners, restaurants, private families, parties, festivals, receptions and other occasions. A force of from twelve to fifteen assistants and five wagons are employed in the service, and his trade is almost wholly within the city, but some ice cream is shipped outside.

P. Harity—Umbrella and Parasol Manufacturer; 43 Virginia avenue.—The manufacture of umbrellas and parasols carried on by P. Harity at the above location, was by him established in 1876, and by his thorough knowledge of the business in all its minutest details has steadily increased the extent and importance of his trade in the city and surrounding territory. He occupies a neatly fitted up store at 43 Virginia avenue, directly opposite the site where he originally located, where he carries large stocks of materials and makes a specialty of covering and repairing. His supplies include the latest fashionable designs in umbrellas for ladies and gentlemen, parasols, etc., of the best qualities and products of the best class of workmanship. He also keeps in stock silk of every hue and color, alpaca, muslin, and other goods for purposes of covering, together with gold, silver, carved ivory and fancy wood handles in great variety. His establishment is well known and popular, his stock is complete and choice, his materials of the best character and description, and his service prompt and reasonable. He gives his personal attention to the manufacture and repair of goods, and does a large trade in the city and surrounding country, throughout which the house enjoys a well deserved reputation for reliability and honorable enterprise.

W. F. Rupp & Co.—Merchant Tailors; 23 East Washington street.—This firm, composed of W. F. Rupp and Gust. Rossberg, was organized in 1861, and has, during its career of nearly thirty years, contributed in no small degree to the elevated standard in gentlemen's dress which prevails in this city. Their apartments are each 20x130 feet in dimensions, and most attractively equipped and furnished. They carry full lines of the finest imported fabrics of the latest patterns, also cloths, cassimeres and vestings, the output of the most celebrated American looms, in addition to trimmings, linings and novelties for gents' wear of the most recent styles and elegant finish. They make to order only, their range of manufacture embracing suits for every service or occasion, besides overcoats, ulsters, and single garments generally, in the latest fashion and the most substantial manner, guaranteeing the perfection of fit and an appearance that will meet the demands of the most fastidious of patrons. They are prepared to promptly furnish samples, suits, or single articles of wearing apparel to customers at a distance, and are so versed in the art of cutting and fitting that the latter, by sending their measure, can rely upon superiority in these respects as if they were present. They employ from twenty-five to thirty experienced assistants, and do a large trade in the city and vicinity, as also with old established customers in other portions of the State.

The Boston Store—Jackson, Porter & Alderman, Proprietors; Wholesale and Retail Dry Goods, Hosiery, Notions, Etc.; 26 and 28 West Washington street.—The Boston Store was established in this city March 1, 1889, by Messrs. W. F. Jackson, A. W. Porter, and F. W. Alderman, composing the firm of Jackson, Porter & Alderman. The members of the firm are from Boston, Mass., and all have had a long and exceptionally desirable experience in the

business in the East. Their location is the most available in the city, the premises occupied having been the dry goods house of M. H. Spades for years. They consist of a four-story and basement building, 50 feet front on West Washington street and 150 feet deep, the entire interior space of which is devoted to the storage and sale of dry goods, novelties and notions. They are handsomely arranged and appointed, equipped with the latest improved elevator and telephone service, and provided with every facility for the business. Their stocks are very large and comprehensive, embracing full lines of foreign and domestic silks and dress fabrics, velvets, satins, laces, embroideries, ribbons, hosiery, gloves, ladies' and gents' furnishings, corsets, shawls, wraps, white goods, linens, domestics, flannels, blankets, upholstering goods, European and American novelties, Yankee notions, nick-nacks, etc., in almost endless profusion, and of the latest and most approved patterns. They are imported direct and obtained from first hands, and present an array of unsurpassed attractions suitable to the taste of the most fastidious and the most conservative of customers. The house is in every particular representative in its character and management, and an acquisition to the city's commercial interests of very large importance and value. The members of the firm give their personal attention to the conduct of the business in all its departments, and have founded an enterprise the success of which is being daily demonstrated. They employ from thirty to thirty-five assistants and cater to a trade in the city and State.

Frank A. Blanchard—Undertaker and Embalmer; 66 North Pennsylvania street; Telephone No. 411.—F. A. Blanchard began the undertaking and embalming business here in 1885, and occupies the main floor and basement of the premises above mentioned, each being 25x150 feet in dimensions, and gives to the details of the business intrusted to his care prompt and careful attention. His arrangements are complete, and his furnishings and appointments are appropriate and of the latest styles. A full and complete assortment of fine caskets, coffins, etc., are kept in stock, also funeral robes, shrouds, trimmings, ornaments, etc., adapted to every want. The establishment is provided with a morgue, in addition to its other appointments, and he is prepared to embalm bodies for preservation by a process producing permanent effects. His equipment also includes funeral cars, hearses, carriages and other auxiliaries necessary to the service, and he elicits respectful commendation for the nicety he brings to the discharge of his duties. A full and experienced staff of assistants, including a lady attendant, are employed, and he responds to calls by day or night, also to telegrams for services at a distance.

The When Clothing Store—Men's and Boys' Clothing, Hats, Caps, Furnishing Goods, Etc.; 30 to 40 North Pennsylvania street.—This store was established in this city during 1875, as one of many branches of a house under the same management at Utica, N. Y. They are located in an elegant four-story and basement building, of which they are owners, carry large stocks of clothing, hats, caps, furs and furnishing goods, and do a large trade in the city and among transients.

Domestic Laundry—Steam Laundry; Lace Curtains a Specialty; 73 North Illinois street.—Among the laundries of this city, none is better known or more generally patronized than the Domestic Laundry, which was established by Henry Richters, the present proprietor, in 1884. The premises occupied consist of the basement and main floor, each 25x100 feet in dimensions, well arranged and equipped with every facility for the promotion of the work, both in respect to quantity and quality, including all the latest inventions in machinery for washing, ironing, etc., and other special appliances, operated by a five-horse power engine, put in during the spring of 1889. The cleansing of lace curtains, of the finest quality, is made a specialty by Mr. Richters, and his success in this line has secured for his establishment a very large and select class of patrons. Fine family and hotel work are not less specialties, and the same care is exercised, and extra attention is paid to these lines, such being particularly the case with ladies' wear, collars, cuffs, etc. None but competent and experienced assistants are kept in the service, each department of which is personally supervised by Mr. Richters, and nothing is left undone that will contribute to giving the fullest satisfaction to patrons. Orders receive prompt attention, prices for work are reasonable, and a large business is done in the city and vicinity, giving employment to from ten to twelve hands, and two wagons.

Jos. F. Kunz—Merchant Tailor; 159 East Washington street. The business carried on by Jos. F. Kunz, and established in this city by that gentleman in 1887, has commanded a success both pronounced and gratifying. He is located at one of the most desirable and available business sites in the city, and otherwise convenient to customers. The premises occupied are 25x100 feet in dimensions, neatly appointed and attractively arranged for the tasty displays of his lines of goods, and the transaction of business. He carries selected stocks of the choicest description of foreign and domestic cloths, suitings, overcoatings, etc., in the latest patterns of style, of the finest finish, and appropriate to every service. He also carries vestings, trimmings of silk, satin and velvet, and a general line of commodities adapted to a first-class establishment of the kind. He is prepared to fill orders promptly for suits for weddings, receptions and other social occasions, as also for the counting room and business purposes, for ulsters, overcoats and heavy wear generally, in addition to single garments, made up in the best manner, and in fit and appearance the most perfect embodiment of fashion and superior workmanship. His stocks are complete, his make unsurpassed, and his prices low. He employs from ten to fifteen journeymen with their assistants, and the house caters to a large and growing city trade.

H. H. Hutchins—Manufacturer and Dealer in Fine Boots and Shoes; 243 East Washington street.—The emporium of H. H. Hutchins, devoted to the manufacture and sale of the finer and medium grades of boots and shoes, was established by Mr. Hutchins in 1868. His experience in the business, intimate familiarity with the wants of the trade, and the careful attention he gives to the selection of the stock handled, have secured him deserved success. Located as above, where he has remained continuously for the past sixteen years, he occupies premises 25x100 feet in dimensions, attractively fitted up and handsomely appointed for the business. He carries very full and complete lines of footwear for men, women, youths, boys and misses, in varied assortments and of the best qualities. They are the productions of leading eastern manufacturers in French calf, morocco, kangaroo, kid and other choice descriptions of leather, made up in button, lace, elastic and other styles, and adapted to every service and occasion. They are made specially for this market, and in workmanship and materials are not inferior to custom made products, besides being purchased in large invoices for cash by Mr. Hutchins, he is able to offer very substantial inducements in prices to customers and the trade. Mr. Hutchins is, in addition, prepared to execute orders promptly, and his house has acquired an extended and invaluable reputation, not only among patrons who have availed themselves of the advantages he has offered for more than twenty years, but also with customers of a more recent date, in the city and throughout the surrounding country.

The New York Store—Wholesale and Retail Dry Goods, Notions, Millinery and Boots and Shoes; 25, 27, 29 and 31 East Washington street. The New York Store was established by Glenn Bros., during 1855, in one of the stores of the Bates House block. It passed through several changes prior to 1887, when the present firm was created. They occupy very commodious and handsomely equipped premises, 50x195 feet in dimensions. They carry heavy and diversified stocks, employ a force of 150 assistants, and do a large and constantly increasing business in the city and State.

George Hotz—Merchant Tailor; 124 South Illinois street.— One of the oldest and most popular merchant tailors in Indianapolis is George Hotz, who has been thus engaged for more than thirty years, during all of which time he has been located on South Illinois

street in his present vicinity. He occupies the main floor and basement, each 20x100 feet in dimensions, attractively apportioned and appointed, and containing all requisite facilities for display and sale purposes, as also for the speedy and finished production of his lines of supply. He carries a well assorted stock of cloths, woolens, cassimeres, vestings, overcoatings, etc., the best grades of imported and domestic manufacture from which to make selections, and is prepared to fill orders for suits or single garments appropriate to social occasions or business purposes. His products are models of fashion and elegance, unsurpassed in fit and appearance, and samples of superior workmanship. His stocks all around are as comprehensive as they are desirable, and obtainable at low prices and upon reasonable terms. He is an experienced cutter and fitter, who gives his personal attention to the requirements of the trade, in which he is also assisted by a force of from fifteen to twenty operatives, and does a large annual business, mainly in the city and surrounding country, besides filling orders for customers in all parts of the State, throughout which he has enjoyed an enviable reputation as a proficient factor and dealer for upwards of a quarter of a century.

John Shingler—Dealer in Queensware, Glassware, Lamps, Etc.; 78 Massachusetts avenue.—The queensware and glassware house of John Shingler, who established it in 1886, is one of the most prosperous and ably managed in the city. He occupies the main floor and basement at the above location, 20x100 feet in dimensions, handsomely appointed and well provided with facilities for the displays of stock and the sale and shipment of orders. He carries large and full lines of china, glass and queensware, silverware, tableware, cutlery, hanging and swinging lamps, students' lamps, etc., of the latest and most elegant designs, also fancy goods, ornaments and novelties generally, in great variety, and well adapted to the high grade trade to which he caters. His stock, in all departments, is very choice and complete, the products of the leading potteries of Europe and America, and in every particular well calculated to please the taste of the most fastidious and conservative of buyers. He carries a full line of porcelain dinner sets of the best English potteries, and his chamber sets are of the best ware and best designs. He does a large trade in the city and vicinity, which is steadily increasing.

Herman Bamberger—Dealer in Hats, Caps, Furs and Gloves; 16 East Washington street.—Mr. Bamberger began business in 1858, and for the past thirty years has occupied the site now utilized by his business. His premises consist of the basement and main floor, each 20x120 feet in size, affording every accommodation for his business. He carries very large stocks of hats by the leading makers, being sole agent for Youman's celebrated stiff and silk hats. Besides these, he deals in caps, straw goods, furs, fur robes and gloves, of standard makes and qualities, and all the latest styles of goods usually handled by a first-class hat house. He is also a manufacturer of silk hats, making those of a $5.96 and $4.25 per dozen quality, supplying a large trade which is rapidly extending. Special orders received in the morning can be shipped the same day, affording facilities that cannot be had at distant cities. He deals in ladies' furs and for trimmings of every description, and also makes a specialty of altering and repairing all kinds of fur garments, making over, re-lining, etc. In this department, Mr. Bamberger's long experience, and the fact that he gives it his personal attention, enables him to make better terms, and give his patrons a still further advantage and guarantee as to the goods purchased.

The Famous Eagle Clothing Store—Men's and Boys' Clothing and Furnishings; 13 West Washington street. Benjamin Gundelfinger, proprietor of the "The Famous Eagle," one of the largest and best known clothing establishments in the city, has been engaged in the same line of business since 1860, when he was connected with the firm of Glazier Bros. & Co., with whom he had been for many years previous clerking at the old Oak Hall clothing store here. Afterward he established two other concerns which he disposed of, and, in the year 1882, established his present headquarters where he has remained since. In this department the house is known as the

Famous Eagle Clothing House. His location is one of the best in the city, on the leading retail trade thoroughfare, and in every way desirable. He occupies the main floor and basement, fronting twenty feet on West Washington street and running back two hundred feet to Pearl street. They are commodious, handsomely appointed, and provided with all facilities for the business. He carries very full and complete lines of clothing for men, youths, boys and children, the products of the leading local and eastern manufactories, of the best materials and in the latest styles of the fashion, made up for use and embodying the best class of skilled workmanship. His lines of furnishing goods are full, complete, embracing all that is new and desirable in that line, such as shirts, collars, cuffs, neckwear in endless varieties, hosiery, gloves and handkerchiefs, and choice selections of underwear. They are obtained direct from producers and Mr. Gundelfinger is enabled to offer the most advantageous inducements in respect to prices and quality to customers and the trade.

F. Koester & Co. Furniture and House Furnishing Goods; 98 East New York street. The house furnishing establishment owned and conducted by F. Koester & Co. though a recent addition to the commercial resources of Indianapolis, has acquired the confidence and patronage of a large and increasing trade distributed throughout the city and vicinity. The firm was organized and commenced operations in 1888, and are located at the above number on New York street, where they occupy the main floor and basement, each 25x100 feet in size, of premises in every way adaptive. They sell for cash or upon the installment plan, and in the matter of prices, liberal terms, quality of materials, and other invaluable inducements, are not excelled by any similar house in this city. Their stocks, which are full and complete, embrace general household furniture of the best make, and according to the latest patterns, carpets, oil-cloths, handsomes, pictures, ornaments, bric-a-brac, china, glass and queensware, cutlery and tinware, mattresses and bedding, stoves for coal, wood or gas, and household sundries generally. They are prepared to furnish a residence of the most commodious dimensions at the shortest notice with every article necessary to comfort or luxury, ready for occupancy, and in the most attractive manner.

Andrew Oehler Dealer in Watches, Clocks, Jewelry, Etc.; 20 South Delaware street. Andrew Oehler has enjoyed an experience of thirty-eight years in the business, thirty years of which has been passed in this city, he having established himself here in 1858. He carries full and select lines and does a large retail trade. He occupies a substantial four story and basement brick building, 25x100 feet in dimensions, at a location both desirable and available. His stocks embrace every article of utility and ornament dealt in by first-class houses of the kind. Mr. Oehler's specialties are optical work, fine watch repairing, and the manufacture of special features in gold, silver and filigree work. He carries the best foreign and American makes of watches in solid gold, silver and filled cases; solid gold and rolled gold jewelry; solid silver and electro-plated ware; marble, bronze and other fancy clocks; statuettes, vases, etc.; fine specimens of ceramics; opera glasses and optical goods generally; charms, gold-headed canes, bric-a-brac, novelties, etc., of exquisite design and in great variety.

William Kiemeyer—Successor to Maas & Kiemeyer, Manufacturer and Dealer in Cigars and Tobacco; 141 East Washington street.—One of the leading and prosperous houses engaged in the manufacture of cigars and tobacco in Indianapolis is owned and conducted by William Kiemeyer. The enterprise was established in 1872 by the firm of Maas & Kiemeyer, and was continued under their joint management until February, 1888, when Mr. Maas retired and Mr. Kiemeyer succeeded to the sole ownership. He is located at a most desirable site for the convenience of the trade, where he occupies handsomely equipped and well appointed premises for the manufacture and sale of his line of productions. The latter are limited to the choice productions of cigars, which are well known to the trade under brands that long since were recognized as superior, and became standard articles of general consumption. He also carries

full lines of imported Havana cigars, also Key West and other selected brands of domestic make, chewing and smoking tobaccos, pipes and smokers' articles in great variety, in addition to a general assortment of sundries adapted to the demands usually made upon his line of business. His stocks can always be relied on as fresh and pure, and their sale is always made at low rates and upon liberal terms. He employs a force of competent operatives, and his trade is large locally and throughout the State.

New York Shoe Store—John Mahoney, Proprietor; Dealer in Fine Boots and Shoes; 71 East Washington street. A prominent retail boot and shoe dealer of this city is Capt. John Mahoney, located as above. He has been identified with, and actively engaged in, the business from boyhood. When the War of the Rebellion broke out, he devoted his energies to raising a company for active service, and Company A, 35th Regiment Indiana Volunteers, was speedily enlisted and he was selected Second Lieutenant, and after some service was commissioned by Gov. Morton as Captain, and his company was assigned to the Army of the Cumberland, and participated in many of the memorable engagements of the war. After the surrender of General Lee he tendered his resignation at Nashville and returned to this city, and at once resumed operations as a retail dealer in his present line of commodities, in which, excepting a brief period when he was occupied with real estate transactions, he has since been prosperously engaged.

Roman Oehler Watchmaker and Jeweler, 183 West Washington street.—One of the oldest and most favorably known jewelry houses of Indianapolis is that conducted by Mr. Roman Oehler, at 183 West Washington street. Mr. Oehler is a native of Germany, and was born in the Province of Wurtemburg in 1846. He learned his trade of jeweler and watchmaker in his native land, came to this country in 1864, landed at New York, and came direct to this city. He was unable at first to secure work at his trade, but being determined not to remain idle, he accepted such odd jobs as sawing wood, etc., and thus finding work in a bakery kept by Mr. Herman Kenich, on South Illinois street, where he remained about a year, when, having found work at his trade, he went to Mr. George Feller, on Washington street, where he remained until the breaking out of the Rebellion, when he enlisted in the service of his adopted country as a member of Captain Clause's battery. He was subsequently assigned to duty as orderly on the staff of Brigadier General Jefferson C. Davis, of Indiana, and was in active service for two years, receiving an honorable discharge at the expiration of his term. Returning to this city he began business on Virginia avenue, in 1864. In 1867 he purchased a lot, 20x100 feet, on West Washington street this present place of business, where he built a one-story house, 20x40 feet in dimensions, and removed to it in 1869. In 1872 he enlarged his building by making it three stories high, again enlarging it in 1880, by building an addition, making present dimensions 20x100 feet. In 1884 he patented a watchbox and ring-pilfer, and in 1885 made a trip through England, Germany and Switzerland to get them manufactured, and since then has added this manufacture to his present business.

Boston Clothing House—Adolph Kahn & Co., Proprietors; Men's, Boys', and Youths' Clothing; 1 East Washington street. The Boston Clothing House, an extensive and ably managed concern, engaged in the ready-made clothing trade, was established in 1886, and is composed of Adolph Kahn, who has had twenty years' experience in this business, and Maurice Brunswick. They are located on Washington street, the second door east of Meridian, an invaluable site, where they occupy store premises 25x100 feet in dimensions. They are handsomely fitted up and appointed, being provided with spacious accommodations. They also conduct a branch store at 102 South Illinois street. They carry large and select stocks, the products of the best Eastern manufacture. They embrace suits, overcoats, etc., for men, youths and boys, models of fashion, fit and superior workmanship; also gents' underwear, hosiery and furnishing goods, in silk, woolen and flannel, of the best imported and domestic make and qualities, together with the almost endless variety of ties, scarfs, mufflers, etc., to be had only of first-class dealers in such commodities.

Bargain House— D. R. McDonough, Proprietor; Wholesale and Retail Dealer in Queensware and Glassware in all the Styles and Varieties, Etc., 63 North Illinois street. The Bargain House, owned and directed by D. R. McDonough, was established by him in 1883. He

is located as above, in premises admirably adapted, having a frontage of 25 feet on North Illinois street with a depth of 120 feet, and is provided with every facility and equipment for the business. His stocks are large and complete, ranging from the choicest to medium grades, in every pattern from the plainest to the latest samples of the antique, embracing Limoges, Haviland, and other productions of the leading French potteries, American, English, French, Belgian, and other glassware, Meakin's famous English white granite ware, also tinware, cutlery, lamps, and housekeepers' furnishing goods generally, 5 and 10 cent goods in great variety, at every price and for every service. These goods are imported direct and obtained from first hands at prices and upon terms that enable Mr. McDonough to offer the most advantageous inducements to patrons and the public, and in such invoices that he is prepared to fill and ship orders promptly without regard to magnitude or destination. Mr. McDonough also handles as a specialty three particular grades of oil for illuminating purposes, which are sold at the most reasonable market prices. This special branch of the business includes the best 74° deodorized gasoline.

CHARITABLE HOMES AND HOSPITALS.

ORPHANS' ASYLUM.

THE claims of humanity and the cause of charity are neither neglected nor forgotten by the citizens of Indianapolis. Institutions for their protection and promotion abound under State and municipal direction, and under private control, for the care of the sick and destitute, and to forms of human suffering or necessity need want for remedies or relief. The charitable and benevolent institutions of State and city are well located, handsomely built, adaptively arranged and appointed, and liberally supported and sustained. Experienced attendants are enlisted in the service, and the treatment of the sick, the maimed, and the diseased in mind, body or estate is characterized by humanity and fidelity to the admonition promul-

gated nearly 2,000 years ago by the Man of Nazareth, who spake as never man spake, and whose teachings were still further emphasized by the career of the chief of His apostles, who impressed upon his followers the duty of mankind to bear one another's burdens, and so fulfill the law.

INSANE ASYLUM.

The Insane Asylum is located at the western terminus of Washington street, two miles from Illinois street, where it occupies a tract of land 160 acres in extent. The male department was erected in 1848, and the wings added late in the fifties. The latter contains twenty-four wards. The building is of brick, 625 feet front by 150 feet in depth, containing all the latest improvements, and is provided with accommodations for 640 patients. The female department, which is located north of the male department, occupies a commodious building, also of brick, completed in 1880, at a cost of $300,000, and is in every respect one of the most complete institutions of the kind in the country. It is four stories high and built according to the Kirkbride system, by which plan every room in the immense edifice is perfectly lighted and ventilated. It has a frontage in a direct line of 1,096 feet, a depth through the center of 381 feet, and has a total capacity for 850 patients. The institution on April 1, 1882, contained 1,490 inmates exclusive of the superintendent and his staff of assistants.

BLIND ASYLUM.

The State Asylum for the Blind occupies the square bounded by North Meridian, St. Clair and Pennsylvania streets, with a total area of eight acres. The old building was completed in 1848. The present structure was completed in 1851, and occupied in January, 1853. The main building is 90 feet front, and 60 feet deep, the adjoining wings are each 83x30 feet in dimensions. The main entrance is reached by way of a handsome portico, 30x25 feet, enclosed by Corinthian columns, 25 feet high. The buildings are of brick, handsomely appointed, and divided into school rooms, operating rooms, dormitories, etc., equipped with every facility and convenience. It is open to residents of the State, between the ages of nine and twenty-one years, and is supported out of the general fund of the State, set apart for charitable purposes.

DEAF AND DUMB ASYLUM.

The Deaf and Dumb Asylum is located at the corner of Washington and State streets. The education of deaf mutes was instituted under the authority of the State in 1843, with a class of thirteen pupils. In 1844, the asylum was first established in Indianapolis, and, in 1850, the present improvements were begun. They are situated in the center of a lot of ground, 105 acres in extent, and consist of the main building, five stories high, 60x61 feet in dimensions, with wings four stories in height and 35x85 feet in dimensions, on either side, with a building in the rear used as workshop, laundry and for other industrial purposes, and well equipped with machinery and appliances. During 1882 the improvements were increased by the addition of a building for school room purposes, with a capacity for 520 pupils. The institution is open to applicants between the ages of ten and twenty-one years, residents of Indiana, all of whom receive an intellectual and industrial education, and otherwise fitted for the duties of life. During last year the institution contained 300 pupils.

INDIANA REFORM SCHOOL.

The Indiana Reform School is located north of the Deaf and Dumb Asylum, occupying a series of two-story brick buildings situated in the midst of an attractive lawn planted with trees and shrubbery. The main building is 63 feet front with side and transfer wings, each 54½ feet front and 30 feet deep. The premises are substantially built and finished and contain accommodation for 300 inmates.

THE CITY HOSPITAL.

The City Hospital was first completed and occupied in 1859. It is located in the northwestern part of the city, and originally cost $30,000. For some years after the premises became ready for occupation, they were in the possession of the government for military hospital

purposes. In 1866, however, the city authorities resumed the direction of affairs, and have since appropriated the building, to which additions have been made since it was first erected to the uses for which it was intended in the first instance. Accommodations are provided for a large number of patients, an ample corps of physicians is in attendance daily, and the management is efficient and acceptable. The institution is supported by the city, and during 1888 $22,371.91 was appropriated for that purpose.

ST. VINCENT'S HOSPITAL.

St. Vincent's Hospital is one of the largest and most complete institutions of the kind in the State. The premises occupy the site of the old Bay Hotel at the southeast corner of Delaware and South streets, which was purchased at a cost of $20,000, and upon which has been erected an hospital building at an additional cost of $130,000. It is divided into an operating room, private and public wards for the sick and injured, for whom the best medical and surgical aid known to the profession are provided. The second floor of the building contains the male wards, the female wards occupying the third floor, with a general ward on both floors. Particular regard has been paid to lighting and ventilation; the premises, and the wards and rooms are furnished with open grates in which natural gas is used as fuel, the building being also heated by steam. It is equipped with all desirable appliances and is in charge of eight Sisters of Charity.

HOME FOR FRIENDLESS WOMEN.

The society which provides a home for friendless women is composed of the ladies of Indianapolis and was organized in July, 1863, for purposes fully explained in its corporate title. For a number of years they occupied private residences, but in 1870 erected the edifice, corner of Tennessee and Ninth streets, since known as the "Home for Friendless Women." It is three stories high, 57x75 feet in dimensions, and contains upward of fifty rooms, which are available for temporary residence to those for whose benefit and protection it is designed. The institution is under the direction of a Board of Trustees and a Board of Managers, the latter composed of lady members of the society, to whose unselfish efforts its maintenance is largely due, assisted by contributions and allowances.

INDIANAPOLIS BENEVOLENT SOCIETY.

The Indianapolis Benevolent Society was organized in November, 1835, for the purpose of affording relief and aid to the destitute poor. Membership is acquired by the donation of money or other contributions, which are in turn distributed by the executive officers upon the recommendation of managers who investigate the cases requiring relief, in the various districts into which the city is divided for this purpose.

THE INDIANAPOLIS ORPHANS' HOME.

The Widows' and Orphans' Society was organized in 1849, for the care of orphans, and in 1855 erected the Home, corner of College and Home avenues, the same costing $1,500. Since then, additions have been made and improvements effected, and the society is now one of the most valuable and important charitable associations in the State. Its government is directed by an executive and a managerial board, and its support is derived from donations and aid from the State. There are accommodations for about 100 inmates, who enjoy in addition to their maintenance, facilities for obtaining an education.

GRANT BARNELL ALLEN, M. D., THE DISTINGUISHED ORTHO-PEDIC SURGEON, PRESIDENT OF THE NATIONAL SURGICAL INSTITUTE.

THE GERMAN PROTESTANT ORPHAN ASYLUM.

One of the leading instrumentalities in the work of benevolence in Indianapolis is the German Protestant Orphan Asylum, organized in 1867. Subsequent to that date, the association purchased a tract of seven acres in the southeastern portion of the city, upon which is the asylum was built and still remains. Its capacity is between 100 and 150, and its source of support is contributions, etc.

of their special lines of instruments, the latter provided with every facility and appointment for operations and treatment. In the spring of 1889, requiring additional accommodations in the latter department, they completed an annex 30x100 feet in dimensions, which is elaborately furnished and equipped with over $20,000 worth of machinery of their own invention. Adjoining the Institute, the National Surgical Institute Hotel is located. It consists of a four-story

INDIANA HOSPITAL FOR THE INSANE—DEPARTMENT FOR WOMEN.

THE NATIONAL SURGICAL INSTITUTE.

Allen & Wilson, Proprietors; South Illinois and Georgia streets. The National Surgical Institute was established in this city during 1858, by Horace R. Allen, M. D., and others. Subsequently it became an incorporation, with Dr. Allen as President, and Charles L. Wilson, M. D., Vice-President; but as there are few stockholders, and no stock available to purchase, they are seldom designated by their official titles. The career of the Institute since its foundation, over thirty years ago, has been devoted to an exemplification of the example of the Good Samaritan, and obedience to the divine admonition: "Bear ye one another's

and basement edifice, 150 feet front on South Illinois street and 100 feet deep on Georgia street, containing accommodations for nearly 500 patients, and always fully occupied by residents from all portions of the world, whose confidence in the reputation and skill of the management is attested by their traveling thousands of miles to avail themselves of opportunities for their restoration to health, available nowhere else. It is provided with nursery for the care of children as companying their parents, a kindergarten school being also sustained for their entertainment and education, and no pains or expense are spared to render the patient contented and comfortable. Their lines

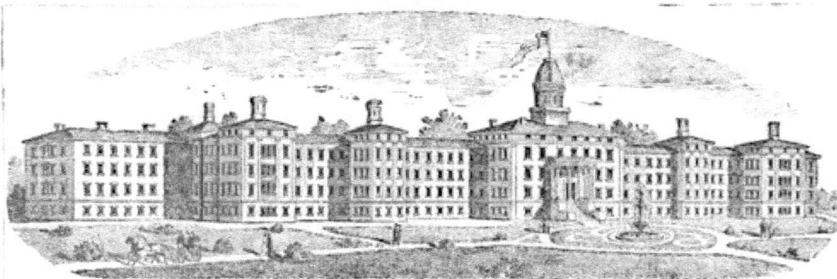

INDIANA HOSPITAL FOR THE INSANE—DEPARTMENT FOR MEN.

burdens." It was established for humanitarian objects, and under its dispensations the paralyzed have been made to walk, the lame and deformed have been permanently cured, and the sick and afflicted successfully treated. The Institute proper, located as above, near the new Union Depot, occupies a three-story and basement brick building, sixty feet front by two hundred feet deep, containing manufacturing and treatment departments, the former equipped with all the latest improved machinery and appliances for the successful production

of production include orthopedic and surgical appliances, the inventions of Dr. Allen, for every species of deformity and operation connected therewith, necessary to perfect a cure. Samples of these were exhibited at the Centennial Exhibition of 1876, a case 36 feet long, 12 feet high and 10 feet wide being required for the purpose, at an outlay of $10,000 for the samples alone, which in number were five times greater than those of all the world besides, and were awarded the first premiums. Their departments of treatment are devoted to spinal diseases, lateral curvature of the spine, hip diseases, paralysis and its resulting deformities, bow legs and knock-knees, club feet, diseases of the bones and joints, deformities, wry neck, rheumatism, tumors, piles, fistula, catarrh, etc., in all of which their success has been exceptional with patients from every State in the Union, Canada, England, Scotland, Australia, Mexico, South America, and other portions of the globe. These facts are borne out by testimonials from prominent citizens and residents, testifying to the efficiency of the services rendered, and confirmatory of the Institute's claims to patronage, superiority and perpetuity. This is the oldest and largest institution of its kind in the world, upon which Dr. Allen has spent thirty-one years of his life, and over $500,000 in building up to its present enviable standing. During that period thousands of helpless cripples, given up by physicians, have been restored in the shortest possible time and with little pain, of which number many have been sent to the Institute by physicians, who in so doing publicly admit its worth. Full information regarding terms, etc., will be mailed applicants, and the Institute's great work, and the results it has accomplished, are part of the daily record of current events in Indianapolis, and of the benefits conferred upon humanity in all parts of the world.

In addition to the above, there are the German Lutheran Orphans' Home; the Colored Orphan Asylum, established in 1870; Home for Aged Poor; Friendly Inn; Flower Mission; Bobb's Free Dispensary; Young Men's Christian Association; Newsboy's Home, and other institutions of a benevolent character distributed throughout the city, adequate to the requirements of the service in which they are severally engaged.

THE COURTS.

INDIANAPOLIS is the judicial center of Indiana, the Federal and Supreme Courts of the State being located here, in addition to the County and Municipal Courts. The State of Indiana is attached to the seventh judicial circuit and comprises one judicial district. The Federal Court is held in the Government building on the first Tuesdays in May and November, and is presided over by Associate Justice John M. Harlan, of the United States Supreme Court, the Circuit Court by the Hon. Walter Q. Gresham, of Chicago, and the District Court by the Hon. William A. Woods, of Indianapolis.

SUPREME COURT.

The Supreme Court of Indiana is held in the Supreme Court room at the State House, the terms commencing on the fourth Monday of May and the fourth Monday of November of each year. The bench is composed of one Chief Justice and four Associate Justices.

MARION COUNTY COURTS.

There are two courts of general civil jurisdiction, the Marion Circuit Court and the Superior Court of Marion County, also a court of criminal jurisdiction called the Criminal Court of Marion County. The Circuit Court has exclusive original jurisdiction in all cases at law and in equity whatsoever, also in the settlement of estates and of guardianships, and in all other causes, motions and proceedings where exclusive jurisdiction thereof is not conferred by law upon some other court, with such appellate jurisdiction as may be conferred by law. This court holds five terms each year, commencing on the first days of September, November, January, March and May.

SUPERIOR COURT OF MARION COUNTY.

The Superior Court has original, concurrent jurisdiction with the Circuit Court in all civil causes except slander, and concurrent juris-diction with the Circuit Court in cases of appeal from Justices of the Peace, Boards of County Commissioners, also in all actions by or against executors or administrators, and all other appellate jurisdiction now vested in, or which may hereafter be vested in Circuit Courts. The court is composed of three Judges who sit and try causes separately, and together constitute an Appellate Court from which appeals are taken to the Supreme Court. There are ten terms of the Superior Court, one for each month in the year except July and August.

THE CRIMINAL COURT OF MARION COUNTY.

The Marion County Criminal Court possesses exclusive jurisdiction, within the county, of all crimes and misdemeanors, except where jurisdiction is by law conferred upon Justices of the Peace, and such appellate jurisdiction in criminal cases as may by law belong to the Circuit Court in counties having no Criminal Court. This court has two terms of six months each, commencing on the first Mondays of January and July of each year.

THE POLICE COURT.

The Police Court has original jurisdiction over cases of misdemeanor and violations of the city charter and ordinances, as also in cases of felony committed within the territorial limits of the municipality. Daily sessions are held at the Police Court room in the basement of the Marion County Court House, the Mayor of the city presiding. There are seven Justices of the Peace, located at various convenient points throughout the city, whose jurisdiction extends to causes in which the amount involved does not exceed $200; also to the preliminary examination into cases of defendants charged with the commission of offenses. The bar of Indianapolis is composed of able men, nearly all of whom are engaged in active practice, and support a well equipped library, having commodious accommodations in the Court House.

LIBRARIES.

THE public library, under the direction of the School Board, was established in May, 1882, and opened in 1873, with 8,000 volumes. Subsequently the association acquired 4,000 additional volumes, the same having been donated by the Indianapolis Library Association, on condition that access to the Public Library should thereafter be free to applicants. The High School building was first occupied for library and reading room purposes, whence they were removed in January, 1875, to the old Sentinel building. In February, 1880, the directory purchased, for $60,000, the present site, corner of Ohio and Pennsylvania streets, which has since been occupied. The library is divided into two departments, the circulating department, from which books can be taken out under proper regulations, and the reference department, in which books are available for examination, but can not be taken from the premises. On the 30th of June, 1888, there were 45,252 books and 3,619 pamphlets in the library, circulation 317,108, card holders 31,018 and from 15,000 to 18,000 in regular use. The expenses of the library are paid by a tax of two cents on the assessed valuation of city property. Besides the Public Library there are the State Library, containing 23,000 volumes; the State Law Library, 18,600; the Agricultural Library, 1,000; the Horticultural Library, 500; all of which are located in the State House; the Marion County Library, 3,600 volumes; and the Bar Library, 1,000 volumes, both at the Marion County Court House; the Masonic Library, 1,750 volumes, Catholic Library, 2,000, and St. Cecilia with 700 volumes. In addition to these, there are collections of valuable works on historical and other subjects, owned by private individuals, but the above constitute the libraries in the city open to the public.

TABLE OF CONTENTS.

PROMINENT ILLUSTRATIONS.

INDEX TO BUSINESS HOUSES.

Interior view of Pullman Sleepers and Drawing Room Reclining Chair Buffet Cars running on the O., I. & W. Ry (I., B. & W. Route).

Between PEORIA and CINCINNATI, Between CHICAGO, INDIANAPOLIS and SPRINGFIELD

THE DANVILLE ROUTE

THE BEST LINE BETWEEN

Indianapolis & Chicago.

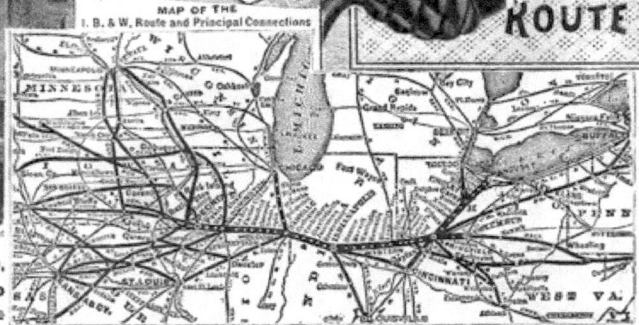

Through Tickets and Baggage Checks to all Principal Points, East, West, North, South, at Lowest Possible Rates.
C. E. HENDERSON, Gen. Manager.   M. M. BRONSON, Gen. Pass. Agt.

INDIANAPOLIS, DECATUR & WESTERN RAILWAY

ELEGANT RECLINING CHAIR CARS RUN DAILY

. . . . BETWEEN . . . .

CINCINNATI, O., INDIANAPOLIS, IND., DECATUR, ILL.

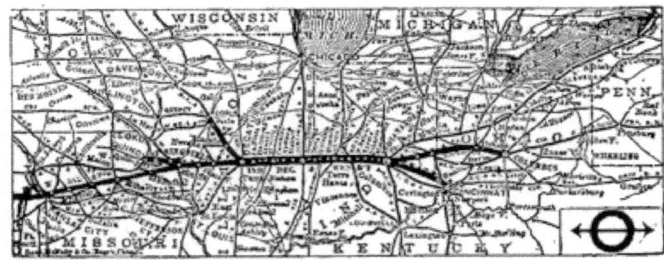

SHORTEST LINE BETWEEN INDIANAPOLIS AND KANSAS CITY BY 25 MILES

SPRINGFIELD, ILL., JACKSONVILLE, ILL., KEOKUK, IA.

Ticket Offices: 134 S. Illinois St., and Union Depot, Indianapolis.

H. B. HAMMOND,   L. A. BOYD,   JNO. S. LAZARUS,
PRESIDENT.   SUPERINTENDENT.   GEN. PASS. AGENT.